CW01151785

Experiencing the Beyond

Challenges of Life

Essays on philosophical and cultural anthropology

Edited by
Gert Melville and Carlos Ruta

Volume 4

Experiencing the Beyond

―

Intercultural Approaches

Edited by
Gert Melville and Carlos Ruta

Editorial Manager
Laura S. Carugati

DE GRUYTER
OLDENBOURG

ISBN 978-3-11-052853-4
e-ISBN (PDF) 978-3-11-053077-3
e-ISBN (EPUB) 978-3-11-052867-1

Library of Congress Cataloging-in-Publication Data
A CIP catalog record for this book has been applied for at the Library of Congress.

Bibliographic information published by the Deutsche Nationalbibliothek
The Deutsche Nationalbibliothek lists this publication in the Deutsche Nationalbibliografie;
detailed bibliographic data are available in the Internet at http://dnb.dnb.de.

© 2018 Walter de Gruyter GmbH, Berlin/Boston
Typesetting: Konvertus, Haarlem
Printing: CPI books GmbH, Leck
♾ Printed on acid free paper
Printed in Germany

www.degruyter.com

Gert Melville and Carlos Ruta
Preface

This volume harkens back to a symposium that took place in Buenos Aires from 27 to 30 September in 2016 under the academic supervision of Carlos Ruta, President of the National University of San Martín, and of Gert Melville, Director of the FOVOG at the University of Dresden, Germany. Following upon its predecessors dedicated to the topics of "Life Configurations", "Thinking the Body as Basis, Provocation, and Burden of Life", and "Potency of the Common", this symposium was the fourth in a series of international meetings with the title "Challenges of Life". Throughout these meetings, specialists with different scientific horizons have been invited from all across the world to reflect upon problems and topics considered essential for a manifold understanding of the human being, of its place in the world, and of the fundamental challenges that life presents in various forms. It lies in the nature of the human being to be aware of his or her existential limitations, to recognize him or herself as a deficient being. Of course, one instinctively senses that life holds many challenges. Yet, more importantly, one also reflectively accepts one's life as a challenge in itself, seeking to discern the conditions and to devise the means with which to tackle it.

The spirit of the meetings is decidedly interdisciplinary and cross-cultural. The topics will be approached from different perspectives of knowledge such as, among others, those emerging from the fields of anthropology, philosophy, historical sciences, sociology, politology, law, medical sciences, and biology. The core topics will be examined by looking at different civilizations, which will make it possible to achieve results by means of a comparison and to become receptive to the diversity of world cultures. At the same time, the lack of chronological limits should also allow access to a range of periods and to the corresponding changes and transformations.

The symposium of 2016 attempted to determine more closely the phenomenon of the "beyond" as a challenge of life. At this endeavour three main sets of questions were in the background:
- Where is the „beyond" embedded? Where does it reside? – In the underworld, in heaven, in the fauna or flora, at holy places (e.g. mountains or sacred groves), among inanimate nature, or in a parallel world that is ever present yet not immediately perceptible?
- To what extent is this „beyond" linked with personal (acting or non-acting) divinity, angels, devils, demons, or spirits? Or does it only require one absolute, transcendent point of reference – such as for instance the general numinous or the ‚great laws' of the cosmos, of universal history, etc.?

- These questions are intimately linked with, and nearly identical to the question of religion – yet only to the extent that a rather broad concept of religion is put forth, which not only regards dogmatically elaborated religious teaching, but also magical practices, superstition, and sacred myths as well as the secular ‚religions' in terms of ideas of the state, ideologies, material worth (e.g. money), etc.

With this backdrop in mind, it is worthwhile to ask first of all what sort of a challenge the knowledge of the existence of a „beyond" constituted for the individual person, for a group, for a society and how it was encountered. It is therefore not a matter of simply presenting the respective ideas of the beyond or even of religions. Rather, we wish to analyze challenges that emerged as a result of such ideas.

The „beyond" presents a problem in the following ways:
- The knowledge of the limits that are placed on humankind (mortality, the determined nature of one's destiny, limitation of ability) represents a challenge either to overcome them by means of one's own strength (e.g. by way of innovations) or to commit to a higher power of the „beyond" (e.g. by all forms of spirituality, hope in miracles, etc.).
- The fear of this higher power, given that it seeks to determine one's destiny – or to the contrary the effort to know the will of the 'Gods' (e.g. by means of prophecies, fortune telling, oracles)
- The desire to make these powers accessible to this world, to know them, to acquire them for oneself, to learn how to be able to direct them (e.g. by way of gaining the Gods favour in the form of sacrifices, mystic contemplation, shamanism, priesthood or by circumventing the destiny by magic and sorcery).
- The concern to be able to defend oneself from the powers of the beyond (e.g. by warding off evil in the form of masks, etc.)
- The compulsion to have to obey the powers of the beyond as the utmost moral and/or legal authority (e.g. by means of divine judgment, ordale, Ten Commandments)
- The desire to be able to reach the beyond (by way of self-sanctification, purchase of means of salvation, martyrdom, etc.)

A broadly comparative approach that spans different historical structures and cultural identities besides general philosophical and anthropological aspects was once again imperative for the conference and consequently also for this book.

Contents

Gert Melville and Carlos Ruta
Preface —— V

General Aspects

Horacio A. Gianneschi
There is no "Being Itself" Beyond Beings – The Progressive Oblivion of an Original Metaphysics —— 3

Santiago González Casares
The Beyond: Death, Aesthetics and Phenomenology —— 16

Axel C. Lazzari
Beyonds, Factishes, and Fetishes
Reflections on a Ritual of Restitution of Human Dead Remains —— 25

Carlos Rafael Ruta
Beyond the Self Circle
Beyond Poetry —— 39

Gustavo A. Ludueña
Spirit World as the Beyond from an Anthropological Perspective
Making Sense "Reasonably" of Afterlife Ontologies —— 54

Sandra Baquedano Jer
Beyond the Species, or the 'Beyond' of Human Life?
Challenges of a Non-Speciesist Ethic —— 66

Historical Structures

Jaime I. Araos San Martín
The Question of Beyond
Previous Considerations from Aristotle's *Metaphysics* —— 81

Gregor Vogt-Spira
Ideas – Presences – Practices
The Beyond in Ancient Roman Culture —— 95

Jörg Sonntag
The Horror of Flawlessness
Perfection as Challenge of Life in the Middle Ages —— 107

Mirko Breitenstein
Living with Demons
The Horror of the Beyond as a Challenge of Life in the Middle Ages —— 121

José Emilio Burucúa
Transcendences in the Italian Renaissance
Regarding a Wood Panel by Jacopo del Sellaio and a Miniature by Reginaldus Metropolitanus —— 138

Cultural Identities

Guillermo Wilde
The Mission as "Beyond" and Beyond the Mission —— 153

Gideon Bohak
Expelling Demons and Attracting Demons in Jewish Magical Texts —— 170

Terry Kleeman
Many Paths, Many Souls: Traditional Chinese Views of the Other World —— 186

Klaus-Dieter Mathes
Liberation through Realizing the Emptiness of Dependent Origination
A Modern Interpretation of the Buddhist "Beyond" in the Light of Quantum Physics —— 198

Faye Kleeman
Here, There, and "Beyond" – Japanese Views on the Afterlife —— 212

Uriya Shavit
Can the Metaphysical Be Rationally Proven?
Islamic Modernism Revisited —— **229**

Pablo Wright
Ontological Thresholds in Contemporary Shamanisms —— **243**

Raquel Romberg
The Beyond as Partner of the Here and Now
The Actuality and Indeterminacy of a Spiritual Semiotics within Spiritism —— **256**

About the Authors —— **268**

General Aspects

Horacio A. Gianneschi
There is no "Being Itself" Beyond Beings – The Progressive Oblivion of an Original Metaphysics

I Aristotle

The eleventh aporia of *Metaphysics* B expounds a thesis, there ascribed to the Pythagoreans and to Plato, in accordance with which being and one are the *ousíai* of beings (οὐσίαι τῶν ὄντων), and each one of them is what each one of them is, i. e., being and one, without being some other thing (οὐχ ἕτερον τι), that is to say, each one of them is, respectively, being itself (αὐτὸ ὄν) and one itself (αὐτὸ ἕν), and their φύσις, their οὐσία, is, respectively, to be being and to be one (τοῦ ἑνὶ εἶναι καὶ ὄντι).[1] The main argument against this thesis is that if we admit some being itself and one itself (τι αὐτὸ ὄν καὶ αὐτὸ ἕν), there could not be anything different, any other thing (ἕτερον), apart from (παρὰ) them, which, in the respective cases, can be or can be one, for that which is different from being is not, and that which is different from what one is, is not one, which necessarily leads us to the Parmenidean monism whereby differences are demolished.[2] This consequence, as noted by Enrico Berti,[3] not only contrasts with the undeniable multiplicity arising from experience, but also aims to hurt the very heart of Plato's doctrine in the *Sophist*[4] (we abstract ourselves from the Pythagoreans), under which that which is different is a being (ὄν), and reality – even within the domain of that which is the most real, i. e., at the level of Ideas – is multiple. This Aristotelian argument implicitly carries with it an assumption,[5] which Aristotle explicitly expresses in other texts,[6] in accordance with which acknowledging an αὐτὸ ὄν necessarily entails attributing a univocal significance to ὄν, i. e., it means that being is a unique *ousía*, a unique nature,

---

1 Cf. ARISTOTLE, *Metaphysics*, 1001 a 5–12, 27–29; 996 a 5–9.
2 Cf. ARISTOTLE, *Metaphysics*, 1001 a 29–b 1; b 3–6.
3 Cf. Enrico BERTI, "Le problème", 97.
4 Cf. PLATO, *Sophist*, 256 d–259 c.
5 As well noted, e. g., by ALEXANDER OF APHRODISIAS, *In Met.*, esp. 226, 7–9; Enrico BERTI, "Le problème", 96–98; "Being", 481 (cf. "Aristotélisme", 314). BERTI has better than anyone else devoted to the theme object of our analysis. The discrepancy which in respect of his interpretation we will be introducing towards the end does not affect the core of his position.
6 Cf. ARISTOTLE, *Physics* I 3, 8; *Metaphysics*, 1088 b 35–1089 a 19.

DOI 10.1515/9783110530773-001

consisting in being no other thing but being, which in turn implies that if such *ousía* is common to all things, all things will thus possess this same unique nature, unique *ousía*, and all things will not be anything different from, any other thing but, being, anything apart from being being. Analogously happens with the admission of an αὐτὸ ἕν.

II Thomas Aquinas

Aquinas's renowned doctrine in accordance with which God, the creator of the universe in his conception, is the *esse ipsum subsistens* or *ipsum esse per se subsistens*, i. e., an *ens per essentiam* whose *substantia*, whose *essentia*, is the *ipsum esse*, an *ens*, the *unum primum ens*, to which *essentialiter convenit esse*,[7] is closely related to Aquinas's interpretation of Aristotle's god, the first unmoved mover in the latter's conception (and also in Aquinas's).[8] In his commentary on *Metaphysics* B, Aquinas claims that Aristotle's arguments against the admission of an *ipsum ens* and of an *ipsum unum* do not constitute the final expression of the Stagirit, but, rather, the expression of a doubt phase, and for the solution of this *dubitatio* we are referred here to *Metaphysics* Λ, as, according to Aquinas, it is there that Aristotle effectively acknowledges *aliquod separatum, quod sit ipsum unum et ens*, which although it is not the *substantia omnium eorum quae sunt unum*, as claimed by the Platonists, it is indeed the *omnibus unitatis causa et principium*.[9]

Now, firstly, Aquinas's reference to Λ for the solution of the eleventh aporia as well as his assertion that there Aristotle proves that there is an *ipsum unum et ens* lack legitimacy. Indeed, on the one hand, it is Aristotle who introduces a solution to such aporia, by explicitly referring to it, not in Λ, but in I,[10] there[11] making definitely his own, as he does in other passages,[12] the arguments against the admission of a being by essence and of a one by essence. And, on the other hand, in Λ, Aristotle does not assert that the first *ousía* – the first unmoved mover – is to be understood as being itself or one itself, i. e., as something whose nature or *ousía* should not be anything but being or one, but, rather, he claims that it is

---

[7] Cf., e. g., THOMAS AQUINAS, *Summa contra gentiles* I 22; II 15, 52; III 65; *Summa theologiae* I, q. 3, a. 4; q. 4. a. 2; q. 7, a. 1 *ad* 3; q. 12, a. 2 and a. 3 *ad* 3; q. 13, a. 11; q. 44, a. 1; q. 61, a. 1.
[8] Cf. THOMAS AQUINAS, *Summa theologiae* I, q. 2, a. 3.
[9] THOMAS AQUINAS, *In Met.*, L. III, l. XII, n. 501.
[10] Cf. ARISTOTLE, *Metaphysics*, 1053 b 10.
[11] Cf. ibid., 1053 b 16–26.
[12] Cf. ibid., 1040 b 6–19; 1088 b 35–1089 a 19.

a determinate being whose essence is thinking.[13] Aristotle's first principle, first unmoved mover, which is eternal, *ousía* and act, is one, but it is not the same as the one, i. e., its essence is not unity, it is not the Platonic αὐτὸ τὸ ἕν.[14] In this regard, it is worth noting that Aquinas does not make any allusion to *aliquod separatum, quod sit ipsum unum et ens* in his commentary on Λ, as should be expected given his own reference to Λ for this purpose.[15] Secondly, Aquinas asserts, as expounded above, that the *ipsum unum et ens* – in his view acknowledged by Aristotle in Λ – is not, as regarded by the Platonists, substance of all the things that are one, but the cause and principle of their unity; and it is clear that, at the same time, he also means that such Aristotelian *ipsum unum et ens*, though not the substance of all the things that are beings, is the cause and principle of their being. Therefore, the difference between the Platonic *ipsum ens* (let us dispense with the *ipsum unum*) and the – in the opinion of Aquinas – Aristotelian *ipsum ens*, would reside in that the former would be *substantia*, essence, or formal cause, of all beings, whereas the latter, though an *ipsum ens* or being by essence, just like the Platonic one, would not be, like the Platonic one, formal cause, but, we should assume, efficient cause of all beings. This same difference is again established by Aquinas in his commentary on *Metaphysics* I 2, one of the passages where Aristotle takes a final position on the eleventh aporia. Aquinas here acknowledges that Aristotle solves the aporia *ostendendo quod unum et ens non sunt substantiae eorum de quibus dicuntur*, or, as Aquinas will expound in more specific terms – for 'one' is the matter at hand here – later, *quod unum non est substantia subsistens, de qua dicitur quod sit unum*. Aquinas himself accepts the Aristotle's argument[16] consisting in claiming that a universal – 'one' and 'being' are universals – is not *substantia* in the sense of *per se subsistens* because *omne universale commune est multis*, whereas in order to be *substantia subsistens* it would be required that, instead of being, somehow – i. e., to the extent it is *aliquid praedicatum de multis* –, *unum in multis*, rather be *unum praeter multum, et ita non [...] commune, sed [...] quoddam singulare in se*. But Aquinas immediately adds, on his own, an exception to this last consequence: *Nisi forte diceretur commune per modum causae. Sed alia est communitas universalis et causae*. Indeed, Aquinas goes on, whereas, on the one hand, *causa non praedicatur de suis effectibus*, on the other hand, *universale est*

---

13 ARISTOTLE, *Metaphysics*, 1072 b 18–21, 1074 b 33–35, 1075 a 3–5, 5–10. In addition to *esse ipsum subsistens*, AQUINAS expresses that God is *ipsum intelligere subsistens* (*Summa theologiae* I, q. 54, a. 1; cf. q. 14, a. 4 *ad* 2 *et* 3; cf. *Summa contra gentiles* I 45), regarding the latter characterization as reconcilable with the former.
14 Cf. ARISTOTLE, *Metaphysics*, 1054 a 7–8; 1054 a 10–12.
15 Cf. Enrico BERTI, "Aristotélisme", 317–319.
16 Cf. ARISTOTLE, *Metaphysics*, 1053 b 16–21.

commune, quasi aliquid praedicatum de multis; et sic oportet quod aliquo modo sit unum in multis, et non seorsum subsistens ab eis. Therefore, on the basis of this exception, Aquinas believes there can be *unum* (and *ens*), which is precisely said to be essentially *unum* (or *ens*), understood as *substantia subsistens*, which is *unum* (or *ens*) *praeter multum* and at the same time *commune*, but *commune* in the sense of the *communitas causae*. In this manner, Aquinas seems to be pointing to his own conception of God as *ipsum esse per se subsistens*, in respect of whom he himself considers it may be said – following *De divinis nominibus* by Ps.-Dionysius –: *omnia est, ut omnium causa*.[17] But Aristotle does not say, and cannot say, such thing here, because in his view 'being' and 'one' are not substances precisely because they have no other *communitas*, in Aquinas's words, than the *communitas universalis*. For Aristotle, there is no 'one' or 'being' conceived of as subsistent, separate substances, said to be essentially 'one' or 'being' and whose *communitas* is the *communitas causae*. Aquinas himself seems to acknowledge Aristotle's strict position in this passage of his commentary on the *Metaphysics*, since as soon as he introduces, on his own, the exception in question, he takes up his commentary on Aristotle as follows: *Sed oportet ens et unum magis universaliter et communiter de omnibus praedicari. Non ergo sunt ipsa substantia subsistens, quae dicitur ens vel unum, sicut Plato posuit.*[18] Aristotle's god, the first unmoved mover, is not *omnia*, not even *ut omnium causa*. It is *omnium causa*, but not *omnia* for that reason. It is *primum ens*, to the extent it is *omnium causa*, but not *ipsum ens* for that reason, or, in a more determined way, *ipsum ens per se subsistens*.

Having assumed the above-mentioned difference between the Platonic and the Aristotelian *ipsum ens* (or *ipsum unum*), in his own theology Aquinas will stand on the side of the separate *ipsum ens* he attributes to Aristotle. Hence, in *Summa contra gentiles*, having proved that God is *esse per essentiam*, Aquinas formulates several arguments to show that this in no manner entails attributing to God a formal causality in relation to the other beings. God, he claims, *non est esse formale omnium*, as some may have believed on the basis of the misunderstood assertion contained in *De Caelesti Hierarchia* by Ps.-Dionysus: *esse omnium est superessentialis divinitas*; indeed, in the context of Ps.-Dionysius's text – in which it is argued that the *divinitas* is *super omnia*, thus showing that *secundum suam naturam ab omnibus distinctum et super omnia collocatum* –, by *divinitas esse omnium* Aquinas believes the aim pursued is to show that *a Deo in omnibus quaedam divini esse similitudo reperitur*. Another reason Aquinas thinks may have led to this same mistake is connected with the *modus loquendi* employed

---

[17] Cf. Thomas Aquinas, *Summa theologiae* I, q. 4, a. 2
[18] Cf. Thomas Aquinas, *In Met.*, L. X, l. III, nn. 1961–1965.

when we say that *Deus in omnibus rebus est* without understanding, in fact, that He is in all things *non [...] quasi aliquid rei, sed sicut rei causa quae nullo modo suo effectui deest*. Among other consequences of admitting that God is the *esse formale omnium*, Aquinas draws here – in Aristotelian fashion – that of the Parmenidean monism: *Si igitur esse divinum esset formale esse omnium, oporteret omnia simpliciter esse unum*; or: *Si enim Deus est esse omnium, non magis dicetur vere lapis est ens, quam lapis est Deus.*[19]

Now, how has Aquinas come to attribute to Aristotle, and to forge for himself, such conception of a god that is *ipsum ens, esse per essentiam*, cause – though not formal – of the being of all things? The path is, in most cases, his particular interpretation of the argument from *Metaphysics* 993 b 24–26, in accordance with which the cause of a determination possesses that same determination in the highest degree. Aristotle's example there is that of fire, which, being the cause of the determination 'hot' occurring in hot things, has such determination in the highest degree (fire, indeed, is "the hottest"). Aquinas cites this Aristotelian argument around forty-four times explicitly and even more often implicitly;[20] and he applies it to God on several occasions as follows: since God is the cause of being of all things, He is more being than they all are, i.e., He is being in the highest degree (*maxime ens*), or even *esse ipsum subsistens*.[21] But, in the passage discussed, Aristotle requires[22] that the determinations in question be synonymous,[23] i.e., determinations which do not only share their name, but whose definition, whose essence, whose form (εἶδος),[24] is also the same,[25] as in the Aristotelian example of hot things insofar as they are hot, which are all called by the name "hot" and it is about their same hot essence, nature, form, although their intensity may vary, that we speak when they are said to be hot.[26] Being, in contrast,

---

19 Cf. THOMAS AQUINAS, *Summa contra gentiles* I 26 (also I 27). Cf. *Summa theologiae* I, q. 3, a. 8.
20 Vincent DE COUESNONGLE, "La causalité I", 433, with note 1; "La causalité II", 667, note 23.
21 For the passages: Vincent DE COUESNONGLE, "La causalité I", 433–444; "La causalité II", 658–680.
22 As recalled by ALEXANDER OF APHRODISIAS, *In Met.*, 147, 28–29, but even by AQUINAS, *In Met.* L. II, l. II, n. 292.
23 Cf. ARISTOTLE, *Metaphysics*, 993 b 24–26: ἕκαστον δὲ μάλιστα αὐτὸ τῶν ἄλλων καθ' ὃ καὶ τοῖς ἄλλοις ὑπάρχει τὸ συνώνυμον (οἷον τὸ πῦρ θερμότατον· καὶ γὰρ τοῖς ἄλλοις τὸ αἴτιον τοῦτο τῆς θερμότητος).
24 Cf. ARISTOTLE, *Physics*, 257 b 9–19.
25 Cf. ARISTOTLE, *Categories*, 1 a 6–12 (cf. 3 b 7–8).
26 ARISTOTLE's *Posterior Analytics* 72 a 29–30 contains a more general formulation of the argument, applicable not only to συνώνυμα: αἰεὶ γὰρ δι' ὃ ὑπάρχει ἕκαστον, ἐκείνῳ μᾶλλον ὑπάρχει, οἷον δι' ὃ φιλοῦμεν, ἐκεῖνο φίλον μᾶλλον. In fact, the example of φίλον specifically refers to heterogeneous realities, as is the case of means and ends, connected with each other by anteriority-posteriority relations. AQUINAS here (*In Post. An.*, L. I, l. II, n. 33) glides –with legitimacy

as is common knowledge, is not a synonymous determination for Aristotle.[27] If we apply the argument in the context of synonymous realities or determinations, it occurs that both cause and effect share the same essence, nature or form, as their determination, and they differ from each other, as possessors thereof, only on account of the degree or intensity with which the determination in question is present in that which possesses it; therefore, if the Aristotelian argument is applied in the sphere of beings considered as beings, God, understood, as by Aquinas, as the being itself by essence, should, insofar as it is the cause of being of all other things, be necessarily conceived of as formal cause, i. e., as cause that has (or, in this case, that is) the same form, or essence, as its effects, i. e., the same form or essence held by the rest of the things as beings. And it is precisely this consequence that Aquinas seems to be unable to fully elude, despite repeatedly trying to depart from the Platonists in this respect, i. e., despite his intention to deny that God can be understood as the *esse formale omnium*. In fact, in some passages, Aquinas even asserts that God, insofar as He is only being, is, somehow, *species* of all the subsistent forms which participate of being.[28]

---

given the general formulation, though, seemingly, without discerning any differences between the two– from this example to that of the hot thing. Now, when the argument is applied to realities connected by an anteriority-posteriority relation, the adverb μᾶλλον does not indicate *a more intense degree* of the same nature or essence of the determination in question, but a nature or essence which is, *in a primary manner* (πρότερον), the common determination which occurs heterogeneously and secondarily as well in the other things. For the equivalence between μᾶλλον and πρότερον in this type of argument: *Protrepticus*, fr. 14 Ross (B 81–82 DÜRING) and Émile DE STRYCKER's interpretation ("Prédicats", 597–618; "Sur μᾶλλον", 303–304). Cf., however, e. g., Bertrand DUMOULIN, *Recherches*, 156–158; Donald MORRISON, "Degrees", 397–401.

27 The context in which the argument is used in *Metaphysics* – that in which ARISTOTLE aims to show that "the science of truth", insofar as it is the science of causes, is also science of the first causes – contains a reference to god ("principle of the things that are eternally", 993 b 28), but about it, as the first cause of everything that is (993 b 28–30), ARISTOTLE claims it is true in the highest degree, although this does not entail its being conceived of as the highest degree of a same essence common to all things. The expression αἴτιον... τοῦ εἶναι means cause of being which tallies with what is true, as evidenced by 993 b 21 sq., πῶς ἔχειν, being a certain way, not being *simpliciter*. The assertion "so, *to the extent to which* a thing has being, *to that extent* it has truth" (993 b 30–31) does not involve a question of degree, of intensity, but, rather, one of mode, of genus, of being, as evidenced by the use of adverbs of manner (ὡς..., οὕτω...). Therefore, the concepts of μᾶλλον and of μάλιστα, if referred to god, should be understood in the sense of πρότερον. (Cf. BERTI, "Le problème", 115, notes 116 sq.).

28 THOMAS AQUINAS, *De Potentia*, q. 6, a. 6 *ad* 5 (context: the doctrine in accordance with which angels, despite being creatures, are pure subsistent forms): Ad quintum dicendum, quod secundum philosophum, etiam in causis formalibus prius et posterius invenitur; unde nihil prohibet unam formam per alterius formae participationem formari; et sic ipse Deus, qui est esse tantum,

III Philip Merlan

Philip Merlan,[29] seeking to regard Aristotle as one of the first Neoplatonists,[30] denies the existence of a *metaphysica generalis* in Aristotle. To this effect, he believes it possible, and necessary, to isolate the texts in which he considers that Aristotle defines metaphysics *ex professo*, sc. *Metaphysics* Γ, E 1 and K 3-7.[31] According to Merlan, studied in and by themselves, this set of texts shows that they were written in the Academic tradition. To justify this he, among other things,[32] provides a peculiar interpretation of the set of terms which only appears in the aforementioned three *Metaphysics* books, sc. τὸ ὄν ᾗ ὄν. Having stated that ᾗ ὄν qualifies τὸ ὄν and thus determines the nature of τὸ ὄν – so that it turns it into "the being" that "only is and is not something",[33] "the being" that is "fully indeterminate",[34] in the sense that it is "a form which is not form of anything"[35]–, Merlan considers that τὸ ὄν ᾗ ὄν always means "nothing else but the supreme being, in other words the divine",[36] that τὸ ὄν ᾗ ὄν "always designates, in Aristotle, the πρώτη οὐσία", in the sense of οὐσία ἀκίνητος,[37] that is, τὸ ὄν ᾗ ὄν "is only another expression for the subject-matter of theology".[38] In other words, "Aristotle's

---

est quodammodo species omnium formarum subsistentium quae esse participant et non sunt suum esse. "Species" is applied to God because, within the framework of the objection (*De Potentia*, q. 6, a. 6, arg. 5), AUGUSTINE was cited calling God species prima, a qua omnia sunt speciosa. The use of such vocabulary in order to make reference to the form is reminiscent of the relation between form and beauty – the latter characterized by the *claritas* – in things (cf. AQUINAS, *In De divinis nominibus*, c. IV, l. 5).

To express the relationship between God, understood as *esse ipsum subsistens*, and all the other beings, AQUINAS resorts to the notion of "participation" (*Summa contra gentiles* II 15; *Summa theologiae* I, q. 44, a.1; II, 1, q. 61, a. 1; *Compendium theologiae* I 68). He weakens (*In Met.*, L. I, l. X, nn. 153–156; L. I, l. XVII, n. 259; L. VIII, l. V, n. 1765) the Aristotle's critique of the Platonic notion of participation (*Metaphysics*, 987 b 13, 991 a 20–22, 992 a 28–29, 1045 b 7–9) and emphazises that ARISTOTLE's critique of the function of Ideas as *exemplaria* does not exclude that the *divina scientia* is *rerum omnium exemplar* (*In Met.*, L. I, l. XV, n. 233).

29 Cf. Philip MERLAN, *From Platonism*, 1–5, 160–220, 228–231; "Metaphysik", 87–92; Id., "Postskript", 148–153; Id., "Being-qua-being", 174–194.
30 For what MERLAN means by "Neoplatonism": *From Platonism*, 1, note.
31 Ibid., 210, 205 sq., 229 sq.
32 We can only highlight the salient points of MERLAN's consideration of these texts (cf. ibid., 161 sqq.).
33 Philip MERLAN, "Postskript", 148. Cf. ibid., 153.
34 Philip MERLAN, *From Platonism*, 212.
35 Ibid., 215.
36 Ibid., 214. Cf. ibid., 190; Id., "Metaphysik", 88.
37 Philip MERLAN, "Postskript", 151.
38 Philip MERLAN, "Being-qua-being", 186.

being-*qua*-being is something transcendent – something like Plato's ideas. It is not, like Aristotle's forms, something immanent".[39]

In addition, making his own interpretation difficult to reconcile with what has been discussed so far, Merlan believes that these Aristotle's texts, having shared "the Academic metaphysical system", conceive the "being-*qua*-being" as an "element" – similar or identical to the Academic (or Platonic) One – present, together with the non-being as the other element, not only in the supreme sphere of being (i. e., that of unmovedness, divinity) but also, though in a different way (no longer as the being "in its pure form, unalloyed", but as "being something"), in the other spheres of being. It is because the being as an element is present everywhere that it is καθόλου ("common", "unrestricted and omnipresent"). According to Merlan, Aristotle also admits here the derivation of the various spheres of being from the supreme one, and, to that extent, it was him who, along with other Academics, gave rise to Neoplatonism.[40]

Now, Merlan acknowledges that the doctrines he attributes to the Aristotle that wrote these texts are harshly criticized in other parts of the *corpus aristotelicum* and especially of *Metaphysics*,[41] thus creating, as recognized by our interpreter, an "even more glaring" contradiction than any of the contradictions that his own exegesis aims to resolve within the set of texts *ex professo* dealing with the object of metaphysics. According to Merlan, Aristotle's metaphysical texts thus reveal a rift.[42] The author gives four possibilities to explain it,[43] but considers that which of them is adopted is irrelevant because here his sole purpose is "to establish the notion of an *Aristoteles Neoplatonicus*".[44] He recognizes that this is not the whole Aristotle, but, according to him, the "traditional" one (that who "professes one entirely consistent system of philosophy")[45] is not the whole Aristotle either.[46]

Merlan's audacious exegesis of the texts from where he intends to extract this *Aristoteles Neoplatonicus* practically exempts us from making any comments. With these texts at hand, we cannot but agree with Jesús de Garay: "what Aristotle is not, in any case, is a Neoplatonist".[47]

---

39 Ibid., 190.
40 Philip MERLAN, *From Platonism*, esp. 169 sqq.
41 Cf. ibid., 165, 169 sq., 172 sq., 184, note 173, and esp. 189–193, 193 sq.; cf. also 198–202, 204, 205, 206 sq., 210.
42 Ibid., 209 sq.
43 Ibid., 210–212.
44 Ibid., 212; cf. ibid., 231.
45 Ibid., 210.
46 Ibid., 212.
47 Jesús DE GARAY, *Aristotelismo*, 20.

IV Final remarks

It is important, with regard to what we have said so far, to address the anteriority-posteriority orders conceived by Aristotle in the field of the different types of *ousía*. We can only make some brief remarks here.

If we consider the ontological priority (ontological-causal dependency relations) explicitly established in this field,[48] the application of the unit model τῷ ἐφεξῆς[49] can be noted here. The problem, due to that the logical priority is not explicitly established in this field, consists in whether or not Aristotle here maintains, just as in the '*ousíai* – accidental determinations' relation, a correlation between the ontological and logical priorities. The solution to this dilemma is key to the interpretation of the Aristotelian metaphysics.[50] Enrico Berti is in favor of the second alternative, among other things, because he believes that, should the first option be chosen, which, according to him, results from a Platonic or Neoplatonic interpretation of Aristotle, Aristotle's first unmoved mover would be the *esse ipsum subsistens*.[51] We agree with Berti when he regards the interpretation of Aristotle's first unmoved mover in the latter manner as non-Aristotelian; however, we are in favor of the first alternative, although we believe that, should it be admitted, the consequence is not the one Berti wants to avoid. Precisely from the manner in which Aristotle understands the "logical priority", i. e., so that the understanding or conceptual circumscription of the prior is a necessary (but not sufficient) condition only for the full or complete understanding or conceptual circumscription (in its ultimate foundations) of what depends on it,[52] it inevitably follows that what is prior in the realm of being (both at the level of the different

---

48 Cf. ARISTOTLE, *Metaphysics*, 1072 b 13–14; *De generatione et corruptione* II 10; *De caelo*, 279 a 28–30.
49 For the distinction πρὸς ἕν and τῷ ἐφεξῆς: *Metaphysics*, 1005 a 8–11 (in 1004 a 2–9 the order τῷ ἐφεξῆς is attributed to the parts of philosophy as a reflection of the existing order among the various types of *ousía*).
50 Cf. Enrico BERTI, "Priorità", 261 sq.
51 In "Brentano", 109–111, Enrico BERTI, criticizing some interpreters for claiming that it is the πρὸς ἕν relation – which, unlike τῷ ἐφεξῆς, which involves, according to BERTI, only the ontological priority, also involves the logical priority – that which governs the various types of *ousíai*, expresses: "Ma, se Aristotele avesse compiuto questo passo, avrebbe cocepito Dio come l'Essere per eccellenza, o come l'Essere per essenza (*Esse per essentiam*), cioè l'essere stesso (*ipsum Esse subsistens*), come è accaduto nel neoplatonismo (Porfirio) e nella Scolastica, il che invece non si può dire."
52 For ARISTOTLE's common use of the logical priority: Alejandro VIGO, "Prioridad y prioridad ontológica", 105. The κατὰ λόγον priority in *Metaphysics* Δ 11 is broader than the logical priority usually employed by ARISTOTLE (cf. Alejandro VIGO, "Prioridad ontológica y lógica", 191).

types of *ousíai* and at the level of the 'ousía – accidental determinations' relation) cannot be understood in Aristotelian terms as *ipsum esse*, as *esse per essentiam*.

In his critique to Michael Frede,[53] who considers that the unmoved *ousía* is logically prior to all other types of *ousía*, Berti states, on the one hand, that he cannot agree with this interpretation since he is unable to see how the definition of the moved *ousía* can contain the notion of the unmoved *ousía*.[54] On the other hand, he states that he can agree, as a legitimate interpretation of Aristotle, with Frede's statement "ultimately, nothing is intelligible unless it is understood in its dependence on God",[55] but only if by "dependence" we mean ontological dependence,[56] in the sense of causal dependence.[57] Furthermore, Berti asserts that he can agree with Frede on that the Aristotelian god is the way of being "in terms of which all the other ways of being have to be explained",[58] but only if "in terms of which" means "in dependence on which" and the dependence in question is ontological dependence in the specified sense.[59] Having said that, what we fail to understand well is how assertions such as that indicating that in Aristotle "nothing is intelligible unless it is understood in its 'ontological' dependence on God" or that the Aristotelian god is the way of being "'in ontological dependence' on which all the other ways of being have to be explained" can be accepted as legitimate interpretations, without assuming what that is on whose ontological dependence all the other things have to be understood, without assuming what that is on whose ontological dependence all the other ways of being have to be explained, that is, without assuming precisely what the Aristotelian god is in understanding what the other *ousíai* and, in general, the other beings, are if what is sought is a full or complete (i. e., in their ultimate foundations) understanding of them, always regarded as beings; in other words, without assuming the logical priority of god in respect of the other beings. To sum up, the Aristotelian logical priority does not necessarily mean formal causality, i. e., the causality that explains the essence of a being. We agree with Berti on that, from Aristotle's point of view, the form of the material *ousíai* (matter-form composites) is logically prior to them because it is the formal cause of their being – understood here as being

---

53 Michael FREDE, *Essays*, 81–95.
54 Our disagreement with BERTI as to certain details regarding this matter mainly lies in how we interpret ARISTOTLE's characterization of "logical priority", particularly in how to understand the requirement that the λόγος of the prior instance *be contained* (ἐνυπάρχειν) in the conceptualization or explanation of the secondary instance. We do not have space here to address this topic.
55 Michael FREDE, *Essays*, 89.
56 Cf. Enrico BERTI, "Multiplicity", 203 sq.
57 Cf. Enrico BERTI, "Being", 474 sq., 479.
58 Michael FREDE, *Essays*, 84, 87.
59 Cf. Enrico BERTI, "Being", 479.

something determinate –, whereas the immaterial *ousía*, the separate form, is not the formal cause of the material *ousíai*, just like – we would add –, at the level of the different categorical ways of being – where Aristotle explicitly establishes the logical priority –, the first of the beings, i. e., the *ousía*, understood here as "substantial form", is not the formal cause of the other categorical ways of being. In short, the first of the beings, either at the level of the different types of *ousía* or at the level of the categories, is not, for Aristotle, the *forma formarum*.

The Aristotelian priority of god, once again, is not conducive to interpreting it as *ipsum esse*; on the contrary, it prevents such interpretation. It should be noted that Berti correctly interprets that Aristotle's assertion regarding the logical priority of the *ousía* over accidental categories does not mean that the *ousía* is the *ipsum esse*, but quite the opposite;[60] and so we cannot understand well how this same anteriority-posteriority relation can operate differently in the relation between the various types of *ousía*, this time meaning that the first being (the first *ousía* in the sense of the first unmoved mover) is *ipsum esse*. Similarly, Berti rightly considers that the logical priority of the *ousía* over all other categories, which implies, as recalled by himself, that the notion of *ousía* is included in that of the accidents, does not mean in any way that the notions of accidents can be derived from the notion of *ousía*; therefore, it is incomprehensible why, for Berti himself, this same type of priority when applied to the relation between the different types of *ousía*, which would mean that the notion of the anterior type of *ousía* is included in the notion of the posterior type of *ousía*, would now mean that the notion of the posterior *ousía* can be derived from the notion of the first *ousía*, thus resulting in a deductive metaphysics.[61]

Putting aside these considerations, after our discussion on Aquinas and Merlan, listed from the most to the least Aristotelian, what matters now is that we can somehow conclude that the Aristotle's criticism to the Platonic ousification of being and one, as well as his understanding of the order of priority between the various beings, apparently imply a critique *ante litteram* of the Medioplatonism, Neoplatonism and scholasticism, and seem to be an attempt to present an original metaphysics.[62] If this is so,

> It is time that Aristotle should be read through Aristotle, and not through Plato or the Neoplatonists or Aquinas.[63]

---

60 Cf., e. g., Enrico BERTI, "Being", 473–475.
61 Cf., e. g., Enrico BERTI, "L'analogia", 148 sq.
62 Cf. Enrico BERTI, "Le problème", 90, 117–119. Cf. Id., "Aristotélisme", 311, 314.
63 Walter LESZL, *Logic and Metaphysics*, 538.

Bibliography

Alexander of Aphrodisias, *In Aristoteles Metaphysica Commentaria*, edited by Michael Hayduck. Berlin, Reimer, 1891.
Aristotle, *Categoriae et liber de interpretatione*, edited by Lorenzo Minio-Paluello. Oxford, Oxford University Press, 1949.
Aristotle, *De caelo / Du ciel*, edited by Paul Moraux. Paris, Les Belles Lettres, 1965.
Aristotle, *Fragmenta selecta*, edited by William D. Ross. New York, Oxford University Press, 1955.
Aristotle, *Metaphysics*, 2 vols., edited by William D. Ross. Oxford, Clarendon Press, 1924.
Aristotle, *On Coming-to-be & Passing-away*, edited by Harold H. Joachim. New York, Oxford University Press, 1926.
Aristotle, *Physics*, edited by William D. Ross. Oxford, Oxford University Press, 1936.
Aristotle, *Prior and Posterior Analytics*, edited by William D. Ross. London, Oxford University Press, ^{2}1965.
Aristotle, *Protrepticus*, edited by Ingemar Düring. Göteborg, Elanders Boktryckeri Aktiebolag, 1961.
Berti, Enrico, "Aristotélisme et néoplatonisme dans le commentaire de Saint Thomas sur la *Métaphysique*". In Id., *Dialectique, Physique et Métaphysique*. Louvain-la-neuve, Peeters, 2008, 311–327.
Berti, Enrico, "Being and Essence in Contemporary Interpretations of Aristotle". In Id., *Nuovi studi aristotelici*, vol. IV/2. Brescia, Morcelliana, 2010, 459–484.
Berti, Enrico, "Brentano e la metafisica di Aristotele". In Id., *Nuovi studi aristotelici*, vol. IV/2. Brescia, Morcelliana, 2010, 99–119.
Berti, Enrico, "L'analogia dell'essere nella tradizione arisotelico-tomistica". In Id., *Nuovi studi aristotelici*, vol. IV/1. Brescia, Morcelliana, 2009, 139–154.
Berti, Enrico, "Le problème de la substantialité de l'être et de l'un dans la Métaphysique". In Études sur la Métaphysique d'Aristote, edited by Pierre Aubenque. Paris, Vrin, 1979, 89–129.
Berti, Enrico, "Multiplicity and Unity of Being in Aristotle", Proceedings of the Aristotelian Society 101/2, 2001, 185–207.
Berti, Enrico, "Priorità logica e priorità ontologica fra i generi di sostanza in Aristotele". In Id., *Studi aristotelici*. L'Aquila, Japadre, 1975, 261–273.
De Couesnongle, Vincent, "La causalité du maximum. L'utilisation par Saint Thomas d'un passage d'Aristote", *Revue des sciences philosophiques et théologiques* XXXVIII/3, 1954, 433–444.
De Couesnongle, Vincent, "La causalité du maximum. Pourquoi Saint Thomas a-t-il mal cité Aristote?", *Revue des sciences philosophiques et théologiques* XXXVIII/4, 1954, 658–680.
De Garay, Jesús, *Aristotelismo*. Sevilla, Thémata, 2007.
De Strycker, Émile, "Prédicats univoques et prédicats analogiques dans le *Protreptique* d'Aristote", *Revue Philosophique de Louvain* 66, 1968, 597–618.
De Strycker, Émile, "Sur un emploi technique de μᾶλλον chez Aristote", *Mnemosyne* 22, 1969, 303–304.
Dumoulin, Bertrand, *Recherches sur le premier Aristote*. Paris, Vrin, 1981.
Frede, Michael, *Essays in Ancient Philosophy*. Minneapolis, University of Minnesota Press, 1987.
Leszl, Walter, *Logic and Metaphysics in Aristotle*. Padova, Antenore, 1970.

Merlan, Philip, "Metaphysik: Name und Gegenstand", *The Journal of Hellenistic Studies* 77, 1957, 87–92.
Merlan, Philip, "*Ón heî ón* und *próte ousía*: Postskript zu einer Besprechung", *Philosophische Rundschau* VII, 1959, 148–153.
Merlan, Philip, "On the terms 'Metaphysics' and 'Being-qua-being'", *The Monist* 52/2, 1968, 174–194.
Merlan, Philip, *From Platonism to Neoplatonism*. The Hague, Martinus Nijhoff, ²1960.
Morrison, Donald, "The Evidence for Degrees of Being in Aristotle", *The Classical Quarterly* 37/2, 1987, 382–401.
Plato, *Sophist*. In *Platonis opera*, vol. 1, edited by John Burnet. Oxford, Oxford University Press, 1900.
Thomas Aquinas, *Compendium Theologiae*. In Id., *Opuscula theologica*, vol. 1, edited by Raimondo A. Verardo and Raimondo M. Spiazzi. Torino, Marietti, 1954, 13–138.
Thomas Aquinas, *De potentia*. In Id., *Quaestiones disputatae II*, edited by Pius Bazzi. Torino, Marietti, ¹⁰1965, 7–276.
Thomas Aquinas, *In Aristotelis libros Peri Hermeneias et Posteriorum Analyticorum expositio*, edited by Raimondo M. Spiazzi. Torino, Marietti, ²1964.
Thomas Aquinas, In *duodecim libros Metaphysicorum Aristotelis expositio*, edited by M.-R. Cathala and Raimondo M. Spiazzi. Torino/Roma, Marietti, 1964.
Thomas Aquinas, *In librum beati Dionysii De divinis nominibus expositio*, edited by Ceslaus Pera. Torino/Roma, Marietti, 1950.
Thomas Aquinas, *Summa contra gentiles*, 3 vols., edited by Ceslaus Pera, Petrus Marc, and Petrus Caramello. Torino, Marietti, 1961.
Thomas Aquinas, *Summa theologiae*, 4 vols., edited by Petrus Caramello. Torino, Marietti, 1962–1963.
Vigo, Alejandro, "Prioridad ontológica y prioridad lógica en la doctrina aristotélica de la sustancia", *Philosophica* 13, 1990, 175–198.
Vigo, Alejandro, "Prioridad y prioridad ontológica según Aristóteles", *Philosophica* 12, 1989, 89–113.

Santiago González Casares
The Beyond: Death, Aesthetics and Phenomenology

> And thou shalt know the origin of all the things on high, and all the signs in the sky, and the resplendent works of the glowing sun's clear torch, and whence they arose. And thou shalt learn likewise of the wandering deeds of the round-faced moon, and of her origin. Thou shalt know, too, the heavens that surround us, whence they arose, and how Necessity took them and bound them to keep the limits of the stars
>
> Parmenides, Poem X

Every metaphysical endeavor in the history of western thought to posit a definition of what is ultimately real, every effort to give an account of the substance out of which every existing thing is made, has systematically been forced to give some definition of the Beyond. It is not accidental given the fact that philosophy, when taken seriously, must uncover that which lies beneath it all and would ultimately explain the human purpose. Throughout its trajectory it has come up with different names for this fleeting object: Being, Substance, spirit, etc., in an attempt to explain that which eludes all explanation and nevertheless defines every definition.

Beyond, from a phenomenological standpoint, may suggest a couple of figures such as the transcendence beyond intentional consciousness (Husserl)[1] and the Beyond and Otherwise (au-delà et autrement) (Levinas). Husserl's transcendental reduction would suggest a Beyond as interior and within, while Levinas' entails a definite exterior. First paradox of the beyond: interior and exterior. As St. Augustine would say, that which is *interior intimo meo et superior summo meo* makes me who I really am, intimately and authentically. The Beyond would appear here as that for which I do not have a name, cannot assign a place, and nevertheless exerts an address, a Calling onto me. It is not by name nor by a question but through the vindication of this Calling that I may acquire my authentic selfhood.

On the other hand, it can be argued that there is no Beyond, that any positing of a beyond is nothing more than traces of outdated values. *Non plus ultra*, nothing beyond this world, nothing more than will to power (Nietzsche). As Gilbert Ryle would put it, "the official doctrine" (the Cartesian road) posits that we all carry around with us two distinct substances, body and mind. They co-exist

---

[1] See Edmond HUSSERL, *Meditations Cartésiennes*, 56–98.

in the individual ego until its last breath in which the body perishes and the mind continues on and may or may not somewhat transform.[2] Philosophy has more often than not prioritized the concept of mind (soul, spirit) over the notion of body, positing the mind as the governing substance. Attributing Reality, Good and Truth as well as access and provenance to and from the beyond, to the mind while the body held the opposite. To ask the question of the beyond is to invoke nothing less than that which governs all philosophical inquiry from Descartes' *cogito* back to the original astonishment of the first philosopher, the birth of man's questioning.

It is the purpose of this essay to examine the philosophical problem of the Beyond not only from both positions but as a constitutive one of all philosophical reasoning and, at the same time, a profound paradox that haunts philosophy since its beginnings. Let us remember that since Aristotle, medieval interpretation and modern times, the debate over the primacy of philosophy was discussed as the study of an exceptional domain, separated immutable and divine. We will begin by the end, by its annihilation, its utter disappearance; its impossibility. Nietzsche.

Death and *Destruktion*

Death has haunted the history of philosophy since its initial breath. More often than not, it has appeared as a liberation in which, by merit of its occurrence, a new dimension was conquered; the soul separated from the body and the interior detached itself from its exterior. The interior (the soul) would appear as that which is private and the exterior (the body) as that which is public. In the modern era, Descartes argued that these were to distinct substances in which the soul preceded and hence controlled the body. While the latter was worthy of all mistrust, the former was the only access to reality as such. The body was advanced as that which can easily mislead while the soul was the only trustworthy guarantee of my existence. This duality implies a difference in ontological status, they are not made of the same matter, one is in space and time and the other is limitless, impossible to contain, outside of time and space. The body is sensible while the soul is *supra sensible*. This relationship between body and soul has prolonged itself since Plato up to Descartes and constitutes, along with Christianity, the basis for Nietzsche's critique of nihilism.

Nietzsche does not only acknowledge the death of the Christian God but argues ultimately for the destruction of the concept of a *supra sensible* in itself. All possible notions of a beyond are discarded, either as an impossible reality

---

[2] See Gilbert RYLE, *Descartes' myth*, 296–297.

or as the actual absorption of any external foundation by subjectivity. The soul becomes the stomach and body and spirit forge an alliance superseding any of the two isolated substances. He denounces the fact that all solid foundation has succumbed to the unscrupulous sword of the doubting-*cogito*. No-thing of the ever powerful Beyond has remained, all Otherness has fallen victim of the formidable might of solipsism. Nietzsche does not attempt to reconstruct such a di-stance, but to declare its utter annihilation, the most solemn of all deaths, the death of that which cannot die, that which is by definition eternal: the Death of God and annihilation of all that is transcendent. The center of the universe and metaphysical foundation are incarnated in man's understanding, owner of the ultimate truth and proprietor of fundamental reality. Nietzsche calls the descent into nothingness that implies the emergence of the modern era as Nihilism. Nihilism not only implies the disappearance of the beyond as the correlate of all truth and warrant of transcendence, but also the de-valuation of all the values that originated from the hypothesis of the ultra-sensible. As the unpublished "Will to power" reads, nihilism is when "the highest values devalue...the goal is missing, the answer to the "Why?"[3] Nietzsche will argue that all values that up to now have been anchored in the *supra*-sensible, have lost all their value and lead to the profound decadence of civilization. It is only through the destruction and revaluation of all values that new values, affirmative values of *this* existence, will arise. It is only by negating the nihilistic foundation of all values that we can create new and overpowering values capable of affirming the life founded on the moment (*Augenblick*) and the aesthetic possibility of fully experiencing that moment. It is through aesthetic creation that we can avoid the ascetic nature of all values rooted in the ultra-world. In order to affirm our existence we must assert the reality of the body and question that which we can only posit through reason and speculation. Nietzsche will ponder on the idea that that which is immediate is the certainty of the sensible, that which is given to us by the body and soil of our lives. True existence can only be explained through action in the moment, and not the construction of an ulterior world.

Disnaturing the western reflex to mistrust the sensible and bringing forth a *Destruktion* of the history of values instituted from and by the *ultra et supra*, Nietzsche proposes to re-valuate those values that are rooted in the ever-after. It is through the declaration of an aesthetic experience of the vital, that he thinks this life as an end in itself (this body, this land), without a necessary correlation with any sort of beyond. This experience is based on his doctrine of the "eternal recurrence"[4] of the moment (*Augenblick*). To live this life as if it were to eternally recur,

---

3 Friedrich NIETZSCHE, *The Will to Power*, aphorism 2.
4 See Friedrich NIETZSCHE, *Le gai savoir*, par. 341.

repeat itself over and over, in the same succession of events, and nothing in it will ever be different. This formula is not intended to explain the state of the universe, of a finite number of things in an eternal time cycle, it constitutes a metaphor to incite human beings to embrace life, without an appeal to any ulterior instance. Nietzsche's effort lies in eliminating the tendency to look away from existence as it is given to us and construct Reality as inaccessible in this life-time. He posits time and life as an intricate relationship of the expression and becoming of the will to power (*Wille zur Macht*).

The body, in nietzschean philosophy, is that which is immediate, it is what is nearer when we feel, what we feel to be alive. The body incarnates the only certain assertion of existence, contrary to the entire history of western thought that has attempted to insure the precedence of the intellectual, the mindful and the soulful. Reality can only be reached through the graces of the all powerful thought-process, our inherent capacity of understanding, anything that we can bring into question will immediately exist, that is the exceptional quality of the mind-soul, to be able to put into question its own existence. Nietzsche will subvert the Cartesian cogito by the potency of the now! that is and will always be governed by the body. The body is now, and the will to power that emanates from it, is what is ultimately real.

Aesthetics as a First Philosophy

Man is an instance to be transcended, he must be sur-passed. Inicipit! a man that is over with man, an overman (*Übermensch*). This notion constitutes Nietzsche's great paradox, an *aporia* that will accompany the whole of his philosophy. There is no agenda but there is one, there is no transcendence but there is one, to transcend the human being.

It is recurrent in philosophy to understand the human problem in this matter, to be human is to question mere possibility, to expose the useful and uselessness of its natural habitat. Reason appears as the source of this systematic rebellion, it is the human attribute that defies the whole of nature's configuration. Even our Initial astonishment falls victim to this inherent gesture. We have put everything in question, even the question itself, to the point that the question has become the actual definition of human habitation. It is the question that differentiates humans from all other forms of the living, let it be plants, insects, animals; the only living creature capable of the question is the human. Man has even become a problem to himself (Scheler),[5] the question is the distinctive characteristic and

---

5 See Max SCHELER, *Man's place in nature*, 3–10.

the access to human *essentia*. At the same time, it implies the tendency to challenge what is given us and defy the place that has been assigned to us. It is the systematic and methodical questioning that faces us with the beyond, either as a foundation or as a destination. It does not seem likely that a farm animal would be disturbed by any sort of metaphysical consideration about what is most profoundly real, if he is hungry, he will eat, no matter the protocol. The trans-human is the instance capable of living the present as if it were to eternally recur, without any regard for what came before or what comes after. The trans-human could be an animal, it could be a child; it could be an artist. The artist as a sort of aesthetic reduction could be postulated as a "*Destruktion*" of all pre-disposed and pre-established values in order to create new ones, aesthetic ones. It is the earth and the body (*aisthetikos*, sentient) speaking through that creation and emerging from abyssal times of recurring eternity: *Er-eignis*! The eternal recurrence of creative eventfulness.

Could it be possible to see here a predecessor of Heidegger's poet? As a phenomenological figure, Heidegger's poet speaks from and towards somewhere that looks a lot like an elsewhere, from a language (pré-dire originaire) that seems a lot like an "otherwise than being". It is the poetic word (*Gedicht*)[6] that transcends all possible words, always retreating from what is expressly being said. The poetic gesture would set free (un-veil) that which remains veiled to language. That which poetry reveals is impossible to be "said", heard or seen. It is rooted in a different sort of space, it is indeed not yet *in* space, but the condition of possibility of their being such a construct as space, or spatiality. It is a Situation (*Ort*), an artistic situation. Inhabiting that situation opens all possibility for aesthetic creation in general. It constitutes a certain type of resolution and a definite response to a Calling. To incarnate this convocation is to liberate that which is hidden and live in the permanent peril of artistic life. It is the artist who ends up responding to the Calling that situates him in the pure "Ereignis" (eventfulness) that reassembles all creation.

The existing dialogue between poetry and thinking as an attempt to get at Being, manages to describe its status and verify its uncertain and forgotten pro-venance. It unveils Being as having "epochs", different figures describing the whole of reality, what is ultimately real. Being as a sort of presence-becoming (*Anwesen, Parousia*): 'Εν, the One unifying unique, *logos*, *essentia*, *idea*. Each and every instance of these historiographical figures of Being, results in its last expression, no longer the Idea nor the *actualitas*, but its eventfulness. This term

---

[6] Martin HEIDEGGER, *Acheminement vers la parole*, 38. HEIDEGGER refers to Trakl's *Gedicht* that in german does not only imply the poetic word or poem, but also a certain unity that sets the tone (*Ge*) of a meaning that is always retreating from what is being said literally.

subtends all efforts of the late Heidegger and seems to result in the saying of the poet that, through the eventfulness his "engagement", liberates the Verb in its purest form. The poet creates an eventful space-time (*Zeit Raum*) that enables him to evoke that which cannot be said.

Phenomenology

But up to this point, we have not yet unraveled the mystery of the Beyond, we have ignored the real question pertaining to the Beyond, and that is, what does the Beyond truly entail? What does philosophy mean when she so easily implies such a notion? What do we mean when we imply that something is beyond? Beyond what? It could be argued that the notion of the Beyond is attached to our incapacity to understand certain instances that seem to elude our pre-determined structures of comprehension. That which is beyond is nothing more than that which we are not able to comprehend. That is, that the pre-existing structures of our conscious activity is not able to predict, there is no possible *adequatio*, no logical correlation to our intellectual capacity. It is beyond our understanding. All names that have been attributed to an all-encompassing explanation have been a result of our own shortcomings. We have shaped the concept of the divine from the limits of our gnoseological possibility. That which we do not understand lies beyond, and it is therefore primary and ultimately fundamental. We have, since the beginning of philosophy, posited the beyond as the proper explanation to that which is closest and immediate. It has been the modern assumption that all that is sensitive (sensible, sentient) in our existence is innately subject to higher scrutiny, slave to the power of the almighty spirit. The mind, as we have stated above, puts the body into question and by the same gesture submits it to its superiority. Certainty emerges from the mind and not the body, which falls second to all philosophical consideration. But the power of the mind has been submitted to question, all the ontological security that it provides comes from its own gnoseological incapacity to be certain of what it prescribes. Why do we then deposit all of our trust in the information supplied by our minds? Why do we base our existence in the mistrustful limits of our understanding and subsume the predictable workings of our bodies to this complication?

As we have argued before, subjectivity has been understood since the modern era as that which *solus ipse*, absorbs the world, reality and swallows its foundation, interiorizing at the same time all origin and source of knowledge. This gnoseological gesture implies the radical doubting of none other than our mere existence. Situating the subject as the pole and center of all intentions, generator of reality. The beyond could appear as its counterpoint, as that which, from its intuitive excess, subverts the subject's capacity of comprehension: counter-intention, counter-intuition – counter-experience. The Beyond is the other 's capacity to resist all subjective attempts to encompass the world and reality. It is what lies before and otherwise, that which is beyond our understanding, and for which we lack concepts, dwells inside and constitutes us from within. This paradox holds the mystery of the rapport that we entertain with existence. It de-lineates the dis-tance (Marion),[7] de-noun-ces the *differance* (Derrida)[8] and de-notes the asymmetry (Levinas)[9] of our relationship to Otherness. This liaison is constitutive of our selfhood for we are as far as we come from some otherwise and elsewhere, we are in as much as we differ from ourselves, that we are unequal to ourselves. That which we know and understand does not say anything about who we truly are or what our purpose is. That which fulfills our categories and pertain to our sensibility in space and time can only give us an objective account of our experience. It is beyond our conceptual capabilities that hides the truth (*Aletheia*) of our resolve.

Phenomenology in its latest methodological evolution, has attempted to describe the giveness of these counter-phenomena that transform subjectivity and escape comprehension. For Levinas, that which is beyond appears as Infinity, the idea of infinity or the Infinite in our thought, is the irreducible negation of what is finite, "the difference between the infinite and the finite, is a non-indifference of the infinite in the place of the finite and the secret of subjectivity".[10] This secret is the "infinité-en-nous" (infinity in us) that is transmitted through the de-finite *Calling* of the Responsibility-for-the-Other. Infinity appears as what emerges of the face-to-face dual. Duel for life and for love, materializing the asymmetrical dual of You and I – the Commandment Thou shall not kill! It is the appearance of the other human that establishes the interdiction of murder. It is indeed Infinity that lies beneath this novel relationship and founds existence in an ethical abyss. It is the Other's precedence that defines the hierarchy of the face-to-face. It is nothing more than providing an answer to the Calling, offering the subject's deepest treasure – his selfhood – as a vindication of the living. This Otherness is constitutive of subjectivity as its abyssal origin (*Ab-grund*). Levinas uses the concept of infinity (inspired in Descartes) as the foundation of the Impossible to found. Infinity installs a dia-chronical time that cannot be contained in any synchronical finitude or synthesis of the subject's understanding. It implicates the installation of an exterior or an outside (*Dehors-là-bas*) as the condition of

---

7 See Jean-Luc Marion, *L'idole et la distance*, 247.
8 See Jacques Derrida, *Marges*, 1–29.
9 See Emmanuel Levinas, *Totalité et infini*, 236–38.
10 Emmanuel Levinas, *De dieu qui vient a l'idée*, 108. Our translation.

possibility of a here, inside and now. The Beyond is the Other One ('*Ev*) defined by the infinite di-stance of the ethical difference (*differance*). That which is in front of me is the furthest, what is nearer is beyond me. The interpellation of the face of the Other reveals the endless obligation not only towards my fellow neighbor but to all humanity that transpires in the third person, testimony of justice. The appearance of the infinite Beyond renders subjectivity passive and helpless, all its rational apparatus is subverted by the incomprehensible signs of a limitless hermeneutics. It is because those conceptual structures that allow us to have an experience are incapable of coping with the amount of intuition that such an event entails. All our categories seem to fall short in explanations and any sort of rationalization. Their parameters are unable to contain all the implications of the overflowing of information implied in the otherwise (*Saturation*).[11] Levinas thusly installs ethical responsibility as a first philosophy. It is the interruption of ontology by the incommensurable Beyond of the Other's otherness ("otherwise than being") that allows Levinas to repatriate the Beyond to the world of the living and perhaps not access it but include its unattainability into a possibility in this life.

We have posited three distinct approaches to the concept of the beyond. Initially, we proposed to think with Nietzsche the beyond as the origin of the negation of life and the body for modern western thought. And how the *Destruktion* of this ascetic conception of the beyond could allow the possibility of an aesthetic life in the moment. The second approach departs from the aesthetic experience of life from the poetic word, the inhabitation of existence through eventful artistic creation. The third and final approach, is an attempt to think this aesthetic existence from an ethical point of view, attempting to recognize the beyond in that which is immediately closer, the face of the Other human being.

Bibliography

Derrida, Jacques, *Marges*. Paris, Editions de minuit, 1972.
Heidegger, Martin, *Acheminement vers la parole* (Collection Tel, 55), traduction français par François Fédier. Paris, Gallimard, 1976, 1981. German edition: *Unterwegs zur Sprache*. Stuttgart, Klett-Cotta, [14]2007.
Husserl, Edmond, *Méditations Cartésiennes*, traduction française par Gabrielle Pfeiffer et Emmanuel Lévinas. Paris, Armand Colin, 1931, Vrin 1947, 1992. German edition: Husserl, Edmund, *Cartesianische Meditationen*, edited by Elisabeth Ströker. Hamburg, Meiner, 2012.
Levinas, Emmanuel, *Autrement qu'être ou au-delà de l'essence*. La Haye, Éditions Martinus Nijhoff, 1974.

---

[11] See Jean-Luc MARION, *De Surcroît*, chap. I.

Levinas, Emmanuel, *De dieu qui vient à l'idée*. Paris, Vrin, 1982, 1986, 1992.
Levinas, Emmanuel, *Totalité et infini. Essai sur l'extériorité* (Phaenomenologica, 8). La Haye, Martinus Nijhoff, 1961.
Marion, Jean-Luc, *De Surcroît. Études sur les Phénomènes Saturés* (Perspectives critiques). Paris, PUF, 2001.
Marion, Jean-Luc, *L'idole et la distance* (Figures). Paris, Grasset, 1989.
Nietzsche, Friedrich, *Fragments posthumes*, vol. 14. Paris, Gallimard, 1977. German edition: *Sämtliche Werke*, 15 vols., edited by Giorgio Colli and Mazzino Montinari, vol. 7–13: *Nachgelassene Fragmente, 1869-1889*. München, Dtv, Walter de Gruyter, 1999, 2005.
Nietzsche, Friedrich, *Le gai savoir* (GF Flammarion), présentation, traduction, notes, bibliographie et chronologie par Patrick Wotling. Paris, Flammarion, 1997. German edition: *Die fröhliche Wissenschaft*, edited by Karl-Maria Guth. Berlin, Contumax – Hofenberg, 2016.
Nietzsche, Friedrich, *The Will to Power*, translated by Anthony M. Ludovici, New York, Barnes & Noble, 2006. German edition: *Der Wille zur Macht*. Paderborn, Voltmedia, 2005.
Ryle, Gilbert, *Descartes' myth in Classics of analytic philosophy*, edited by Robert R. Ammerman. Indianapolis/Cambridge, Hackett, 1990.
Scheler, Max, *Man's place in nature*, translated by Hans Mayerhoff. New York, Noonday, 1961. German edition: *Die Stellung des Menschen im Kosmos*, edited by Wolfhart Henckmann (Philosophische Bibliothek, 672). Hamburg, Meiner, 2015.

Axel C. Lazzari
Beyonds, Factishes, and Fetishes
Reflections on a Ritual of Restitution of Human Dead Remains

The Beyond, Going Beyond, and Factishes

"The Beyond" is commonly placed within the semantic field of religion and magic, describing a field of forces and entities in sharp contrast with the mundane realities of human life. Since its beginnings anthropology has made of this dichotomy between the sacred and the profane one of its major topics. Prayer, spells, spirit possession, rites of passage, along with dogmas and myths, are typical examples of an intercourse with The Beyond.[1]

All these phenomena involve the workings of fetishes. In its classical socio-symbolic conception, the fetish is a negative condition consisting in the power of a thing over a subject who cannot recognize that the source of this power is a social projection fixed in an otherwise passive material. Ideological, religious or sexual fetishes are thick "screens" which thwart the proper access of conscience to reality through signs. Not only would the fetishist conflate in a thing the signified with the signifier, the image with the reference, thus loosing track of both facts and signs, but also he or she would approach the outcome with veneration, respect, avoidance, confusion or even terror.

The fetish is also usually related to ritual action in anthropological theories. The various kinds of ritual are, in a nutshell, fetish-oriented actions that interrupt or bend the social process of signification thus awakening the participants to the experience of The Beyond. These theories consider that the semiotic *impasse* brought about by the fetish is tendentially channeled within ritualistic circuits.[2] Insofar as the fetish can be given a meaning, regardless its function as

---

[1] Classical landmarks of socio-anthropological studies on "religion and magic" are, among others, Edward B. TYLOR, *Primitive Religion*; Emile DURKHEIM, *Les formes élémentaires*; Bronislaw MALINOWSKI, *Magic, Science, and Religion*; Victor TURNER, *The Ritual Process*; Clifford GEERTZ, "Religion as a Cultural System".
[2] See Catherine BELL, *Ritual*.

Axel C. Lazzari, Consejo Nacional de Investigaciones Científicas. Professor of Anthropology at the Instituto de Altos Estudios Sociales, Universidad Nacional de San Martín.
Note: A previous version of the text was delivered at the Conference "The Beyond as Challenge of Life", fourth session of the Conference Series "Challenges of Life", Buenos Aires, September 28–30, 2016.

reinforcement or critique of the *statu quo ante*, inherited perspectives on ritual are predominantly homeostatic. In other words, fetishes, in general, and fetishes in ritual, in particular, are to be grasped as meaningful socio-cultural facts. But can the fetish be calmly constructed as an object of analysis given that its very nature is to de-stabilize and interrupt objectivity as well as subjectivity? Perhaps, but provided that instability be the epistemic keynote of theory.

Actor-Network Theory (ANT by its acronym) helps us with some important insights. This conceptual apparatus conceives of "sociality" as any action of linking, following, representing, affecting, translating, mediating, in sum, actions of "gathering" but also of "going beyond" from a point to another. The social is not a formal or substantive domain as in the social and human sciences, but a movement between the more or less stabilized network or assemblage of actors and their rhizomatic actions. Latour states that "an actor in Actor-Network Theory is a semiotic definition – an actant –, that is, something that acts or to which activity is granted by others. It implies no special motivation of human individual actors, nor of humans in general. An actant can literally be anything provided it is granted to be the source of an action".[3] If social action is neither the privilege of humans nor does it presuppose an inner motivation, all beings, by mere existence and reproduction, are effecting mediations and links with many others. The relevant problem is not The Beyond or The Human confronted to a "super-human" or "non-human" but the constant assembling, de-assembling and re-assembling of human and non-human actants according to the weight, number and type of the allies they mobilize.[4]

If, in consonance with these tenets, fetishes are actants, why are they considered proxy forces and secondary realities? This brings us to the problem of the fetish as the opposite of fact, which echoes the homologous dichotomies of constructed and spontaneous reality, on one hand, and subject-object, on the other. Whereas the "believer" would behave towards the fetish as if it were a spontaneous active reality, for the "critic" it would amount to a constructed and passive thing to be debunked. Subsequently, the "critic" could take two ways, deeming the fetish either as an unmade fact, independent of the observer (the positivist stance), or as a socio historical one (the constructionist standpoint). In terms of the contrast subject-object, facts fall on the object side of the divide (the subject is elided) while fetishes are the figments of beliefs (the object is just a support). This dicothomy privileging fact over fetish can be, according to Latour, deconstructed by the magic bullet of "action" as an ongoing "fabrication" or "creation". From the standpoint of actions (and actants), "projected" and "spontaneous reality",

---

3 Bruno LATOUR, "On Actor-Network Theory", 373.
4 See Bruno LATOUR, *Nunca fuimos modernos*; Id., *Reensamblar lo social*.

"subject" and "object" must be symmetrically approached as constructions. The real is constructed (networked) and constructions are real (have effects); besides, neither subjects nor objects exist but only quasi-subjects and quasi-objects always already "thrown" into actions, being reconstructed through action. This argument allows Latour to introduce the concept of *factish*, a noun conflating fact and fetish. A factish is a type of action prior to the bifurcation between fact and belief, being the common condition of both. In effect, factishes are becomings, events involving both human and non-human actants in the move. Latour calls these events "the slight surprise of action" and we name them as "going beyond". Factishing equals assembling or de-assembling of actants before they cristallize in facts and fetishes. Indeed, both facts and fetishes can be acknowledged as such only insofar as they reveal their "well fabricated" nature, their constructedness and links.[5]

Our purpose can be now stated as the re-examination of a "ritual of restitution" of aboriginal dead remains in Argentina – the so-called Retirn of Mariano Rosas to his Home- from the perspective of networks, factishes and fetishes. We will specifically dwell on the ways in which an event involving *a human faint before a skull*, and *a human vision and invocation of a spirit* can produce "beyonds" that subvert the hegemonic representation of a successful ritual act of aboriginal recognition.

The Event

In June 2001, in the province of La Pampa, a crowd gathered in an open clear in the countryside to welcome back a skull, the only remnant of Rankülche Chief Mariano Rosas. The skull, with many other Indian skeletal and organic remains, had been kept in the Natural Science Museum of La Plata for more than a century, where it had arrived after the Argentine military profaned the Chief's grave during the conquest of the Rankülche homeland in 1879. It was from this institution that the skull was returned, not without previous negotiations among Rankülche activists,

---

[5] Bruno LATOUR, *Pandora's Hope*, 266 sq. See also Bruno LATOUR, *Sur le culte moderne*. Latour's endeavor is but another twist in the ongoing rehabilitation of the otherwise negative concept of the fetish. For instance, William PIETZ deems the fetish as "always incommensurable with (whether in a way that reinforces or undercuts) the social value codes within which the fetish holds the status of material signifier [...] The fetish might be identified as the site of both formation and revelation of ideology and value-consciousness" (William PIETZ quoted in Emily APTER, "Introduction", 3). Among many other authors that tend to associate the fetish to a double-edged formation, a border crossing, a pact, or even the vortex of sociality, see David GRAEBER, *Fetishism as social creativity*; Michael TAUSSIG, *The Devil and Commodity Fetishism*.

and government and Museum officials, to the contemporary Rankülche people and "re-buried" inside a pyramidal mausoleum built accordingly. The occasion was framed by official discourse as a solemn ceremony whose main purpose was to redress an evil of the past. In this sense the acknowledgement of aboriginal history and identity was subordinated to the recognition of the whole provincial and national collective, the bearer of both the guilt and the capacity to forgive it.[6]

Fig. 3.1: "The remnants of Mariano Rosas already rest in Leubucó"
Front page of provincial daily La Arena

---

6 For a detailed ethnography see Axel LAZZARI, *Autonomy in Apparitions*.

However, during the ritual performance something "went beyond" the script. We quote from our previous analysis the event we wish to focus in:

> People wandered around the memorial grounds, always returning to contemplate the skull housed in the pyramid. In one of these human swarms, I suddenly found myself next to an old Rankülche woman who, wrapped in her poncho and on the arm of her daughter was approaching the pyramidal tomb for the first time. *Agitated and squeezed by the crowd, once in front of the skull, she let out a sigh, exclaimed "Marianito!" ("Little Mariano!") and fainted dead away, falling into the arms of those of us around her.* Surprised, we opened up a space in the crowd so that she could breathe. A few seconds later she came around. People commented on what had happened, and soon *rumor had it that the old woman's fainting was irrefutable testimonial proof that the skull belonged to Mariano Rosas.* I also remember asking the old woman *what had happened and her answering that she didn't know, that upon seeing the skull, she neither saw nor remembered anything else.* Her lapse, however, was anxiously filled with the words of her daughter, along with mine and everybody else's: *"She saw Mariano."*[7]

The Event as Fetish in Ritual

In order to fully grasp the specificity of an ANT perspective let us first advance an interpretation of this event according to a socio-symbolic analysis of ritual. The ceremony of the skull's restitution can be partially illuminated by the double burial model proposed by Robert Hertz in his seminal essay on death as a social phenomenon. A double burial is a ritual of passage performed in two phases, starting with the burying of the "wet" body and followed, after a certain period, with the definitive placing of the "dry" parts (bones) in some sort of grave or vessel.[8] The obvious difference between this model and our case is that the two phases, the first circa 1878 and the next in 2001, are not connected by a smooth cultural script shared by the same social collective but by the historical accident of the profanation of Chief's tomb (and the destruction of indigenous sovereignty). In this sense, We should properly speak of an interrupted rest and a redressive re-burial rather than a double-burial. Yet the argument developed by Hertz holds some important insights. Focusing on the wet and dry opposition,

---

7 Ibid., 361–362.
8 HERTZ interpreted the distinction between "wet" and "dry" phases of the ritual within the classical homeostatic frame of Durkheimian *sociologie*. The wet phase referred to the dangerous manipulations of the rotting corpse and sociologically corresponded to the removal of the personal identity of the dead, and to the mourning of the kin. During the dry phase the bones of the dead were incorporated to the collective memory creating feelings of respect, and therefore absorbing death into society. See Robert HERTZ, "Collective Representation of Death".

corresponding to the pairings personal/collective identity, corpse/skeleton, and pollution/meaning, we ask whether the "sociological" transition from one pole to the other is ever attained.

Fig. 3.2: An attractive skull inside the mausoleum
Credit: Axel Lazzari

The skull – the fetish – starts wet and ends up as a dry one. In effect, the polluting quality of the headbone is triggered by the event of the old woman's faint and her vision and utterance of the name "Marianito" during the performance. The fainting iterates the symbolic condition of wetness, the dead weight of the woman's unconscious body resembling a transient cadaver. For a moment, the forgotten "corpse" of Mariano Rosas reappears in the scene; we can even say that "Marianito" possesses, as the spirit of the corpse, the woman who then loses consciousness. But this symbolic and emotional climax swiftly dies away once the old lady regains consciousness and the skull is collectively identified as Chief Mariano's. These analytical steps would comply with an interpretation of ritual as accomplished reparation with fetishes playing the role of affective decoys before leaving the scene for the re-unification of social persons. The event would also admit a counter-hegemonic reading if we track down the interpretations brought about by the faint-vision from different quarters. In any case, The Beyond, here the contact with Mariano, is understood from within a perspective whereby the fetish is ultimately contained within a circuit of social facticity and signification.

The Event as a Network of Factishes "Going Beyond" Ritual

Let us now reconsider the unexpected event of the woman's faint-vision-naming as an assemblage of human and non-human actants, a working of factishes. In so doing, we do not assume that a ritual is necessarily successful, even less that it can exist without a constant labor of boundary keeping performed by certain agents. "Ritual", in any case, would be a possible outcome of an entanglement of translations between human and non-human actors rather than a symbolic dimension of social practices. We ask then how is it that the reburial of the Mariano Rosas's skull acquires, for most of the participants, the status of a ritual of reparation. Conversely, aren't there misrecognized factishes pushing beyond ritual?

The recognition of the Return of Mariano Rosas as a ritual hinges on recruiting different actants around the leit motif of *reparation of a crime*. This is confirmed by the consensual interpretation of the vision of "Marianito" by the old woman as an act of gratitude coming from The Beyond, and therefore a proof of a symbolic redress. Images, tales, rumors, news, even scholarly articles, all these and other human and non-human actants, translating one into the other, following each other, contributed to disseminate this reading of a debt being paid. Of critical importance for this idea of successful reparation to hold on is the connection of this cluster of actants to other networks that would attest to the notion of the crime occurring in the past.

The political negotiations among government officials and Rankülche leaders that predated the celebration of the Return of the Mariano recognized that the opening by Argentine military of the Chief's tomb in 1878 and the subsequent series of actions including anthropological measurements of the skull, and later on, its exhibition and custody in the Museum grounds, were events amounting to a "desecration" of the dead. We suggest that these past assemblages of human and non-human actants around "war" and "science" created the conditions to recognize a crime and the need of ritual reparation in the present.

A document from 1878 describes the search for the tomb of Mariano Rosas and the "exhumation" (sic) of the cadaver.[9] The discovery of the grave, however, comes with a revelation:

When the body was discovered, one saw that it was completely and perfectly mummified.[10] The black *skin* attached to the *bones* from head to feet formed a veritable *drum* in the thoracic and abdominal regions. He had all his *hair* and the few hairs that he had had in his *beard* when living. The empty *eye* sockets were covered by the skin of the *eyelids*, which still showed their eyelashes. The *fingernails* (were) very long

---

9 P., "Párrafos de la carta".
10 The mummy could not, had not to mean anything more than chance since, as P. puts it, the Rankülche were ignorant of the "inimitable art of the ancient Egyptians", and "in my humble opinion that state was due, purely and simply, to the silicon qualities of the soil." P., ibid.

The mummy evokes uncanny sentiments. It is death wrapped up in the appearance of life as though the cadaver has not stopped dying. The candid purpose of "getting an idea of the customs of these barbarians and what these [funerary] practices reveal about their religious customs and what they think of death",[11] cannot prevent the mummy from acting as a factish in a manner that obstructs the usual recognition of a corpse as a fact or even a (wet) fetish. The naturalist description can hardly hide this thing (a body?, Mariano?, both?, none?) which disturbingly throws out partial objects such as skin, bones, hair, beard, fingernails, eye sockets, eyelids, and a drum! Insofar as these non-human actants cannot be orderly recruited to represent the details of strange "religious customs", desecration is already hovering around the alleged "exhumation".[12]

Later on the network of factishes expands into a science atmosphere. Once again it strikes the difficulty to align non-humans for the task of objective description and explanation of facts. The following example lays bare the contradictory attempts to make of the skull both a scientific object and a fetish.

After the dismemberment of the mummy and a long journey through private hands Mariano's skull finally arrived at the Museum of Natural Sciences of La Plata in 1889 as part of a donation. In 1893 Hermann Ten Kate, a Dutch anthropologist who had spent some time in Argentina, included Mariano Rosas's skull in his work on Araucanian "cranial deformations". The skull was given number 292. This number was written down in a card along with the name of the Chief Mariano Rosas, and printed in the skull itself with the word "Araucano" attached to it. The identification procedure already reveals an instability produced by an

---

[11] Ibid.
[12] The text itself a document of a misrecognized desecration. "We are going to Mariano Rosas' tomb, where Captain Rodríguez awaits us with a phalanx of funerary sappers." The "funerary sappers" uncover a scene that obliges to obsessive "ethnographic" detailing as a way of purifying the factish: "With his head pointing east and his feet west, the old Ranquel lay with his body wrapped in seven blankets and his forehead with seven scarves, each and every scarf and blanket by the hand of each and every one of his seven wives. His head rested on his saddle, with silver riding gear and stirrup to the right, alongside his body he had his sword [...] and near his shoulder a demijohn of water. To the left he had some folded rags, some ribs of beef, like the remains of a barbecue, a *mate* with *yerba* and a silver *bombilla*, and on his chest, in the place and position where Christians place a crucifix on their dead, the General had a bottle of anisette, a corkscrew, a rag with the molars he had lost while living, and a brush for painting his face." The not-yet a fact of the mummy haunted P.'s rationalizations once again. "These remains constitute a truly precious object. Speaking, of course, from a scientific and not aesthetic point of view." By disavowing this vision by means of "science," he could take pleasure in the preciousness of the thing. The "exhumer" seemed to have been eroticized. See P., ibid.

unexpected factish entanglement. Specimen "292" of the racial series "Araucano" cannot easily be separated from card "292" and "Mariano Rosas". On one hand, Ten Kate's scientific publication states that certain numbers in the series "have belonged" to certain personal names and, on the other, an all too denotative plate of skull 292 is displayed on the page.

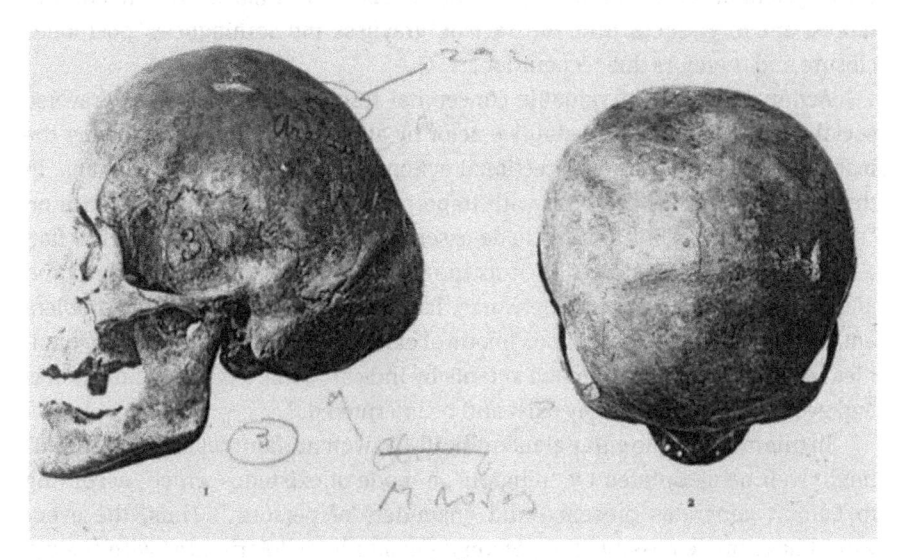

Fig. 3.3: Skull number 292, Mariano Rosas's skull? From Ten Kate 1893

Here is a network comprising numbers and personal names *in text* and a numbered skull *in image*. Despite the bridge offered by number 292 which would have made the name "Mariano" signify the skull and viceversa, there seems to be an excess at both ends. We know the skull belongs to an "Araucano" but it cannot be irrefutably affirmed it is Mariano's since this name is nowhere printed in the bone. The result is a free floating personal name and a cranium not attaining the status of a sheer scientific fact. Neither a "well-constructed" object nor a fetish (a war trophy) the skull stays as a factish. Albeit negatively, this undecidability allows for "desecration" to be chosen *a posteriori* as the master trope for the process of restitution.

Let us now turn back our attention to our event skull-old woman-faint-vision-"Marianito". Can we identify something else than the symbolic play of permutations between wet and dry skull? The vision and faint of the old woman came with her own commentary: "I saw gray and then I saw nothing." It is our conjecture that this phrase indicates unrecognized factishes at work. We should take this grayness and nothingness literally as the boiling vortex of forces not yet congealed in fetishes and facts. The old lady puts in words a liminar experience leaving no ground for the participants to identify with something in common. This stands in stark contrast with the emotion-ridden name of "Marianito" and its iteration "she saw Marianito", a doubled fetish. Sure, naming "Marianito" allows for the creation of a symbolic space and pushes the ritual in the direction of redress and forgiveness. Still, the trace of "grayness and nothingness" postpones closure and therefore due recognition.

Action-network is a valuable conceptual resource that permits to traverse social domains and any substantive actor by applying the rule of following the inscriptions left by the non-directional actions of humans and non-humans. In this sense, ANT does come up with important novelties with its insistence on "symmetrizing" actants as a key to de-assemble institutions.[13] However, the "flattening" effect produced by ANT runs the risk of misrecognizing the values and affects that circulate through networks. Latour has acknowledged this problem and tackled it with the concept of "mode of existence". A mode of existence qualifies translation practices among actants by indicating the keys as to how things and events should *felicitously* exist and be interpreted.[14]

In this manner, the entanglement skull-old woman-faint-vision-"Marianito" might well be modulated by "religion", a mode of existence which, according to Latour, generates presence and engenders of persons.[15] Thus, the event would have made possible the personal encounter of "Marianito" with the old woman for, more than anything, naming is presentification, the invocation of a being before a person towards which he or she becomes a witness of. If we pay respect to this key we might reconsider the apparition of "Mariano Rosas" as a (non-human) presence translated into a (a non-human) skull translated into a (human) person by means of fainting and visioning.

It seems that factishes are constantly becoming within an immanent though discontinuous space of networks and modes of existence, but where does this force come from? In other words, do assemblages *and* modes of existence "lay on" something else? Is there after all an Absolute Beyond if not before the Human at least in relation to networks and values? Again, Latour plays his card: "plasma"

---

13 See, for example, the arguments about the networks of science and nature-politics in Bruno LATOUR, *Ciencia en Acción* and Id., *Politiques de la nature*.
14 A comparative research on modes of existence is being carried out by Latour and his associates with the objective of establishing the conditions for a cosmopolitical parliament. LATOUR identifies fifteen modes of existence belonging to the "a-modern" as the first step in a cross-cultural comparison. See Bruno LATOUR, *Investigación sobre los modos de existencia*.
15 Ibid., 289 sq.

which, as a reserve of forces, is but another name for Being as Other, a non-absolute Beyond.[16]

Conclusion

We should recapitulate our itinerary. Our first step was to analyse the event of faint-vision-"Marianito" as entailing a symbolic code in a ritual (*wet/ dry*). We went on to unravel the construction of the fact of desecration, which justifies the ritual of reparation, indicating the works of human and non-human assemblages (*a mummy in pieces, a skull and a name going astray*). Then we identify in some verbal traces (*gray, nothing*) the possible operation of an assemblage of actants prior to fetishes and facts. We finally introduced the concept of mode of existence to make justice and account for the ritual as a religious experience. The following diagram represents the main "stations" we have connected in our trajectory.

The Beyond

GODS/SPIRITS

▼

beyond "The Beyond"

(*social facts* of "fetish", "sacred", "belief", "ritual", etc.)

SOCIETY/CULTURE/HISTORY

(anthropologism)

▼

beyond "the social beyond of The Beyond"

(*network* of human and non-human actants, *factishes*)

TRANSLATION OF PRESENCE

▼

---

16 Both Action-Network Theory and the theory of modes of existence relate to a "flat" ontology within which Being is conceived of as a movement of othering. Unlike the metaphysics of Being as the Same, differences are irreducible to a transcendental plane, and are to be understood as mini-transcendences, othering "jumps" of hiatuses. See Bruno LATOUR, "Le plasma"; Bruno LATOUR, *Investigación sobre los modos de existencia*.

beyond "the beyond as network"

(*mode of existence* of religion)

BEINGS OF PRESENCE

▼

beyond "network *and* modes of existence"

(*plasma*)

NON ABSOLUTE BEYOND

The Beyond reproduces itself in many guises. "Society", "culture", "history" perform the role of displaced "divinities"; presences constantly reappear as that which has to be deferred and translated along networks until they are recognized as such yet under the caveat of the mode of existence of religion and, again, dissolved in the non-absolute beyond of plasma.

A complementary diagram depicting the relations among sign, fetish, factish, mode of existence, matter and plasma may add more clarifications.

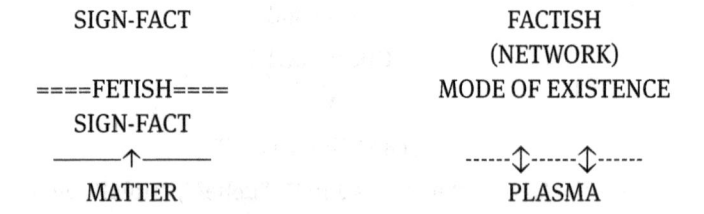

SIGN-FACT	FACTISH
	(NETWORK)
====FETISH====	MODE OF EXISTENCE
SIGN-FACT	
──────↑──────	──────⇕──────⇕──────
MATTER	PLASMA

The left column shows the script of sign-fact-//fetish//sign-fact that depicts socio-cultural perspectives of The Beyond. Signification and reference are, respectively, "relations of rupture" between present and absent (hidden presence) signs, and present signs and the "referred" reality of facts. The fetish is that which, through its manifestation, disrupts the "relations of rupture" of signification and reference. This, notwithstanding, the fetish is deemed recoverable for signification and referentiality. In the right column we aligned factish (network) and mode of existence. Factishing brings together (translates, bridges, delegates) active entities that are not completely closed (quasi-objects and quasi-subjects). The "jumps" between dis-continuous actants determines the expansion of the network. When the network is stabilized by the force of certain actants there appear boundaries such as facts and fetishes, and actants perform as signs and referents (left column). The stabilization of boundaries can also be understood as modes of existence. The mode of existence entails certain purification with the emphasis placed on the value adscribed to mediating actants, and on the specific tone it lends to the different kinds of beings that are constructed within it. Finally, a supplementary row features "matter" and "plasma". Matter is separated from sign//fetish//sign by a full line and an arrow which intends to evoke a breaching, a radical rupture inscribed in the fetish. Next to it "plasma" is connected to factishing by a dotted line traversed by bidirectional arrows, which means that plasma is not a pure transcendence, as it would be the case in dualist ontologies.

Bibliography

Apter, Emiliy, "Introduction". In *Fetishism as cultural discourse*, edited by Id., and William Pietz. Ithaca and London, Cornell University Press, 1993.
Bell, Catherine, *Ritual. Perspectives and Dimensions*. New York, Oxford University Press, 1997.
Durkheim, Émile, *Les formes élémentaires de la vie religieuse*. Paris, CNRS Éditions, 2008 (1912).
Geertz, Clifford, "Religion as a Cultural System". In Id., *The Interpretation of Cultures*. New York, Basic Books, 1973 (1966), 87–125.
Graeber, David, "Fetishism as social creativity or, Fetishes are gods in the process of construction", *Anthropological Theory* 5 (4), 2005, 407–438.
Hertz, Robert, "A Contribution to the Study of the Collective Representation of Death". In *Death and the Right Hand*, edited by Rodney Needham, and Claudia Needham. New York, Free Press, 1960 (1917).
Latour, Bruno, *Ciencia en acción. Cómo seguir a los científicos e ingenieros a través de la sociedad*. Barcelona, Labor, 1992.
Latour, Bruno, "On Actor-Network Theory: A Few Clarifications", *Soziale Welt* 47 (4), 1996, 369–381.
Latour, Bruno, *Pandora's Hope. Essays on the Reality of Science Studies*. Cambridge, Mass./London, Harvard University Press, 1999.
Latour, Bruno, *Politiques de la nature. Comment faire entrer les sciences en démocratie*. Paris, La Découverte, 1999.
Latour, Bruno, *Nunca fuimos modernos. Ensayo de antropología simétrica*. Buenos Aires, Siglo XXI, 2007.
Latour, Bruno, "Paris, ville invisible: le plasma". In *Airs de Paris*, edited by Daniel Birnbaum, and Valérie Guillaume. Paris, Centre Pompidou, 2007, 1–7.
Latour, Bruno, *Reensamblar lo social: Una introducción a la teoría del actor-red*. Buenos Aires, Manantial, 2008.
Latour, Bruno, *Sur le culte moderne des dieux faitiches*. Paris, La Découverte, 2009.
Latour, Bruno, *Investigación sobre los modos de existencia. Una antropología de los modernos*. Buenos Aires/Barcelona/México, Paidós, 2011.
Lazzari, Axel, *Autonomy in Apparitions: Phantom Indian, Selves, and Freedom (on the Rankülche in Argentina)*. Unpublished Ph. D. Thesis. Anthropology Department, Columbia University, 2011. Accessed July 8, 2014: http://udini.proquest.com/view/autonomy-in-apparitions-phantom-goid:864737978.

Malinowski, Bronislaw, *Magic, Science, and Religion, and Other Essays*. New York, Paul Reynolds Inc., 1948.

P., "Párrafos de la carta de un expedicionario (episodio de la campaña a Nahuel Mapu)". In *La Tumba de Mariano Rosas*. Santa Rosa, La Pampa, Daily *La Arena*, 1969. Copy of an original article published in *La Prensa* in 1878.

Taussig, Michael, *The Devil and Commodity Fetishism in South America*. North Carolina, The University of North Carolina Press, 1980.

Ten Kate, Hermann, "Contribution a la craniologie des araucans argentins", *Revista del Museo de La Plata*, 4, 1893, 211–220.

Turner, Victor, *The Ritual Process. Structure and Anti-Structure*. Ithaca, Cornell University Press, 1991.

Tylor, Edward. B., *Primitive Culture*. New York, Harper Torchbooks, 1958 (1871).

Carlos Rafael Ruta
Beyond the Self Circle

Beyond Poetry

> Was not writing poetry a secret transaction, a voice answering a voice?
> Virginia Woolf

1. There is perhaps a border beyond which it is hard, at least today, impossible imagining or foreseeing with more clarity the moment and the way in which the man set the decisive step towards language.[1] Anyway, this path in their vicissitudes and determinations would not mare or condition in anyway the implicit potentiality of this phenomenon (of language) that was rising in that moment. It is there at stake the projective horizon language that per the descriptions of its aims or proposes is setting the profile of its deep nature as well.

We should remember that within this problematic field the phenomenon of language that determines and characterises us can also be defined in its essential specificity as "poetic". This description lined through an intellectual tradition that finds in Humboldt one of its primary steps understands that each linguistic expression is the manifestation of a possibility of human creativity that goes through language. That is way its nature and its dynamics utterly exceed the urgency of practical necessities. It is in that sense that such tradition places in an essential harmony the display of poetic writing and language itself because of that creative disposition that gives life to language. From that perspective, poetry is not the other of language but language itself and it is in this direction at the same time that results in its transparency and opacity a privileged zone to approach our estimation of both the limits and possibilities of language. It exposes us inevitably to the task of give details and of thinking the essential roots of this phenomenon as it is set in this dilated soil that concerns the limits and possibilities of human condition in itself.

This link could never be underseen, the challenge consists of rehearsing the questioning and the thinking in its density and aim its plains and articulations and the base from where it rises and that responds to this creative disposition of language itself and in this case the phenomenon of poetic writing.

In the domain of poetry itself, Rainer Maria Rilke, wondered precisely about the origin from where that life destined to name the silence of the world emerged

---

[1] Jürgen TRABANT, *Die Sprache*, 88 sq.

and answered that unveils the temporal structure over which it is set and it is claiming to be thought of:

> *Siehe, ich lebe. Woraus? Weder Kindheit noch Zukunft*
> *werden wenigerÜberzähliges*
> *Dasein entspringt mir im Herzen.*[2]

Childhood and future see each other and are supposed here as radicular instances of plenitude that end up in the fecundity of the poetic word, and that writing "verbally inventive".[3] Rilke's assertion seems to inscribe the poetic work and task in an arch set in extremes of openings as if they were in vanishing lines of an unlimited temporal fruitfulness. Nevertheless, the defining horizon on which it might be possible to inscribe the (always) creative experience of the language does not seem to be other than the fundamental finiteness that identifies human life and of course establishes its entire ontological projection as conceptual mesh of the sense of being.

The ninth piece of Rainer Maria Rilke's The Duino Elegies provides, in this regard, some guidance (on the problems of the language). The poem states the purpose of a poet's job precisely ingraining it in such reality and experience of finiteness that ascribes meaning to the poetic word. It might perhaps be even possible to search therein for the origin of what Kierkegaard called our essential literary property. Word and existence would interweave their essence there precisely in the projective sense which such finiteness entails.

Even though in the course of the poem a much greater parable is described, one of the central axes establishing its direction, insofar as it constitutes one of the supporting points that shape its motion, points to and depicts what is perhaps the most transparent, defining and clear-cut aspect of our essential finiteness. The expression which marks and summarizes – in Rilke's words – our profound reality and our experience is Ein Mal.

> *Us, the most vanishing of all. Once*
> *for each, only once. Once and no more*
> *And we, too: just once. Never again. But*
> *to have lived this once, even if only this once,*
> *to have been of earth – that cannot be taken from us.*

The fleetingness of everything. Perhaps the passing-by nature of everything. Describing a transient, even paradoxically definitive course. Everything is not but once, only once. And we too, once, just once. Just like everything else, we are

---

[2] Rainer Maria RILKE, *Die Gedichte. Duineser Elegien. Die Neunte Elegie*, 661 sq.
[3] Terry EAGLETON, *Cómo leer un poema*, 35 sq.

fleeting too. Such fleetingness entails the lightness inherent to our own *Dasein*, using Rilke's expression. The transience characterizing the lightness of that which, lacking the gravity of that which is unstable appears prone to be swept away just by the breeze of the passage of time. The meaning of what is seems to be determined by its passage. A transience which in turn points, in its precariousness, to the demarcation of its own space: our time is this time and only this time. But such lightness of that which floats while passing by, that lightness that is a sign of need, soars up into a sky of change from the strength of an uncontestably supporting argument: Ein Mal. Just once. And such Ein Mal embodies all the faces of our own unicity. Of the unique nature which makes us what we are. The unrepeatability that defines us and distinguishes us as time, perhaps just one note, unique in the melody and tonality (Stimmung) of the world. But also the unrepeatability of that which does not come back. Of that marked by the time limit which thus determines our inherent expiration date. Marked by that we will never be. Marked by the negativity which constitutes us. But Rilke believes that here we also find the density of meaning and experience which gives such fleeting nature the name of "worldly" (irdisch), thus enunciating, at least, the strength of a root in which he accepts the fullness of fleetingness that weaves the harmony and tonality of all things and their destiny. Without a doubt, the limit that signals the end inherent to our unicity is also sealed by the unicity which such end – unlike everything else – entails for us, to wit, death. Even if we refer to it, as does Rilke in this very same poem, as that *friendly death (vertraulicher Tod)*. We know that the unrepeatability of our time is rooted in the unicity of our limit. Of the meaning death carries just for us as the final and defining threshold of our journey. There is nothing but irreversibility beyond such threshold. However, we should ask ourselves whether the Only Once expressed by Rilke in the poem also points to an absolute absence of any "beyond," especially if we believe that, in Rilke's view, the crucial determination of the poetic discourse, or, even more, of a language, resides in such Ein Mal. It is worth wondering, therefore, if there is no "beyond" for the poem that accompanies us to the final and defining threshold of our destiny. And we wonder if such transit could co-mean something beyond the simple permanence that writing gives by transcending the temporal limits of its origin.

It is about questioning about the thread of meaning that poetry inserts in the threshold of human life. A threshold that constitutes that future founding all the past that we are. The threshold we know marks or reveals a foreshortening of the complex human time structure to which obviously, our own linguistic strength is not indifferent or foreign. In this frame, we could pose the place of poetry as the opening of a possible beyond experience and human time. Even when reaching it seems diffuse and inconsistence. It is obvious that this questions have their roots in experience and poetic writing but they spread their relevance to the hole phenomenon of language. And therefore, this problematic design leads us to question ourselves what our beyond is in the language that comes with us and crosses the border of our time. The reference to Rilke, to Rilke's poetry, is here crucial to define the territory demarcated by this search. Poetry casts the clarity of such night against the shadows; it inscribes light in the thickness of its mist. And it unveils, in its own density, the mark coined by all languages.

Nevertheless, the question unwraps even towards the interior of poetic experience. We already know that it does not ask simply for the beyond of the poem that in its writing transcends the temporal limits of the poet and thus spreads its presence beyond its own space in the earthly time. The question inscribes within the knot that is woven in the poem by time and meaning. Primarily in the experience of its writing. But also referred to the beyond that can open in the precarious time of its reception. It then has to do with the time of its origin and the time of its persistent and always renewed reception.

In any case, the most thought-provoking aspect of the question is the view focusing on the manner in which poetry may itself become a beyond for our life as humans. This not only introduces issues of hermeneutical theory, but also confronts us with the possibilities of poetry itself with regard to the limitations and deprivations everyday life reproaches us for. Not only are these issues relevant to the essence of poetry but they also open up a wider horizon to discern and consider the core of a language.

2. Just like us, poetry may not escape confronting or refusing to confront the final threshold of the life in which it finds one of its limits and where it more clearly exposes itself to its own challenges and dangers. Ultimately, it is about the risk of incurring – upon making the final, decisive move – the loss of the roots of one's own poetic work diluted in artificial craft, thus departing from the genuine creative energy. The risk of losing the true "tonal rectitude," an expression used by Eavan Boland in an essay on Elisabeth Bishop's poetry in which the author wonders where poetic tone plunges its roots. He finally argues that "its origins must always be in a suffering world rather than a conscious craft".[4] Commenting on this passage, Seamus Heaney suggests as follows: "This last sentence is a wonderful formulation of what we seek from any poet's undermusic...". As the best poetry of the western world witnesses – and he revises – this tradition is full of a kind of "old wisdom". This is poetry imbued with a power ingrained in a world of life that has been lacerated or essentially defined by pain, a suffering world of life that with every defeat of destiny faces the challenge of confronting death.

---

4 Seamus HEANEY, *La reparación de la poesía*, 184.

In an honest effort to rescue Dylan Thomas's work from certain criticism, Heaney focuses on the poem "Do not go gentle into that good night". In his view, there the poet fulfils the promise because his craft has not lost touch with the suffering world. The poem speaks, of course, about the threshold of death. It was written in one go and without hesitation, in a late stage of the poet's short life, just when his father was dying of cancer and his marriage had come to a halt. However, as suggested by Seamus Heaney, there we can hear the wail of the poet's child-self in the face of his father's departure. There the son gives solace to the father, but it could also be construed that the child poet inside Thomas consoles the histrionic old man he had become. "Do Not Go Gentle is a lament for the disappearance of the maker in Thomas himself as well as an adieu to his proud and distant schoolteacher father." The poem fulfils the technical requirements and thus escapes the emotional claustrophobia. Its wording has turned into an extraordinary force. And the structure of the composition is a "vivid figure for the union of opposites, for the father in the son, the son in the father, for life in death and death in life".[5] As argued by Heaney, there is also something Rilkean therein "for we are here in the presence of knowledge transformed into poetic action." I would like to quote a letter written by Rilke in which he speaks about The Duino Elegies:

> *Death is the side of life averted from us* [...]. *The true figure of life extends through both spheres, the blood of the mightiest circulation flows through both: there is neither a here nor a beyond, but the great unity in which the beings that surpass us, the angels, are at home.*

It is precisely in such unity, in the experience of such unity, that poetry can exert its overwhelming force born out of a sensitivity which matured together with the methods of expression. Poetry can thus identify the path along which to move forward through what Thomas himself had defined as "creative destruction, destructive creation" so as to prevent the "suffering world" from fleeing from its own composition and intimate substance. It is as if Orpheus's most daunting challenge were to be fought off again, the challenge of putting the power of his lyre to the test facing the gods from the underworld and hauling life back from death. As stated above, in such answer poetry not only risks its voice but also defines its own essence and value. It imperils its own worth and its fate. It confronts the challenge of being its own beyond.

However, the tonal and stylistic attitudes or arrangements may vary greatly upon embracing the ultimate instance of our finiteness at the heart of poetic activity. This is not only about the manner in which poets assume or confront,

---

5 Ibidem, 190.

whether personally or through their work, that final moment and its meaning; it is also about perceiving the consequences or resonances for poetry itself in view of its own human or aesthetic value. How much can poetry tell us, from the profound disposition conceived, about the moment we are in the presence of the threshold of life? An instance which anticipates its memory every day with every No uttered by reality throughout the years. In a counterpoint essay, Seamus Heaney analyses some poetic pieces composed by Philip Larkin and W. B. Yeats, even being aware of, and calling into question, Larkin's rejection of the purportedly romantic stance assumed by Yeats. Heaney considers Larkin's poem "Aubade". "Death is no different whined at than withstood," an observation lying at the heart of the poem's message. The poem thus assumes or considers that any rhetorical or imaginative ploy which might mask the realities of the body's dissolution and the mind's disappearance after death is mystification. Religion, courage, philosophy, drink, and the routines of work and leisure are regarded by Larkin as placebos. As he grew older, he assumed a tougher stance on the inexorability of his own extinction. Human wisdom, therefore, seemed to him a matter of operating within the limits of mortality, and of giving up any false hope of transcending or outfacing the inevitable. Yeats, from a non-naive view, made it possible to glimpse that there is no hideaway, that individual human life may not find a shelter where to feel safe from the coldness of the universe. We are well aware, however, of Yeats's embrace of the supernatural, which was not at all naive; he was as alive as Larkin to the facts of bodily decrepitude and the destructive force of death, but he deliberately resisted the dominance of the material over the spiritual. This is why all of his "supernatural machinery" was nothing but, in his own words, "stylistic arrangements of experience [...] They have helped me to hold in a single thought reality and justice".[6] This is why Larkin's poem, beyond its technical finds, is the "definitive post-Christian English poem, one that abolishes the soul's traditional pretension to immortality and denies the Deity's immemorial attribute of infinite personal concern". The reader is left on the edge of the abyss, in the midst of immense emptiness, a place where, as Yeats puts it, "the cold winds blow across our hands, upon our faces, the thermometer falls".[7] For Yeats, however, these circumstances were not symptomatic of an absence but, rather, the ecstatic presence of the supernatural. It would be therefore logical to assume, as suggested by Seamus Heaney in the essay herein addressed, that Yeats would not only reject Larkin's poem Aubade, but he would also endorse Milosz's views on the same work despite recognizing

---

6 Ibidem, 202.
7 Ibidem, 210.

the poem's integrity and coherence, which "comports to the sensitivity of the second half of the 20th century". In Milosz's view, Larkin's poem endows death with the supreme authority of Law and universal necessity, while man is reduced to nothing [...]. "But poetry by its very essence has always been on the side of life. Faith in life everlasting has accompanied man in his wanderings through time, and it has always been larger and deeper than religious or philosophical creeds which expressed only one of its forms".[8] In Milosz's opinion, we can find a rationalization there which entails a betrayal of poetry as to its history and destiny. But perhaps it is not. Perhaps it can never be, as full poetry, even if unaware of it, is always on the side of life. But there is indeed the risk of reneging on the "spiritual intellect's great work".[9] Reneging on what Seamus Heaney considered: "the goal of life on earth, and of poetry as a vital factor in the achievement of that goal, is what Yeats called in "Under Ben Bulben" the "profane perfection of mankind". From Heaney's perspective, the poetic vision of reality which poetry offers should be transformative. "The poet who would be most the poet has to attempt an act of writing that outstrips the conditions even as it observes them [...] will transfigure the conditions and effect thereby what I have been calling the redress of poetry. That experience of a transformative relation with the language." If we resort to poetry, to literature, as noted by Heaney, to be forwarded within ourselves, that concerns us at the heart of the paradoxes of our time structure. It is an experience like "foreknowledge of certain things which we already seem to be remembering".[10] And such poetry sets in motion a new world in the fresh capacity of creation. It can thus manage to pronounce a final Yes. And that Yes, such affirmative answer, is very valuable because its weight and significance reside in its capacity to contain a No. In Heaney's opinion, Yeats' poetry confirms that courage is good. "It shows how the wilful and unabashed activity of poetry itself is a manifestation of joy and a redress, in so far as it fortifies the spirit against assaults from outside and temptations from within –temptations such as the one contained in Larkin's attractively defeatist proposition that death is no different whined at than withstood."

Such redress of poetry, time and time again referred to by Seamus Heaney, arises from what he calls, along with Robert Pinsky, the responsibilities of the poet. The artist needs the promise to respond. The free and creative answer to human life's negativity tells us "be whole again beyond confusion" (Robert Frost). The poet implies that the imaginative transformation of human life is the ideal means to truly understand it. There poetry perfects its beyond in itself. It is

---

[8] Ibidem, 212.
[9] Ibidem, 213.
[10] Ibidem, 214.

the glimpse of a potential order of things lying beyond confusion. In this manner, poetry fixes its own borders, drawing the line which separates the real conditions of our daily life from their imaginary literary representation and the social discourse of the world from the world and the poetic language. Poetry thereby focuses on the world's potential for change offered by the answer imagined. The poem makes a showing as to how poetry may lead men to a more complete life, beyond the closing of a pure and barren negativity. Beyond the epochal prison of time.

3. Even though underlying this are all the questions that begin to surface in view of the mystery surrounding the connection between time and meaning, we should identify, at least, the interplay of time forces which puts together all poetic foreshadowing, structured as an arch stretching its significance potential beyond its own historical present. It even appears to transcribe its knowledge and doings in circular fashion, always engaging the past and the future from the crux of the present. Such doing makes it possible to discern a foreshortening which in addition refers to a type of unfathomability that transcends, permeates and communicates all times. However, these considerations are not only fragmentary and unreliable: they consist in anticipations which require more careful and even closer examination of a poet's work and of poetic composition. In an essay written in 1958, Albert Camus, in an attempt to "situate" René Char's poetic work, provides some guidance to enlighten us as to the touch of originality which singles out great poetic work.[11] In Camus's opinion, what occurs in the case of Char is a *"révolution poétique,"* a "startling" originality. But the suggestive thing is that Camus argues that such originality rests on its link to the past. A view which, in this case, would need to recover the tragic optimism of the pre-Socratic Greece to be on a par with the "disasters" of his time, a post-war time. Camus states that it is by reason of such poetry that our night shines and in such way teaches us to walk through the heart of obscurity. A type of poetry which (in the case of René Char) fiercely struggled against totalitarianism and denounced the allied nihilisms crossing and determining the atmosphere of sense of its present, thus opening "une route d'espérance". In view of such poetry that "habite justement l'eclair," Camus asks: What can one ask of a poet today? And he answers: To find again love, peace, liberty in the treasures of the present. Just as Char did. In other words, his acceptance of his own present, his settling in the midst of "our dismantled citadels," his being at the heart of the conflict, the fact that he never rejected anything of his time, all of that is what turns Char into "poète de nos lendemains." A type of poetry constituting our beyond by reason of a time texture

---

[11] Albert CAMUS, *René Char*, 1163 sq.

which accepts its own present and ingrains it in the light of a past. However, the key to such web of times which gives rise to both sense and meaning, which gives rise to "originality" is, in Camus's view, the "rigor" of that obscurity that is bound together with a job of furious condensation of the image.

4. Even though it may be irreverent or at least provocative in the case of Camus, it does not seem unreasonable to refer here to some of Paul Valery's indications, in this case commenting on a legendary French translation of the Spiritual Canticle of St. John of the Cross.[12] Having the features of its own genre, the Canticle represents and promotes a temporary expansion, in the vital core of its attempt, i. e., the union of man and God. And, therefore, the overcoming of the present time towards a beyond that began in this life, but transcending the limits of the present to get beyond all ephemeral time in the image of eternity. Valery recognizes this mystical feature of the Canticle, but is only concerned with and interested in the purely poetic aspects of the text. In this regard, and making reference to the comments on this Canticle, Valery insists that verses are never limited to a single referential meaning; they rather create what he calls "valeur du sentiment." From memory games or foreshadowing emerges a resonance that engages the subject in a "poetic universe" and pure sound amid the noise makes it anticipate an entire musical universe. Poetic words make their way into that poetic universe in which time and meaning expand beyond the originary senses of their historical present. Valery thinks that the only certain thing in poetry is the dispossession which, from such poetic universe, makes its way into another and absolutely different time. The poetry used to refer to this matter profoundly transforms all values in the text. "For us, it is about living and breathing in a different, second life, and it represents a state or a world in which objects and beings, or their images, have other liberties and ties that are different from those which belong to the practical world." There is a transformation of all nature and experience operated from within the language, and it all ends in the poetic beauty as the result of "sustained" and "hard work." This temporary opening towards its own beyond is achieved through the language and is the consequence of hard work on the language. We know that Valery spent years and made great efforts to analyse and reflect on this vital core of a poet's work.

5. The above considerations, collected from fragmented, diverse and limited records of writing experiences, result in a series of philosophical hermeneutics questions which are based on the search for the roots of the act we call poetry and from which we can glimpse the foreshortening of potential of every language.

---

[12] Paul VALERY, *Cantiques Spirituels*, 445 sq.

Within the framework of the phenomenology of the word, in all of its implications, the central and perhaps decisive question could focus on clarifying the ontological roots of the phenomenon of poetry. That question should lead to the clarification of poetry as our potential beyond, i. e., opening an exploration path to clarify the temporary exodus that poetry creates from our ontological determination.

It would then be about elaborating an analysis that could allow to rethink from its ontological root this capacity that seems to incarnate poetry to open the possibility of transcend the temporal determinations that are imposed to human existence.

Even limited, centrally, to the reflections elaborated in *Sein und Zeit*, Heidegger's work wakens fundamental suggestions to think "the poetic" in its temporal texture and therefore in its potential of opening time and meaning.

At the beginning of the work (paragraph 5), when the author precisely refers to the task of elaborating the question about being (the central ontological question), Heidegger clarifies the ontic-ontological primacy of *Dasein*, i. e., the entity that should be questioned to grasp the meaning of being. The entity that will play the role of the primarily interrogated.[13] How can we make this *Dasein* accessible to understanding interpretation? That is the question that presides the thread of questions that knot the paragraph and that is at the same time the central key of its paradoxes. Because it is not enough to access its primacy in the interpretative labour but we need to make clear the correct way of accessing it.[14] The whole paragraph can be read, in this sense as an expression and a review of difficulties to access to the being and to the *Dasein*. To this *Dasein* that "we are in each case ourselves". And in it, it is necessary to precise for Heidegger, that this entity (dieses Seiende) because its ontic proximity is ontologically further away. Nevertheless, we can enhance this *Dasein*, as the proper way of being corresponds the inherence of an understanding of this being. And so we live in an interpretative state about our own being. We behave in every moment in a certain interpretative state.[15]

It is not insignificant for us that this interpretation, always pre-ontological is carried out as a tendency from that we relate to constantly and immediately in our behaviour that is the world. Even when this last thing has decisive resonance to think poetry it is important here to underline the ways of being of

---

13 Martin HEIDEGGER, *Sein und Zeit*, 15.
14 Ibidem, 15: "[...] eine ausdrückliche Aneignung und Sicherung der rechten Zugangsart zu diesem Seienden gefordert ist."
15 Ibidem, 15: "Zwar gehört zu seinem eigensten Sein, ein Verständnis davon zu haben und sich je schon in einer gewissen Ausgelegtheit seines Seins zu halten."

that interpretative state. *Dasein* – according to Heidegger – develops the understanding of its being through multiple forms of interpretation. Even if the list of this diverse paths (verschiedenen Wege) goes through the science of the spirit it includes as one of such ways poetry without any doubt in a broad sense (Dichtung).[16] It carries out what other ways have also done; those different disciplines that "have questioned through different paths and variable proportions the behaviours faculties strength possibilities and destiny of the *Dasein*". The Dichtung is part of a whole of forms that develop the ways of making the *Dasein* accessible to itself. They deploy that interpretative state in a diverse exercise of the language. The poetry is precisely one of this ways of being (*Seinsart*) that deploy in a peculiar way what was pre-ontologically given.

It is undoubtedly relevant to point out that for Heidegger it is necessary to enhance that the *Dasein* "being" is comprised by and comprises something as the being; but also to enhance the need to show that that from which the *Dasein* comprises the being without expressing in its origin is the time. Here underlies Heidegger's hard or lost search for clarification of time as the horizon of all understanding of the being and every way of interpreting it and therefore the irremediable attempt to rethink time and within it the temporality inside the *Dasein*. In any case, from both sides, poetry is seen interwoven with the way of being constitutive of the *Dasein* that refers it to its intimate interpretative determination and at the same time roots it in its own temporal character. Poetry, from its genuine features, deploys and deepens into the potential of opening sense that points the *Dasein*; it does so within an engagement even though it is only foreseen with its constitutive and essential temporal determination.

Paragraph 34 of the same work introduces an interpretation of language whose purpose, according to Heidegger himself, was "to show the ontological place of that phenomenon within the creation of the *Dasein* being".[17] This attempt is based on the intention to clarify, for the purposes of philosophical investigation, the horizon for the question that delves into the way of being that is appropriate for the language. With regard to these exploratory questions and analyses, Heidegger makes an almost passing reference to poetry. More precisely to the "poetic discourse" (*dichtende Rede*). The whole phenomenon of language is thought from the perspective of the "discourse" (*die Rede*) as one of the existential features of *Dasein*, along with "understanding" (*Verstehen*) and "affective disposition" (*Befindlichkeit*). The analysis of these last two existential features helps us clarify the place of interpretation and its derivation: the statement. Amid

---

16 Ibidem, 16.
17 Ibidem, 160 sq.

these elements we can find the concepts of "saying" and of use of the language, both of which are closely related to one of the meanings of the statement, that is, "involvement" as "expression" (*Mitteilung – Heraussage*). In this sense, for Heidegger, discourse is "the existential-ontological foundation of language." Based on the references in this regard, Heidegger suggests that the poetic discourse "may" have as its goal the involvement (*Mitteilung*) of the existential possibilities of the affective disposition (*Befindlichkeit*).[18] In order to explain this statement, we must first establish all the defining features of "discourse" which should refer, in this case, to the "poetic discourse".

In the co-implication of the three defining features describing the physiognomy of *Dasein*, understanding undoubtedly plays an important role, without disregarding the fact that its possibilities are essentially linked to the other two components: emotional tone and discourse. The comprehensibility underlying the circuit of these existential features classifies its components into the same interpretation by which *Dasein* takes the understanding. Discourse has the specific function of "articulating comprehensibility," that is, articulating sense and, through it, all meanings. Therefore, the ontological roots of language are found there. The phenomena related to involvement, expression and communication of sense and meaning prolong the fundamental fact that defines discourse in its reciprocity with comprehensibility. However, discourse as well as understanding and emotional tone are co-originating existential features. In this regard, in order to discover their unity and specificity, it is of crucial importance to pay attention to what "arises" from them in terms of the *Dasein* phenomenon.

The bottom line here is that these three existential features determine and give rise to the opening of being-in-the-world which defines us as the *Dasein* we ourselves are in each case. Therefore, the language itself has its roots in the constitution of this opening of *Dasein*. And on the basis of this phenomenon of language, discourse (*die Rede*) articulates comprehensibility, as we have seen, meaning comprehensibility of "there," the existential space that *Dasein* creates as opening of its being in the world and, thus, of all its possibilities. Discourse is thus involved in this function of opening the world that *Dasein* creates as only it has its own being, as being-in-the-world. Discourse itself is the "existential constitution of opening of *Dasein*" and, therefore, constitutes its existence. This is also related to another critical dimension of the functionality of discourse. Since the comprehensibility that opens our being in the world is always "being with others" (*Mitsein*), and since that comprehensibility is articulated in the

---

[18] Ibidem, 162: "Die Mitteilung der existenzialen Möglichkeiten der Befindlichkeit, das heißt das Erschließen von Existenz, kann eigenes Ziel der 'dichtenden' Rede werden."

"discourse", living or being with each other *(Miteinandersein)* is discursive, is articulated by the discourse. Living together is talking to one another (even if we refuse to do so). And the structure of this discourse implies, according to Heidegger, the fundamental phenomena of listening and being silent.

Even though each of the features we have identified as relevant to "discourse," according to Heidegger's perspective, could or should apply to the "poetic discourse," we need to first establish the essential link between this "poetic discourse" and "affective disposition" *(Befindlichkeit)* as one of the existential features of *Dasein*, which is the involvement – and the sharing – of its existential possibilities. The key here is still the "opening" of the existence indicated and created by *Befindlichkeit* (affective disposition). Disposition to meet again oneself again within the originary phenomenon of the mood, the disposition, the "emotional tone", the Stimmung. The emotional tone is the ability to control our opening of the being there, of the existential spatiality of *Dasein*, which opening is prior to any and all knowledge.[19] In this tonal opening *Dasein* rediscovers itself because in the opening of the world it is always placed in front of itself.

It answers to *(Befindlichkeit)* what in the ontic order is the better known and the everyday, that is the mood and the affective disposition. It is in that sense that Heidegger's considerations imply to rethink these phenomena, and not to let them go unseen, because truly they are not ontologically a nothingness. Within the Befindlichkeit there is an originary opening that exceeds the possibilities of opening of knowledge (Erkennen). Because Stimmung is an originary way of the being of the *Dasein*. And in that sense the Befindlichkeit opens the *Dasein* to its condition of thrownness (Geworfensein), let to its own responsibility. The facticity of giving oneself to oneself. Of the opening thanks to which one receives and takes its *Dasein* (existence) as the being that has to be by existing. The Stimmung opens to the *Dasein* its own There. In this originary phenomenon the *Dasein* is its there, its Da, its existential space. The *Dasein* is open in its condition of being thrown and therefore given to the world. Constantly given to the world, affected by it. In there then the world appears but in such a way that is always our matter.

At the base of this phenomenon is the experience of the same affective tone (Stimmung) as that given to the tonal range of the world.[20] This tone gives *Dasein* its own tone; it determines how and in which manner this being is. And this is so since Heidegger considers that there is actually a world melody such that "being in the world" means that there you can reconnect (in that being) with all the harmonicas of the world. Stimmung, the tone, is precisely the fundamental mode

---

19 Ibidem, 29, 134 sq.
20 Martin HEIDEGGER, *Gesamtausgabe A*, 29/30, 101.

in which we dwell in our being there, our own existential space, being in the world as if we were put there to exist, also receiving our own existence from that opening. The purpose of all Stimmung is undoubtedly to reveal oneself, but our bond with the body, which is to inhabit it, is also revealed there, such that tones remove us from our bodies and expose us to the outside. This is also the basis of the possibility of the word and the tone that the word itself acquires in "the way of speaking". *Dasein* expresses itself in such discourse because being-in-the-world, understanding, is already being outside. Moreover, according to Heidegger, what *Dasein* refers to is that "being outside," its status of being exposed, of being an open place.

The poetic discourse is thus responsible for such aligning such tonal resonance of the world. That poetic discourse is involved in and shares the possibilities of that originary opening of tones that makes it possible to find out about oneself and the world in a tonal arrangement. The poetic discourse is involved in this tonal phenomenon in the existential possibility of speaking that is listening. Listening in the sense of being open to the others, the world and originarily to ourselves. To the "primary and authentic opening of *Dasein* to its own may-be".

In an enigmatic and suggestive formula, Heidegger claimed that tones (*Stimmungen*) are "background events of the power of time".[21] The poetic discourse that holds all poetry together but which also mints, in terms of the language, our "legitimate literary property" is tonal opening to the full power of time, to all its possibilities. It opens those possibilities in the tonal arrangement it hears, but says nothing about it in its own time. But it also creates in its linguistic doing an opening power where all times can establish new openings beyond the closure of their present. In that poetic discourse *Dasein* always seeks the possibility of leaving itself, of transcending in a tonal opening that is not limited to any closure of meanings but which precisely opens up free projection possibilities in each present, and mints the potential of this opening in listening, thus leading to a permanent and infinite sharing of its own beyond. Itself as its own beyond increasingly open to the potency of time, of each time.

What can we take to the other side? Wondered Rilke in the same ninth Elegy. Very little and nothing remains – for him – as a promise. Nevertheless, he felt that facing the experience of fugacity and finiteness, we always would like to hold the world in our hands, and give it, but give it to whom? And ¿*what can we take to the other side?* Finally, ... and almost only ... "*the acquired word*" (erworbenes Wort). From this our time: *the time of what can be said* (Hier ist des Saglichen Zeit), that has here its own land.

---

21 Martin Heidegger, *Gesamtausgabe*, 38, 130.

We are here to say: house, bridge, hole, door, bowl, fruit tree, window... And these things ... fleeting, confide in our saving them, and we are more fleeting.
Everything that is here needs us, this that is so fugitive that strangely is our concern.[22]
We are here to say...

Bibliography

Camus, Albert, "René Char". In Id., *Essais*. Collection Bibliothèque de la Pléiade, Paris, Gallimard, 1965, 1163–1166.

Eagleton, Terry, *Cómo leer un poema*. Madrid, Akal, 2010.

Heaney, Seamus, *La reparación de la poesía. Conferencias de Oxford*. Madrid, Vaso Roto Fisuras, 2014.

Heidegger, Martin, *Sein und Zeit*. Tübingen, Max Niemeyer Verlag, 1984.

Heidegger, Martin, *Gesamtausgabe. II. Abteilung: Vorlesungen 1923-1944*. vol. 29/30: *Die Grundbegriffe der Metaphysik. Welt – Endlichkeit – Einsamkeit* (Wintersemester 1929/30), edited by Friedrich-Wilhelm von Herrmann. Frankfurt am Main, Vittorio Klostermann, ²1992.

Heidegger, Martin, *Gesamtausgabe. II. Abteilung: Vorlesungen 1919-1944*, vol. 38: *Logik als die Frage nach dem Wesen der Sprache* (Sommersemester 1934), edited by Günter Seubold. Frankfurt am Main, Vittorio Klostermann, 1998.

Rilke, Rainer Maria, *Die Gedichte. Duineser Elegien. Die Neunte Elegie*. Frankfurt am Main, Insel, 2002.

Trabant, Jürgen, *Die Sprache*. München, C.H.Beck, 2009.

Valery, Paul, *Cantiques Spirituels*. Collection Bibliothèque de la Pléiade, Paris, Gallimard, 1957.

---

22 Rainer Maria RILKE, *Die Gedichte. Duineser Elegien. Die Neunte Elegie*.

Gustavo A. Ludueña
Spirit World as the Beyond from an Anthropological Perspective
Making Sense "Reasonably" of Afterlife Ontologies

In his masterpiece, *The Idea of the Holy*, Rudolf Otto defined the notion of the numinous as a consciousness that awakes in the believer, invoking a profound feeling of existence; furthermore, it represents the "irrational" component of religion, it is something "felt as objective and outside the self".[1] Additionally, the numinous is compounded by the so-called *mysterium tremendum*. While *mysterium* distinctly refers to the unknown, occult, esoteric and other aspects of the religious experience, the numinous evokes mental states stimulated by the individual's encounter with the holy. The latter, in Otto's view, represents a challenge to the knowledge of something envisioned as divine, which cannot be expected to be purely attained by the mere intervention of common reason. In this regard, the important assertion made by this author is that religion is not only a rational enterprise – as proposed by theological thinking, for example – but involves irrational components as well, which occur in the personal experience with the numinous. Because of its relation to the worshiper's mental realm, a corollary of such a perspective is that this experience is not only religious but also epistemological. Consequently, this concept will constitute the focus of the remainder of this article.

By assuming that such knowledge rests on the cultural order of things, this study will focus on the cognitive effects of the numinous, herein materialised in the spirit as a particular ontology according to the Spiritualist movement. The spirit introduces disorder into the elements that define that which is strictly human. In this sense, a latent danger exists in relation to the order of things. If the spirit could be considered to be normal from a certain perspective, the opposite is also possible if another cultural scheme is considered. In the author's fieldwork among spiritualist groups in Buenos Aires, such a contradiction was encountered. In this regard, analysing the coexistence and connections of opposite models of thinking in relation to the spirits, the spirit will be taken as the area of dispute in terms of the beyond being accepted by some, while being rejected by others. Hence, while spirits become a source of fear, distrust, existential hesitation and ultimately risk for some; for others, their presence in everyday life is

---
1 Rudolf OTTO, *The Idea of the Holy*, 11.

natural and not necessarily dangerous.[2] These positions reveal the competition of different strategies comprehending the beyond – whether in a negative or a positive fashion. By analysing the epistemologies in dispute, namely science and Spiritualism, the aim of this work is to investigate the diverse thinking about the spiritual within these groups. In doing so, three strategies of reasoning about the numinous will be identified, which reveal the principles of causality, plausibility and verification. It will be stated that they collaborate in the formation of a specific mode of thought. Moreover, the article argues more broadly that such a mental mechanism is also applicable to the exploration and knowledge of the beyond in contemporary scientific culture.

Spiritual Interactions: The Principle of Causality

Although spirits are not envisioned as humans, they are largely acknowledged to possess humanlike characteristics, notably awareness. Thus, one of the main characteristics of the spirit is the absence of a human body. Such an ontological condition is complemented by the sociological aspect, where, according to Spiritualism, there exists an epistemological certainty about the possibility to be known; remarkably, to be described, perceived, interrogated and so forth. This knowledge is public; it is disseminated among the members of the group and has the mission of establishing the order of reality. In particular, this savoir acquires relevance in the ritual process where it functions as a mental disposition to the numinous. This cognitive dimension was present in the narration of Nicolás.

I encountered Nicolás during one of his visits to the branches of the spiritualist movement where I was conducting fieldwork.[3] He was the responsible person of the branch, representing the authorities of the movement. Nicolás was an old man with extensive experience as a member of the institution, and positively welcomed enquiries into the group's spiritual practices. All discussions occurred in Nicolas' office, where both parties sat opposite each other in a confined space, separated by a desk. A photo of the spiritual guide of the branch was displayed on the closest wall. The guide had been a member of the branch until his death many

---

2 Cf. Paul STOLLER, *The Taste of Ethnographic Things*.
3 The referred movement is the Basilio Scientific School which was founded in 1917 in Buenos Aires by French immigrants. In its beginnings, it was characterized by a strong presence of cosmological and ritual elements from Catholicism and Allan Kardec's Spiritualism; its mission was the restoration of Jesus' spiritual principles later abandoned by, according to the historical narrative, the Catholic Church.

years previously; Nicolás expressed a significant level of sympathy for him and made references to his memory on a daily basis. According to spiritualist beliefs, the spirit reflects the consciousness of someone who has passed away, proving the existence of life beyond the own self in the afterlife.

On many occasions during the conversations, he was observed to glance at the photo while talking. It is assumed that the mission of the guide is to protect and orientate people who come to the branch in search of assistance. Nicolás advised that he maintained a close relationship with him and often asked for guidance. "When I want to talk with the guide I see the photo and ask him about different things and then he responds to my questions". In this sense, the guide became the indexical sign of an afterlife existence. This functions as a form of consciousness which exceeds human existence. One of the stories Nicolas narrated in order to exemplify this relation was about a member of the movement – called José – who was diagnosed with bladder cancer. In this vein, it is important to note that, in native etiological theories, all illnesses have – in the last instance – a spiritual origin.[4]

Furthermore, he explained the function of the practice of the "spiritual fluid", which is intended to transmit purified spiritual particles into the body of an affected person. This action normally involves two people; one who receives the fluid and one who gives it. Usually, the first person assumes a calm seated position on a chair, while the second person, in a standing position behind the receptor, is responsible for applying the fluid. The latter gently caresses the head and shoulders of the person receiving assistance, applying the fluid in the form of a smooth vibration. It is assumed that the purified particles (i. e., the fluid) will revitalise the affected organs or the parts of the body impacted by the disease. In this sense, and under the principle that all diseases have a spiritual root, Nicolás said that he applied this fluid to José for one year on a regular basis. Once the doctor decided that surgery was necessary for the patient, he asked the guide for assistance with the aim of ascertaining the result of the operation in advance.

In this vein, it must be stated that the relation with science in general – and medicine in particular – is simultaneously perceived, both positively and negatively. The positive aspect is due to its legitimacy and power of explanation regarding the physical world; while the negativity emanates from the insistence on denying the very existence of other realms that are distinct from the empirical world. The coexistence of both systems of knowledge engenders a constant tension. Thus, when Nicolás asked the guide to predict the outcome of the

---

[4] See Miguel ALGRANTI, "Teorías etiológicas de la enfermedad" and, for Kardecian Spiritualism, Elizabeth MORENO and Juan CORBETTA, "Locura y Espiritismo".

intervention, he advised that the surgery would be successful. In fact, and with the notable surprise of the doctor after long and intensive surgery, the cancer had disappeared. Nonetheless, following this event, José was overwhelmed by a form of depression and refused to either eat or leave the hospital. Finally, after several days experiencing this condition, he died, and his wife noticed Nicolás at this juncture. In the interview, he advised that he was sadly surprised by the news, as well as extremely upset because of both the failed prediction made by the guide and the time and effort he had invested in assisting José through the extensive period imposing spiritual fluids to aid his recovery.

In his words, "I was angry with the guide... then I asked him why... what had happened with José. He told me that he had decided to stay". When he transmitted the guide's explanation to José's wife, she was highly reluctant to accept this assertion and to believe in the spirit itself. In part human and in part non-human, the spirit's affirmed and neglected existence by part of different people shows the contradiction among opposite cosmologies. In epistemological terms, the spiritual world – synonymous with the beyond – refers to an undiscovered field through which common understanding cannot penetrate; in other words, the beyond delineates the limits of the known world. Ultimately, the wife rejected Nicolás' explanation because she considered it to be a falsehood. From the outset, she was hesitant to accept his account, rejecting the effectiveness of the fluid and experienced self-doubt regarding the guide's intervention.

This story is an illustration of the assiduous interpersonal relationships with a spirit and its agency, as well as the naturalisation of the spiritual world and resultant effects on the world of the living. In this case, this notably refers to the fluid applied to support José's health and his decision to remain in the beyond, even when the illness had been cured. Throughout Nicolás' narration a floating sense of predictability manifested, and therefore security, in relation to the results that were expected from the spiritual intercession (i. e., the spiritual fluid used for helping José and the request for his recovery). Even though unwanted results could generate an apparent contradiction through the cause-effect principle, ulterior Nicolás' interpretations of the consequences allowed for comprehension of the unpredicted contradictory outcomes. This opinion on the spiritual agency is based on the knowledge believers, Nicolás and others alike, hold about the composition of the human body and the power of spiritual particles. The death of the patient was ultimately understood as a decision that José's spirit made by itself, following the universal law of free will; in other words, each personal action – in this case, a choice – or a ritual performance, such as the like the giving of fluid, can have significant consequences.

Seeing Beyond: The Principle of Plausibility

The spirit is a sui generis ontology; it is non-empirical, and possesses an abstract being and self-consciousness. Spirits are ambiguous and threaten the limits between the human and non-human. For these reasons, the spirit owns, in Mary Douglas' words, an "anomalous" ontology that – for non-spiritualists, at least – jeopardises human beings. As she argued, an anomaly is "an element which does not fit a given set or series".[5] Moreover, Douglas affirms that "[a]ny given system of classification must give rise to anomalies, and any given culture must confront events which seem to defy its assumptions".[6] It is accepted by spiritualists that spirits are not composed of matter – neither biological or other – and are only visible through so-called spiritual vision; this refers to visual mediumship, more commonly known as clairvoyance.

After one of the conversations, I maintained with Nicolás, I was led to the "spiritual saloon", where the weekly practice of the so-called "worship to god" occurred. This ritual action involves the participation of six "mediums" who, while sitting at the front of the room, are supposed to incorporate non-evolved spirits into their bodies, in order to provide them a medium through which they can speak.[7] It is assumed that these entities, throughout the duration of the session, employ the body and mind of the mediums as channels for conveying a message or purely to express an opinion about life, people, human behaviour, and so forth. They are used to express their message to the public for several minutes and then receive a response from the person responsible for overseeing the coordination of the practice. Prior to commencing the round of speeches, each spirit is described by the respective host, who possesses the ability of clairvoyance, so that the physical appearance of the spirit can be described to the audience. The routine of visualisation is led by the coordinator; however, this frequently includes the participation of other ritual assistants, who can either partially or fully perceive the characteristics of the entity. It is important to note that, along with the visual mediumship, there is also the so-called "intuitive" visual mediumship. In this case, it is supposed that the medium intuits the characteristics of the spirit that he or she is communication with and observing. Most people declare to hold this competence. This intervention, which transforms the

---

5 Mary Douglas, *Purity and Danger*, 38.
6 Mary Douglas, *Purity and Danger*, 40.
7 The medium is conceived of as the holder of the mediumship, which refers to a form of communication with the world of the spirits; for instance, though the vision, hearing, writing, intuition, etc.

process into something more collaborative, operates as a social device for the re-construction and certification of the spirit's appearance and – sometimes – even its attitude (e. g., aggressiveness, sadness, etc.). Therefore, the acknowledgment of the identity is finally acquired through the mediumship; this would allow the medium both to access a non-empirical order of reality as well as the possibility of establishing information about the spiritual world that is not perceptible by conventional means.

Indeed, these visual experiences are also demonstrated in other cultures. For example, Edith Turner[8] highlighted the importance of seeing spirits for the Ndembu healers of Zambia for developing witchcraft diagnoses. She described her vision of a plasma-like figure departing the body of a patient in a *Ihamba* healing ceremony performed by a ritual doctor. "I saw with my own eyes a large gray blob of plasma emerge from the sick woman's back. Then I knew the Africans were right, there is spirit affliction, it isn't a matter of metaphor and symbol, or even psychology".[9] On the other hand, also in Africa, Paul Stoller narrated his fieldwork experience among the Songhay of Nigeria, where an epistemological intersection appeared between the worlds of the ethnographer and natives.[10] While living among this people, he was initiated as a *sorko*, which is a praise-singer to the Songhay spirits who is trained as a healer in order to combat magic, witchcraft and spirit sickness.[11] The list of these ethnographic situations in cross-cultural perspective is sufficiently broad that it can be traced back to the British anthropologist Edward E. Evans-Pritchard's experiences with the Azande people,[12] and even the earlier fieldwork conducted by Edward B. Tylor's among the nascent spiritualist movement in the United Kingdom in the late nineteenth-century. A lucid conclusion regarding the relation of the researcher with these experiences is provided by Barbara Myerhoff through her experience of taking peyote under the guidance of Ramón, a shaman of the Huichol Indians from Mexico. She experienced a sense of disappointment over having lost contact with a presence because of her own reaction: "It was my Western rationality, honed by formal study, eager to simplify, clarify, dissect, define, categorize, and analyze".[13] Put in Turner's terms,

---

[8] Edith TURNER, *Experiencing Ritual*.
[9] Edith TURNER, "Training to See What the Natives See", 260.
[10] Paul STOLLER, *The Taste of Ethnographic Things*.
[11] Cf. Paul STOLLER, *The Taste of Ethnographic Things*, 46.
[12] Edward E. EVANS-PRITCHARD, *Brujería, magia y oráculo entre los azande*.
[13] Barbara MYERHOFF, "I Found Myself Impaled on the Axis Mundi", 157.

> [t]here seems to be a kind of force field between the anthropologist and her or his subject matter making it impossible for her or him to come close to it, a kind of religious frigidity. We anthropologists need training to see what the natives see.[14]

In this perspective, to deliberate or to comprehend the extra-ordinary from people's cosmological parameters may be one of the most defiant challenges offered by the beyond; a corollary of this is that one of the problems related to the unknown is how to explain it based on the known.

Besides these methodological issues that question naïve anthropological objectivity and neutrality, there are also comprehensive difficulties. This is because the challenge of the spirits is epistemological; it subverts the episteme about the known world.[15] In other words, the problem with the beyond becomes the problem of the incursion of the unknown world into the known world. Hence, extraordinary experiences make the frontiers between the two realms less defined. This vague situation exposes ordinary assumptions about the world and suspends the associated knowledge. More precisely, this fact leads to the cognitive contradictions involved in the convergence of the normal and the abnormal, as well as its rationalisation. When Nicolás invited me to sit in the saloon, he maintained proximity and asked if I could perceive anything that was reflected in the mediums. This was certainly a surprising question; in that environment, it was very clear that what appeared to be exceptional for the bystander was in fact normal for the participants. Despite this fact, I endeavoured to look directly at the mediums and made serious attempts to perceive alterations in their faces or bodies. After several seconds, I was unsuccessful; my assertion that "I can't see anything", was disappointing for Nicolás.

Although spiritual vision functions as empirical proof of the existence of spirits and the spiritual world, a limited number of people declare that they have this capability. Consequently, an implicit principle of plausibility operates over the spiritual existence, which derives from the membership of the "community of believers", according to whom, afterlife is an existential fact. This plausibility seems to function effectively, as it is clear in the ritual previously described through the assertion that, "if some people with visual mediumship affirm the presence of an entity, so I believe that the entity is there, even when I cannot see it". However, the space of the plausible also engenders ambiguity regarding what

---

14 Edith TURNER, "Training to See What the Natives See", 262. On extraordinary fieldwork experiences, see also Jean-Guy A. GOULET and Bruce GRANVILLE MILLER, eds., *Extraordinary Anthropology*.
15 For the same problem in relation to witchcraft, see Jean FAVRET-SAADA, *Les Mots, la mort, les sorts*.

can be expected; this necessarily places the believer in the situation where they must search for techniques in order to reduce uncertainty.

Coping with Uncertainty: The Principle of Verification

Associated with the principle of plausibility is the so-called "comprobación" (i. e. personal verification), which is valid for believers and impure spirits (who, in a spiritualist's view, are required to achieve awareness about their evolutionary situation). It is important to mention that the identity of Spiritualism as a "spiritual science" is based upon this principal. This implies that the only truths that are accepted are those tested by an individual rather than through an act of authority. In doing so, it is supposed that this tests the action of the spiritual over people's lives. In this vein, it should be stated that the modern rationalisation of reality emanates to a high degree from scientific thinking; scientific culture provides the fundamental schemes that construct our understanding of the world. In the modern world, things that defy such a science-based cosmology are either anomalous or – as a minimum – ambiguous.[16] For that reason, this study focuses on the notion of the anomaly, because it enables people to confront the difficulties caused by the symbolic order of things.

As previously stated, although spiritualist believers recognise the existence of spirits as well as the possibility of communicating with them, they do not refute scientific knowledge. In their perception, the world is a manifestation of a spiritual condition, which is invisible to the common senses. The beyond is compounded by those aspects that are not evident to the senses. Then, as the senses are the channels of connection to the known world, the unknown world has a structural difference that is centred around a radical ontological composition. In this case, the beyond illustrates the tensions between the spiritual and the material as a metaphysical distinction, upon which worshippers make sense of their existence. The spirit, as a liminal figure, seems to satisfy the articulations between both worlds. For this reason, when the beyond emerges into everyday life, this could be disruptive and provoke confusion in the scheme of social classification and the comprehension of reality. Although "[i]t is not impossible for an individual to revise his own personal scheme of classifications", it should be

---

[16] Spiritualist's tensions with medicine where described elsewhere, Gustavo A. LUDUEÑA, "Popular epistemologies and 'spiritual science'".

said that "no individual lives in isolation and his scheme will have been partly received from others".[17] This means that, in each spiritual experience, the individual refers to the cultural taxonomy under which the situation could make sense. The next paragraph will introduce an example to demonstrate this concept.[18]

In the mid-1970's, Blanca – an elderly woman with a well-known reputation for her mediumistic abilities – collaborated as a medium in one of the branches of the Basilio Scientific School. On one such occasion, she was accompanied by her husband who was waiting among the audience. The general practice was that the so-called "familiars and friends" of the subject that had passed away, would come to converse with the assistants. Blanca was seated at the forefront of the spiritual saloon, accompanied by other mediums. As was customary in such spiritual practices, they were incorporating spirits; this implies that the medium lends his/her body to the spirit so that it can be employed as a means of communication. The expectation of the assistants was naturally to receive the opportunity to meet people who they loved and to hear a "message" from the beyond. The person with authority over the ritual described the spirits in detail individually, enumerating the personal and physical features. Based on these indications, at the end of the description, each member of the audience was invited to identify the spirits accordingly by announcing their names. The process was operating smoothly until an unexpected event occurred. Blanca recalled that, at one moment, there was a problem with the identification of a spirit that had incorporated her body.

The appearance of the spirit had been described very clearly: it was a young blonde woman in her late twenties, with blue eyes, a white dress and boots, among other characteristics; she was "like a bride", she said. Despite this detailed description, three or four names suggested by the audience proved to be incorrect. The spirit replied negatively each time, before the names were proclaimed by the people. The coordinator became nervous because of what was interpreted as a lack of "spiritual elevation" among the assistants. Ultimately, she felt the "intuition" that the spirit was actually there for the medium, Blanca; therefore, she proceeded several steps towards the back of the room where Blanca's husband was located and asked him if he was aware of any close associate who could meet the description of that particular spirit. He hesitated for a while and, although plagued by uncertainty, replied to the person in charge that there was a friend of her daughter – called Marta – who had disappeared several days previously. The responsible person of the practice encouraged him to ask the spirit if that name was indeed correct, and then he said: "are you Marta Shelter?"

---

17 Mary DOUGLAS, *Purity and Danger*, 39–40.
18 For a wider description of this case see Gustavo A. LUDUEÑA, "Estado, nación y espíritus desaparecidos".

The spirit – through the medium – answered with a clear and resounding "yes". The experience was vividly emotional for both Blanca and her husband, during and after that spiritual practice. Upon returning home, she experienced a high level of concern and was uncertain of the veracity of that event. "Was it really the spirit of Marta? Could have I committed a big mistake? How should I tell my daughter if that meant that Marta was dead?", the worried Blanca berated herself after the experience. Consequently, she asked God for "proof".[19]

The requested proof materialised after several days. Blanca's daughter received a telephone call from a friend advising her that Marta and two acquaintances, all of whom had been kidnapped by the military forces as it was later determined, had been discovered murdered along with other individuals. In this story, Blanca was unsecure about the spirit that had incorporated her body. This was an ambiguous situation given that it involved what appeared to be a dubious identity. Such ambiguity was dangerous because of its implications for the medium and her daughter. However, the proof arrived and was so convincing that it reinforced Blanca's faith in the power of mediumship. Contrarily to people to whom spirits are predominantly signified as a radical alterity synonymous with an anomaly – like José's wife whose attitude was of general disbelief regarding the numinous – Blanca's reaction was of careful hesitation. This indicates that it was juxtaposed between unbelief and belief, although never of uncertainty in relation to the beyond. Nevertheless, the alteration of the order of things depends on events which create extraordinary conditions by suspending the efficacy of the systems of valuation and making them temporarily ineffective.

Conclusion

The beyond, as vividly symbolised by the spirit, exists outside the parameters of the scientifically cognoscible. Spirits are ambiguous and compromise the limits between the human and non-human. For these reasons, the spirit possesses an anomalous ontology, which threatens the human existence. To summarise, this work has analysed the reception of spirits as a signal of at least one of the many forms of the extraordinary conditions of the beyond. In this sense, it can be said that secular society has not eradicated spirits despite the advanced developments in science and technology. Furthermore, spirits are not restricted to – nor

---

[19] The notion of "proof" has an important value in the cosmology of this movement and is anchored in its self-definition as a "spiritual science". See Gustavo A. LUDUEÑA, "Cosmología y epistemología espiritualista".

are they necessarily subsumed to – any singular religion but rather to a universal secular culture of the beyond. They are still present in our society though disparate images, narratives, cultural products, and so forth. This manifestation of the beyond in our society is also a signal which implicitly demarcates the boundaries of the world that it is possible to know and the unknown world.

As an ontology of the "in-between", and in the light of the scientific culture, the spirit represents – and is usually presented as – an abnormal alterity. In doing so, the beyond confronts the accepted and legitimate models of knowledge through the action of a differential – and even opposite – epistemology demonstrating its subversive power. Furthermore, in cognitive terms, neither dealing with the numinous nor the direct experience associated with it, produces "irrational" results. The intervention of at least three principles of reasoning have been described, which feature a singular way of thinking in Spiritualism. However, because of its parallelism with the scientific culture, it could be more appropriate to approach the beyond in a broader sense. These identified principles are causality, plausibility and verification. They operate relationally in order to understand reality under the umbrella of a religious culture, characterised by a specific knowledge and a moral system. Additionally, it has been demonstrated that this interaction is not always consistent with spiritualist values; nonetheless, empirical data in each case demonstrates that the agents constantly attempt to rationally comprehend the beyond. Further research should be conducted in order to gain a new understanding on the reasoning criteria in relation to the beyond in other cosmological systems.

Bibliography

Algranti, Miguel, "Teorías etiológicas de la enfermedad y algunos principios terapéuticos en las prácticas de la Escuela Científica Basilio de Buenos Aires", *Scripta Ethnologica* XXIX, 2007, 109–119.

Douglas, Mary, *Purity and Danger. An analysis of the concepts of pollution and taboo*. London/New York, Routledge, 2001.

Evans-Pritchard, Edward, *Brujería, magia y oráculo entre los azande*. Barcelona, Anagrama, 1976.

Favret-Saada, Jeanne, *Les Mots, la mort, les sorts. La sorcellerie dans le Bocage*. Paris, Gallimard, 1997.

Goulet, Jean-Guy A., and Bruce Granville Miller, eds., *Extraordinary Anthropology. Transformations in the Field*. Lincoln/London, Univ. of Nebraska Press, 2006.

Ludueña, Gustavo A., "Cosmología y epistemología espiritualista en la Escuela Científica Basilio", *Ilu. Revista de Ciencias de las Religiones* 6, 2001, 67–77.

Ludueña, Gustavo A., "Estado, nación y espíritus *desaparecidos*. La imaginación política en el espiritismo porteño durante la dictadura militar, 1976–1983", *Historia, Antropología y Fuentes Orales* 47–48, 2012, 181–216.

Ludueña, Gustavo A., "Popular epistemologies and 'spiritual science' in early twentieth-century Buenos Aires". In *Handbook of Religion and the Authority of Science*, edited by James R. Lewis and Olav Hammer. Leiden, Brill, 2011, 609–631.

Moreno, Elizabeth N., and Juan M. Corbetta, "Locura y espiritismo: etiología espírita de la salud mental y las técnicas terapéutico-rituales de la 'desobsesión'", *Ciencias Sociales y Religión / Ciências Sociais e Religião* 22, 2015, 120–135.

Myerhoff, Barbara, "I Found Myself Impaled on the Axis Mundi". In *Shamans through Time. 500 years on the path to knowledge*, edited by Jeremy Narby and Francis Huxley. London, Thames and Hudson, 2001, 154–157.

Otto, Rudolf, *The Idea of the Holy*. London, Oxford Univ. Press, 1923.

Stoller, Paul, *The Taste of Ethnographic Things. The Senses in Anthropology*. Philadelphia, Univ. of Pennsylvania Press, 1989.

Turner, Edith, "Training to See What the Natives See". In *Shamans through Time. 500 years on the path to knowledge*, edited by Jeremy Narby and Francis Huxley. London, Thames and Hudson, 2001, 260–262.

Turner, Edith, *Experiencing Ritual. A New Interpretation of African Healing*. Philadelphia, Univ. of Pennsylvania Press, 1992.

Sandra Baquedano Jer
Beyond the Species, or the 'Beyond' of Human Life?
Challenges of a Non-Speciesist Ethic

Awareness of death and the mystery of suffering have lead humanity, throughout its history, to search for philosophical and metaphysical explanations of the world. With the aid of fantasy, human species has been able to configure a variety of projections about a 'beyond', in order to bestow some kind of ultimate sense on the phenomenon of existence.

The more adverse, irrational, disconcerting or worrying that reality is in the present, the more intensely de we tend to rely on fantasy as a means of representing a reality beyond the one that we currently inhabit. According to this principle, fantasy is able to give the world what it is lacking in the form of myth, belief, vision, utopia, social or economic targets, or simply as a regulative fiction.

Composed by unreal elements, as much as by real elements, fantasy is able to constantly search for new hopes, in order to change or improve the world or the life, feeding ethics with the challenges that beliefs, or representations of a 'beyond', bestow upon humanity. In this context, it is important to question what happens with other species – how do they relate to this 'beyond'? What is the role of other living beings in the challenges or dynamics that come with the possibility of being a participant in this transcendence?

This paper, will provide a brief introduction to the sense and meaning of speciesism, in order to subsequently approach the implicit or explicit ways in which this form of discrimination has been embedded within our tradition and its representations of the 'beyond' since time immemorial. Finally, it will demonstrate, the extent to which the concept of nature, coupled with the metaphysics of Western thought, not only validates certain shortcomings in traditional ethics, but also give rise to new ethical challenges for the inclusion of non-speciesist moral motives.

What is Speciesism?

Speciesism is a fundamental issue within all environmental philosophy. However, the sense and meaning of the term are poorly understood, even amongst a great number of people who claim to have a profound interest in issues relating to biodiversity and the ethical perspectives toward non-human species.

DOI 10.1515/9783110530773-006

Speciesism is derived from the word species, in the same way that racism is derived from race. Speciesism regards humanity in its entirety, in the same way that racism regards specific races. The latter works on an intraspecies level, whilst the former looks beyond the species. The intention is not to suggest that these phenomena are the same, or even substantially similar, only they are mentioned as referential analogous, although in both cases the comparison points at instances of discrimination.

The popularization of the term speciesism can be credited to Peter Singer, but its origin has a double history, both in its beginnings as a fact, and in the coining of the concept itself. In the first case, the origin is prehistoric, whilst the birth of speciesism as a term is a more recent event, with its first appearance in Richard Ryder's paper of 1970, "Experiments on Animals", which highlights the cruelty of experiments carried out on animals in laboratories.[1]

Ryder explains this conduct by affirming that humans experiment in order to increase their knowledge to the benefit of their own species; however, Singer claims that humans act without taking into account the idea of an evolutionary socio-physiobiological continuum.

The term speciesism is generally applied to the affirmation of superiority of one species, to the detriment of all others. It requires, amongst other things, the separation of species or groups in conditions of discrimination. Examples include the cases of speciesism against non-human animals within artificial habitats, such as abattoirs, laboratories, or circuses to name a few.

Broadly speaking, certain patterns are shared by those who defend such discriminatory practices: not avoiding, but encouraging – directly or indirectly – suffering amongst non-human animals.

Channelling Pain in the Representation of the 'Beyond'

Suffering is such a complex and profound phenomenon, that it cannot be compared, in terms of the intensity of the experience, with any other capacity. From a biological perspective, pain can be defined as an unpleasant sensory or emotional

---

1 Cf. Richard RYDER, "Experiments on Animals", 79. For more information by the author in relation to the use of animals in laboratories, and the development of the concept of the 3 Rs (*replacement, reduction,* and *refinement*) within the world of laboratory vivisection, see also: "Speciesism in the Laboratory" in: Peter SINGER, ed., *In Defense of Animals*, 96.

experience, encountered in relation to some kind of real or potential injury. It is the reaction in the face of this injury that stimulates action.

When defensive mechanisms do not help us to channel pain, turning, instead, against the person who endures it, a sort of obstruction occurs that can be identified more with the term *suffering* than pain. Spaemann takes this perspective: "The German term 'suffering' has, in a manner that is analogous to its corresponding term in other languages, a double meaning. It means sadness (unhappiness, unpleasantness...), and also, simply, passivity (in the sense of *passibilitas*), or, in a manner of speaking, frustration."[2]

Starting from a certain degree of intensity, pain, as such, becomes suffering. The passing of one into the other occurs when the depth of the ailing makes any projection for the future, positive or negative, disappear; when the hope of any real relief is lost, and with it, the channelling that reduces or removes its intensity is hindered. In this situation, to speak of pain is no longer adequate, and suffering becomes the word that best expresses the totality of the physical and emotional state.

According to Bentham[3] and Singer,[4] the only defendable limit, at the moment of concerning ourselves with the interests of others, is that of sensitivity. This refers, not only to the capacity for suffering, but also for enjoyment.

In the case of human beings, the pain of the person who experiences it, as well as that of someone who merely knows it, without necessarily being affected directly, can be an incentive for sounding out representations of a dimension that transcends this "valley of tears": the place where all desires, anxieties and the evil that claim existence reside. Specifically, the need to free oneself from the fear of death, as much as from the avatars and miseries of life, has provided fantasy with a fundamental role in the formulation of transmundane beliefs or representations.

Nonetheless, the possibility of avoiding this obstruction by channelling suffering through abstractions that liberate the mind from mundane pain, have forged diverse representations of a 'beyond', which – one way or another – have manifested, from the origins of Western metaphysics, a certain vexatious subordination of those species that are considered to be inferior to the dominant one: the human species.

---

2 Robert Spaemann, "Über den Sinn des Leidens", 118.
3 Cf. Jeremy Bentham, *Introduction to the Principles of Morals and Legislation*, chap. 17.
4 Cf. Peter Singer, *Animal Liberation*, chap. 1.

Evidence of Speciesism in the Origins of Western Metaphysics and their Respective Transmundane Projections

From the dawn of Western metaphysics, there is a classical ontological hierarchy between the sensory and the intelligible world. Regarding this, Socrates points out that death can mean the point of entry to a more elevated state,[5] but he also warns that wisdom does not lie in seeking it out – as this would imply an attempt to take a life, which could constitute a criminal act – [6] but in maintaining a willful disposition toward virtue, being, throughout one's life prepared and longing for death. Within this worldview, the wise person must develop his or her spiritual sphere through education and the good use of straightforward reasoning to ensure the soul's transmigration toward higher states. Throughout his work, Plato uses various myths to present the theory of metempsychosis, according to which, if a person has become accustomed to a degree of vice in his or her life, their soul will transmigrate to lower animal states:

> And he that has lived his appointed time well shall return again to his abode in his native star, and shall gain a life that is blessed and congenial; but whoso has failed therein shall be changed into woman's nature at the second birth; and if, in that shape, he still refraineth not from wickedness he shall be changed every time, according to the nature of his wickedness, into some bestial form after the similitude of his own nature.[7]

On the contrary, if someone had cultivated the habit of virtue throughout his or her life, their soul would transmigrate to the life of other, superior humans:

> Those who have indulged in gluttony and violence and drunkenness, and have taken no pains to avoid them, are likely to pass into the bodies of asses and other beasts of that sort (...) And those who have chosen injustice and tyranny and robbery pass into the bodies of wolves and hawks and kites (...) and those who go to the best place, are those who have practised, by nature and habit, without philosophy or reason, the social and civil virtues which are called moderation and justice? (...) Is it not likely that they pass again into some such social and gentle species as that of bees or of wasps or ants, or into the human race again, and that worthy men spring from them? (...) And no one who has not been a philosopher and who is not wholly pure when he departs, is allowed to enter into the communion of the gods, but only the lover of knowledge.[8]

---

5 Cf. PLATO, *Phaedo*, 114d–115a.
6 Cf. ibidem, 61c.
7 PLATO, *Timaeus*, 42b–c.
8 PLATO, *Phaedo*, 81d–82a.

The Providential Subordination of Species in the Middle Ages

With the passing of the ancient universe to the medieval, the subordination that existed amongst living beings, as presented by Plato and Aristotle[9] – which was inherited, in turn, by the Stoics – [10] resurfaces, with the providential verticality of species as the official posture of the church. In this context, it must be considered that all sins in the mediaeval universe, including that of killing, are referred to as acts against God, or against human beings, without taking other life forms into consideration. Augustine, for example, allows this exclusion to be glimpsed with greater clarity upon condemning voluntary death. He upholds the idea that self-homicide violates the fifth commandment (Exodus 20:13), due to the fact that the Decalogue does not specify that "thou shall not kill" refers exclusively to others. Therefore, he claims that this omission proves that suicide would also mean killing a human being. However, the fifth commandment does not take non-human species into account. Augustine even elaborates in various writings on the permissibility of this act on non-human animals:

> When we say, Thou shall not kill, we do not understand this of the plants, since they have no sensation, nor of the irrational animals that fly, swim, walk, or creep, since they are dissociated from us by their want of reason, and are therefore by the just appointment of the Creator subjected to us to kill or keep alive for our own uses.[11]

From this perspective, it is legitimate, for example, to sacrifice an animal if one is its owner; or – if this were not the case – to do so with the will of the owner – in the case of doing so without the owner's permission, the wrong that has been incurred would fall within the intrahuman sphere: that is to say, the injustice is against the person who was the owner, and in no way against the slaughtered animal. In this respect, Thomas Aquinas, goes beyond legitimizing theologically this right to property, not only bestowing upon the sinner the crime of theft or looting, but also claiming that within natural life, the laws of creation that order the animal and vegetable kingdoms through a divine disposition, centered on mankind, are revealed. Upon him fall the power of dominion and administration of the rest of the species:

> *Respondeo dicendum quod nullus peccat ex hoc quod utitur re aliqua ad hoc ad quod est. In rerum autem ordine imperfectiora sunt propter perfectiora: sicut etiam in generationis*

---

9 Cf. ARISTOTLE, *Politics*, vol. 1, 1256b.
10 Cf. Henricus SCHENKL, *Epicteti Dissertationes ab Arriano digestae*, 1.6.18–22.
11 AUGUSTINE, *The City of God*, vol. 1, chap. 20, 142.

via natura ab imperfectis ad perfecta procedit. Et inde est quod sicut in generatione hominis prius est vivum, deinde animal, ultimo autem homo: ita etiam ea quae tantum vivunt, ut plantae, sunt communiter propter omnia animalia, et animalia sunt propter hominem. Et ideo si homo utatur plantis ad utilitatem animalium, et animalibus ad utilitatem hominum, non est illicitum.[12]

Even though Thomas Aquinas explains that there are three celestial hierarchies, relating to three ways of rationally knowing all created things, he also makes evident that the vertical organization of these worlds is not reduced to an angelic order. In line with the principle of subordination of the relative and absolute, and of the imperfect and the perfect, he defends this providential order of species, headed by the human layer that is conceived in the upper centre of creation.

With the remnants of the ancient universe, but fundamentally during the Middle Ages, both nature and the world have transcendent meanings. This is because, even though nature conserves the idea of an autonomous whole, endowed with its own laws, humanity does not belong to that natural order, but to a supernatural one. As a result, morality is not guided by the premise of *naturam sequi*, because in the end, what is sought is not conformity with nature, but orientation and adaptation to the supernatural.

Although the term *natura* has been applied to various classes of beings, in the Middle Ages, nature was associated above all else with the intramundane beings in existence, including the remainder of living beings. By conceiving this whole as *natura*, there is the tendency to seek that which, in every one of its manifestations contains of itself *natura*. And here we have it that, amongst all of the existing manifestations, only one was attributed with the principal role: that of the human being. According to this point of view, ethical exclusivity is a trait of our species in which only intrahuman relationships are regulated. In the realm of nature, mankind experiences freedom, but she no longer offers the measure of morality. Starting from this premise, both nature and intrahuman moral motives only acquire sense and value in reference and relation to God.

The Modern Paradigm and Human Exclusivity in Access to Transcendence

Descartes, one of the key representatives of the defining paradigm of modernity conceives essentially two realities: thought and extension. Two principles of

---

[12] St. Thomae Aquinatis, *Summa Theologiae*, 2-2, Quaestio 64. a. 1-2, 410–411.

movement are released from the Cartesian dualism: the first is incorporeal, concerning the spirit, soul or thinking matter; whilst the second is entirely mechanical and corporeal. The mechanistic vision of the organisms conceives them as very complex machines. The correspondence of the soul, conceived as a thinking *thing* with its own body-machine, implies that it will eventually know and interpret both intra and extrahuman nature, in a mechanical fashion, as if it were dealing with an inert object, which, therefore, must be exploited technically.

According to Descartes, the animals, despite sharing anatomical similarities with human beings, are separated hierarchically by the nature of the soul. It is the unique, superior qualities of man that allow his soul to enjoy immortality:

> (...) there is none which is more effectual in leading feeble spirits from the straight path of virtue, than to imagine that the soul of the brute is of the same nature as our own, and that in consequence, after this life we have nothing to fear or to hope for, any more than the flies and ants. As a matter of fact, when one comes to know how greatly they differ, we understand much better the reasons which go to prove that our soul is in its nature entirely independent of body, and in consequence that it is not liable to die with it. And then, inasmuch as we observe no other causes capable of destroying it, we are naturally inclined to judge that it is immortal.[13]

The thesis that animals are not capable of suffering was sustained implicitly by declaring that animals are automata,[14] explaining all of their movements through mechanical principles.

Following a very similar line, albeit through other concepts, Kant retakes key aspects of the Cartesian paradigm to argue that both man and animals alike are subject to the needs of nature; that is to say, by being empirical, they remain subordinate to its instincts and inclinations. More like a person, the human being forms part of an intelligible world, which is concerned with moral law. In other words: in his natural sphere, he forms part of the determinism that prevails in the phenomenic and empirical world, but, at the same time, he is a free subject of morality, as he forms part of the noumenal being. This frees him from the chains of need that operate in the phenomenic world, and allows the human being – unlike all other species – to move toward transcendence. When the moral value of an act is measured by the intention that motivates it, this depends on a subjective reasoning. The concept of morality requires that the principle that directs the action of an individual should be applicable universally. However, the anthropocentrism within this idea, which can lead to a speciesist legitimation,[15]

---

13 René DECARTES, *Discourse on the Method*, 60.
14 Cf. ibidem, 59.
15 Cf. Hans JONAS, *Das Prinzip der Verantwortung*, 36.

is uncovered in the categorical formula that this subject of morality must uphold through the Kantian imperative: "act in such a manner that you treat the humanity in your own person, and also that which is in others, always as an end, and never just as a means."[16] The status of an end in itself, exclusive to mankind, would be derived from certain properties of the species. However, this imperative does not contemplate the remaining living beings, or the biosphere as a whole, which, in their omission may be reduced to mere means for the speciesist purposes of man, infringing upon them in a discriminatory fashion and destabilizing the balance of nature, which is necessary for the conservation of biodiversity on the planet:

> Allein weil Tiere nur als Mittel da sind, indem sie sich ihrer selbst nicht bewusst sind, der Mensch aber der Zweck ist, wo ich nicht mehr fragen kann: "Warum ist der Mensch da?", welches bei den Tieren geschehen kann, so haben wir gegen die Tiere unmittelbar keine Pflichten, sondern die Pflichten gegen die Tiere sind indirekte Pflichten gegen die Menschheit.[17]

Both the conversion of natural elements into mere economic or energy resources, as the transformation of all other species into means of consumption and exploitation are part of the same problem that separates speciesist way man from nature, and which, despite being characteristic of the Modern Age, we have already shown to be rooted in the earliest beginnings of Western metaphysical thought, in the diverse mythological or philosophical representations that point to a life beyond this one.

Through an instrumental interpretation of the biosphere in general, and the rest of living beings specifically, the scientific revolution of the 16th and 17th Centuries has highlighted the way in which written history has celebrated the progress achieved by modern man in working against his ecological being.

The subject has moved on to conceive the world as a field of objects for exploitation, extraction and manipulation. This objectification has become the starting point for man's domination of nature, as his reified external other. The world modeled through objectification is left to one side, whilst at the other extreme lies the subjective power through which humanity dominates and reifies nature, together with all other living beings.

In this hermeneutic ecorreification, one acts and feels not only cleaved from a 'beyond', but also from the natural self. Born in this irreconcilable dichotomy, the innate aggression of 'civilized' man against the natural environment presupposes

---

[16] Immanuel KANT, *Kant's gesammelte Schriften*, vol. IV: *Grundlegung zur Metaphysik der Sitten*, 429.
[17] Immanuel KANT, *Eine Vorlesung über Ethik*, 256.

not only the alienation that the artificial sphere of the big city has thrust upon wild nature, but also, and foremost, a pseudo-objective way of understanding that this ends, in a more critical phase, institutionalizing the collective depersonalization of humanity.

Although it is not fair to suggest that Bacon and Descartes originated the environmental damage of the 21st Century, it cannot be denied that in epistemological terms, both the denaturalization implicit in the belief in the idea of manipulating nature for the purposes of knowledge,[18] as also the notion of *res extensa* (possible by the *cogitans* and *infinta*) ideologically consolidated the hermeneutic ecorreifying by academizing and legitimizing via the technical and mechanistic notions of reality. The safeguarding or destruction of the natural environment belongs to this ideological tendency, which results in incurring a ruthless speciesism.

Conscious of the dichotomous interpretation of nature alongside all other living beings as the "other", or that which is distinct from oneself, it is possible to probe the tracks of the ontological wall – existing between the 'I', and that which is foreign to this rotund individuality – in such extended dynamics of dominion and exploitation, as may be the case with speciesism, a form of discrimination that is forged and institutionalized, even, when the *principium individuationis* is erected as the law of being.

Metaphysical Projections of Nature: Ethical Challenges for the Inclusion of Non-Speciesist Moral Motives

The complex and dissimilar meanings of nature, preceded by historic and philosophical notions of the term do not provide a unique meaning through which to understand it. However, it is that conceptual diversity that makes creates the opportunity for a new dynamic in our relationship with other species, which is different to the one we have inherited from industrialized western civilization and its mercantilist valuation of the environment. Exploring this relationship takes us on a journey that goes beyond mere touristic interest, because before journeying to a far-flung reserve – where travellers pay to see landscapes that are free from human commerce – one must first journey into one's own interior, where it is possible to measure, question and suspend that same *ratio sufficiens* and its distorted appreciation of the self.

---

[18] Cf. Francis BACON, *The New Organon*, CXXIX, 118–119.

In this sense, nature precedes and makes possible the physical place to which one is travelling. This is more than a park or an unsurmountable fence, with determined aesthetic features that must be maintained, because it is not only a place that is outside of the house, office or city – it is the shared environment that is inherited from other life forms, that have not necessarily been intervened through the lens of an ecorreifying hermeneutic. When this is imposed, the natural elements become instrumentalized resources for achieving mankind's ends, and the remainder of living beings become objects for consumption and exploitation. This interpretation hides the pristine and disinterested concept of nature from anyone who rates and probes nature in this way. It cannot be the essentially other, if it is the shared environment on top of which the culture of each present moment builds itself.

From an ethical context, the fundamental aspect of humanity, in contrast to the rest of the species, is not the capacity to create abstract or metaphysical representations, but above all, the possibility of being able to take responsibility for all other living beings, through conditioning its own behavior. The change in direction away from speciesist habits surges from compassion, the moral motive that is directed against certain innate tendencies of human beings that turn out to be speciesist.

Until now, non-human animals have not been able to defend themselves from speciesism directed at them, nor from human complicity, as endorsed in the West through a broad spectrum of discriminatory practices, which often transcends the creed, race, or society of those who foster them.

Just as the theoretical knowledge of understanding and reason is incapable of modifying morality, there is a different sensibility that is present in the phenomenon of compassion. Nobody can be obliged to feel compassion, nor would there exist any mandate that could allow it to be felt. With just reason Schopenhauer considers it to be the only authentic moral motive, as it means to directly 'suffer with' (*Mit-leid*) the pain of the 'other' in his/her pain. That is to say, compassion is more immediate than reason. Apparently it would appear that it is felt or it is not felt, it is had, or it is not had. This requires that in some way, one is identified with the other, to know that the radical differences that separate the 'I' from the others (the same distinction on which selfishness is based) is annulled. This occurs when one participates immediately in the suffering of the 'other', without requiring reflection in order to wake that sensibility; only there does the 'not-I' becomes 'I'.[19]

Pain, by being more specific than suffering, clearly has a biological usefulness, seeing as it should improve a species' chances of survival, permitting the

---

19 Cf. Arthur SCHOPENHAUER, *Kleinere Schriften*, 743–744.

avoidance of sources of harm, and, therefore, of suffering, independent of the race, species, or gender of a living being.[20]

Compassion is born from the act of seeing that the true 'I' does not exist only in the individual, but in the sum of all of the rest. From the moment in which it has been liberated from the characteristic barriers of *principium indivduationis*, all pain that is experienced – both one's own, as well as that of others – will move and affect an individual in the same way. Charity, kindness, altruism and saintliness arise when the individual assimilates and transcends toward the common and universal pain; all of these serve to mitigate the ailments of those who suffer.

Compassion or pure love come from the act of becoming conscious that our true self does not exist only in each one of us, but it is also the product of everyone else. By reaching a dimension beyond the *principium individuationis*, all pain, both of oneself and of the species that appear to be most alien to us can be experienced with the same intensity,[21] which results in moral motivations that attempt to minimize the pain of the other, regardless of species, race or gender of whom suffers from it.

Bibliography

Aquinatis, St. Thomae, *Summa Theologiae*, vol. 3. Madrid, Biblioteca de Autores Cristianos, 1963.
Aristotle, *Politics*, edited by Jeffrey Henderson, translated by H. Rackham. London, Harvard University Press, 2005.
Augustine, St., *The City of God*, vol. 1, translated by Marcus Dods. Chicago, University of Chicago by Encyclopedia Britannica, 1952.
Bacon, Francis, *The New Organon and Related Writings*, edited by Fulton H. Anderson. New York. The Liberal Arts Press. 1960.
Bentham, Jeremy, *Introduction to the Principles of Morals and Legislation*. London, The Athlone Press, 1970.
Descartes, René, *Discourse on the Method*, translated by Elizabeth S. Haldane. Chicago, University of Chicago by Encyclopedia Britannica, 1952.
Jonas, Hans, *Das Prinzip der Verantwortung*. Frankfurt a. M., Suhrkamp, 1979.
Kant, Immanuel, *Eine Vorlesung über Ethik*, edited by Gerd Gerhardt. Frankfurt am Main, Fischer Taschenbuch Verlag, 1990.
Kant, Immanuel, *Kant's gesammelte Schriften*, vol. IV: *Grundlegung zur Metaphysik der Sitten*, edited by Preussische respectively Deutsche Akademie der Wissenschaften. Berlin/Göttingen, Georg Reimer, 1902.

---

20 Cf. Peter SINGER, *Animal Liberation*, 17.
21 Cf. Arthur SCHOPENHAUER, *Die Welt als Wille und Vorstellung*, vol. 1, chap. 66.

Plato, *Phaedo*, vol. 1, translated by Harold North Fowler. London, Harvard University Press, 1961.
Plato, *Timaeus*, vol. 7, translated by R. G. Bury. London, Harvard University Press, 1961.
Ryder, Richard, "Experiments on Animals". In *Animals, Men and Morals. An Enquiry into the Maltreatment of Non-Humans*, edited by Stanley and Roslind Godlovitch and John Harris. London, Victor Gollancz, 1971.
Schenkl, Henricus, *Epicteti Dissertationes ab Arriano digestae, Fragmenta, Enchiridion ex recensione Schweighaeuseri, gnomologiorum Epicteteorum reliquiae*. Leipzig, Teubner, 1916.
Schopenhauer, Arthur, *Die Welt als Wille und Vorstellung*, vol. 1 (Sämtliche Werke, 1). Stuttgart/Frankfurt, Suhrkamp Taschenbuch Verlag, 1986.
Schopenhauer, Arthur, *Kleinere Schriften* (Sämtliche Werke, 3). Stuttgart/Frankfurt, Suhrkamp Taschenbuch Verlag, 1986.
Singer, Peter, *Animal Liberation*. New York, HarperCollins Publishers, 2002.
Singer, Peter, ed., *In Defense of Animals. The Second Wave*. Oxford, Blackwell Publishing, 2006.
Spaemann, Robert, "Über den Sinn des Leidens". In Id., *Einsprüche, christliche Reden*. Einsiedeln, Johannes Verlag, 1977, 116–133.

Historical Structures

Jaime I. Araos San Martín
The Question of Beyond
Previous Considerations from Aristotle's *Metaphysics*

In this paper, I would like to discuss from a philosophical point of view the question of beyond in all its generality: the conditions that make it possible and some of its anthropological, ontological and epistemological implications. My intention is to do so through the lens of Aristotle's thinking, particularly, in his work *Metaphysics*, which, as its name suggests, and as I propose, can be interpreted as a work of research on beyond in itself.

1 Life as a Challenge

The first challenge of life is to live. But to live is not just to exist and brave the elements as rocks do. Living is different from surviving. In fact, sometimes a necessity that arises within life itself leads to a living being risking and even losing its own life, like many animals when trying to save their offspring, or some humans, that we call heroes, when standing up for dignity and justice. "In the case of living things, their being is to live", Aristotle wrote about this in his book *On the Soul*.[1] In this context, this means at least two things: a) life is not subjected to being, being is subjected to life; b) life is immanent action, *actus, enérgeia*. Life is the act, the realization of a living being, of his being. So life can have many challenges, but, above all, life itself is a challenge, the challenge and the task of every living thing is to follow the impulse of it being and reach fulfilment according to its nature. This nature manifests itself as a living being's immanent purpose, as an intrinsic call to display and realize its potential, as its *télos*.

So, if the first challenge of life is to live, this means to carry out the possibilities of realization and improvement of every living being, according to its own nature. In the most basics forms of life the vital impulse is fulfilled with acts of nutrition, growth and reproduction. At a higher level, one can add local movement, sensory knowledge, opening animals up to the environment, and the desire for sensitive goods and pleasure. In the case of human life, its own fulfilment requires living in a political community and the exercise of the higher faculties

---

[1] ARISTOTLE, *De anima*, B 4, 415 b13. In *The Complete Works of Aristotle*, vol. I. We will quote ARISTOTLE's Works according to this edition.

of the spirit, i. e. intellect and will, which are operatively enabled by ethics and dianoetics virtues, through the essential process of education or *paideía*. Now, the human being is subject to different desires, some of them aimed at pleasure, others honour, power, knowledge, present goods, future goods, etc. Some of these desires may be contrary to each other, thereby introducing enormous life complexity, to the point that learning to live is largely about learning to channel one's wishes according to the rule of reason. Such is the objective of ethics. But there's a desire that stands out above all others, a desire that distinguishes and elevates itself above other living beings all the while being a constituent of what a human being is: the desire to know. It is the thesis that Aristotle puts forth in the first line of *Metaphysics*: "All human beings by nature desire to *know*".[2]

2 The Desire to Know

What does the term "knowledge", the English translation from the Greek *eidénai*, mean in this phrase? Since the generation of various forms and degrees of knowledge, ranging from sense perception (*aísthesis*) to wisdom (*sophía*), through the empirical knowledge (*empeiría*), technical (*téchne*), ethical and scientific (*epistéme*), is attributed to this desire, it is common to interpret it in abstract terms, as indeterminately referring to knowledge in general. This interpretation may be incorrect. In philosophical works, the term *eidénai* refers to knowledge that is sought after for its own sake, and not for another purpose, knowledge that is the fruit of love for the truth[3] and the human impulse to understand. Thus, it is opposed to useful and productive knowledge, which is not for its own sake, but for instrumental objectives, which are different from knowledge.[4] *Eidénai* therefore means the freedom of knowledge, what perhaps we might call, in the words of Heidegger, truth as freedom.[5]

Then, what is affirmed on the first pages of *Metaphysics* is that in all classes and degrees of human knowledge, not only in terms of philosophical knowledge, there is some degree of freedom, of complacency in the truth, a trace of love of knowledge by itself, because somehow all are born from of the same desire: the desire to know. But this desire doesn't find complete satisfaction in any of them: only in "wisdom" (*sophía*), defined as the "science of first causes and principles".[6]

---

[2] ARISTOTLE, *Metaphysics*, A 1, 980 a1. Translation – with modifications by me –, D. W. Ross, in *The Complete Works of Aristotle*, vol. 2.
[3] Cf. ARISTOTLE, *Metaphysics*, A Elatton 1, 993 a30, b 30–31.
[4] See Hermann Bonitz, *Index Aristotelicus*.
[5] Cf. Martin HEIDEGGER, *Wegmarken*, 177 sq.
[6] Cf. ARISTOTLE, *Metaphysics*, A 1, 981 b26–982 a3.

One must ask: First causes and principles ... of what? Aristotle gives no answer in this chapter or in the chapters or books that follow, until Gamma. If a philosopher known for his rigorous and careful use of language makes no mention of this, it is highly significant, and one must take this into account for a correct interpretation.

To determine certain knowledge as the science of first causes and principles, without specifying its object or content, involves bringing all the attention to the concepts of cause and principle for themselves. What is a cause (*aitía*)? As is well known, this question does not allow for a simple answer, because the term has a variety of meanings. Aristotle expresses it as follows:

> "Causes are spoken of in four senses. In one of these we mean the substance, i.e. the essence (for the 'why' is referred finally to the formula, and the ultimate 'why' is a cause and principle); in another the matter or substratum, in a third the source of the change, and in a fourth the cause opposed to this, that for the sake of which and the good (for this is the end of all generation and change)".[7]

To these concepts apply the most simplified denominations, of scholastic origin, by which the Aristotelian four causes are traditionally known: formal, material efficient and final, respectively. Now, formal cause is so opposite to material cause as is efficient cause respect to final cause: their differences are irreconcilable; however, there is a point of convergence: they are all, one way or another, an answer to the question *why*. For example: ¿Why is something the way it is? Why does something possess a certain property? Why does it thunder? There is a cause behind these phenomena, insofar as a cause gives an answer to the question why, allowing us to understand one thing or state of affairs. In other words: cause is what responds somehow in some degree to the natural human desire to know, to understand.

Aristotle associates the concept of cause with that of principle. What is a principle? Also this word has different meanings, but they can be brought together, as proposed by Aristotle himself, in following definition: "It is common, then, to all <principles> to be the first point from which a thing either is or comes to be or is known".[8] In this formula we are also able to grasp the meaning of cause, since, as the Greek philosopher says, "all causes are principles".[9] However, the reverse is not true: the principle of non-contradiction, for example, cannot be considered a cause; nor does it cause the beginning or start of a race, etc. The meaning of

---

[7] Ibid., I 3, 983 a26–32. Cf. ibid., V 2, 1013 a24 sq.; *Physics*, II 3, 194 b23–195 b21. Translation by W. D. Ross.
[8] ARISTOTLE, *Metaphysics*, D 1, 1013 a17–19. Transl. W.D. Ross.
[9] Ibid., D 1, 1013 a17.

principle appears to be wider than the cause. Now, without having to deal thoroughly with the semantic field of two terms, one can establish that when Aristotle puts them together in the usual formula "first causes and principles", it can be read by understanding the conjunction "and" (*kaí*), as is common in Aristotelian writing, with an explanatory, rather than additive, sense: "first causes, *that is*, the principles". And the association of the "principle" concept with the "first causes" concept also serves to underline the status of "first" of these causes and distinguish them from the second and instrumental causes.

3 The Desired Science

That being said, what does it mean then, when certain knowledge is defined as the science of first causes and principles? If investigating the causes is equivalent to seeking out the *why*, to wanting to understand, then, investigating the first causes and principles means seeking there and beyond until reaching the first why;[10] in other words, the desire to understand there and beyond until reaching the highest intelligible. Now, to what entity does this title belongs? Until this question is answered, the universal science of first causes and principles will remain undetermined. And yet, there is no answer in *Metaphysics Alpha*, the book in which this new and distinct science is presented. Evidently, Aristotle does not deem it necessary. In fact, he continues to deem it unnecessary until the book *Gamma*, where he identifies the concept of "being as being" as its own object, and the book *Epsilon*, where he identifies, by way of hypothesis, the science of being as being and the theological science, a hypothesis he wouldn't resolve until book *Lambda*, where he proceeds to demonstrate the existence of God as the first principle upon which the movements of heaven and nature depend.

What initially defines metaphysics, then, is neither an object, nor content. It is a movement of the soul: the desire to know carried beyond empirical data, productive techniques, and theoretical particular sciences such as physics and mathematics. It is the unrestricted desire to know and understand carried beyond limits, to the field of freedom. Aristotle says: "As the man is free, we say, who exists for himself and not for another, so we pursue this as the only free science, for it alone exists for itself".[11]

---

10 "We say we know each thing (*eidénai hékaston*), write Aristotle, only when we think we recognize its first cause" (*Metaphysics*, I 3, 983 a25-26), and (...) "the ultimate 'why' is a cause and principle" (*aítion dè kaì archè tò dià tí prôton*)" (*Ibid*. 983 a29).
11 Aristotle, *Metaphysics*, A 2, 982 b24–28. Transl. W. D. Ross.

It is the only science that is free, in effect, first, because it is not subordinate to production or anything different from knowledge: therefore it is called "science of truth".[12] Second, because it is not limited to a particular object: hence it is called, as opposed to the particular sciences, "universal science" (*kathólou epistéme*).[13] Third, because it is science of first principles, therefore, it is free from assumptions or hypotheses: it is a "non-hypothetical science".[14] Fourth, because it constitutes the open space where the desire to know goes beyond, until its culmination. For this reason Aristotle also refers to it as "the sought-science" or rather, "the desired science" (*zetouméne epistéme*),[15] that is, science which is defined by the desire to know.

4 The Science of Beyond

"Wisdom", "free science", "science of truth", "universal science", "desired science": these are the expressions that Aristotle chooses to present the knowledge that he considers the highest and most desirable. They are not really names, because they do not identify either the object of this science, its subject or content. Or perhaps are names that identify it otherwise, quasi negatively by attributes that, to describe any other science would be accidental, relative and insufficient, but in this case become more revealing than any definition by genus and specific difference. Each of these expressions reveals intimately and rigorously what this science is and what is at stake: truth and freedom, wisdom and universality, desire and the nature of the human being. Metaphysics is the unsatisfied science, the science that wants to go further.

Here is also the first reason – first not only in chronological sense – to call this science "meta-physics". Regardless of whether Aristotle used the term or not, the concept is undoubtedly in the work bearing this name. But perhaps not even this name is able to do justice to this science. Because, it is defined in terms of physics, whose content, as in the science of movement, is perfectly determined.

---

12 Cf. *Met.* A. Elátton 1, VI 1.
13 Cf. *Met.* A 2, 982 a22; G 1, 1003 a22–26.
14 Cf. *Met.* G 3, 1005 b14–17.
15 Cf. *Met.*, B 1, 995 a24; Z 1, 1028 b2–3. Also LEIBNIZ, referring to Aristotelian *Metaphysics*, translated *zetouméne epistéme* by "desired science": "Unde nemo mirari debet, scientiam illam principem, quae Primae Philosophieae nomine venit et Aristoteli dicta est desiderata seu quaesita (*zetouméne*), adhuc inter quaerenda mansisse": "No one should be astonished that this primordial science, to which the name of first philosophy belongs and which Aristotle called desired or sought, remains today among the sciences to be sought" (*De Primae Philosophiae Emendatione et de Notione Substantiae*, p. 468).

Even if this name is misunderstood in a purely negative way, as is common today, as the science of the non-physical, it is misunderstood in relation to the physical. However, according to the first books of *Metaphysics*, the part that we must rescue from the traditional title is more than the noun "physics", the Greek preposition *metá* "beyond", so it is displayed as "science of beyond".

But does the absolute use of a preposition, more precisely, of the preposition "beyond" make sense? Is it a legitimate use of language?

5 Beyond

Prepositions, just as adverbs, conjunctions, negations, etc., belong to the group of terms that medieval logicians, inspired by developments made by the Stoics and that went back to Aristotle's *Peri Hermeneias*, they called *syncategoremata*,[16] that is, "co-significants". These are terms which by themselves have no meaning,[17] but they acquire them joined to other terms that do have meaning by themselves. I refer to *categoremata* terms, which include firstly the names[18] and, secondly, the verbs. It follows that *syncategoremata* terms, since they have no meaning by themselves, can not be used in ordinary language in an absolute way, that is, separated from a name or other categorematic term, next to which and by which they acquire a definite meaning. Now, if this is true in general for any syncategorematic term, it seems to be especially for an expression like that which concerns us here: "beyond". It would be nonsense to talk of a "science of beyond" or "colloquium of beyond" since in both cases there is an absolute use of the term "beyond", as if it were a name, a noun. The problem is not whether or not there is a beyond, but what is meant when talking about it. We could organize a colloquium on sirens and discuss whether or not there is a science of the sirens, and it makes perfect sense. But when we talking about the science of, or a colloquium on, beyond, the meaning of the expression remains incomplete and in suspense: *beyond*, in relation to what?

Indeed, the concept of "beyond" is structurally associated with another concept, the limit, for this is the inescapable reference point with respect to which something can be located "here" or "beyond". The limit is what makes "here" or

---

[16] The origin of this name seems to be in a passage of *Institutiones Grammaticae*, of Prisciano, 64. Cf. Julián Velarde, *Historia de la lógica*, 131.

[17] More precisely, they have not a full and defined meaning.

[18] It is called "name", in this tradition, mainly nouns, but also descriptive adjectives and personal pronouns. Cf. John of Saint Thomas, *Ars Logica*, ed. B. Reiser, Turin: Marietti, 1930, pp. 13b–16b; Jaime Araos: *La filosofía aristotélica del lenguaje*, 101–126.

"beyond" possible. If the limit is eliminated, then the difference between being here or being beyond is also eliminated ipso facto. In general, the term "beyond", when used correctly and therefore in a full sense, is expressed with reference to this limit: "beyond the wall", "beyond good and evil", "beyond your nose".

This is in general terms. But how is it when we get down to particulars? Does language allow for any exceptions? Of course yes. And an interesting course of action in these cases, assuming some intelligence and wisdom is inherent in the current language, is to try to understand this exceptional use, before condemning it. Perhaps the absolute use of the expression "beyond" is justified when the implicit limit is, in a way, also absolute. I call "absolute" in this context a limit that is natural and invincible, but at the same time is subjective, in the sense that it is always a "limit for". This is what happens in ordinary language when people who know how to speak, speak in an absolute manner about beyond. The absolute extends only to say, not what is said or to the respective thought. This means that there is a limit, but it is implied. This limit is human life, our life. The expression "beyond" refers to the limit of human life. Its absolute use makes clear the absolute limit, which does not say, but it means, as Heraclitus says of the Oracle of Delphi.[19]

This limit is natural and not merely conventional. A conventional limit is, for example, establishing a certain number of years as the age of reaching adulthood: many countries set it at 18, but some at 14, and others at 21. Other limits combine nature and convention. The speed limit on the highway has some natural base, catered road conditions, vehicle power and reaction capacity of human beings, but ultimately it is conventional: it could be 10 kilometres farther or 10 kilometres less. And as such, it could easily change. It is a vincible limit. Other limits are natural, but not invincible. Beyond the precise point that divides us, the Andes mountains is a kind of natural limit between Argentina and Chile, and the Atlantic Ocean, a natural limit between Europe and America. We can't change these limits, but we can overcome them, fighting against the elements. The army of General San Martín demonstrated this, when it crossed the mountains to aid Chile's independence; and Admiral Columbus, when he crossed the ocean to reach America (which he believed to be India).

Like the above, it is beyond the natural limit of life. But unlike them, the Beyond is, for us, an absolutely invincible limit. Life is the limit; beyond, is the dark. Is there life beyond life? Or just death? Is there punishment beyond life, or reward or nothing at all? Are there paradise and purgatory and hell? There is darkness; this is what we can say from rational evidence. But there is no absolute

---

19 Cf. Hermann Diels y Walther Kranz, *Die Fragmente der Vorsokratiker*, vol. 1, 22B 93.

darkness, since we asked for this limit, for the beyond. Because we named it, it might seem that the Beyond is a concept. But it is not nor could it be. The concept, as Socrates taught, is what answers a question: the question of *what is* a thing (*tí estin*). Or, if the essence or nature of the thing is unclear, as taught by Plato's *Meno*, the concept is what hypothetically gives answer to the question about how is a thing (*hopoîon estin*). What we call beyond, however, is not a concept, because it is not an answer to any question about life or death or the afterlife. We know nothing nor can we know about the beyond, nor do we have experience of beyond, and yet, we wonder about it. And it is not a casual or fashionable question, but one that man has previously pondered and now and always, a question that is part of what it means to be human. Strictly speaking, what we call "beyond" only appears and is shown to thought and to reason in this question: it therefore constitutes an absolute limit, and the same absolute limit that is characteristic of the desired science, the science of first causes and principles.

6 *Metaphysica Naturalis*

Asking for the beyond absolute, that is, by beyond of an absolute limit, like life, being or knowledge, confronts us with the kind of questions that belong to what Kant calls *metaphysica naturalis*, questions that haunt human reason in such a way that, as affirms in the Preface to the first edition of the *Critique of Pure Reason* (1781), "cannot be ignored, because they spring from the very nature of reason, and which cannot be answered, because they transcend the powers of human reason".[20] Of an acute observation like this, that can be understood, in my opinion, as a successful interpretation of the natural desire to know that lies at the gateway to the *Metaphysics* of Aristotle, i. e., metaphysics as a *naturalis dispositio hominis*, it is possible to draw very different conclusions. And the conclusion that the Prussian philosopher drew was the necessity for the reason self would limit, moderate his passion for knowledge and renounce asking this kind of questions, the metaphysical questions or limit questions, because they would be the product of an illegitimate use of pure reason, as revealed in the critique of knowledge. According to Kant, the theoretical use of pure reason, according to which it has the outrageous claim of attaining knowledge of the highest things, without support and touchstone in experience, is illegitimate. This is what happens when you ask about, for example, the immortality of the soul, freedom of will or the

---

[20] Inmanuel Kant, *Kritik der reinen Vernunft* (KrV). I will quote according to the Spanish translation of Pedro Ribas:*Crítica de la razón pura*, p. 38.

existence of God: because these problems are not amenable to experience, they cannot be the subject of theoretical knowledge, because this is limited to phenomena. Hence, Kant denies them legitimacy in the field of metaphysics, but then grants them legitimacy in the field of morality, as postulates of practical reason. Kant summed up in one sentence his thoughts on the matter: "I had to suppress knowledge, to make room for faith".[21]

What could have led Kant to such a differing conclusion to that reached by Aristotle? Perhaps knowing their differences on some key points help us to outline and better understand the scope of Aristotelian thought about the beyond. We can begin by the difference in the concept of metaphysics. Kant understands this science as opposed to physics: its object is what is not physical, and therefore is not susceptible to experience. Through a process of translations and betrayals that should be very appealing to historians of science, and that among the nearer thinkers to Kant include Baumgarten, Wolff, Leibniz and Suarez, metaphysics has gone from being a necessarily linked physical science and hardly distinguishable from it, as is evident in the work of Aristotle, to being completely separate from the physical to such an extent as to be defined by its denial, as is usually understood by science today.[22] It has forgotten the meaning of the Greek metá "beyond", part of the title of this science, reducing it to mere denial. Now this proposition can be read underlining the sense of transcendence of its object, *trans*, especially like the Neoplatonists did; or underlining its sense of later in the order of research, *post*, as did the first commentators on the Aristotelian text[23] – both, moreover, complementary – , but not as a mere negation. The positive link with physics is evident in the various books of the *Metaphysics*, not only those containing extensive and detailed examinations of physical issues, such as Zeta, Eta, Theta and Kappa, but even in Lambda, where Aristotle is given the task of demonstrating the existence of a separate, eternal and immobile substance. Indeed, the analysis of physical and perfectly perceptible phenomena, such as time and circular movement of celestial bodies, is what serves as the basis for the demonstration.[24] It is not outside the movement, but the phenomenological analysis of this, which leads us to conclude, by logical necessity, the existence of "an eternal and immobile principle, which depend the heavens and the world nature":[25] this is the genius of Aristotle's argument.

---

21 Immanuel KANT, *Kritik der reinen Vernunft*, Preface to the second edition, 20.
22 GRONDIN y HABERMAS are, among others, notable exceptions. Cf. Jürgen HABERMAS, *Nachmetaphysisches Denken*; Jean GRONDIN, *Introduction à la métaphysique*.
23 Cf. Pierre AUBENQUE, *Le probleme de l'être chez Aristote*, Presses Universitaires de France, Paris, 1962, chap. 1.
24 Cf. ARISTOTLE, *Metaphysics*, L 6.
25 Ibid., L 7, 1072 b13–14.

The experience of time and movement is experience of finitude, of what it is neither absolutely being nor absolutely nothing, but rather unity of being and not being. This experience of finitude of the cosmos and the self and one's own understanding is the existential background of desire to know, to know beyond, of the *metaphysica naturalis*, which we might call *éros metaphysikós* or, more properly, *órexis metaphysikés*.

The posture that man must assume in the face of this natural desire is not one of self-restraint, Aristotle thinks, but rather one of its provocation and drive. Man does well if he follows his own desires, which are according to his nature – that is the ethical mandate –, and none is more typical or can take him further. This desire is natural, but there are several circumstances that can cause it to fade it or divert off course: sophistic persuasion, prejudice, ideology, and in general, anything that causes us the illusion of knowledge. Hence the importance of their provocation. What causes and moves the desire to know is the state of awe, wonder and perplexity: "Men always – writes Aristotle – start and began to philosophize moved by the wonder".[26] In the state of awe and wonder, man recognizes that it does not know and this goads and releases that intimate desire to know under the form of questions. These are the questions that, when well conducted, will lead him to escape from ignorance and rejoice in truth. However, for that very reason, what is important and decisive here are not the answers but rather the questions.

7 The Progress of Science

As we have seen, Kant proposed a self-limitation of the desire to know constitutive of metaphysics and human beings, to prevent reason from asking questions to which it cannot respond. His ideal of science is taken from Newton´s *Mathe-matical Principles of Natural Philosophy*,[27] in which he took charge of fundamental problems of physics and his responses found universal acceptance, free of controversies. Kant wants to submit philosophy, and particularly metaphysics, to this model. He thinks this is the only way metaphysics can stop being "a battlefield of endless disputes", and change the contempt that it has been subjected to, for the title of "queen of the sciences", that it once received.[28] The road is one alone, according to Kant: the criticism of pure reason against dogmatism that has led metaphysics to its present condition.

---

26 Cf. ARISTOTLE, *Metaphysics*, A 2, 982 b12–13.
27 Isaac NEWTON, *Philosophiae naturalis principia mathematica*.
28 Immanuel Kant, *Kritik der reinen Vernunft*, Preface to the first edition, 8.

Aristotle has a very different conception about the particular way science progresses. If science is an attempt to answer the question "why", then the development of questions is paramount for its progress, while answers are secondary and relative to these questions. "The question – says Heidegger- is the piety of thinking".[29] This is true for all sciences, but especially for metaphysics as a science of the first causes and principles. Accordingly, science does not advance, as Kant believes, by adding answers, but instead by adding questions. On the other hand, this is not achieved in the framework of a self-enclosed reason – whether this the individual or transcendental *Ich denken* –, but a reason involved in a dialectical and dialogical context,[30] in a game of questions and answers, as Socrates and Plato taught masterfully, and Gadamer has lucidly described it in our time.[31]

This is the reason why Aristotle, at the beginning of an investigation, always starts collecting and valuing the opinions of his predecessors, not only like-minded thinkers, but also of those with whom he disagrees; even those who have erred. Indeed, that's the way "the philosopher" performs, as shown in his Alpha Book of *Metaphysics*, and makes this position explicit at the beginning of the Book Alpha Elátton, in which he writes: "It is just that we should be grateful, not only to those whose opinions we may share, but also to those who have expressed more superficial views; for these also contributed something, by developing before us the powers of thought".[32] Therefore, Philosophy is understood as a traditional and collective activity, a spirit well collected by the medieval scholastics that incorporated it in the method of *lectio*, *quaestio* and *disputatio*. The battlefield that Kant would like to avoid, is something that Aristotle and his following tradition has appreciated and learned to employ as an open laboratory of thought.

The method of questions and opposing reasons takes an even more elaborate form in Aristotle: the diaporectic method. By this, a) first the *aporíai* or puzzles that are about a subject, that is, statements or opposing arguments, that stop the thought (*aporeîn*) are identified; b) then, with thought tied to the thing under investigation, these *aporíai* are developed in their various aspects (*diaporeîn*); c) finally, the exit or solution of the *aporía* (*euporeîn*) needs to be found. Aristotle compares the *aporía* with a knot: one who does not know the knot, cannot untie it; the same happens with the one who does not discover the *aporía*; they cannot solve it: "Those who seek without stopping early in the aporíai resemble those

---

29 Martin HEIDEGGER, *Die Frage nach der Technik*, 36.
30 Cf. Enrico BERTI, *Aristotele. Dalla dialettica alla filosofia prima*. Terence H. IRWIN, *Aristotle's First Principles*.
31 Cf. Hans-Georg GADAMER, *Wahrheit und Methode*. I will quote according to the Spanish translation of Ana A. Aparicio and Rafael de Agapito: *Verdad y método*, 439–58.
32 *Met.* A Ellaton, 1, 993 b11-14. Trans. W. D. Ross.

who ignore where to go, and even ignore whether they've found or not what they wanted".[33] By contrast, the state of perplexity of mind reveals the problematic "of the thing itself" and fixes attention on it, with a view to their understanding.

8 Knowledge of not Knowing

Kant's phrase that we quoted an earlier above, will allow us to address another important point. Kant said: "I had to suppress knowledge, to make room for faith". This statement, not only manifests the primacy that the German philosopher grants to faith, but also the dialectic opposition between knowledge and faith: both are mutually exclusive. This is due to a conception of knowledge, which, as is common to the thinking of the Enlightenment, requires full and seamless clarity. Any shade that could be introduced works against the value of knowledge.

On the contrary, Aristotle, who was heir to a tradition founded on the human experience of finitude, focuses on the upward path of research and search rather than descending path of demonstration – which in practice is limited to mathematics[34] – and this leads him to consider knowledge as a complex interplay of light and shadow. This is what Plato had seen in the *Meno*: it is not possible to investigate nor what is known nor what is not known, but what lies in between both extremes.[35] This also applies, in an even more pronounced way, for the most desired science. In the same chapter in which Aristotle presents the attributes that elevate science of first causes over all other knowledge, he affirms the proximity of this science and the myth: "*Philómythos* – in other words, the 'myth lover' –, is in a certain way *philósophós* – meaning, lover of wisdom –, because myth <as philosophy> consists of marvellous elements".[36] The marvellous, is what shines by the perfection of its being and at the same time what gives us some darkness, because it exceeds the power of our cognitive capacity. That is therefore why, although following Parmenides and Plato, Aristotle affirms a directly proportional relationship between the being and the intelligibility of a thing, for "each thing is in respect of being, so is it in respect of truth",[37] it does not follow that we have more intelligence of the *per se* clearest and truest things, for "the

---

[33] Ibid., B 1, 995 a35.
[34] Cf. Enrico BERTI, *Le ragioni di Aristotele*, cap. 1. There is Spanish translation of H. Gianneschi y M. Monteverdi, *Las razones de Aristóteles*.
[35] Cf. Plato, *Meno*, 80d sq.
[36] ARISTOTLE, *Metaphysics*, A 2, 982 b18–19.
[37] Ibid., A Elátton 1, 993 b30–31.

understanding of our soul behaves towards the clearest things by nature, as the eyes of the bat with respect to the light of day".[38]

In this explanation an important distinction from Aristotle is implicit:[39] what is most clear and intelligible by nature, that is, first causes and principles, is not most clear and intelligible to us. The most clear to us are sensible things. Therefore, according to the order that naturally follows our understanding, ranging from the effects to the causes, the first causes represent the end of investigation and the limit of our knowledge. This means that metaphysical knowledge progresses as much as the human understanding experiences its finiteness. There is no danger of a metaphysical *hybris*. The marvellous, the mysterious, the amazing, that is beyond, is discovered and hidden at the same time. It is discovered in the truth of its being, and it is hidden as an invincible limit of desire and understanding. However, the metaphysical knowledge has recognized the limit as such, and to that extent it has broken its closure and in a certain way has overcome it. Metaphysical knowledge, as knowing of the limit, is a knowing of not knowing. The knowledge of not knowing is the knowledge of an absolute beyond, invincible by pure reason, the precise moment when reason, for an intimate and proper motion, is called to surpass itself as faith.[40]

Bibliography

Aquinas, Thomas, *Corpus Thomisticum*, edited by Enrique Alarcon. Online available at: http://www.corpusthomisticum.org (accessed May, 2017).
Araos, Jaime, "Eros metafísico: el movimiento constituyente de la filosofía primera". In Pierre Aubenque, Enrico Berti, Tomás Calvo et al., *Dialéctica y ontología. Coloquio Internacional sobre Aristóteles*. Santiago de Chile, Instituto de Filosofía, UC, 2002, 153–195.
Araos, Jaime, *La filosofía aristotélica del lenguaje*. Pamplona, EUNSA, 1999.
Aristotelis Opera (Scriptorum Classicorum Bibliotheca Oxoniensis). Oxford, Oxonii e Typographeo Clarendoniano, 1894–1969.
Aristotelis Opera ex recensione Immanuelis Bekkeri, 5 vols. Berolini, Academia Regia Borussica, 1831–1870; Berlin, De Gruyter, 1961².
Aristotle, *The Complete Works of Aristotle. The Revised Oxford Translation*, edited by Jonathan Barnes, 2 vols. Princeton New Jersey/Oxford, Princeton University Press, 1991 (1984¹).

---

38 *Ibid.*, A Elátton 1, 993 b9–11.
39 Cf. Aristotle, *Physics* A 1, 184 a10-26; *Anal. Post.* A 2, 72 a1.
40 Negative theology from the Middle Ages, represented by Pseudo Dionysius, Thomas Aquinas and Meister Eckhart, among others, the philosophy of "abandonment of the mental limit" by Leonardo Polo, the "philosophy of the limit" by Eugenio Trías, and the philosophy as think in the limit by Jorge Millas, are some emblematic developments, among others, who have followed the path opened by Aristotle.

Aubenque, Pierre, *Le probleme de l'être chez Aristote*. Paris, Presses Universitaires de France, 1962.
Berti, Enrico, *Aristotele. Dalla dialettica alla filosofia prima*. Padova, Cedam, 1977.
Berti, Enrico, *Le ragioni di Aristotele*. Roma/Bari, Laterza e Figli SpA, 1989. There is Spanish translation of H. Gianneschi and M. Monteverdi: *Las razones de Aristóteles*. Buenos Aires, Oinos, 2008.
Bonitz, Hermann, "Index Aristotelicus". In *Aristoteles Opera*, vol. 5. Berolini, Academia Regia Borussica, 1831–1870; Berlin, De Gruyter, 1961.
Diels, Hermann, and Kranz, Walther, *Die Fragmente der Vorsokratiker*, 3 vols. Berlin-Grunewald, Weidmann, 1951–1952.
Dionysius the Areopagite, *Corpus Dionysiacum I* (DN), edited by Beate R. Suchla. Berlin, De Gruyter, 1990. Corpus Dionysiacum II (CH, EH, MT, Letters), edited by Günter Heil and Adolf M. Ritter. Berlin, De Gruyter, 1991.
Gadamer, Hans-Georg, *Wahrheit und Methode*. Tübingen, J.C.B. Mohr (Paul Siebeck), 1975. There is Spanish translation of Ana A. Aparicio and Rafael de Agapito, *Verdad y método*. Salamanca, Ediciones Sígueme, 1993.
Grondin, Jean, *Introduction à la métaphysique*. Montréal, Herder, Les Presses de l'Université de Montréal, 2004.
Habermas, Jürgen, *Nachmetaphysisches Denken*. Frankfurt am Main, Suhrkamp Verlag, 1988.
Heidegger, Martin, "Die Frage nach der Technik". In Id., *Die Technik und die Kehre* (Opuscula, 1). Pfullingen, Neske, 1962.
Heidegger, Martin, *Wegmarken*. Frankfurt am Main, Vittorio Klostermann, 1976.
Irwin, Terence H., *Aristotle's First Principles*. Oxford, Oxford University Press, 1988.
John of Saint Thomas (Juan de Santo Tomás, João Poinsot), *Ars Logica*, edited by Beato Reiser. Turin, Marii & Marietti, 1930.
Kant, Immanuel, *Kritik der reinen Vernunft*. Hamburg, Felix Meiner, 1967. English edition: *Critique of Pure Reason*, translated and edited by Paul Guyer and Allen W. Wood. Cambridge/New York/Madrid/Melbourne, Cambridge University Press, 1998. Spanish edition: *Crítica de la razón pura*, translation by Pedro Ribas. Madrid, Taurus, 2005.
Leibniz, Gottfried W., "De Primae Philosophiae Emendatione et de Notione Substantiae". In Id., *Die philosophischen Schriften*, vol. 4. Hildesheim/New York, Georg Olms Verlag, 1978, 468–470.
Meister Eckhart, *Die deutschen und lateinischen Werke*, published on behalf of the Deutsche Forschungsgemeinschaft. Stuttgart, 1936 sqq. New edition: Stuttgart, Kohlhammer, 1987–2003.
Millas, Jorge, *Idea de la filosofía*, 2 vols. Santiago de Chile, Editorial Universitaria, 1970.
Newton, Isaac, *Isaac Newton's Philosophiae Naturalis Principia Mathematica*. The Third Edition with Variant Readings, edited by Alexandre Koyré and I. Bernard Cohen, 2 vols. Cambridge, Harvard University Press and Cambridge University Press, 1972.
Plato, *Meno*, translated by Walter R. M. Lamb (The Loeb Classical Library). London/Cambridge, Mass., Harvard Univ. Press, 1990 (Reprint 1924).
Polo, Leonardo, *Antropología trascendental*, 2 vols. Pamplona, EUNSA, 2010.
Polo, Leonardo, *El Ser – I: La existencia extramental*. Pamplona, EUNSA, 1997.
Priscianus Caesariensis, *Institutiones Grammaticae,* edited by Martin Hertz, vol. 2. Leipzig, Teubner, 1955. Reprinted: Hildesheim, Georg Olms, 1961.
Trías, Eugenio, *Lógica del límite*, Barcelona, Destino, 1991.
Velarde, Julián, *Historia de la lógica*. Oviedo, Universidad de Oviedo, 1989.

Gregor Vogt-Spira
Ideas – Presences – Practices
The Beyond in Ancient Roman Culture

Ancient mythology has created a number of characters who have to endure immense, never-ending punishments for their crimes in a ghastly underworld: Sisyphus, who has to ceaselessly roll a boulder uphill and watch it fall back down again each time; Ixion, who is bound to a wheel; Tityos, who is staked to the ground, where a pair of vultures come to tear his continually regenerating liver to pieces; the Danaides, who for eternity pour water into buckets full of holes. In short, the realm of Tartarus, guarded by Cerberus, is a place of horror. In his Epicurean didactic poem, *De rerum natura*, the Roman poet Lucretius strongly attacks the widespread fear of these horrors, saying that none of this exists or could possibly exist. He explains that the myths of the underworld are only allegories for misdeeds and fears experienced in life itself and that if men wanted to envisage a change for the worse after death, then they foolishly made life hell for themselves.[1]

For the purposes of our enquiry, this exceedingly graphic and colourful passage teaches us three things about the 'beyond'. First of all, there are widespread ideas about the beyond in which the notion of horror plays a role – even if we take into account that Lucretius exaggerates the picture of the underworld on account of the aim of his line of argument, which is to free men from fear. Secondly, there are educational movements which question the existence of a beyond – this not only applies to a few schools of philosophy but is a widespread position in formal education. Thirdly and finally, the beyond is connected with the question of survival after death and is therefore understood to be one of the great challenges. In Hellenistic and Roman philosophy, whose central concern is to prove that fear of death is unfounded, it is even seen as the greatest challenge.

In fact, Greco-Roman culture developed an abundance of ideas about the beyond. The beyond is seen to have a presence in the multifaceted and interrelated living world and there are many different practices to be dealt with. They vary from cult rituals to mystery religions and deeds of magic. Nevertheless, there remains one essential characteristic feature: in pagan Greco-Roman culture, the beyond never develops into one uniform, generally imagined space.

---

[1] LUCRETIUS, *De rerum natura* 3, 978–1023. On LUCRETIUS' allegorical interpretations see Christoff NEUMEISTER, "Lukrezens Umgang mit dem Mythos", esp. 23–26.

Note: I am most grateful to Gabrielle Kirov for translating my text into English.

DOI 10.1515/9783110530773-008

Different ideas about the beyond coexist and there are different levels of abstraction related to these ideas too, without this becoming a complete, totalitarian, systematic model that could be generally accepted as a valid world view, as in the case of Christianity.

There is a simple reason for this absence: a generally formulated, visually specific idea of the beyond has no integral place in the anthropomorphic Greco-Roman concept of the gods. The communication between men and gods is oriented towards life and is not primarily organised according to the idea of what will be after life. Typically, traditional handbooks of ancient religion do not mention the lemma 'beyond'.[2] It is true that the death cult plays an important role – and it is often mentioned, as are specific ideas about the beyond, especially the underworld – but in principle we can state the following: in the case of the ancient pagan world, we must view with some caution the hypothesis, formulated in the introduction to this volume, that the 'beyond' might be "intimately linked with, and nearly identical to the question of religion". There are overlapping ideas but nothing identical, since the concept of a beyond in the transcendent sense does not organise this world, rather the beyond is much more likely to be formed as a complement to this world and as such, does not represent a central problem for ancient religion.

This still needs to be clarified from two angles. If one creates a broad concept of religion,[3] in fact the picture changes. The ancient world is defined by a co-presence of religion in this broad sense, on very different levels of abstraction and indeed

---

[2] The lemma is completely absent from the extensive history of religions in the *Handbuch der Altertumswissenschaften*, which has been reprinted many times: the Greek history, Martin P. NILSSON, *Geschichte der griechischen Religion* and the Roman history, Georg WISSOWA, *Religion und Kultus der Römer*. However there is a mention, albeit brief and cursory, in the new edition by Kurt LATTE, *Römische Religionsgeschichte* and also in Ulrich von WILAMOWITZ-MOELLENDORFF, *Glaube der Hellenen*. The lemma is absent again from the indices of a work published throughout the world, Walter BURKERT's *Griechische Religion* (chapt. IV 2, 300–306 however, includes the title "Die Jenseitsmythologie" within the text). It is also absent from Jörg RÜPKE's introduction *Die Religion der Römer*. Even in classical studies lexica the lemma is of no greater importance. Whilst it is not listed in *Paulys Realencyclopädie der classischen Altertumswissenschaft*, the latest great undertaking of *Der Neue Pauly* nevertheless includes a short article by Fritz GRAF, half of which is admittedly dedicated to Etruscan culture, as well as to the Old and New Testament. The situation is fundamentally different when Christianity is viewed systematically. Significantly, there are large-scale and comprehensive entries in the *Reallexikon für Antike und Christentum*. It even includes two articles with the lemmas "Jenseits" and "Jenseitsreise" (written by several authors; author of the sections on pagan antiquity is Peter HABERMEHL). From a cultural studies perspective, the lemma has now entered companion guides to the ancient world, e. g. Nanno MARINATOS and Nicolas WYATT, "Mythological Conceptions".

[3] Suggested in the formulation of the third question in the introduction of this volume.

in no way specific to levels of differentiating practices. This is, however, a further indicator that a homogenization of ideas about the beyond is not necessary.

Secondly, the beyond does not necessarily need to be thought of only in chronological terms as a place of abode for human beings after death but can also be understood in more abstract terms as that which is 'beyond' human access or any possibility of taking action or gaining knowledge, consequently as that which surpasses, or rather, transcends, human life. When one understands 'beyond' in this sense as a term for the fundamental movement of 'trans', it is obvious that the ancient gods as a whole are included. However, there are a large number of further instances such as fate, coincidence, the cosmos etc. which all lie 'beyond' individual human powers. Thereby the type of questioning changes from religion to philosophy, not to mention that the problem of transcendence has its own implications. For our purposes it is sufficient to stipulate that even so, one finds no tendency towards one homogenized idea of the 'beyond'. What is imagined and discussed much more is the interplay between this human life and the exceedingly high number of concepts of the beyond, perceived extremely differently and individually.

This leaves us with the conclusion that in the ancient Greco-Roman world, there was no systematic need for one uniform concept of the beyond. It is much more a matter of different views existing together, which in practice in no way exclude one another.

In the following section I want to concentrate on pagan Rome, which in this context is of interest in so much as we can observe here particularly clearly the superimposition of several completely different levels: firstly an old Italian tradition which is organised not around personalised gods but around ritual dealings with the dead; secondly, a tradition absorbed from Greek culture with its world of gods, which establishes the public ritual and its world of images and at the same time, brings with it its own rationalistic solutions; furthermore, discussions on the question of the immortality of the soul, both from a philosophical and a religious point of view; and finally, a discourse covering all layers, which is directed towards what lies beyond the powers of human action and which defines the 'what goes beyond us' as the personalised concept of a force of destiny which governs the whole of human life.

I

One of the key questions is, where is the 'beyond' embedded, where is it located? If we are asking about the geographical location, it appears that here different spatial ideas merge into one another. Firstly there is the beyond located on the 'ends of the huge earth' and then there is the beyond, 'far beneath the earth.' Both terms are used a few verses apart in Hesiod's *Theogony*, and so are not seen as contradictory.[4] The immeasurable depths are illustrated again in the assertion that an iron anvil falling from earth would take ten days to reach Tartaros.

Homer provides the most graphic picture and through him the images for the whole of the ancient world were canonised. Odysseus's travels culminate in the journey to the underworld, the Nekyia, the epitome of transgression, to which Circe shows him the way.[5] His ship is said to be carried by the north wind towards Oceanus, thus to the edge of the world – for Oceanus is a river that encircles the earth with its lands and seas. It is related that he must land there and go into the dank house of Hades and on to the point at which two rivers flow into the Acheron with a tremendous roar.

If we combine the many different messages together, it appears that the focus is not a coherent geographical whole but the creation of the characteristic 'outermost limits'. 'Beyond' is, in this respect, the 'other world' translated into geographical terms. However, there are certain shifts insofar as the image of the 'dank depths' takes precedence over the edge of the world. In Rome, Orcus is generally depicted as a dark cave that is connected with the Upper World through different narrow, localised chasms. Nevertheless, elements from both geographical images are combined: the picture of the ferryman, Charon, who ferries the dead across to the other side, goes rather better with the image of the river around the world.[6]

On Odysseus's journey, Hades is not primarily connected with horrors. It is only at the end, when 'the myriad tribes of the dead came thronging up with a wondrous cry', that he is seized with fear.[7] In the course of time, however, there is a growing intensity in the sense of horror. Literature especially contributes to this idea.[8]

---

[4] HESIOD, *Theogony* 720; 731. Cf. HESIOD, *Theogony*, ed. Martin L. WEST, 356–379, esp. 358: "The underworld that emerges from Hesiod's account is not one of which one could draw a map or construct a world".

[5] HOMER, *Odyssey* 10, 508–515.

[6] Usually interpreted as referring to a variety of sources cf. Martin L. WEST, *The East Face* as well as Nanno MARINATOS and Nicolas WYATT, "Mythological Conceptions", which take rather a harmonising approach, yet in the conclusion make the important observation (405), "the geography of the *Odyssee* is comprehensible if we take into account that the Beyond is not just Hades but also the sky".

[7] HOMER, *Odyssey* 11, 632 sq.

[8] This is particularly the case in Roman literature. For an in-depth study of this see Annette M. BAERTSCHI, *Nekyiai*.

Parallel to the exclusion of an 'Otherworld', is an approach to integrate it into the world of the Olympian gods. This view is likewise evident in Homer.[9] He explains how the world was divided between the three sons of Cronos: Zeus, Poseidon and the third one, Hades, who is lord of the nether regions. He relates that everything has been divided into three and assigned by lot: Zeus having obtained the broad heaven, Poseidon the grey sea and Hades the murky darkness. However the earth and Olympus remain common to all. This is undeniably a vertical division of space. Olympus, which also becomes synonymous with heaven, thus eludes a spacial location, however.

Nonetheless, seen from another viewpoint, the idea of the beyond not being within the construction of a single space comes undone. An especially rich topography and prosopography of the underworld is proposed in the sixth book of the *Aeneid*, in which Vergil also has his Aeneas descend into the underworld, an imitation of the Nekyia of the *Odyssey*. This time the arrival is relocated to the well-known topography of Lake Avernus, near the Gulf of Naples, where it has been noticed that birds that fly over it fall down dead. Here Vergil conflates ideas about the beyond from different mythological and philosophical sources and from now on imprints his image in a way which compares with Dante later on. After Aeneas has walked through the halls, which are beleaguered with the personification of negative abstract qualities such as care, age, want and war, he reaches a point at which the path divides. To the right lies Elysium, to the left is 'godless Tartarus', where the wicked are punished.[10] The underworld, into which Aeneas descends, the realm of Hades or Pluto, in Latin, therefore combines both concepts: hell and paradise.

Both are painted with great intensity. On the left side is a massive wall, encircled by a flood of devilish, whirling flames; within it is set a huge gate, which even the gods may not break open. Next to this is an iron tower where the monster Tisiphone keeps watch, in a blood-coloured cloak and girded with vipers and whips. Then behind the gate are the fifty-headed Hydra and the gaping depths of Tartarus.[11] From the visual aspect we move to the acoustics where all is accompanied by unbearable clanging, clinking and rattling. The "awfulness [...] brought closer to the listener's senses through strong painting with language"[12] is also described poetically. In short, a topography of horrors. Since antiquity, man has tried in vain to bring them into a coherent, spacial order.[13]

---

9 HOMER, *Iliad* 15, 187–193.
10 VIRGIL, *Aeneid* 6, 273–281; 540–543.
11 Ibid. 548–558; 576–579.
12 Eduard NORDEN, *Aeneis VI*, 272 in the comment on place.
13 Ibid. 273. This certainly does not prevent a wealth of visual representations: cf. Antonie WLOSOK, "Vergils Unterwelt in der Buchmalerei".

On the other side, then, is Elysium, where the blessed reside. It is described with refined discretion as a place filled with joy, with the charming green of blissful groves, through which a crimson light shines through, with its own sun and its own stars.[14] The idea of Elysium can already be found in the *Odyssey*, where it is situated, like Hades, on the edge of the earth, beyond the river of Oceanus.[15] There it is described as being the easiest life for men, where there is no snow, nor wintry weather, nor rain and where Oceanus continuously sends up blasts of the west wind, to cool the men – the images of paradise are evidently dependent on the climatic conditions of the particular environment.

The concept of the beyond on which we have focused our special attention until now and whose localisation we have questioned, is that of classical Greek mythology, which was also adopted by the Romans. It belongs to the world of the Olympian gods and understands the beyond to be a residence for the dead, trying to integrate it into a world order, without there being a need to develop this into a coherent spacial location. In its organisation in particular, elements of the specific living environment are frequently recognised. So, for example, Vergil has assigned characteristics of the Naples area to his portrayal of the underworld, which conveyed the impression to those travelling in Italy in the early modern era that they could wander through the beyond of ancient times at the Gulf of Naples.[16]

Meanwhile, alongside this, a second localisation of the beyond appeared not in the underworld but, on the contrary, in heaven: an idea which began to develop in the fifth century BC and became of significant importance to intellectuals until late antiquity. Fundamental to this was the scientific worldview of astronomy, according to the Academy and the Aristotelian school. It divides the cosmos into an area subjected to change, in which men's lives are located, and the eternal realms of the celestial bodies. As the moon acts as a boundary, one area is designated sublunary and the other supralunary.

The location of the beyond is to be seen in the context of the question of the immortality of the soul. This is a problem that plays a key role in the contemporary discourses and pervades the various schools of philosophy just as much as it extends to the domain of mystery religions. The borderline between religion and philosophy becomes blurred on this occasion.[17] Especially successful in this respect was a myth by Heraclides Ponticus, a pupil of Plato, who had the souls of

---

14 VERGIL, *Aeneid* 6, 637–641.
15 HOMER, *Odyssey* 4, 561–569.
16 Cf. Ekkehard STÄRK, *Kampanien*, esp. 37–62.
17 Jan N. BREMMER, *After Life* gives a short history of the concepts of the immortal soul, cf. esp. chapter 2 "Orphism, Pythagoras and the Rise of the immortal Soul". Peter HABERMEHL, "Jenseits", 273–287 gives a good overview.

the dead wander the milky way and either be pulled further upwards into heaven or, if they still had to be purified, return back down to earth.[18] Later the Milky Way would then generally be thought of as the abode of the blessed as, for example, in Cicero's *Somnium Scipionis*, in which the evidence of the immortality of the soul is based on the latest findings in the field of astronomy.[19]

However, in Roman times it was not enough to have these two co-existing ideas about the beyond. In addition, two further ideas appear, which are on very different levels of abstraction, although they extend through all layers. On the one hand, there is the belief in Fortuna, the central goddess of the Hellenistic-Roman world, who in a certain sense supersedes the old Olympian world of the gods. Structurally, this is an abstract concept and here the 'beyond' is the sum of that which lies beyond human powers of action or cognition, that is, what is quite simply unavailable to man. At the same time, it is in turn made accessible as a personified abstract concept and thereby raised to the level, even, of a universal deity. This means that the field of action of this 'beyond' is potentially the whole world. The correct way of dealing with this therefore becomes a key theme, which to a wide extent determines the ethical discourse.[20]

Added to these was a fourth idea which dates from the early Roman period and remained effective and established rites and customs until the imperial period by virtue of Roman society being strongly bound to tradition. It is expressed by the formula, "In the world view of the early Romans, the beyond was the realm of the ancestors."[21] Behind this lies the idea that the deceased continue to exist as spirits – the key term is *manes* – and they would be included in the ritual funeral procession and burial among the *di manes*. So the ghosts of the dead are seen as gods, who however continue to exist in an imprecise, indistinct way and are not seen as individuals but are thought of as a collective. It is important that they are recorded as having been buried amongst the *di manes*, as, if they are left unburied, they wander around without becoming one of the gods.

Di manes is the most common expression for the ghosts of the deceased. In particular it is used in the inscriptions on gravestones, where the deceased is addressed with the stereotyped wording, 'for the ghost-gods' – *Dis manibus* ... In addition there are also other expressions for the ghosts of the departed such as *di*

---

18 HERACLIDES fr. 96 WEHRLI, *Herakleides Pontikos*, with the comment 93. Cf. also Martin P. NILSSON, *Geschichte der griechischen Religion*, vol. 2, 240 sq.
19 Cf. Reinhold F. GLEI, "Kosmologie".
20 For more details, Gregor VOGT-SPIRA, "*Carpe diem*" in the first volume of this series, and generally on the subject in *Dramaturgie des Zufalls*. On the divine nature of chance, Martin P. NILSSON, *Geschichte der griechischen Religion*, vol. 2, 200–210.
21 Peter HABERMEHL, "Jenseits", 289.

parentes, which emphasises the aspect of relationship, or *di penates*, which brings the reference to the home into the foreground. These can be traced back genetically to different ritualistic origins but through usage they merge fluidly together.

What is crucial here is that the deceased are not situated in a beyond that is totally divorced from the world of the living. Ancient Rome created no vivid pictures of the beyond. The verdict evident in the histories of religion is that "no living image of life after death or goings-on in the shadowy realm" was developed.[22] What persists much more, is a close connection between the living and the dead, to the extent that the deceased Roman has "a social function" and "plays a role in the life of Roman society"[23] in a very different way than he would in the modern world. For one thing, it is assumed that the ghost-gods take part in the life of their descendants, support them favourably but also sanction violations. We can also see engraved on a tombstone from the second century BC,[24] "I have gained the commendation of the ancestors, so that they are pleased to have given birth to me". The presence of the dead extends so far that wax masks of them are put on display in the atria of the houses of the ruling elite – the striking similarity to the original is often emphasised – and are carried along at the funeral of a family member. In this way the link between generations is constantly kept alive for each individual both in outer representation and also as an inner duty.

Finally, another indication of the unbroken link to the dead is also to be seen in the state feasts celebrating the dead. At the end of the Roman year, in the second half of February, the feast of the Parentalia is celebrated, with the view that the ghosts of the dead return to earth and ceremonies involving food for example are held at the tomb. The second great Roman feast for the dead has a quite different character: this is the feast of the Lemuria held on the 9, 11 and 13 May. Ovid offers an impressive description of this rite:[25]

---

22 Georg WISSOWA, *Religion und Kultus der Römer*, 238. See also Kurt LATTE, *Römische Religionsgeschichte*, 100: "Es gibt keine Vorstellungen von einem Totenreich, einem Jenseits, in dem sie weilen, oder von einem Herrn dieses Reiches".
23 Wilhelm KIERDORF, "Totenehrung", 84 sq.
24 Epigraph for Cn. Cornelius Scipio Hispanus (*Corpus Inscriptionum Latinarum* I² 15 = *Inscriptiones Latinae Selectae* 6): *Maiorum optenui laudem, ut sibei me esse creatum | laetentur; stirpem nobilitavit honor.*
25 OVID, *Fasti* 5, 429–444: *Nox ubi iam media est somnoque silentia praebet, | et canis et variae conticuistis aves, | ille memor veteris ritus timidusque deorum | surgit (habent gemini vincula nulla pedes), | signaque dat digitis medio cum pollice iunctis, | occurrat tacito ne levis umbra sibi. | cumque manus puras fontana perluit unda, | vertitur et nigras accipit ante fabas, | aversusque iacit; sed dum iacit, 'haec ego mitto, | his' inquit 'redimo meque meosque fabis.' | hoc novies dicit nec respicit: umbra putatur | colligere et nullo terga vidente sequi. | rursus aquam tangit, Temesaeaque concrepat aera, | et rogat ut tectis exeat umbra suis. | cum dixit novies 'manes exite paterni' | respicit, et pure sacra peracta putat.*

> When midnight has come and sleep brings peace and the dogs and the flock of colourful birds are quiet, then the Roman who remembers ancient rites and fears the gods, rises. He wears no shoes on his feet and makes a sign with his thumb encircled by his fingers (the fist), lest an insubstantial shadow stands in his way in the silence. Thereon he cleanses his hands in spring water and turns around. First he takes some black beans and throws them backwards with averted face. As he throws, he says, 'I offer these (to the dead). With these beans I throw, I redeem me and mine.' He says this nine times without looking back. It is thought that the shadow gathers up the beans and follows behind, unseen. Again he touches water and sounds the gong of Temesan bronze and asks the shadow to leave his house. Thereby he calls out nine times, 'Ancestral spirits, depart!'. He looks around and considers the sacred rite to have been fulfilled.

Unlike the feast of the Parentalia, whose main feature constitutes a 'loving connection with the ancestors', the feast of Lemuria is defined 'by an attitude of repulsion towards the spirits of the dead'.[26] The *lemures* are represented as ghosts and nightly monsters, which the pater familias must chase away from his house all year long by performing the apotropaic ritual. During the imperial period the *lemures* are generally identified with the ancestral ghost-gods, so the spirits of the deceased were imagined to be wandering around at night.

There remains the question of the link between ideas about the beyond and characters who do or do not act. Passing through the three different localisations of a beyond, something has become implicitly clear. For instance, the last type, the *di manes*, as a rule thought not to be anthropomorphic, belongs to the level of belief in spirits and demons, which runs through all ancient religions as an underlying structure and is still alive in such apparently abstract forms as a belief in fate. However, the idea that deceased people become gods is not restricted to the depersonalised ghost-gods. This honour can be bestowed on outstanding figures, heroes, in particular. The beyond in which they are located is then the actual living space of the gods.

The strongest connection with the beyond and gods is to be seen in the world of myth, in which the forces of the underworld take on powerful forms. First of all there are the mirror images which complement the gods which exist above ground, as with Hades. At times both the domains of this life and the beyond are linked, as with Persephone, for the daughter of Zeus, abducted from a Sicilian meadow by the lord of the underworld and forced to marry him, spends half the year above the ground and the other half of the year underground. In addition, there are also some monsters from hell which, in the course of time, have been woven into downright excessive stories, especially in the literature.[27] Here

---

[26] OVIDIUS, *Fasten*, vol. 2, 315.
[27] We have already met Tisiphone in VERGIL (cf. supr. n. 11); an important role is also played by Allecto, who is so hideous that even Pluto and her own sisters of the underworld abhor her (VERGIL, *Aeneid* 7, 324–329). For more characters see Annette M. BAERTSCHI, *Nekyiai*.

the belief in demons offers many links, so that it is not always easy to separate the layers.

II

Within the framework of these four different concepts of the beyond which coexist in Rome and characterise the life of the individual, a number of different modes of behaviour with respect to the beyond have already become clear. In conclusion, the main question of this volume, 'The Beyond as Challenge of Life', might be reconsidered, specifically with respect to the connection between the beyond and this life.

The basic schema to explore and overcome the boundaries of this life is one of the most productive narrative structures in Greek culture. As a rule, it is worded as a 'Voyage into the Beyond'. Many heroes undertake such journeys in unknown border areas, where physical distance and descent to the underworld go hand in hand. The journeys of Odysseus, particularly the Nekyia, have been especially influential in literature.[28] This type of journey into the beyond, a version of which became the ascension, was so widespread that it has meanwhile been satirized and mocked. For example in a comedy by Plautus, a fraudster dressed as a long-distance traveller boasts that he has even been up to heaven to Jupiter's throne. He says, however, that he did not just simply go up to heaven but he even rowed upstream in a boat. But he did not meet the father of the gods as he had just gone to his country house to distribute food to the slaves.[29]

In the history of religion it is accepted that at the origin of the journey to the beyond lies the schamanistic journey of the soul: ecstatic experiences in which a living person penetrates into places in the beyond. The reports of such characters are varied. One prominent character is Epimenides of Crete, of whom it is told that he lived for a long time in the secret cave of Zeus on Mount Ida.[30] It is said that he consorted with the spirits of darkness, went on a strict fast, experienced long periods of ecstasy of the soul and then, enthusiastic and proficient in wisdom, returned to daylight in order to wander through the country, from then on, as a seer, a priest who conducted purificatory rites and a healer.

---

[28] See Maximilian BENZ, *Jenseitsreisen*. An overview is given in Peter HABERMEHL, "Jenseitsreise".
[29] PLAUTUS, *Trinummus* 939–947.
[30] Cf. Erwin ROHDE, *Psyche*, vol. 2, 96 sq.

Generally speaking, a close relationship between this life and beyond applies to all beliefs in the supernatural. Here the challenge is faced through ritual practices. We have seen examples of this in the *di manes* and the Lemuria. It should at least be mentioned that in both the Greek and Roman cultures there exist alongside institutionalised rituals considered to be mandatory, a wide range of magical practices, which, in some cases, are met with hostility.

To what extent all such ideas about the beyond were actually believed is disputed. We have already mentioned at the start Lucretius's criticism of the fear of the horrors of Hades. There are many others too, who reject the popular beliefs in such mythical pictures of hell.[31] Admittedly, one should not therefore necessarily conclude that there is a general lack of belief. There is scepticism, rather, with regard to the concrete visual shapes and the concrete stories. The awareness of the existence of a supernatural presence infuses Roman culture at every social level, influences the patterns of public activity and, by no means least, provides fertile ground for the numerous mystery religions which are very popular.

To conclude, what we can retain here is that this is profoundly different from all the religions which offer a doctrine of salvation. For there is no evidence of a wish to enter into the beyond. Death is no doubt seen as a central challenge in life: for more than five hundred years the philosophical and popular philosophical discourse bears witness to this. So the struggle is led, not from a 'beyond' but from this world, as a process of liberation from fear.

Roman culture provides an example of how multiple heterogeneous beliefs can be reconciled without the need to resolve the 'beyond' in a rationalistic way. The pragmatic approach to this heterogeneity has an integrative and stabilising effect and is therefore to be regarded as a cultural strength.

Bibilography

Baertschi, Annette M., *Nekyiai. Totenbeschwörung und Unterweltsbegegnung im neronisch-flavischen Epos*. Berlin, Humboldt Universität, 2013.
Benz, Maximilian, *Gesicht und Schrift. Die Erzählung von Jenseitsreisen in Antike und Mittelalter*. Berlin/New York, De Gruyter, 2013.
Bremmer, Jan N., *The Rise and Fall of the After Life*. London/New York, Routledge, 2002.

---

[31] Representative of the views of the educated classes: CICERO, *Tusculanae disputationes* 1, 10 sq.; 36 sq.; *De natura deorum* 2, 5 and repeatedly. It is characteristic too that the main feature of the *Aeneis* comments is that all the stories of the underworld are said to be fiction (SERVIUS, *Aen.* 6, 596 and repeatedly).

Burkert, Walter, *Griechische Religion der archaischen und klassischen Epoche* (Die Religionen der Menschheit, 15). Stuttgart, Kohlhammer, 1977 (English, French and Italian translations).

Corpus Inscriptionum Latinarum, vol. 1^2, pars 2, fasc. 1: *Inscriptiones Latinae antiqvissimae ad C. Caesaris mortem*, edited by Ernst Lommatzsch. Berlin, Georg Reimer, 1918.

Glei, Reinhold F., "Kosmologie statt Eschatologie: Ciceros 'Somnium Scipionis'". In *Tod und Jenseits im Altertum*, edited by Gerhard Binder and Bernd Effe. Trier, WVT, 1991, 122–143.

Graf, Fritz, Art. "Jenseitsvorstellungen", *Der Neue Pauly* 5, 1998, 897–899.

Habermehl, Peter, Art. "Jenseits, hier B. nichtchristlich. IV. Griechenland; V. Rom; VI. Der Synkretismus der Kaiserzeit", *Reallexikon für Antike und Christentum* 17, 1996, 258–329.

Habermehl, P., Art. "Jenseitsreise, hier B. nichtchristlich. III. Griechenland/Rom", *Reallexikon für Antike und Christentum* 17, 1996, 502–534.

Hesiod, *Theogony*, ed. with prolegomena and commentary by Martin L. West. Oxford, Oxford U.P., 1966.

Kierdorf, Wilhelm, "Totenehrung im republikanischen Rom". In *Tod und Jenseits im Altertum*, edited by Gerhard Binder and Bernd Effe. Trier, WVT, 1991, 71–87.

Latte, Kurt, *Römische Religionsgeschichte*. München, Beck, ^{2}1967.

Marinatos, Nanno and Nicolas Wyatt, "Levantine, Egyptian and Greek Mythological Conceptions of the Beyond". In *A Companion to Greek Mythology*, edited by Ken Dowden and Niall Livingstone, Malden. MA/Oxford/Chichester, Oxford U.P., 2011, 383–410.

Neumeister, Christoff, "Lukrezens Umgang mit dem Mythos". In *Die Allegorese des antiken Mythos in der Literatur, Wissenschaft und Kunst Europas*, edited by Hans J. Horn and Hermann Walter. Wiesbaden, Harrassowitz, 1997, 19–36.

Nilsson, Martin P., *Geschichte der griechischen Religion*. 2 vols., München, Beck, ^{3}1992.

Norden, Eduard, *P. Vergilius Maro. Aeneis Buch VI*. Darmstadt, WBG, ^{4}1957.

P. Ovidius Naso, *Die Fasten*, edited and translated with a commentary by Franz Bömer, 2 vols. Heidelberg, Winter, 1957–1958.

Rohde, Erwin, *Psyche. Seelencult und Unsterblichkeitsglaube der Griechen*, 2 vols. Freiburg i.Br./Leipzig/Tübingen, Mohr, ^{2}1898.

Rüpke, Jörg, *Die Religion der Römer. Eine Einführung*. München, Beck, ^{2}2006.

Stärk, Ekkehard, *Kampanien als geistige Landschaft. Interpretationen zum antiken Bild des Golfs von Neapel*. München, Beck, 1995.

Vogt-Spira, Gregor, *Dramaturgie des Zufalls. Tyche und Handeln in der Komödie Menanders*. München, Beck, 1992.

von Wilamowitz-Moellendorff, Ulrich, *Der Glaube der Hellenen*, 2 vols. Darmstadt, WBG, ^{2}1955.

Wehrli, Fritz, *Herakleides Pontikos* (Die Schule des Aristoteles. Texte und Kommentare, 7). Basel, Schwabe, 1953.

West, Martin L., *The East Face of Helicon. West Asiatic Elements in Greek Poetry and Myth*. Oxford, Oxford U.P., 1997.

Wissowa, Georg, *Religion und Kultus der Römer*. München, Beck, ^{2}1971.

Wlosok, Antonie, "Vergils Unterwelt (Aeneis VI) in der Buchmalerei von der Spätantike bis zur Renaissance". In *Leitbilder aus Kunst und Literatur*, edited by Jürgen Dummer and Meinolf Vielberg. Stuttgart, Steiner, 2002, 95–153.

Jörg Sonntag
The Horror of Flawlessness

Perfection as Challenge of Life in the Middle Ages

Throughout the Middle Ages, the perfection of God was seen as an unreachable goal which every member of medieval society had to approach as best as he or she could in order to enhance the *bonum commune* on earth and to find individual salvation in the hereafter. In his most influential *De civitate Dei*, Augustine discussed this challenge, this search for eternal beatitude on the laborious way to immortality after the fall. According to Augustine, world history was shaped by two parallel states (*civitates*) still mixed on earth. The deep human insecurity of belonging to the predestined *civitas Dei* of the "good" (angels, saints, good Christians), or to the *civitas terrena* of the "bad" (devil, demons, bad Christians) made, indeed, the 'perfect' imitation of God, Christ and many other holy role models who obviously belonged to the *civitas Dei*, the most obvious and striking way to master this challenge and to face that horror of flawlessness.[1]

Therefore in the Middle Ages, imitation was in fact, a cultural principle, which extended across, determined and formed all spheres of life in a nearly omnipresent way. Beyond the motif of *imitatio Christi*, we can find an immense number of ideal types, whose deeds and thoughts were imitated in manifold ways. Medieval queens were to act like Eve, Ester, or Jael. The ecclesiastical hierarchy found its analogies in the heavenly hosts or the servants of the temple of Salomon. Bishops and abbots sat on the thrones of Moses and Aaron. Mythological warriors like Hector and Achill as well as Roland and Iewein modelled the aristocratic knightly culture. In the late Middle Ages, men and women took the nine heroes and heroines from Antiquity, the Ancient Testament and Christian tradition as examples to follow. Models also derived from nature (as for example the bee-state), or artistically arrangements in iconography, music or literature. Imitation in all its facets was everywhere.

However, the phenomenon of imitation was naturally bound to plenty of challenges itself because it depended on diverse logics of perception that underlay individual tastes of judgmental recipients, who are at once integrated into a social milieu borne of and situated in specific and constantly changing group dynamics. Different role models sometimes applied in different areas of life, sometimes the same role models got different use in a competing way; sometimes they just complemented or overlapped each other.

---

1 Sancti Aurelii Augustini, *De Civitate Dei libri I-X*. On the reception of this highly influential treatise, see Elena CAVALCANTI, ed., *Il "De civitate dei"*, or Blaise DUFAL, *Repenser l'autorité du Père*.

DOI 10.1515/9783110530773-009

This model mixing in and between societal or (more specifically) institutional subsystems that additionally differed in time and space, is not the only challenge when analyzing imitation as a cultural matrix. Another one is the problem of definition because imitation in fact correlates with many phenomena such as the canon, allegory, typical and a-typical, emulation, variation, reception, simulation, the *exemplum* and others.

The following contribution tries to face these challenges. It addresses imitation as an act of conscious mimicry of ontic entities (persons, animals, things) and of ideas, actions or techniques in light of omnipresent patterns of orientation, behaviour, and education in the Christian Middle Ages. Imitation is therefore perceived as a reflected and concrete *actio*, in the sense of *imitating*. Due to this, it always has a function that can be described and differs in self and foreign perception. An act of imitation goes from an original pattern in the past to the imitated in the present. At all times, imitation creates a situation that can be referred to "as if". In this way, it functions by means of illusion.[2]

This article focuses on the paradigms and paradoxes of this kind of imitation and the different ways, qualities, or quantities of imitation practices within medieval society. In doing so, it addresses three examples based on different types of sources, areas of life and windows of time. The first example is the so-called mirrors for princes from the 9th century. The second one discusses the monastic customaries as handed-down to us in the so-called *consuetudines* from the 11th and 12th century. A third example uses moralizing treatises on games from the 14th and 15th century. These treatises are attributed to all members of the late medieval society, in special to townsmen and the lower nobility. What all case studies from courtly, religious, or urban life have in common is their perspective: moral education on the way to perfection. Here, the phenomenon of imitation played an important role, maybe the most important.

1 Perfection According to Early and High Medieval Mirrors for Princes

Plenty of research is done on the medieval mirrors for princes, texts that named good and bad examples to be used or avoided in order to become a good ruler.[3]

---

[2] On this definition, see Gerald SCHWEDLER and Jörg SONNTAG, "Imitieren".
[3] Cf., for instance, Hans Hubert ANTON, *Fürstenspiegel und Herrscherethos*; Wilhelm BERGES, *Die Fürstenspiegel*; Angela DE BENEDICTIS, ed., *Specula principum*; Hans-Otto MÜHLEISEN, Michael PHILIPP, and Theo STAMMEN, eds., *Fürstenspiegel der Frühen Neuzeit*; or Rob MEENS, "Politics, mirrors of princes and the Bible", 345–357.

The *Liber de rectoribus christianis* written by Sedilius Scottus around the year 850 is not only one of the first medieval texts of this genre, but also a paradigmatic example of the 9th century. In twenty chapters, Sedilius tried to teach the prince piety, justice, strength, wisdom and many more of such good qualities. He argued that a king had to approach the highest King that is Christ himself. For this goal, a good king should be pious like David and fair like Salomon. He should build churches as the emperor Constantine did, and decorate churches with treasuries as Salomon did in the Temple.[4] Pious kings should also consider the admirable wisdom of their (sometimes) intelligent wives as in the case of the Emperor Theodosius and Placilla.[5] No one should become guilty by ignoring the crimes of others, as the Old Testament priest Eli did.[6] In his *Eruditio regum et principum*, the Franciscan Gilbert of Tournai († 1284) gave a short overview of the most famous role models used such as Falvius Vegetius Renatus (4th c.) for attacking or defensing a city, Palladius (4th c.) for perfect agriculture, Vitruv († after 15 BC) for building perfect houses, Euclid (3rd c. BC) for perfect geometrical measuring, Socrates († 399 BC) for good logical thinking, or Plato († 348) for his analyses.[7] Such a concentrated and self-contained overview list of the most striking role models is rather odd. However, these models are quite familiar and they appear again and again in scattered instances within most of such educational texts for princes throughout the whole Middle Ages, be it in early treatises written by Sedilius, Jonas of Orleans († 843), Hincmar of Reims († 882), or in the later works composed by Godfrey of Viterbo († 1196), John of Viterbo († after 1228), or the Dominican Vincence of Beauvais († 1264).

Indeed, the best role models for kings have always been David, Salomon, Hiscia, Josia, Trajan, Constantine, Theodosius, Justinian and even Pope Leo. Bad examples were seen in Nero, Caligula, or the Old Testament Isabel for women. The most important models derived from the Old Testament and the Roman Antique.

In most cases, the acts of imitation presented in the mirrors for princes were restricted in its 'magical' force. They were much more bound to the level of immanence and deal more or less with an "earthly beyond" which is thinkable and capable for human beings. Although a king or prince behaved according to these models, he was still acknowledged as himself. Maybe only in the coronation ceremony such boundaries got blurred to a certain degree. In fact, monastic situations could be very different.

---

4 SEDILIUS SCOTTUS, *Liber de rectoribus christianis*, 1, 106–108.
5 Ibidem, 5, 126.
6 Ibidem, 19, 136.
7 GILBERTUS DE TORNACO, *Eruditio regum et principum*, I, 2, 5, 300–302.

2 Perfection According to High Medieval Monastic Customaries

The customs of high medieval monastic life recorded in the *consuetudines* provide detailed insights into many rituals performed in Cluny, Fruttuaria, Bec, Canterbury, Siegburg, Einsiedeln, Gorze or Fulda and in the spiritually depending monasteries of their reform circles.[8]

Out of this multifaceted reservoir of rituals, the monastic table fellowship of the 11th and 12th century seems to be one of the most illustrating examples for the matter of this study: The time of day and the silence at the table were seen as imitations of the Eucharist; the location of the refectory addressed the Heavenly Banquet and Paradise. Likewise, the blessing of the wine and bread imitated the New Testament stories of Christ feeding the multitudes and the marriage feast at Cana. The food itself reminded the monks of Adam and Eve, the children of Israel in the burning oven, Elijah and Christ. When bread crumbs were swept from the table and eaten, the parable of the beggar Lazarus came to mind. Augmented by the symbolism of light, in both the candles and the orientation of the room towards the east, the monks thus created a holy place, a *locus sanctus*. Under the eyes of God, Christ, and the angels – who were all quite intentionally described as the addressees – a real unity between convent and heaven was fashioned and the actors got actually transformed.[9] Since every monk knew quite well about the holiness of this situation and the omnipresent danger of the imitation success, it was vital that the participants immediately atone for every mistake, even the smallest.[10]

Many similar cases could be added here: Monks did penance like Cain and Iob. They washed the feet like Jesus, Abraham, Joseph, Mary of Bethany. They died like Jesus, the poor Lazarus, Lazarus of Bethany or Martin of Tours.[11] Once again, Old Testament models were more prominent than New Testament models. Indeed, plenty of actions from the Bible – the director's book – found their realization, at least via diverse symbolic techniques. Monks extracted specific modules of specific role models and combined them into new hybrid imitation clusters in

---

[8] On this text genre, cf. Gert MELVILLE, "Handlung", 23–39; Idem, "Regeln"; Sébastien BARRET, "Regula Benedicti"; Lin DONNAT, "Coutumes"; Roberto CRISTIANI, "Consuetudini"; Isabelle COCHELIN, "Évolution"; Eadem, "Community and Customs"; or Giles CONSTABLE, "Legislation", 151–161.
[9] Cf. in detail Jörg SONNTAG, "Speisen des Himmels", 259–276.
[10] See, for instance, the *Redactio Fuldensis-Trevirensis*, VI, 22, 285. Cf. with plenty of references, Jörg SONNTAG, *Klosterleben*, 322 sq.
[11] Cf. ibidem, 335–369, 390–442, 469–526, and 580–614.

order to charge up the situation with holy aura and to train the individual souls on the way to perfection. Due to this technique, holy auras of the imitated figures such as Christ, the angels, Lazarus, Mary of Bethany, Adam and Eve, or Martin were internalised and, at the same time, these figures got present in the imitating persons.

In this way, monastic representation portrayed time as a state of simultaneous existence instead of acknowledging the passing and changing of times in the present. According to Augustine's time theory, the eternal Word of God, the *principium*, expresses itself in a temporal fashion in the Bible. Through imitating various biblical role models in a congruent way, the monks expressed this Word, so that the monastic spirit in the course of time would gain a degree of permanence and find eternal truth. The simultaneous assumption of various biblical role models (Mary, Martin, Christ, or Lazarus) did not enable monks to experience 'all things simultaneously' but, as far as it could be felt in this world, 'a multiple simultaneity' which glimpsed and symbolically revealed the "heavenly beyond" and eternity. For the monks, this imitation was more than symbolic: It was indeed an everlasting state. In the eyes of the imitators, such imitation won a magical, a sacred character.[12] A more intense approach to perfection may be impossible. The fascinating educational paradox was to gain perfection in the future by being ostentatiously perfect in the present. In the monastic life, presented as *vita perfectionis* again and again, this kind of symbolism (to symbolise, but to already be) was striking. Through the training in the ritual and the correlation theory of body and soul, those who inwardly developed further via the outward *imitatio* of Christ and other holy figures and thus worked on their souls, won back the godlikeness, which had been lost in Paradise but was aimed at in monastic life.[13]

3 Perfection According to Late Medieval Game Treatises

From the 13th century onwards, there arose plenty of moralizing treatises which assigned specific concepts of meaning to games in order to provide every member of the medieval society with helpful advice concerning her or his status within the world and the corresponding codes of practice. In fact, these texts linked every move within a game with role models showing perfect deeds or warning against imperfect behaviour. They demonstrated the player how to imitate them

---

12 On this monastic strategy, see Jörg Sonntag, "Tempus fugit", 221–242.
13 Cf. Jörg Sonntag, "Der 'gute' Ritualbruch im Kloster", 198 and Idem, *Klosterleben*, 651.

right after the game. The most prominent example is undoubtedly the *Book of Chess* written by the Dominican Jacobus de Cessolis at the beginning of the 14th century. Indeed, the overwhelming literature on this highly influential book, one of the most copied texts in the late Middle Ages, has become barely manageable.[14] Jacobus clarifies the origins of chess. This game would have been invented firstly to improve Evilemordach's control over his own anger, secondly to keep the chess player from being idle, and thirdly to indulge the desire for novelty. By means of many *exempla* taken from Aegidius Romanus or John of Salisbury, Jacob informs on good and bad behaviour of kings, queens, bishops, knights, judges, and eight pawns that represent eight professional groups: the first pawn stands for the farmer, the second one for the smith, the third one for the clothier and scribe. The fourth pawn symbolises the merchant, the fifth one the physician, the sixth one the innkeeper, the seventh one the city guard, and finally, the eighth pawn represents the gambler and courier. What Jacobus did was new at the end of the 13th century. In the spirit of the flourishing northern Italian cities, he implemented the chess game to sketch a social model which, unlike John of Salisbury's *Policraticus*, enhanced the function of the individual members of the society in relation to the king, according to their rights and duties, in favour of the general welfare. From a modern level of observation, one may call this treatise revolutionary.

Out of this tradition, Johannes of Rheinfelden, a Dominican from Freiburg, wrote a *Ludus cartularum moralisatus* in 1377, where he used the card game in order to convey moral behaviour.[15] Around 1428, the Dominican Johannes Nider composed the "24 golden Harps" in which he dedicated every single harp to the virtues of wise model figures from the past (from Moses, Paphnutius, Daniel, or Isaac to Pinufius, Theonas and finally, Abraham).[16] Around 1450, a regular canon from Cologne, a member of the Order of the Holy Cross, authored a *Moralis explicatio lusus pilae palmariae*, where the *Jeu de Paume* (an early form of the modern tennis) was the means for explaining social behaviour.[17]

Such texts functioned quite similar to the mirrors for princes. They mainly addressed the "earthly beyond", in this case virtues clear to and comparatively reachable for everybody. However, there were also game treatises that truly lifted

---

14 Jacobus de Cessolis, *Libellus de moribus hominum et officiis nobilium ac popularium super ludo scachorum*. On this treatise, see Oliver PLESSOW, *Mittelalterliche Schachzabelbücher*, 46–95; Jenny ADAMS, *Power Play*, 15–56 and Jean-Michel MEHL, *Des jeux et des hommes*, 91–162.
15 On this treatise, cf. Arne JÖNSSON, "Der *Ludus cartularum moralisatus*", 135–147 and Idem, "Card-Playing", 359–373.
16 Stefan ABEL, *Johannes Nider. Die vierundzwanzig goldenen Harfen*.
17 On this treatise, see Heiner GILLMEISTER, *Aufschlag für Walther von der Vogelweide*, 205–209. Jan van den Berghe had already used the Jeu de Paume to explain legal procedures. Cf. Jörg SONNTAG, "Erfinder, Vermittler und Interpreten", 259.

up the imitator to a higher level of transcendence, the "heavenly beyond". They enforced a sacred imitation as was done in the monastery.

The Dominican Master Ingold from Basel, for instance, finished the so-called "Golden Game", the *Puechlin von Guldin Spil* in 1432. He argued that by playing seven games the right way, they would transform into golden games against the deadly sins: chess against pride, board games against graving for food, playing cards against incontinence, throwing dice against avarice, shooting against anger, dancing against idleness, and harp playing against jealousy and hatred. This article only selects some aspects of dancing for a closer consideration. When people are dancing, walking or sitting, they should bear in mind that Christ himself was the best dancer. The soul of the dancer would now be invited to a spiritual – a mystic – dance with her bridegroom Christ: Ingold argues that Jesus had danced twelve dances:

1) in the womb of Mary, when she went to the house of Zacharias and Elisabeth in Jerusalem
2) in the womb of Mary, when she went to Nazareth fearing the Jews
3) in the womb of Mary, when she went from Nazareth to Bethlehem
4) when Jesus went from Bethlehem to Jerusalem in order to sacrifice in the temple
5) during the flight to Egypt
6) when Jesus came back and preached in the temple at the age of 12
7) when he pushed the tax collectors out of the temple
8) when he went into the temple on Palm Sunday
9) when he went again into the temple teaching justice
10) when he went into the Garden Gezemaneh to pray
11) when he met his enemies in the Garden
12) when he walked under the cross upwards to the hill of Golgotha.[18]

Ingold presents plenty of such techniques for ball, card or dice games. A player always had to imitate the best player ever, Jesus, and other models of perfection. Again, the main goal was to play physically, but to imitate spiritually while playing. A person who imitated Christ by playing such a spiritual game in mind with him would experience God and earn the realm of Heaven. The audience addressed by such treatises was the lower nobility and the townsmen.

In opposite to most of those imitation strategies found in the mirrors for princes or in monastic rituals, these imitations do not merely function via one to one copying, i. e. via physical congruence, but rather in mind, and via the interpretation of diverse role models from the past. The goal of the imitated pattern

---

18 MEISTER INGOLD, *Das Püchlein vom Guldin Spil*, 72 sq.

and the imitating act was seen as congruent, but not necessarily the physical performance. This technique, of course, is (at least) as old as the four senses of the Holy Scripture. As many other religious authors Honorius of Autun provides us with a model for the symbolisation capacity of the daily hours and the weekdays:

Daily Hours	
Nocturns	Capture of Jesus
Prime	His delivery to the people
Terce	Beating of Jesus
Sext	Crucifixion
None	Death
Vespers	Taking Jesus down from the cross
Compline	Burial
Matins	Resurrection

Weekdays	
Sunday	Conception
Monday	Baptism
Tuesday	Birth as son of God
Wednesday	Betrayal of Judas
Thursday	Last Supper and foot-washing
Friday	Death
Saturday	Burial
Sunday	Resurrection[19]

When the monk as the perfect imitator of Christ was sitting in the choir and singing psalms, he positioned himself into Christ's passion. The past and the present melted together.

In fact, from the 13th century onwards, games got such spiritual goals. This was new, and because of this evolution, games became more and more one additional aspect to the monastic spirituality and the rituals of daily religious life. This was new as well. Those innovative images, games, for communicating commonly acknowledged, mystical contents, however, first became possible as the game had become more and more Christianised. This increasing spiritualization of the game, and its implementations since the 13th century became part of the typical "dingallegorische Erbauungsliteratur" of the later Middle Ages.[20]

---

[19] Cf. HONORIUS AUGUSTODUNENSIS, *Gemma animae*, II, 55–56, 633 D–634 A.
[20] Jörg SONNTAG, "Erfinder, Vermittler und Interpreten", 254–257 and Idem, "Zwischen Spaß und Ernst", 85.

4 Perspectivation: Imitation and the Horror of Flawlessness

One striking problem for both medieval laymen and monks was that God himself – his omnipresence, his face, his plans, (and as a consequence) his perfection – was known as unfathomable. It was not even thinkable for any human being. Strictly speaking, nobody could really know what perfection was and even less, what a perfect imitation of this perfection would be. Perfection belonged to the "heavenly beyond"; it was eternal. Earthly perfection, however, – at least from the modern level of observation – underlay continual changes. Corresponding to this, the one significant strength of imitations within institutional arrangements lies in their potency to function without long explanations and to visualize complete stability but, again, to be in constant flux. More than in any other medieval area of life, imitations were used in the monastery exactly in this institutionalized way and with such a high density. In opposite to imitations presented in the mirrors for princes, imitations here could open a direct gate to the "heavenly beyond" and to eternity. Here, the experts of perfection lived using the only instrument, which – although interpretable – was of eternal truth in their opinion: the Word of God himself that is the role models provided by the Bible. In order to transcend the distance between the perfect and the non-perfect, the perfect was symbolically integrated into the non-perfect. During this symbolization process, as during the imitation act, the symbolization or imitation goal is not only signified, but already present. In other words, again, the aim was to gain perfection by visualizing being already perfect. This is a paradigmatic feature of medieval symbolization theory.[21]

Quite obviously, religious life could be an innovation laboratory even for practices of imitation that found their way into other areas of medieval life. The *Guldin Spil* and his promoted transfer of those (former monastic) spiritual techniques to a lay audience is just one example. Because religious women and men practiced the so called *via perfectionis* to face the horror or flawlessness by implementing congruent and non-congruent imitations, they themselves became one prominent model for modelling.

As argued at the beginning of my short contribution, imitating is always indebted to the illusionary. That is to say that it always creates a situation "as if", whose quality depends on the perception of oneself and the others. When the Cistercian Bernard of Clairvaux, around the year 1140, in his letter to a Canon Regular named Oger called actors imitators, who pretended to be others but were

---

[21] On this symbolization theory, see Jörg SONNTAG, *Klosterleben*, especially 6–10.

not, and the monks players, he pinpointed to this dissolution of illusion directly.[22] The monks would be imitators becoming the imitated themselves. The most prominent figure for this transformation is Francis of Assisi, the *alter Christus*, when he 'represented' and 'became' Christ through imitation, he was the imitated himself. Since there apparently was no "as if" situation anymore, there was no imitation anymore. At least, from the level of modern observation, this may be seen as a fascinating paradox. One could think, the holier an imitation was, the stronger was this paradox. Or, in the eyes of a modern analyst, the holier the imitation was, the more incomprehensible is its process. It seems as unfathomable as God himself. Yet, this paradox is much more complex:

The necessity for the imitation of various role models, above all the *imitatio Christi*, was seen in the Middle Ages to be already founded in the creation. In some situations, in fact, people had no choice but to imitate. We may call this phenomenon "Kulturzwang", the force by culture to imitate. There are already a lot of discussions in the Middle Ages on this normative force of imitation and diverse role models.[23] One may pose the question of how long a culture, in which imitation became a cultural matrix, may need to establish specific indicators that are immediately clear in the cultural memory of a group and generated as *endoxa*.

From this resulted a further productive paradox for the individual and the society as such. Because members of the medieval society strove to retain previous fulfillment that was said to have once existed from before the Fall (prelapsian paradise), they orientated themselves towards certain ideals and thus evoked an imitation until a certain degree of loss of self. In fact, especially a monk, who had promised full renunciation of his self-will at profession, ritually led, not fully but in a large part, the life of others in order to prospectively perpetuate his own life through the inner self-sanctification that he had undergone in this way.

Nevertheless, again, all these paradigms and paradoxes obviously more or less correlate with the phenomenon of perception, since mimicry mostly profits from the attainment of an effect of fast recognition resulting from an imitated pattern, which was thus identified as such. However, human perceptions of old and new, of the allegedly erroneous and correct are always whimsically pronounced and at times unpredictable. Even 'perfect' imitations failed in history again and again: the "Chronicle of the 24 General Ministers of the Minorite Order" tells, for instance, of Juniper († 1258), a Franciscan brother who walked around unclothed like Francis and strove to be like him in every way. He imitated the saint's actions in whatever way he was able. However, he lived in a different time,

---

22 BERNARDUS CLARAEVALLENSIS, *Epistolae*, 87 (ad Ogerium canonicum regularem), 12, 702.
23 See, for instance, Bruce C. BRASINGTON, "*Non imitanda set veneranda*", 135–152.

after the death of Francis, and Juniper's confreres viewed his conduct as a scandal and even considered hanging the man who had wandered astray.[24]

There are even plenty of tolerated violations against common imitation practices. The above mentioned Bernard of Clairvaux departed from numerous quotidian rituals of monastic life and their biblical role models. However, since every charismatic was perceived by his entourage as already holy and perfect in the present moment, he no longer required classical lines of imitation.[25] Francis of Assisi lay nude in nestles and snow. Christ had never done this. The intention – that is, the demonstration of humility and humiliation – of both actors was nevertheless externally acknowledged as a category of congruence with Gospel values. In such a case, the force of perception could grant acceptance to obviously different actions in the concrete act of imitation thereby contributing to its success. Thus, one can imitate the same pattern by doing different things. Again, this exactly holds true for the mystic games composed by Ingold and others.

To conclude, imitation practices unfolded in different ways (congruent, non-congruent). Imitations were (and always are) characterised by a different quantity since one could imitate partly or nearly in total, or combine individual elements to new hybrid imitation clusters. One could obviously choose from a more or less well established pool of models and combine them in a new creative fashion. But how creative could a medieval monk, a bishop, or a king, really be? And how long can a transformed or newly combined imitation still be conceived as imitation and not as new act? Additionally, imitations could be signified by a different quality, i. e. they could address different levels of the beyond. Therefore, I have used the terms "earthly" and "heavenly beyond". These are two heuristic poles, their spheres naturally blended together, even more in the Middle Ages. The first one could be addressed and understood quite easily. The second one, the "heavenly beyond", required much more elaborated techniques of sanctification. Some of them, the non-congruent spiritual imitations, even found their way into the lay world by a (more or less) worldly topic, the game. The flawlessness of perfection was a challenge of life from which nobody could escape. The only way to face the paradoxical situation of gaining perfection by already being perfect was illusion. Indeed, medieval culture functioned through illusion kept alive by the power of imitation.

---

24 Cf., for instance, Achim WESJOHANN, "*Ut ... stultur vel fatuus putaretur*", 203–204.
25 On this and other examples, see Jörg SONNTAG, "Der 'gute' Ritualbruch im Kloster", 189–207.

Bibliography

Abel, Stefan, *Johannes Nider. Die vierundzwanzig goldenen Harfen. Edition und Kommentar* (Spätmittelalter, Humanismus, Reformation, 60). Tübingen, Mohr-Siebeck, 2011.

Adams, Jenny, *Power Play. The Literature and Politics of Chess in the Late Middle Ages* (The Middle Ages Series). Philadelphia, University of Pennsylvania Press, 2006.

Anton, Hans Hubert, *Fürstenspiegel und Herrscherethos in der Karolingerzeit* (Bonner historische Forschungen, 32). Bonn, Röhrscheid, 1968.

Sancti Aurelii Augustini, *De Civitate Dei libri I-X*, 2 vols., edited by Bernard Dombart and Alfons Kalb (Corpus Christianorum. Series Latina, 47, 48). Turnhout, Brepols, 1955.

Barret, Sébastien, "Regula Benedicti, Consuetudines, Statuta. Aspects du corpus clunisien". In *Regulae – Consuetudines – Statuta. Studi sulle fonti normative degli ordini religiosi nei secoli centrali del Medioevo*, edited by Cristina Andenna and Gert Melville (Vita regularis. Abhandlungen, 25). Münster, LIT-Verlag, 2005, 65–103.

De Benedictis, Angela, ed., *Specula principum* (Ius commune. Veröffentlichungen des Max-Planck-Instituts für europäische Rechtsgeschichte – Sonderhefte – Studien zur europäischen Rechtsgeschichte, 117). Frankfurt a. Main, Klostermann, 1999.

Berges, Wilhelm, *Die Fürstenspiegel des hohen und späten Mittelalters* (MGH-Schriften, 2). Leipzig, Hiersemann, 1938.

Bernardus Claraevallensis, *Epistolae*, 87 (ad Ogerium canonicum regularem), edited by Gerhard B. Winkler (Bernhard von Clairvaux. Sämtliche Werke, 2). Innsbruck, Tyrolia, 1992, 688–702.

Brasington, Bruce Clark, "*Non imitanda set veneranda*. The Dilemma of Sacred Precedent in Twelfth-Century Canon Law", *Viator* 23, 1992, 135–152.

Cavalcanti, Elena, ed., *Il "De civitate dei". L'opera, le interpretazioni, l'influsso*. Rome, Herder, 1996.

Cochelin, Isabelle, "Évolution des coutumiers monastiques dessinée à partir de l'étude de Bernard". In *From Dead of Night to End of Day. The Medieval Customs of Cluny*, edited by Susan Boynton and Isabelle Cochelin (Disciplina Monastica, 3). Turnhout, Brepols, 2005, 29–66.

Cochelin, Isabelle, "Community and Customs. Obedience or Agency?". In *Oboedientia. Formen und Grenzen von Macht und Unterordnung im mittelalterlichen Religiosentum*, edited by Sébastien Barret and Gert Melville (Vita regularis. Abhandlungen, 27). Münster, LIT-Verlag, 2005, 229–253.

Cristiani, Roberto, "Le Consuetudini di Cluny. Metodi, linguaggi, percorsi storiografici", *I Quaderni del M.Æ.S. (Mediæ Ætatis Sodalicium)* 6, 2003, 187–198.

Constable, Giles, "Monastic Legislation at Cluny in the Eleventh and Twelfth Centuries". In *Cluniac Studies*, edited by Idem. London, Variorum, 1980, 151–161.

Donnat, Lin, "Les coutumes monastiques autour de l'an Mil". In *Religion et culture autour de l'an Mil. Royaume capétien et Lotharingie*, edited by Dominique Iogna-Prat and Jean Charles Picard. Paris, Picard, 1990, 17–24.

Dufal, Blaise, *Repenser l'autorité du Père. Saint Augustin et le De civitate Dei au XIVe siècle*. Paris, Doctorat d'Histoire, 2014.

Gilbertus de Tornaco, *Eruditio regum et principum*, edited by Hans Hubert Anton (Ausgewählte Quellen zur deutschen Geschichte des Mittelalters. Freiherr-Vom-Stein-Gedächtnisausgabe. Mittelalter, 45). Darmstadt, Wissenschaftliche Buchgesellschaft, 2006, 288–446.

Gillmeister, Heiner, *Aufschlag für Walther von der Vogelweide. Tennis seit dem Mittelalter*. München, Droemer Knaur, 1986.
Honorius Augustodunensis, *Gemma animae*, ed. by Jacques-Paul Migne (Patrologie Latina, 172). Édition originale Paris, 1854 (Brepols, 1995), coll. 543–738.
Jacobus de Cessolis, *Libellus de moribus hominum et officiis nobilium ac popularium super ludo scachorum*, edited by Marie Anita Burt. Austin, University of Texas, 1957.
Jönsson, Arne, "Der *Ludus cartularum moralisatus des Johannes von Rheinfelden*". In *Schweizer Spielkarten*, vol. 1: *Die Anfänge im 15. und 16. Jahrhundert*, edited by Detlef Hoffmann. Schaffhausen, Sturzenegger-Stiftung, 1998, 135–147.
Jönsson, Arne, "Card-Playing as a Mirror of Society". In *Chess and Allegory in the Middle Ages*, edited by Olle Ferm and Volker Honemann (Runica et Mediaevalia). Södertälje, Sällskapet, 2005, 359–373.
Meens, Rob, "Politics, mirrors of princes and the Bible. Sins, kings and the well-being of the realm", *Early Medieval Europe* 7, 3, 1998, 345–357.
Mehl, Jean-Michel, *Des jeux et des hommes dans la société médiévale* (Nouvelle bibliothèque du Moyen Âge, 97). Paris, Librairie Honoré Champion, 2010.
Meister Ingold, *Puechlein vom Guldin Spil = Das Goldene Spiel von Meister Ingold*, edited by Edward Schröder (Elsässische Litteraturdenkmäler aus dem XIV. Bis XVII. Jahrhundert, 3). Straßburg, Trübner, 1882.
Melville, Gert, "Handlung, Text und Geltung. Zu Clunys 'Consuetudines' und Statuten". In *Der weite Blick des Historikers. Einsichten in Kultur-, Landes- und Stadtgeschichte. Peter Johanek zum 65. Geburtstag*, edited by Wilfried Ehrbrecht and Angelika Lampen et al. Köln/Weimar/Wien, Böhlau, 2002, 23–39.
Melville, Gert, "Regeln – *Consuetudines*-Texte – Statuten. Positionen für eine Typologie des normativen Schrifttums religiöser Gemeinschaften im Mittelalter". In *Regulae – Consuetudines – Statuta. Studi sulle fonti normative degli ordini religiosi nei secoli centrali del Medioevo*, edited by Cristina Andenna und Gert Melville (Vita regularis. Abhandlungen, 25). Münster, LIT-Verlag, 2005, 5–38.
Mühleisen, Hans-Otto, Philipp, Michael, and Theo Stammen, eds., *Fürstenspiegel der Frühen Neuzeit* (Bibliothek des deutschen Staatsdenkens, 6). Frankfurt a.Main/Leipzig, Insel Verlag, 1997.
Plessow, Oliver, *Mittelalterliche Schachzabelbücher zwischen Spielsymbolik und Wertevermittlung. Der Schachtraktat des Jacobus de Cessolis im Kontext seiner spätmittelalterlichen Rezeption* (Symbolische Kommunikation und gesellschaftliche Wertesysteme, 12). Münster, Rhema, 2007.
Redactio Fuldensis-Trevirensis, ed. by Maria Wegener and Candida Elvert (Corpus consuetudinum monasticarum, 7, 3). Siegburg, Schmitt, 1984, 257–322.
Schwedler, Gerald, and Jörg Sonntag, "Imitieren. Mechanismen eines kulturellen Prinzips im europäischen Mittelalter. Eine Einführung." In *Nachahmen im Mittelalter. Dimensionen – Mechanismen – Funktionen*, edited by Andreas Büttner, Birgit Kynast, Gerald Schwedler and Jörg Sonntag (Archiv für Kulturgeschichte). Köln, Böhlau, 2017 (in print).
Sedilius Scottus, *Liber de rectibus Christianis*, edited by Hans Hubert Anton (Ausgewählte Quellen zur deutschen Geschichte des Mittelalters. Freiherr-Vom-Stein-Gedächtnisausgabe. Mittelalter, 45). Darmstadt, Wissenschaftliche Buchgesellschaft, 2006, 100–149.
Sonntag, Jörg, "Der 'gute' Ritualbruch im Kloster oder Wenn das Heilige heiligen Ritualen Grenzen setzt". In Büttner Andreas, Schmidt Andreas, and Paul Töbelmann, eds., *Die*

Grenzen des Rituals. Wirkreichweiten – Geltungsbereiche – Forschungsperspektiven (Norm und Struktur, 42). Köln/Weimar/Wien, Böhlau, 2014, 189–207.

Sonntag, Jörg, "Erfinder, Vermittler und Interpreten. Ordensleute und das Spiel im Gefüge der mittelalterlichen Gesellschaft". In Idem, ed., *Religiosus Ludens. Das Spiel als kulturelles Phänomen in mittelalterlichen Klöstern und Orden* (Arbeiten zur Kirchengeschichte, 122). Berlin/Boston, Mass., De Gruyter, 2013, 241–274.

Sonntag, Jörg, *Klosterleben im Spiegel des Zeichenhaften. Symbolisches Denken und Handeln hochmittelalterlicher Mönche zwischen Dauer und Wandel, Regel und Gewohnheit* (Vita regularis. Abhandlungen, 35). Berlin, LIT-Verlag, 2008.

Sonntag, Jörg, "Speisen des Himmels. Essgewohnheiten und ihre biblischen Konzeptionalisierungen im christlichen Kloster des Hochmittelalters zwischen Anspruch und Wirklichkeit", *Saeculum. Jahrbuch für Universalgeschichte* 60, 2, 2010, 259–276.

Sonntag, Jörg, "Tempus fugit. La circolarità del tempo monastica nello specchio del potenziale di rappresentazione simbolica". In *Religiosità e civiltà. Le comunicazioni symboliche (secoli IX–XIII)*, edited by Giancarlo Andenna. Mailand, Vita e Pensiero, 2009, 221–242.

Sonntag, Jörg, "Zwischen Spaß und Ernst. Das Spiel als Heilsgarant in mittelalterlichen Klöstern", *Journal für Religionsphilosophie* 5, 2016, 73–90.

Wesjohann, Achim, "Ut ... stultur vel fatuus putaretur. 'Fehltritte' früher Franziskaner?". In *Der Fehltritt. Vergehen und Versehen in der Vormoderne*, edited by Peter von Moos (Norm und Struktur, 13). Köln/Weimar/Wien, Böhlau, 2001, 203–234.

Mirko Breitenstein
Living with Demons

The Horror of the Beyond as a Challenge of Life in the Middle Ages

In the first decades of the 13th century, the Cistercian Caesarius of Heisterbach († after 1240) arranged a large collection of short stories with mostly fabulous content: his "Dialogue on Miracles". Already with this name, the text refers to its basis structure.[1] It differs from other contemporary texts first and foremost by its arrangement in the form of a dialogue between an inquiring novice and a answering monk. Divided into 12 books, which are thematically arranged, the text contains 746 exemplary short stories. These stories do not represent no-name average persons, but we can read about concrete historical figures, acting at concrete places, which gives the whole narrative a specific background. This, not least, was probably the main reason for the extraordinary success of the text: in addition to more than 100 complete versions, a great number of smaller parts of the text is handed down to us in numerous manuscripts.[2]

Within the Dialogue there is also a story about a lay brother,

> who from his youth to old age had lived both respected and liked by all his brethren, so that none in all the Order seemed stricter than he in the observance of the Rule, or more endowed with virtues [...] Yet by some incomprehensible judgment of God, he grew so melancholy and cast down, that he became completely obsessed with fear of his sins, and altogether despairing of eternal life. It was not that he was troubled with any lack of faith, but rather that he lost all hope of salvation [...] though it is believed that he had never been a great sinner. When his brethren asked him what it was that he feared, and why he despaired, he would reply: 'I cannot say my prayers as I used, and so I am afraid of hell.'[3]

This story is deeply connected with our topic: the given parameters refer directly to the Beyond, the given constellation to its challenges. We can read about: (1)

---

[1] The title is authentic: *Et quia continentia huius Dialogi satis miraculosa est, nomen ei induatur Dialogus miraculorum.* Caesarius of Heisterbach, *Dialogue on Miracles*, Prologue. In this article, references will be given according to the scheme DM, [book.chapter]; for variant titles cf. Fritz WAGNER, "Studien zu Caesarius von Heisterbach", 87.
[2] Cf. Karl LANGOSCH, "Caesarius von Heisterbach", col. 1156.
[3] DM, IV.41.

Note: The present version of the text is a slightly corrected version of the paper given at the Conference "The Beyond as Challenge of Life", San Antonio de Areco, September 2016. I am very grateful for the services rendered by Gabriele Coura in correcting the language of this essay.

DOI 10.1515/9783110530773-010

God, the dominator, who rules this world as well as the other one. His judgment causes all, all that follows; (2) the salvation given by God, which guarantees eternal life; (3) the eternal life after the last judgment, which is every man's goal for the Beyond; (4) the fear of hell, i. e. the fear to lose eternal salvation and to be among the damned instead.

Beside these parameters, there is melancholy and desperation, which are expressions of the lay brother's awareness of the insurmountable differences between the capacity of men and the demands of God – differences that do prevent, as the brother believes, his possibility for reaching eternal life in the Beyond. Instead, it guarantees him eternal death and eternal tortures in hell. The lay brother's challenge is to believe in his own salvation, which was promised by Christ – but even more promised were the eternal tortures for those who did not belong to the few Chosen.

In general, there were two challenges of the Beyond in daily life during the Middle Ages:

1. To live with its presence in this world, which means to know that there are representatives from the other world, and to behave towards them adequately, that is, to search them or to flee from them.
2. To develop strategies in order to avoid hell or to reach heaven within the Beyond after death.

Subsequently, I will focus my presentation on the part of the Beyond that men normally tried to avoid. I shall explore the matter in three stages: First, I am going to present the spaces of the Beyond and their respective protagonists. In a second step, I will introduce the challenges of man while dealing with the presence of the Beyond in this world. This treatment could either be affirmative or by fending and fighting. Finally, I shall present strategies for avoiding the dark sides of the coming Beyond.

Considering the manifold facets of all the various concepts regarding the Beyond,[4] I will base my paper mainly on the previously mentioned Dialogue on Miracles – a text that offers wonderful insights into the Beyond as well as into its meaning and conceptualisation. Caesarius is not a theologian, therefore we can assume that he presents something like the ordinary knowledge of a literate man in a time when concepts of the Beyond – its spheres, places and protagonists – were already well established.

---

4 Instead of many titles, I would like to refer to the lucid general survey by Peter DINZELBACHER, "Eschatology".

1 The Judgment and the Spaces of Beyond

There is no fixed concept of the Beyond for the entire period of time of the Christian tradition from late Antiquity to the Middle Ages. (Some things are still in flux nowadays, as can be seen from the discussion about where the non-baptized should be after death.) Within the 1000 years from the most influential *Visio s. Pauli* from the 3rd century to Dante's journey through the Beyond in the 14th century, we can find different concepts of its places. Generally speaking, there is the heaven, the earthly paradise, the purgatory, the limbo for the fathers, the limbo for the children, the *refrigerium* and the hell. (fig. 10.A1) These seven are the main forms, which are sometimes described as hierarchically subdivided, i.e. from the lowest to the highest heaven, or downside, from the topmost to the deepest hell. While heaven, the two limbos and the hell were thought to be eternal, the earthly paradise, the purgatory and the *refrigerium* were thought of as being temporal only.

Although all these spaces were imagined as spaces of the Beyond, in a way their otherworldly dimension could find its expression only in their non-availability, which means that they are not at man's disposal. For instance, we can find the entrance to hell on earth, which was established by empiric knowledge. In addition, it was proven by the bible that the paradise was located on earth, too. Therefore, it can be determined that some spaces of the Beyond were on the surface of, respectively underneath the earth, but they were restricted and not easily accessible.

Within these spaces, there are transcendental and supernatural forces and powers, but they are in our world as well: primarily God, but also Jesus Christ as his Son, the angels in all their hierarchies, Maria, and men of God like saints. However, there were devils and demons everywhere, too.

1.1 Principles of Judgment

Before dealing with the dark spaces of the Beyond, I would like to make some remarks on the principles of God's judgments, as they were established in the Middle Ages. A case in point here is the relationship between the general judgment at the end of time, announced in the Apocalypse, and the particular *Judgment*, which was supposed to take place immediately after one's death.

In the tradition of the ancient church, the concept of the general judgment was in use: subsequently to the consummation of time and after their bodily resurrection all people were lead to a final judgment, where they were going to be tried and sent either to heaven or hell. All this was conceived according to the pattern given in the Gospel of Matthew 25.31–36 and the relatively simple arrangement described there. However, the Gospel of John (John 5.28f) had already made this simple scheme a little more complex by installing a shortcut to heaven for saints immediately after their earthly death.

Nevertheless, with these two statements the formation of concepts was not over: It was the long time between the individual death and the promised resurrection after the end of time that men were thinking about. The solution was found in the form of the concept of a particular judgment immediately after the death of a person. Therefore, it was assumed that when the soul leaves the body, it was judged instantly and sent to the purgatory, to Heaven, to Hell or to the Limbo, according to their earthly lifestyle and God's providence.

This concept as such represented a rather old idea. Tertullian († after 220) had already written that even before the final judgment, a soul "undergoes punishment and consolation in Hades during the time in between, while it awaits its alternative of judgment, in a certain anticipation of either gloom or glory."[5] This idea of an immediate particular or individual judgment became most influential since the beginnings of the 12th century.[6] However, one might wonder what the function of the general judgment was under these circumstances. The answer is very simple: The general judgment repeated the decisions of the first, the particular judgment and made its sentences public.

1.2 The Spaces

Our short survey of the dark spaces of the Beyond begins with the purgatory. Modern people tend to associate it with a place of shortage and torture, which is true, but first and foremost it is, as Caesarius reports in accordance with tradition "the place of the elect, into which no one enters, unless he departed in love"[7]. These elects, the chosen ones, were brought to the purgatory by angels, not by demons (fig. 10.A1). Caesarius relates what he heard while studying in Cologne:

> Master Rudolph, the Scholasticus at Cologne, whose school I used to frequent, taught us that no demon might ever touch the souls of the elect when they left their earthly prison, but that the blessed angels carried to the places of purgatory all those that were worthy thereof.[8]

---

5 TERTULLIAN, *De anima*, cap. 58.
6 Cf. Jacques LE GOFF, *La Naissance du Purgatoire*.
7 DM, XII.23.
8 DM, I.32.

There is no fixed place where one can find the purgatory. Instead, its location depends on the kind of punishment. When the novice asks: "Where is purgatory?", the monk answers that it is located in several places in this world. Moreover, he adds that everybody who doubts the purgatory should go to Ireland and enter the purgatory of Saint Patrick, and then they would have no more doubts about the pains of the purgatory.[9]

If we survey Caesarius' stories about the purgatory we can state that it is always a place of punishment, but the intensity and quality of this punishment varies. To be in purgatory could mean to suffer real tortures, but it could also mean to be at the mercy of demons and devils. However, even the earthly paradise could function as a purgatory because, as Caesarius reports, the sight of God is denied to the souls there. So this delightful place could also function as a purgatory for those unhappy souls who feel the pain of deferment.[10] In general, Caesarius underlines, in accordance with tradition, that purgatory is a place of punishment, but whoever is sentenced to go there is among the elected.[11]

Nothing is said in Caesarius about two other spaces of the Beyond: the Limbo for the fathers and that for the children. The Limbo for the fathers was the part of the Beyond where the prophets and patriarchs of the Old Testament were imprisoned. On the one hand, according to Paul's epistles (Eph 4.9 and 1. Pt 3.19), it was understood as the hell that was opened by Jesus Christ when he entered the underworld. On the other hand, the *limbus puerorum* was said to be for the unbaptized children. They had to stay eternally without salvation in a place close to hell. Because of their suffering from the original sin, which was not cleansed by baptism, both the fathers and the children were punished. However, unlike the children, Christ himself liberates the fathers for their merits.

There is only one piece of advice in Caesarius' Dialogue concerning the so-called *refrigerium*. The novice is wondering why God lets righteous and holy men die; the monk does not respond to the question. Instead, he informs his pupil about an eschatological certainty: "By whatever death the Just are taken, they will be in *refrigerio*. For to omit many reasons that may be assigned, one is that their hidden virtues may manifest."[12] This concept had its height in late Antiquity. There was considered a room for refreshment for the dead, where they could sleep (fig. 10.A1). Later, for instance during the time of Caesarius, the refrigerium is identified with the bosom of Abraham, where the poor Lazarus stays

---

9 DM, XII.38.
10 DM, XII.37.
11 DM, XII.21.
12 DM, XI.25.

(cf. Lc 16.19ff). This motive became extraordinarily widespread and popular in iconography.

Like heaven, hell was supposed to be of eternal duration. As Caesarius remarks, it is the place prepared by God in order to punish the ones he had damned. Caesarius states in accordance with tradition:

> Of the pains of hell, which are countless, nine are specially noted, which are: pitch, snow, darkness, the worm, scourging, chains, festering, shame, and terror. These have no end and no limit.[13]

Even for Caesarius, hell has different levels. We can infer this from a story where Caesarius refers to a priest

> who gave all his time to gluttony and lust, and entirely neglected the souls committed to his care. When he was dead, his parishioners deceased in his time, pursued him with stones in the eternal regions and crowded round him until he fell into the pit and was no more seen.[14]

As was mentioned before, entrances to hell could be located on earth (fig. 10.A1): Caesarius refers to the Volcanoes Etna and Stromboli by their names.

> They are said to be the jaws of hell, because none of the elect, but the wicked only are sent into them. [...] Hell is supposed to be in the heart of the earth, so that the wicked may not see the light of heaven.[15]

Close to these volcanic mountains one can see devils flying with the damned in order to send them into the fires of hell.

In many respects hell could be compared with the ordinary world: one has to eat, but like all other activities, this is part of the punishment. Caesarius knows that toads and snakes are the infernal food, cooked in sulphurous flames. With numerous examples, he underlines the direct connection between the deeds of men in this world with their fate in the other one. What he describes is a mirrored and equivalent punishment. Concerning the tortures of hell, Caesarius agrees with his contemporaries: They are inconceivably cruel, ceaseless and eternal. Unless God shows his almightiness, there are no human strategies for saving a soul from hell.

It was said that hell is eternal for the damned – but at this point Caesarius offers his own view, which differs from the *sensus communis*. He makes a conclusion by analogy and gives a spark of hope for those in hell: "If God [...] at times

---

13 DM, XII.1.
14 DM, XII.6.
15 DM, XII.13.

recalls the souls of some to their bodies from the joys of paradise, why not the souls of the wicked from the pains of hell?"[16]

2 Challenges of Men when Dealing with the Presence of the Beyond in this World

2.1 Affirmative

Just at the time when Caesarius was working on his Dialogue, the 4th Lateran Council affirmed the traditional view that the devil, hell and all the demons, which were tempting and torturing mankind, were an integral part of God's creation.[17] This was, of course, a statement against a latent dualism, which accompanied Christianity since its beginnings. The function of the forces of hell was primarily to tempt and to prove the faithful. However, it was forbidden to search contact or to unite with them.

Nevertheless, Caesarius knows numerous examples of people of different rank and sex, but especially clerics, who tried to contact demons in order to impose their will on them. However, Caesarius warns his readers: Demons are not controllable.[18] Moreover, even the one who tries to use them with the right intention and in good faith will be damned, at least to purgatory.[19] Caesarius clarifies that the wish to see demons and prayers for this capacity are not punished[20] – it is always the intention behind the will that is crucial. Statements like this are a clear expression of the implementation of the new intentional ethic.

However, he who stops conjuring demons will be saved from hell, as a dead necromancer told his still-living companion:

> Woe is me, for I am eternally lost on account of that diabolical art which I learnt: for it is true death of the soul, as it title shows. And I counsel you as my only friend, to give up this accursed science, and take up a religious life and make amends to God for your sins.[21]

However, necromancy could even have a positive function: Those who are versed in this art are able to persuade those who disbelieve in demons, devils and

---

16 DM, XII.23.
17 *Constitutiones Concilii quarti Lateranensis*, Constitutio 1, 41.
18 DM, XI.60.
19 DM, XII.27.
20 DM, V.5.
21 DM, I.33.

hell.[22] Not believing that there are devils and demons is close to not believing in God himself. Clearly, Caesarius differentiates between the practices of a priest who communicates with the deceased or exorcises demons and devils, and the methods of the conjurers. As was mentioned before, the criterion of difference is their intention. This is certainly shown with an example: even the bishop of Besançon persuaded a former necromancer, who had already finished his pact with the devil, to contact the devil again. The bishop's goal was to get information from the devil about two heretics, also worshippers of the devil, in order to overcome their magic power.[23] However, using the devil's help against the devil was an extraordinary strategy. Normally, one would choose other practices to fight the forces of evil.

2.2 Fending and Fighting Against the Forces of Evil

According to both tradition by empiric knowlege and scripture, it is openly stated that there are innumerable, evil and hostile demons who act against all human beings. Only very few thinkers, like the Silesian philosopher and theologian Witelo († between 1280–1314), stated that visions of demons and devils are first and foremost an expression of mental disease.[24] However, in general they were considered an essential part of the creation, as mentioned before.

Caesarius knows about them: "Some they injure by false promises, others by undermining their faith, some by afflicting them in the body, and others, and this is worst of all, by slaying them with sin. But" – and this seems to be the most important aspect – "none of these things can happen except by the just judgment of God"[25] Here, as well as in many other of Caesarius' stories we can find precautions against the assumption of a dualistic worldview. The Cistercian included numerous examples of dualistic heresies within the chapters on Demons in his Dialogue; in others, Caesarius underlines that the devil is torturing men always with God's consent.[26]

However, everyone could defend himself with some standardised and ritualised forms. Moreover, it is not surprising that prayers, alms and celebrating masses help against the attacks of the demons. In particular, prayers were described as helpful: While praying, the boundaries between earthly existence

---

22 DM, V.5.
23 DM, V.18.
24 Cf. Peter DINZELBACHER, *Angst im Mittelalter*, 97.
25 DM, V.15.
26 DM, V.26.

and the Beyond are crossed, and who prays enters into communication with God or the Saints, especially Maria, who often makes herself present. In addition, signs and rituals were seen as important and extremely helpful: A man who carelessly called the devil is saved just by making the sign of the cross, as the devil himself confesses.[27]

Seeing the devil is described as the highest punishment:[28] A priest could only survive his sight by celebrating a mass immediately before, as the devil confesses.[29] Only God and his followers are able to banish the devil. The words "father", "son" and "holy spirit" captivate even the highest devil, Lucifer, in hell, as another devil says while being exorcised.[30] The most important strategy to avoid devils and demons is to absent oneself from sin. This insight is clearly expressed by the figure of the novice, who says: "the more horror and malice that I hear about the devil, so much the more shall I fear to sin."[31]

3 Strategies to Avoid the Dark Sides of the Coming Beyond

When the still-living necromancer from the last example asked his already dead companion to show him the safest way of living in eternity, the damned replied: "There is no surer path than the way of the Cistercian order; nor if you search through every way of life will you find any that furnished fewer souls for hell than that Order."[32]

Of course not everyone was able to join a religious order; still, this would be the safest strategy. It was the safest because the religious tried to live in this world like in the Beyond; they tried to create a part of heaven in the middle of the worldly desert.[33] Approximation to this ideal should be the main goal. Everyone could follow this paradigmatic way of life – at least partially. Living on earth in a way that was conceived as heavenly anticipated heaven and could help to avoid hell; this was the key point Caesarius wanted to show in his text.

---

27 DM, V.27.
28 DM, V.28.
29 DM, V. 29.
30 DM, V.13.
31 DM, V.28.
32 DM, I.33.
33 Cf. on this the fundamental study by Jörg SONNTAG, *Klosterleben*.

The following three strategies were considered the most promising:
(1) To live according to the rules given by Christ, i.e. to do the powerful works of mercy: freeing the imprisoned, feeding the hungry, giving drink to the thirsty, comforting the sick, clothing the naked, sheltering the travellers, and burying the dead.
(2) To confess all sins. Without confession, nobody could be saved, as Caesarius relates in numerous examples. Hence, one could read:

> Confession of sin is that by which the hidden disease of the soul is laid bare in the hope of pardon. It ought to be voluntary, done without delay and dutifully, modest, general, special, individual, unvarnished, complete, discreet, self-accusing, bitter, anxious, meticulous, true, proportionate, glad, personal and frequent.[34]

(3) To prepare for death with specific rituals. All practices described as *ars moriendi* – the art of dying well prepared – are included.

A priest could even do more: by celebrating mass he was able to help the souls who were in purgatory at the same time. This is depicted in the motive of the Mass of Saint Gregory: Christ himself squirts his blood into the priest's chalice and simultaneously frees souls from purgatory (fig. 10.A3, 4).

All these practices, namely masses, alms, prayers, etc. primarily symbolise the community of the living and the dead. They could not only save one's own soul, but also the poor souls in purgatory. The methods for fighting the devil in this world are also effective for reaching eternal salvation. Moreover, whatever man does for reaching salvation helps to defend himself against devils and demons; this world and the other one are deeply intertwined. Because he is a real man and the real God at the same time, Christ himself connects this world and the Beyond.

Christian conception of history is based on a three-stage soteriological schema of creation, incarnation and Parousia.[35] After the incarnation of Christ, the original sin can be cleansed through baptism. Otherwise, mankind was threatened by the horrors of the Beyond, which were shown and fulfilled by devils and demons in accordance with God's judgment. Therefore, for men in the Middle Ages the challenge of the Beyond primarily meant to persist the challenges of this world. They are the probation for the Beyond.

However, what is more, in this probation, mankind is attacked from two sides: by the devils and demons as well as by God and his angels of death. Numerous

---

34 DM, III.1.
35 Cf. Horst Dieter RAUH, *Das Bild des Antichrist*, 9.

illustrations show this, but also the intercession of saints, particularly of Maria (fig. 10.A5). When we see these pictures, we always have to take into consideration that in the Middle Ages death is not a normal or even natural part of life. Not least, it is the consequence of and punishment for the sinning of Eve and Adam. Moreover, we should be aware that God damns in accordance with his judgment, which is unknown to man – Caesarius remarks, just like St Augustine does, that the church does not pray for the damned.[36]

Summary

After this very short survey through the Beyond, and the presentation of some strategies to handle with its challenges, I would like to summarise a few things and come back to our melancholic brother from the beginning. In general, the Beyond was interpreted as the true home of men in the Middle Ages. The separation between this world and the other was not seen at all because of human guilt: the hell was first created for the fallen angels. However, in consequence of mankind's maliciousness, hell was opened for them. Besides, the number of people who were able to reach heaven was limited: it was the number of fallen angels. Many more were damned. To believe in this, and not in one's own salvation, necessarily results in desperation, as the example at the beginning shows.

Since the 12th century, the Beyond came closer to the individual. This happened in a way that allows us to observe a change from a universal to an individual eschatology: this world and the other one intertwined much deeper than ever before. However, the closer it comes, the more unavailable and intangible it becomes for the established strategies for reaching the Beyond and salvation. Now it was no longer enough to just pray, no longer enough to sing masses or give alms. The development of new ethical concepts of individuality, which gave the responsibility for salvation much more to every individual, had its impact on men's handling the Beyond, too.

Nobody could be sure of reaching heaven, or at least purgatory, because there was no criterion for checking it. Caesarius tells about a monk who said this in the most drastic way: "I should never have thought that the Lord was so severe. For he notices the very smallest faults which have not been blotted out by atonement."[37]

---

36 DM, XII.24.
37 DM, XII.28.

And our brother from the beginning? For fear of hell, he lost all his confidence in and assurance of salvation – in the eyes of his companions, he lived a most holy life, but in his own he was a sinner:

> Because he was afflicted with this vice of melancholy, accidie laid hold of him, and from the two despair was born in his heart. Placed in the infirmary, one morning, having determined upon death, he went to his superior and said: "I cannot fight against God any longer." The other took little heed of his words, but he went away to the fish-pond near the monastery, threw himself in and was drowned.[38]

However, committing suicide did mean hell. Therefore, for fear of hell he had chosen hell.

Bibliography

Caesarius of Heisterbach, *Dialogue on Miracles* = Caesarii Heisterbacensis monachi Ordinis Cisterciensis Dialogus Miraculorum, ed. by Joseph Strange, 2 vols. Cologne/Bonn/Brussels, J. M. Heberle, 1851.

The Dialogue on Miracles [by] Caesarius of Heisterbach (1220–1235), transl. by Henry von Essen Scott and Charles C. Swinton Bland, with an introduction by George G. Coulton, 2 vols. London, Routledge, 1929.

Constitutiones Concilii quarti Lateranensis una cum Commentariis glossatorum, ed. Antonio García y García (Monumenta Iuris Canonici, A: Corpus Glossatorum 2). Città del Vaticano, Biblioteca Apostolica Vaticana, 1981.

Dinzelbacher, Peter, *Angst im Mittelalter. Teufels-, Todes und Gotteserfahrung. Mentalitätsgeschichte und Ikonographie*. Paderborn, Schöningh, 1996.

Dinzelbacher, Peter, "Eschatology". In *Handbook of Medieval Studies. Terms, Methods, Trends*, vol. 1, ed. by Albrecht Classen. Berlin/New York, De Gruyter, 2010, 506–524.

Langosch, Karl, "Caesarius von Heisterbach". In Kurt Ruh et al., ed., *Die deutsche Literatur des Mittelalters. Verfasserlexikon*, vol. 1. Berlin/New York, De Gruyter, ²1978, coll. 152–1168.

Le Goff, Jacques, *La Naissance du Purgatoire*. Paris, Gallimard, 1981.

Rauh, Horst Dieter, *Das Bild des Antichrist im Mittelalter. Von Tyconius zum Deutschen Symbolismus* (Beiträge zur Geschichte der Philosophie und Theologie des Mittelalters, N.F. 9). Münster, Aschendorff, 1973.

Sonntag, Jörg, *Klosterleben im Spiegel des Zeichenhaften. Symbolisches Denken und Handeln hochmittelalterlicher Mönche zwischen Dauer und Wandel, Regel und Gewohnheit* (Vita regularis. Abhandlungen, 35). Berlin, LIT-Verlag, 2008.

Tertullian, *De anima*, ed. Jan H. Waszink. In *Quinti Septimi Florentis Tertulliani Opera*, pars II: *Opera Monastica* (Corpus Christianorum. Series Latina, 2). Turnhout, Brepols, 1954, 779–871.

Wagner, Fritz, "Studien zu Caesarius von Heisterbach", *Analecta Cisterciensia* 28, 1972, 79–95.

---

38 DM, IV.41.

Living with Demons —— 133

Appendix

Heaven

Purgatory

Limbo of Infants   Hell

Refrigerium

Fig. 10.A1: Mestre da Família Artés: The Last Judgment and the Mass of Saint Gregory (Museu de Arte de São Paulo, São Paulo)
(https://commons.wikimedia.org/wiki/File:Mestre_da_Fam%C3%ADlia_Art%C3%A9s_-_Ju%C3%ADzo_Final.jpg)

134 —— Mirko Breitenstein

Limbo of the Patriarchs

Purgatory

Limbo of Infants

Hell

Fig. 10.A2: Miroir du salut humain, Marseille, Bibliothéque municipal, MS 89, fol. 28v
(Das leuchtende Mittelalter, ed. Jacques Dalarun, Darmstadt: Primus ²2006, S. 116)

Fig. 10.A3: Meester van de Levensbron: Gregoriusmis met stichter, Museum Catharijneconvent, Utrecht
(https://commons.wikimedia.org/wiki/File:MCC-108_Gregoriusmis_met_stichter_(1).jpg)

Fig. 10.A4: Meester van de Levensbron: Gregoriusmis met stichter, Museum Catharijneconvent, Utrecht, detail
(https://commons.wikimedia.org/wiki/File:MCC-108_Gregoriusmis_met_stichter_(1).jpg)

Fig. 10.A5: Master of the Göttingen Franciscan Altarpiece, outside of the outer right wing (Das Göttinger Barfüßerretabel von 1424: Akten des wissenschaftlichen Kolloquiums, Landesmuseum Hannover, 28.-30. September 2006, Ergebnisband des Restaurierungs- und Forschungsprojektes, eds. Cornelia Aman / Babette Hartwieg (Niederdeutsche Beiträge zur Kunstgeschichte / NF 1), Petersberg: Imhof 2015, plat 12)

José Emilio Burucúa
Transcendences in the Italian Renaissance
Regarding a Wood Panel by Jacopo del Sellaio and a Miniature by Reginaldus Metropolitanus

I

A visit to the public collection of the *Gemäldegalerie* in Berlin provides an opportunity to explore hundreds of pictures and exercise the intuitive sense of alertness, which may result in the spectator's exhaustion. In the last days of January 2013, a wood panel by Jacopo del Sellaio fascinated me. I was moved by the appeal of the theme and its representation. It was the *Meeting between Jesus and Saint John the Baptist*,[1] an event taking place during their teenage years under the protective gaze of Mary and Joseph. The scene is set by Jacopo in a charming birch forest, where four deer roam or rest peacefully. Just a few centimeters from this object of fascination, I immediately found a bigger wood panel with the same theme, painted by Domenico Ghirlandaio.[2] My first hypothesis was that Ghirlandaio was the first to paint the scene, and that his work had been a source of inspiration for Jacopo del Sellaio. The research I conducted that same afternoon confirmed my hypothesis. On the one hand, the theme and style of Domenico's piece link it to the monumental cycle, dedicated to the life of Saint John the Baptist, which the artist painted at the request of Giovanni Tornabuoni on the right wall of the apse of the Florentine church of Santa Maria Novella, between 1486 and 1490.[3] This fact allows me to date the second wood panel around those years. On the other hand, it is possible that Bartolomeo di Giovanni's presence among Domenico's collaborators in the Dominican church helped to foster an art relationship, and even friendship, between Ghirlandaio and Jacopo, since Bartolomeo di Giovanni had close contacts with Jacopo, evidenced by the fact that both took part in the production of the splendid paintings illustrating the story of Nastagio degli Onesti, made under Sandro Botticelli's direction. Therefore, it can be safely assumed that del Sellaio painted the first wood panel I saw under Domenico Ghirlandaio's influence around 1490.

---

1 Oil on wood panel, 30 x 48 cm, Berlin, *Gemäldegalerie*, inv. 94.
2 Oil on wood panel, 33 x 50.7 cm, Berlin, *Gemäldegalerie*, inv. 93.
3 Giorgio Vasari, *Le vite de'più eccelenti pittori scultori ed architettori*, vol. 3, 260–269.

The meeting between the Holy cousins was a popular theme between the end of the *Quattrocento* and 1600. A tondo, now displayed in the Palazzo Vecchio, attributed to Sebastiano Mainardi and del Sellaio, shows a *Giovannino* lovingly tending to Jesus as a child. What else do both Leonardo's versions of the *Virgin of the Rocks* describe other than the moment in which John, guided and led to Egypt by an angel due to the same reasons that forced the Holy family to flee Bethlehem, recognizes the messiah and pays homage to him while Jesus blesses him? (John's moving to Egypt is suggested in the apocryphal Gospel of James).[4] The theme is repeated in the Burlington House cartoon, displayed at the London National Gallery. Three works by Raphael, dating from the first decade of the sixteenth century, where the influence of the model developed by Leonardo is evident, show the same children as they play and contemplate one another: the *Madonna of the Goldfinch* (Florence, Uffizi), the *Madonna del Belvedere* (Vienna, Kunsthistorisches Museum) and *La Belle Jardinière* (Paris, Louvre). Lucas Cranach may have been the first artist to completely distinguish the children from any other figures in a small panel painted in the early sixteenth century, today on display at the Museum of Bamberg. It is likely that the separation of the infants, imbued with the emotional burden of tenderness, grace and game enjoyment as painted by Leonardo and Raphael, resulted in the much cultivated formula of John and Jesus as children having fun in the midst of nature, reproduced over and over again throughout the seventeenth century. Rubens[5] and Murillo[6] provided the most popular models of the subject, reproduced in hundreds of engravings for more than two centuries. However, a scene like the one in the wood panels in Berlin, where the children have become teenagers, shake hands like serious grown-ups and one of them, Jesus, points to his heart to show his willingness to hear the teachings of the other, John, is a very exceptional representation. I will attempt to provide a historical explanation of this peculiar approach.[7] The search for the iconographic meaning of both works and their intellectual context leads me to suggest an idea of the beyond in the representation that is the object of my lecture.

---

4 Ronald F. HOCK, ed., *The Infancy Gospels*, 70–73; Alphonse MINGANA, *Woodbrooke Studies*, vol. 1, 240.
5 See *Jesus and John the Baptist as Children* on canvas, Munich, Staatsgalerie im Neuen Schloss, Bayerische Staatsgemäldesammlungen.
6 See *Jesus and Infant Saint John or The Boys of the Shell* on canvas, Madrid, Prado Museum, inv. 964.
7 In the monumental work of Louis RÉAU, *Iconografía del Arte Cristiano*, vol. 1.1: *Iconografía de la Biblia*, 505–507, this theme is not included in the very complete list of themes of the Precursor's life.

Let us compare the two paintings that caught my attention. In the case of Ghirlandaio's piece, the figures of the Virgin and Joseph respect the medieval conventions (it is likely that, to better establish Joseph's ascetic appearance, he is dressed in a Franciscan cape or *esclavina*). The Baptist, however, wears a cape and old-fashioned sandals, while Jesus is a decidedly beautiful young man, a feature typical of early Christian mosaics and sarcophagi. The open and bright landscape combines the modern aerial perspective, learned in Florence from the Flemish works imported in the last decades of the *Quattrocento*, with traditional symbolic elements of the Middle Ages, supported by the vocabulary of the *Physiologus*: the fountain of wisdom, the fleeing wild boar –an emblem of darkness and the underworld–, the quail referring to Satan chasing the filial love hoopoe (the theme is a replica of that used in the *Visitation* of the Tornabuoni chapel in Santa Maria Novella), the deer taking the place of good angels and Christ himself, because with their saliva they force the dragons from hell to get out of the crevices of the earth.[8] As to del Sellaio's painting, we find again the iconographic convention of the late Middle Ages in the figures of the Virgin, Joseph and even the Baptist. However, the Paleochristian Jesus not only refers to the old model, his beautiful young figure, but also shows the solar characteristics of the Apollonian Christ. The wooded and gloomy landscape, a place for atonement, where the light is better displayed in both artistic and allegorical terms, displays aesthetic and symbolic meanings that Jacopo adopted from his master Filippo Lippi. The forest animals are again inspired by the *Physiologus*.

Both works allow for a discussion of Erwin Panofsky's theory of the overcoming of the principle of disjunction in the representative arts of Italy in the *Quattrocento*. According to Panofsky, this process signals the dawn of a clear consciousness of historical distance, of a generic beyond which distinguishes Renaissance societies from the ancient world, in regard to ways of life, beliefs and axiology. The German art historian defined the "principle of disjunction" as a couple of tacit rules, working simultaneously, that were adopted by medieval artists from the ninth to the fifteenth century. On the one hand, the artists represented ancient gods and heroes in contemporary clothes or surrounded by contemporary objects, without considering that the material culture of the ancients was different from that of the Middle Ages. On the other hand, if a figure was dressed in the toga or cloak of the ancients, its meaning was invariably subjected to an *interpretatio Christiana*.[9] According to Panofsky, the fact that Renaissance figurative art discovered medieval anachronism between the clothes of historical characters and those of Greco-Roman mythology is not only a major turning

---

8 Cf. Nilda GUGLIELMI, ed., *The Physiologist*, 47, 72, 79–81.
9 Cf. Erwin PANOFSKY, *Renaissance and Renascences*, 82–100 and 104–113.

point in the field of aesthetic knowledge, but also the empirical symptom of a new conception of time (consisting of great disruptions and cultural conflicts, rather than continuities). Panofsky came up with this point of view in the early 50s, and the idea that a new notion of time that arises from the aesthetic change has long been accepted in the historiography of the Renaissance, for example in the works of Eugenio Garin,[10] André Chastel,[11] Peter Burke,[12] John Hale[13] and Christopher Celenza.[14] This is why the paintings that I am analyzing now display oscillations in time references, which might place them before the collapse of the principle of disjunction. The representations of Mary and Joseph and the symbolic networks of the paintings, distinctive medieval features, are intertwined with powerful echoes of Antiquity: the young figures of the Baptist and Jesus, which demand an *interpretatio christiana*.

So far, my argument relies more heavily on historian's *ficta*, than on *facta* coming from the past. It is necessary to continue the search for literary sources of the exceptional meeting between the Holy cousins, because it is likely to provide explicit manifestations of the conflicting transcendences that we inferred from the pictorial representations. We have not found even a hint of the event in the apocryphal gospels, or in Comestor's Scholastic History or in the *Golden Legend*. The *Vita Christi*, written by Ludolph of Saxony in the mid-fourteenth century and widely translated into the vernacular languages at the beginning of the sixteenth century, highlights the passages and chapters dedicated to the life of Saint John the Baptist, who is represented in that text as the prototype of Christian monasticism. Ludolph highlights the Saint's choice of living in contemplation and prayer in the desert from the age of seven.[15] A single clue could have led us to think about the Baptist's meeting Jesus during that eremitic stage of the saint's life. According to Ludolph, the Baptist stayed twenty-three years in the desert stretching from Egypt to the Promised Land, "and there he was fed and waited for the Son of God in solitude".[16] Perhaps someone could have interpreted the passage literally, assuming that John awaited a visit from Jesus at that place and that they actually met. But this is too much of a conjecture, so I continued the search and ran into the text that provided the conceptual and narrative framework to our wood panels.

---

10 Eugenio GARIN, *Medioevo e Rinascimento*, 95–100 and 187–195.
11 André CHASTEL and Robert KLEIN, *El Humanismo*, 91–97.
12 Peter BURKE, *The Italian Renaissance*, 235–247.
13 John HALE, *The Civilization of Europe*, 585–592.
14 Christopher CELENZA, *The Lost Italian Renaissance*, 134–150.
15 We have consulted a French edition: LUDOLPHE LE CHARTREUX, *Le grand vita christi*, chapter VI *in fine*, 60, chapter XIV, 118–121.
16 Ibidem, chapter XIV, 119 d.

The text I am referring to is *De christiana religione*, written by Marsilio Ficino between 1473 and 1474. In this book, the Florentine philosopher attempts to demonstrate the superiority of Christianity over all other religions. He accepts, however, that the truth might be present in other beliefs, although not fully revealed until the advent of Jesus Christ.[17] It is clear that, for Ficino, Plato's theology had presented, in the fourth century B.C., a systematic and true metaphysics, which only lacked the saving and final legitimization of Christ, the Word Incarnate, in history. *De christiana religione* insists, on the one hand, on the historical nature of Platonism as a mature product of the tradition of a *prisca theologia* (dating back to Hermes Trismegistus). On the other hand, the book emphasizes the timeless essence of Christian truth on the basis of several arguments. First, the Christian religion is not based on human wisdom, power or pleasure, but on the sudden emergence of the Savior. This miraculous event was followed by the unstoppable spreading of His message, based exclusively on divine piety, hope and virtue.[18] Second, the conception of the Son of God was *ab aeterno* in the bosom of the Trinity,[19] although it had to be "declared", to become known in human time as a form of the Incarnation. But this temporal manifestation does not contradict the timeless or absolute nature of the Christian truth, which was banned from the eyes of humanity after the fall.[20] Third, prophets, sages and sibyls, among Jews and Gentiles, intuited, foresaw and announced that "declaration" of the Savior before his arrival and the triumph of the Gospel.[21] Ficino carefully studied the prophecies in Chapters XXIV to XXVII of his book[22] and, in Chapter XXX, he elaborated on the fact that Christian truths could be confirmed by Jewish sources (to which Marsilio adds the contribution of the Koran).[23] John the Baptist appears as a conclusion of the whole prophetic tradition, a man whom, according to Ficino, "everybody honors without controversy" and reveres as a "role model of all virtues."[24] According to Marsilio, Josephus praised him and so did the Muslims

---

[17] Cf. Amos EDELHEIT, ed., *Ficino, Pico and Savonarola*, 210–278; James HANKINS, "Marsilio Ficino and the Religion of the Philosophers"; Christopher CELENZA, *The Lost Italian Renaissance*, 100–106.
[18] I have consulted the following edition: MARSILIO FICINO, *De christiana religione*, folios XIr–XIVv.
[19] Cf. ibidem, folios XXIv–XXIIv.
[20] Cf. ibidem, folios XXIIIv–XXIVr.
[21] Cf. ibidem, folio XIv.
[22] Cf. ibidem, folios XXXv–LIIr.
[23] Cf. ibidem, folios LXIv–LXIIIv.
[24] Ibidem, folio LXIIv.

in the *Koran*.[25] All these sources, in addition to the Gospels, stressed the friendship between John and Jesus, to the point that Ficino believed that Jesus chose his first disciples among John's followers.[26] Therefore, it would not be unreasonable to think that the Baptist could have conveyed the messianic conviction and worldly content of the prophetic knowledge to his cousin Jesus.

It seems reasonable to wonder if *De christiana religione* or its references to Saint John were available to Ghirlandaio and provided the meanings of his wood panel and the one painted by Jacopo del Sellaio. Domenico's familiarity with the circle of humanists that gathered around Lorenzo the Magnificent, the Sassettis and the Tornabuonis was proved by Aby Warburg in a famous essay on portraiture and the Florentine bourgeoisie.[27] We might add that in the cycle of frescoes dedicated to the life of the Baptist in the apse of Santa Maria Novella, Ghirlandaio chose a group of four humanists, among the multitude of the inhabitants of Florence, to be present in the scene of Zechariah's sacrifice. To the left of the altar and in the foreground, the painter portrayed Cristoforo Landino, Demetrius the Greek (Calcondilas, successor of Chrysoloras and Argyropulos in the Greek chair of the Florentine Studio), Angelo Poliziano and Marsilio Ficino. The identification has been well known and discussed even by the artists' contemporaries, a fact that can be inferred from Vasari's comment in the life of Domenico Ghirlandaio.[28] Vasari wrote:

> [...] he portrayed a good number of the Florentine citizens who then governed that State, particularly all those of the house of Tornabuoni, both young and old. Besides this, in order to show that his age was rich in every sort of talent, above all in learning, he made a group of four half-length figures conversing together at the foot of the scene, representing the most learned men then to be found in Florence. The first of these, who is wearing the dress of a Canon, is Messer Marsilio Ficino; the second, in a red mantle, with a black band round his neck, is Cristofano Landino; the figure turning towards him is Demetrius the Greek; and he who is standing between them, with one hand slightly raised, is Messer Angelo Poliziano; and all are very lifelike and vivacious.

Ergo, our hypothesis of the existence of a link between the two paintings and the representation of John the Baptist by Ficino in *De christiana religione* could be realistic. It should be considered also that del Sellaio painted twice, in the early 1480s, the meeting between Jesus and the Baptist in the desert. Both times, the

---

25 Ficino might be thinking of Sura No. 3 (The Family of Imran), v. 35; No. 6 (Cattle), v. 85; No. 19 (Maria), v. 13; No. 21 (The Prophets), v. 90, of the *Koran*.
26 Cf. MARSILIO FICINO, *De christiana religione*, folios LXIIv–LIIIr.
27 Cf. Aby WARBURG, "Arte del ritratto e borghesia fiorentina".
28 Giorgio VASARI, *Le vite de'più eccelenti pittori scultori ed architettori*, vol. 3, 265 sq.

scenes were represented on *cassoni* panels.[29] In these cases, John is always subordinate, kneeling before or worshiping his Holy cousin. It is not unreasonable to think that the visual narrative of that meeting, referred in terms of "friendship," as proclaimed by Ficino and thus represented by Ghirlandaio, had a strong impact on Jacopo. Del Sellaio then stepped aside from the formulas used until then to refer to the contemplations of the Son of God by John, who was a monk and ascetic Christian *avant la lettre*. He then came up with the lovely scene on display at the *Gemäldegalerie* which, rather than the *Meeting between Jesus and the Baptist*, should be called *Friendship between Jesus and the Baptist*. We now better understand the close and equal shaking of hands which comes from the ancient pagan representations of greetings and farewells between friends, often on the threshold of death.[30]

Let us try, finally, to describe the matrix that could allow us to link, on the one hand, the anachronisms and implicit temporal conflicts in the exceptional iconography of the two paintings displayed in Berlin and, on the other, the dialectics of the temporal order and eternity, the here and the beyond, developed by Ficino in his *De christiana religione*. The Medieval details, governed by the principle of disjunction, could be the ones that produce the historicity of the visual narrative and allow for the "declaration", in Ficino's terms, of the conception of the Son of the Trinity in time. On the other hand, the early Christian echoes in the figures of John and Jesus, joined by the ancient friendship, symbolized by the handshake, bring us back to the eternity of the Christian truth. The *Nachleben der Antike* would be, in such a case, the vehicle for timeless permanence, rather than awareness of historical distance. The familiar, picturesque scene dominated *prima facie* by an effect of intimacy between people or between nature and humans is impregnated, however, with a sense of something that lies beyond it, a sense of fullness that we experience due to the purely aesthetic remoteness of the representation of Jesus.

---

29 Jacopo del Sellaio, *Temptations of Saint Anthony Abad, Christ finds Saint John the Baptist in the Desert, Archangel Raphael and Tobias, The Penitent Saint Jerome in the Desert, Saint Francis Receiving the Stigmata, The Stoning of Saint Stephen*. Oil on wood panel, Göttingen, *Kunstsammlung der Universität*, inv. 164; *The Baptist worships Christ in the desert, Penitent Saint Jerome, Mary Magdalene in the Desert*. Oil on wood panel, private collection.

30 Nicolás Kwiatkowski has pointed out to me that the deer are presented in pairs in both pieces, as if the animal symbolic world also referred to the friendship linking John and Jesus. In addition, François Hartog has also drawn my attention to the subtle contrast, both in Ghirlandaio's and del Sellaio's works, between the forcefulness of John's step on the floor and Jesus's light way of walking. Perhaps the painters thus echoed Ficino's assertion regarding the exclusively divine character of the Christian presence. It is true that John was a compendium of human and earthly virtues, taken to their highest expression, but only Jesus's nature was based on the highest piety and the heavenly virtues.

II

You must have begun to suspect the consequences of my hypothesis regarding the beyond in the Renaissance period. I believe that it was in the arts, rather than in the other spheres of human activity, where the question of the transcendental foundation of life was settled, in the Renaissance. That period began with the crisis of Scholastic rationalism and the *summum* of ontological, dialectical and contradictory immensity of the world, as postulated by Cusano. It finished in Bruno's threshold of material and eternal infinitude, and in the dawn of philosophical subjectivity proposed by Descartes. The arts explorations in these matters were displayed especially in the representation of the life of Jesus, from the manger in Bethlehem to the lighting provided by the pilgrim of Emmaus. And the whole process seemed to be very simple, which is what Vasari meant when he spoke of Leonardo's *graziosissima grazia* and the artists of the *acmé della rinascita*.[31]

Further evidence of this process can be found in an extraordinary case. The Greek codex No. 4 of Aristotle's *Nicomachean Ethics*, now kept at the Austrian National Library, in Vienna, was signed by "Angelos Konstantinos of Sternataia near Otranto" and illustrated by the painter Reginaldus Piramus Monopolitanus of Apulia between 1496 and 1504. Reginaldus decorated the ten pages that served as the cover of each of the ten books of *Ethics*.[32] The first visual representation in the manuscript is on the initial page of the first book. It is a large allegorical composition in the center of the text –the rational soul, with wings on its head, stretching its cloak and embracing the personifications of the four cardinal virtues–; below, the representation of an exemplary story, mentioned in Aristotle's text –in this case, several episodes of the story of Solon and Croesus told by Herodotus.[33] This set of images displays perfectly the opposition between the two most important philosophical systems of the ancient world: Platonism and Aristotelian realism.

The organization of the painted surface is the same in six of the ten miniatures in the manuscript, but the use of alegoresis, inspired by ancient mythology, extends to the entire figurative *corpus*. However, at the top of the first illustration there is an exceptional scene: Reginaldus has represented Plato's theory of ideas, precisely criticized by Aristotle in the first *Nicomachean* book,[34] as follows: the

---

[31] Cf. Giorgio Vasari, *Le vite de'più eccelenti pittori scultori ed architettori*, vol. 4, 35–51.
[32] Cf. Hermann Julius Hermann, "Miniaturhandschriften aus der Bibliothek", 147–150, 163–167; Otto Mazal, *Der Aristoteles des Herzogs von Atri*, 26–41.
[33] Cf. Aristotle, *Nicomachean Ethics*, I, 6, 1096.11–1097.14; Herodotus, *Histories*, I, 30–33.
[34] Aristotle, *Nicomachean Ethics*, I, 10, 1100.10–31.

golden silhouettes of a man and several animals –lizard, horse, mole, scorpion, snail, mouse, hedgehog, lion, pheasant, fish, worm, snake, donkey, dog, bull, deer, etc.–have been placed on a dark blue sky, crossed by the ecliptic where the shape of the sun can be made out. The silhouettes represent the ideas, from which some golden rays emerge, ending in the sensitive beings to which they give rise in the world. The lobster, fly and ants *methexis* are particularly picturesque. The rays seem to pass behind the triumphal arch that serves as a frame for the allegory of the soul and the virtues. It can be assumed that some of the beings they create on earth are hidden behind the buildings. Apparently, it was Andrea Matteo Acquaviva, Duke of Atri, the manuscript owner and the commissioner of its decoration, who designed the iconographic program of the entire series and devised the staging of the theory of ideas. The core of Platonism, one of the most productive Western philosophical systems, was represented there on the basis of the very notions of similarity and participation (*methexis*). We are in the presence of a beautiful diagrammatic image, based on the correspondence between the object (the theory of ideas) and its representation (what has been rhizomatically represented on the top of the miniature, which displays a new correspondence between the golden silhouette [the idea] and the mimetic simulacrum of the object [the sensible being derived from the idea]). However, the counterpoint with the historical scene at the bottom could not be more violent and, in fact, I believe that this scene prevails in our intellectual and emotional act of contemplation. It does so in spite of the fact that the text of *Ethics* that we will read destroys the beautiful dream of the theory of ideas with reasonable arguments. The counterpoint is achieved through aesthetic means, through the complexity and the attention we must pay to every detail of the visual narrative of the story of Croesus and Solon, as well as to the sequential horizons which we must follow with our gaze. We see Croesus listening to Solon's stories, impressed above all by the death of the young athletes from Argos; this episode is placed on the enlarged center of the picture. Then we see Croesus at the stake made by Cyrus, his defeater; Croesus recalls Solon's warnings. In the wooden panels painted by Ghirlandaio and Jacopo del Sellaio, something from the beyond permeated the scenes and cleared up their meanings. In Reginaldus' miniature, the beyond is just a game of the artist's iconographic creativity. The action described at the bottom of the illuminated pages is what matters in this case, acquiring an illustrative and coherent sense with regard to what we are about to read in the *Ethics*.

During the crisis of metaphysics in the early seventeenth century, the arts of *disegno*, as Vasari called them, provided another example of philosophical visualization. It is somewhat trivial, but compellingly beautiful, and also complemented by Christian hermeneutics. I am referring to a *taille-douce* made by Jan Saenredam of Haarlem in 1604 on the instructions of Hendrik Laurenszoon

Spieghel, a poet, grammarian, and author of Dutch grammar texts, of celebratory New Year poems and "mirrors of the heart."[35] It is likely that he authored the Latin poem in the summary. Spieghel offered the picture to Dr. Peter Paaw, a professor of medicine at the University of Leiden, great anatomist and founder, with Bontius, of the botanical garden in that university.[36] The print is a representation of the "Platonic cave". Inside, a large group of people appears isolated and in the dark. There are statues of gods and men on top of a wall, casting their shadows onto the bottom of the cave. We can see a heated argument between different kinds of individuals: rustic, oriental, coming from different peoples and occupied in diverse trades, soldiers, clerics, some wearing miters and other, togas. A long Latin verse didascalia explains the symbology step by step:

> *Maxima pars hominum cecis immersa tenebris / Volvitur assidué, et studio letatur inani: / Adspice ut obiectis obtutus in hereat umbris, / Vt veri simulacra omnes mirentur amentque, // Et stolidi vanâ ludantur imagine rerum.*
> (Most men, immersed in the darkness, / wallow constantly and perish in vain pursuit. / Look how the gaze sticks to the shadows of objects, / so that everyone loves and admires the simulacra of the true objects, // and fools are deceived by the vain images of things.)

To the left, a smaller group of people examines the lamp illuminating the objects on the wall and calmly reflects on the finding.

> *Quam pauci meliore luto, qui in lumine puro / Secreti â stolidâ turbâ, ludibria cernunt / Rerum vmbras rectaque expendunt omnia lance:// Hi positâ erroris nebulâ dignoscere possunt / Vera bona, atque alios cecâ sub nocte latentes / Extrahere in claram lucem conantur, at illis / Nullus amor lucis, tanta est rationis egestas.*
> (A few men, better than the rest, under the pure light / separate from the stupid crowd, discover the taunts and make direct and balanced judgments / of the shadows of things: // They can recognize the projected darkness of error, / the true and good things, and strive to take / the others from the dark night to the clear light, / for they do not love the light and their reasoning is very poor.)

Behind the second group, there is a corridor to the outside of the *antrum* and only three men are there. They look at and point to the natural source of light in the landscape. The direct representation of Plato's allegory in Book VII of the *Republic* (514 to 517) is explicit, profuse, and compelling. It distinguishes, better than the didascalia, the men that went outside and can see the real things in the world (ideas) and the sun, that is, the Good, from those who still are in the cave.

---

35 Ernst MARTIN, "Spieghel, Hendrik Laurenszoon" (Figure [11.1]).
36 Cf. August HIRSCH, "Pauw, Peter".

These people have discovered that the silhouettes they considered real until then are nothing but shadows cast by the statues under the light of a lamp. The philosophical myth is Christianized by the inclusion of a quote from the Gospel of John (3: 19): *Lux venit in mundu[m] et dilexerunt homines magis tenebras quam lucem.* (Light has come into the world, and men loved darkness rather than light). This idea (probably conceived by Spieghel, the commissioner of the engraving) means that the deception of the senses and the soul in the *Antrum Platonicum* prefigured the blindness of the people, who did not recognize Christ as the savior and liberator of humanity. However, from 1600 onwards, the aesthetic horizon ceased to be the arena for the creative discussion of philosophical topics. That field would be, from then on, the place reserved for dazzling representations of our illusions about the beyond.

Fig. 11.1: Jan Saenredam of Haarlem, *Antrum Platonicum*, 1604

Bibliography

Aristotle, *Nicomachean Ethics*, translated and edited by Roger Crisp. New York, Cambridge Univerity Press, 2014.
Burke, Peter, *The Italian Renaissance. Culture and Society in Italy*. Cambridge, Polity Press, ²1999 (originally published: Cambridge 1986).
Celenza, Christopher, *The Lost Italian Renaissance. Humanists, Historians and Latin's Legacy*. Baltimore/London, The Johns Hopkins University Press, 2006.
Chastel, André, and Robert Klein, *El Humanismo*. Barcelona/Madrid/Buenos Aires/México/Caracas/Bogotá/Rio de Janeiro, Salvat, 1964.
Edelheit, Amos, ed., *Ficino, Pico and Savonarola: The Evolution of Humanist Theology 1461/2-1498*. Leiden, Brill, 2008.
Garin, Eugenio, *Medioevo e Rinascimento. Studi e ricerche*. Bari, Laterza, ³1980 (originally published: Bari, 1954).
Guglielmi, Nilda, ed., *The Physiologist. Medieval Bestiary*. Buenos Aires, Eudeba, 1971.
Hale, John, *The Civilization of Europe in the Renaissance*. New York/London/Toronto/Sydney/Tokyo/Singapore, Simon & Schuster, 1993.
Hankins, James, "Marsilio Ficino and the Religion of the Philosophers", *Rinascimento* 48, 2008, 101–121.
Hermann, Hermann Julius, "Miniaturhandschriften aus der Bibliothek des Herzogs Andrea Matteo III. Acquaviva", *Jahrbuch der Kunsthistorischen Sammlungen in Wien* 19, 1898, 147–216.
Herodotus, *Histories*, translated by Pamela Mensch, edited, with introduction and notes by James Romm. Indanapolis, Hackett Publishing Company, 2014.
Hirsch, August, "Pauw, Peter". In *Allgemeine Deutsche Biographie*, edited by the Historische Kommission bei der Bayerischen Akademie der Wissenschaften, vol. 25. Leipzig, Duncker & Humblot, 1887, 302 sq.
Hock, Ronald F., ed., *The Infancy Gospels of James and Thomas*. Santa Rosa/California, Poleridge Press, 1995.
Ludolphe le Chartreux, *Le grand vita christi en françois*, translated by Guillaume Lemenand. Lyon, Matthias Huss, 1493. Original edition: Ludolphus the Carthusian, *Vita Christi: Text* (Analecta Cartusiana, 241, 1–5). Salzburg, Institut für Anglistik und Amerikanistik der Univ. Salzburg, 2006–2007 (Paris/Rome, Palmé, 1865).
Marsilio Ficino, *De christiana religione*. Venetia, Ottinus Papiensis, 1500.
Martin, Ernst, "Spieghel, Hendrik Laurenszoon". In *Allgemeine Deutsche Biographie*, edited by the Historische Kommission bei der Bayerischen Akademie der Wissenschaften, vol. 35. Leipzig, Duncker & Humblot, 1887, 161 sq.
Mazal, Otto, *Der Aristoteles des Herzogs von Atri. Die Nikomachische Ethik in einer Prachthandschift der Renaissance. Codex phil.gr. 4 aus dem Besitz der Österreichen Nationalbibliothek in Wien*. Graz, Akademische Druck und Verlagsanstalt, 1988.
Mingana, Alphonse, *Woodbrooke Studies: Christian Documents in Syriac, Arabic, and Garshuni*, vol. 1. Cambridge, Heffer, 1927.
Panofsky, Erwin, *Renaissance and Renascences in Western Art*. Norwich/UK, Paladin, ²1970 (originally published: Copenhagen, 1960).
Réau, Louis, *Iconografía del Arte Cristiano*, vol. 1.1: *Iconografía de la Biblia*. Barcelona, Ediciones del Serbal, 1996.

Vasari, Giorgio, *Le vite de' più eccelenti pittori scultori ed architettori, scritte da Giorgio Vasari pittore aretino, con nuove annotazioni e commenti di Gaetano Milanesi*, vol. 3. Florence, Sansoni, 1906.

Vasari, Giorgio, *Le vite de' più eccelenti pittori scultori ed architettori, scritte da Giorgio Vasari pittore aretino, con nuove annotazioni e commenti di Gaetano Milanesi*, vol. 4. Florence, Sansoni, 1906.

Warburg, Aby, "Arte del ritratto e borghesia fiorentina. Domenico Ghirlandaio in Santa Trinita. I ritratti di Lorenzo de' Medici e dei suoi familiari". In Id., *La Rinascita del Paganesimo Antico. Contributi alla storia della cultura*. Florence, La Nuova Italia, 1966, 109–146.

Pictures

Bartolomé E. Murillo, *Jesus and Infant Saint John or The Boys of the Shell*. Canvas, Madrid, Prado Museum, inv. 964.

Domenico Ghirlandaio, *Meeting between Jesus and Saint John the Baptist*. Oil on wood panel, 33 x 50.7 cm, Berlin, Gemäldegalerie, inv. 93.

Jacopo del Sellaio, *Meeting between Jesus and Saint John the Baptist*. Oil on wood panel, 30 x 48 cm, Berlin, Gemäldegalerie, inv. 94.

Jacopo del Sellaio, *Temptations of Saint Anthony Abad, Christ finds Saint John the Baptist in the Desert, Archangel Raphael and Tobias, The Penitent Saint Jerome in the Desert, Saint Francis Receiving the Stigmata, The Stoning of Saint Stephen*. Oil on wood panel, Göttinen, Kunstsammlung der Universität, inv. 164.

Jacopo del Sellaio, *The Baptist worships Christ in the desert, Penitent Saint Jerome, Mary Magdalene in the Desert*. Oil on wood panel, private collection.

Jan Saenredam of Haarlem, *Antrum Platonicum*, 1604.

Peter P. Rubens, Jesus and John the Baptist as Children. Canvas, Munich, *Staatsgalerie im Neuen Schloss, Bayerische Staatsgemäldesammlungen*.

Cultural Identities

Guillermo Wilde
The Mission as "Beyond" and Beyond the Mission

> **Saint Ignatius:**
> *¡Ay! ¡ay! qué tormento,* [Oh, Oh, what torment]
> *vivir lejos de vos,* [to live far away from you]
> *mi Señor, mi Bien, mi Dios.* [my Lord, my Good, my God]
>
> **Aria**
> *¡Oh, vida, cuánto duras!* [Oh, life, so long you are!]
> *¡Oh, muerte, lo que tardas!* [Oh, death, so long you delay!]
>
> *¡Oh dulce amor! ¿Qué aguardas* [Oh sweet Love! What do you wait]
> *en romper ataduras?* [for freeing bonds?]
> *Desátame, y sepárame* [Untie me, and separate me]
> *del cuerpo con la muerte,* [from the body through death]
> *que sin fin deseo verte,* [that I endlessly wish to see you]
> *oh mi Dios, cara a cara.* [Oh my God, face to face][1]

Thus begins the anonymous opera *San Ignacio de Loyola*, composed and first performed in the Jesuit missions of Paraguay, in the middle of the jungle, at certain point of the 18th century. The main characters are Ignatius, founder of the Society of Jesus, and Saint Francis Xavier, the so called "Apostle of the Indies". The first part of the opera is about the battle between Ignatius and the forces of evil that intend to seduce and tempt him. Two angels descend from heaven to encourage Ignatius to fight, giving him support to defeat the devil. The armies of the Good obtain the victory, and sing their triumph in an aria. However, Ignatius is still worried about the fact that there are so many people in the world that have not been reached by catholic faith, the only and true faith. An angel suggests Ignatius that he send an envoy to spread the Christian faith to the Far East. Saint Francis Xavier is the chosen one. The second part of the opera is about Xavier's departure to the distant lands of the East. Xavier doubts about his capacity to accomplish the task, but Ignatius finally convinces him to depart and both do farewell in an aria charged with emotion.

---

[1] *San Ignacio, L'Opéra Perdu Des Missions Jésuites De L'Amazonie.* Ensemble Elyma, dir. Gabriel Garrido. K617 Recordings. Notes by Bernardo Illari. Series: Chemins du Baroque, 1996. CD Booklet. See also "St. Ignatius Loyola – A Mission Opera: An Emblem of the Mission." Introduction. The Jesuit Operas: Operas by Kapsberger and Zipoli. Ensemble Abendmusik. Dir. James David Christie. Dorian Recordings, 2002; Michael ZAMPELLI, "Opera News: Jesuits, Catholic Imagination".

DOI 10.1515/9783110530773-012

The opera is the representation of a voyage towards the exterior Other preceded by a journey to the internal other. Ignatius perfects his spirit after a victory over himself. He overcomes a crisis and depression defeating the Devil, who appears as an allegory of hedonism and joy of flesh. Liberated from the weakness of his body, Ignatius is able to guide others to follow him, and finds in Xavier his *alter ego*, someone who also needs to overcome his weakness and be ready to promote Christian faith among the "deaf gentility".[2]

The musical drama condensate two basic orientations toward the Beyond in early modern missionaries' mind: one related to the idea of overcoming oneself through reflection and experience of internal contradictions, a central aspect of the vanguard's Ignatian spirituality in times of post-tridentine reformation: "Go Beyond yourself in the search for God!." Another dealing with the idea of confronting radical Otherness represented by paganism and infidelity in the four parts of the world: "Go in mission, beyond the frontiers of Christianity. Bring the pagan peoples of the world to the Christian faith since outside the Church there is no salvation" (*extra ecclesiam nulla salus*).[3] Ignatius and Francis Xavier are metaphors of these complementary orientations. They represent two faces of early modern catholic mission, and of what could be defined as a wish for the Beyond. The spiritual exercises were tools to explore oneself deep inside, imagining places, figures and senses, domesticating them, and becoming able to project the internal experience of purification toward the outside. The mission as Beyond is tied to both the greater spiritual narrative of global expansion of Christianity and its universalistic discourse, and to particular circumstances and concrete experiences of confrontation to otherness in local context.

The opera Saint Ignatius was sang in Spanish. But there existed a parallel text written in the indigenous language. Actors performed this text making the story understandable to the indigenous audience. They explained the story and strengthened the moral effect of it. After one of the last scenes, the score indicates that an actor should say in chiquitano language: "Father! I want to go after Saint Xavier/to baptize people/ [...] and with the Good of my death for him/ for baptizing people."[4] The moral function of the parallel text is clear. It proposed a model of imitation for the people referring to the mission as a true redemption and to the missionary as someone capable of abandoning everything (even his life in martyrdom) for promoting his own vision of religion.

---

2 The fragment in Spanish is: "Oh, ciega gentilidad/[...] de tu fuego una centella/ el Oriente ilustrará./ [Messenger 1]: Dichosa tal vez es ella/ ¡oh! y qué feliz quien se va./ [Messenger 2]: Javier es él, es contigo/ eso le puedes mandar,/ vóytelo pues a llamar". San Ignacio.
3 Ibidem.
4 Ibidem.

The Mission as Beyond

> Essendo oggi la festa del glorioso Santo Apostolo dell'Indie Francesco Saverio non ho saputo trovare giorno più a proposito di questo per porgere alla Reverenza Vostra questo mio memoriale [...] soui tanto ferventi desideri di sparger nella Cina la semenza della divina parola [...] Io porre in effetto qualche minima particella di ciò che desiderava fare il Santo Apostolo nella Cina [...].[5]

This excerpt come from one *indipetae* letter sent by the Italian Jesuit Giulio Gori to the General Father of the order. In requesting China as his preferred missionary destination, Gori chooses to begin by reminding Saint Francis Xavier's desire for mission as the inspiration for his own desire. In general, the *indipetae* letters were supposed to express a formal request by potential missionaries for being sent to one of the four parts of the world, but especially a genuine apostolic desire and vocation to go beyond the geographical and symbolic limits of Europe and Christianity, which could even mean a will of dying in the task. From a temporal point of view, the mission expressed a "desire," a preparation for the afterlife, a passage from the life in the world, the temporal life *strictu sensu*, to the eternal life of salvation. The desire for the mission as Beyond, simultaneously implied imagining the beyond of the mission.

Most of these requests were not heard by the Society of Jesus' authorities.[6] The existing corpus of more than 14,000 letters preserved in the Rome's archive, leads to reflect on many possible situations: thousands letters delayed without answer, a few letters with an effective answer, lost letters and letters probably written but never found.[7] There was a spatial and temporal *decalage* between the individual will of the priests expressed in the letters and the bureaucratic and hierarchical organization of the order that processed and eventually answered those letters. A careful account of their contents allows an approach to the images and representations of

---

[5] The complete letter from 1704, is included in the Anex to Anna Rita CAPOCCIA, "Le Destin Des Indipetae", 109.

[6] Fabre suggests that the *indipetae* could be interpreted as a fifth week of the spiritual exercises. Pierre Antoine FABRE, "Un Désir Antérieur". They can express three kinds of "infinities": "[...] trois infinis: celui de son indignité (*humilimus, insipientibus, inconditis*), celui de son infinie désir des Indes (*ferventissimo, ardentissimo desiderio*), celui enfin de l'infinie bonté du Général (*princeps totius bonitatis, inmensa bonitas*)" (ibid., 79). Grâce de partir "formulée comme grâce de 'mourir aux Indes' – et mediter sa vie durante sur l'infinie distance, seulement comblable par une infinie bonté entre l'indignité et l'horizon du voyage. C'est une méditation en soi." (ibid., 79). Fabre notes that from a corpus of 31 letters only four priests that had requested the Philippines as a destination were effectively sent there, cf. ibid., 74.

[7] Cf. Aliocha MALDAVSKY, *Vocaciones Inciertas*.

the Beyond, from a geographical and cultural point of view; representations that circulated amongst educated subjects that had never left the European soil.

The desire of going beyond the limits of Christianity emerged in the framework of the Society of Jesus global expansion and the consolidation of Iberian Empires. Remote missions were a "natural vocation" of the Portuguese crown that, many years earlier than the Spanish crown, sent Jesuit missionaries to Asia and South America.[8] Francis Xavier had put feet in Goa in 1542, and Manuel da Nóbrega was sent to Brazil in 1549 under the protection of the Portuguese *padroado*. Both places became the first overseas missions of the order, and a rehearsal for the development of new missionary methods that would reach their apogee after the Jesuits' arrival in Japan and China.[9]

In the 17th century, the Portuguese assistance of the order had already distributed more than 500 hundred missionaries in the four parts of the world.[10] Years later the Jesuits arrived in Spanish America (in Peru in 1568 and in Mexico in 1572). Toward the end of the 17th century, there were eight Jesuit provinces in the Hispanic American world (included the Philippines) with 17.665 members. Some Jesuit provinces constituted from a geographical point of view an extended territoriality that connected points in both sides of the Atlantic and the Pacific oceans. For instance, Nouvelle France (Canada) belonged to the Jesuit Province of France, the Philippines to the Province of Mexico, and Occidental Africa to the Portuguese Province. As a way of supporting this enterprise, the Roman curia created the *Propaganda fide* congregation in 1622. Not by chance, the same year Ignatius, Francis Xavier and Borgia were sanctified.

In many visual representations of the time both Ignatius and Francis Xavier were depicted as the heart of a network of relations that extended throughout the world. Athanasius Kircher's remarkable "Ignatian tree" shows Saint Ignatius as the basis of a ramification that multiplies its branches giving origin to all the provinces of the Society of Jesus in the world, potential destinations for new Jesuit vocations. Kircher's picture is significantly entitled *Horoscopium Catholicum Societatis Iesu*, which leads to think that the Society of Jesus conceived itself as an allegory of Christianity in the world.

---

8 Cf. Charlotte CASTELNAU DE L'ESTOILE, "Élection et Vocation", 22.

9 The so called "accomodation" method was designed by Italian Jesuit Alessandro Valignano in Japan and after that developed in China by Jesuit Matteo Ricci and in India by Jesuit Roberto de Nobili. For a discussion on this see Elisabetta CORSI, *Órdenes Religiosas Entre América Y Asia*; Joan Pau RUBIÉS, "The Concept of Cultural Dialogue"; Ines G. ŽUPANOV, "El Repliegue De Lo Religioso"; David MUNGELLO, ed., *The Chinese Rites Controversy*.

10 The Society of Jesus also developed a strong policy of "interior missions" in different parts of Europe especially among peasants and muslims. On this see Emanuele COLOMBO, "Jesuitas Y Musulmanes". Also articles included in Charlotte de CASTELNAU-L´ESTOILE, Marie L. COPETE, Aliocha MALDAVSKY, and Ines G. ŽUPANOV, eds., *Missions D´Évangelisation*.

Fig. 12.1: "The Ignatian Tree" engraving in Athanasius Kircher´s *Ars magna lucis et umbrae* (Rome, 1646)

In other images spread throughout the world, Ignatius is usually accompanied by Francis Xavier, both represented as custodians of the catholic faith. A book by Eusebio Nieremberg entitled *De la Diferencia entre lo Temporal y lo Eterno* translated to many languages includes in its Guarani edition printed in Paraguay one engraved image of this type.

One of the most interesting illustrations of Jesuits global ambitions is an anonymous painting from the church of San Pedro, in Lima, made in the 18th century. In *Alegoria de la la Compañía de Jesús y su labor misional en los cuatro continentes*, Ignatius is located on a central pedestal with Francis Xavier and Borgia on both sides. Symbols of writing, preaching and sacramental devotion are respectively represented by each of them. At the feet of the three saints are represented peoples from the four continents praying for their salvation. Smaller figures standing behind and besides the saints represent specific missionaries: Matteo Ricci and Adam Schall, symbols of cultural accommodation and scientific achievement in China, Joao de Britto, Portuguese missionary to Madurai (India) carrying signs of poverty and Brahmin dress, Alexander de Rhodes, French Jesuit who had translated sacred books into Vietnamese and produced maps and histories of the region. On the celestial realm cherubims can be seen surrounding three figures on the left with crucifixes. These are the three Jesuit martyrs of Nagasaki, Miki, Kisai and Goto, killed in 1597. Other three figures on the right may be the three martyrs of the Caaró, Roque Gonzalez de Santa Cruz, Juan del Castillo and Alonso Rodriguez, who died in the Guarani missions in 1628. In his analysis of this painting, Brandon Bayne remarks that in spite of been painted in Peru most of the central missionary figures are not from the Americas, which makes this kind of representation particularly meaningful. "[E]vents on one side of the Pacific – writes Bayne – shaped the evangelization, devotional practice, and colonial expansion on the other side".[11] Pictures like this seem to have promoted a global awareness of missionary activity in which important elements of devotion were gathered in a coherent view. Similar depictions can be found in New Spain, where the figure of the Nagasaki martyrs was particularly prominent, even more than that of local martyrs.[12]

---

11 Brandon BAYNE, "Converting the Pacific", in press.
12 Cf. Clara BARGELLINI, "At the Center on the Frontier".

Fig. 12.2: Engraving from Eusebio Nieremberg´s *De la Diferencia entre lo Temporal y lo Eterno*, translated to Guarani language and printed in the Jesuit missions of Paraguay

Fig. 12.3: Anonymous, Allegory of the Society of Jesus and the pastoral labor in the four continents, Church of San Pedro, Lima, Peru, 18th century.

Anthropological Desire

The Beyond was for the missionaries the place of Otherness, whose diversity could be captured in *ad hoc* taxonomies. From the 17th century on, the Jesuits produced works of comparative ethnology, classifying hierarchically different types of peoples according to their political organization, their civility. One of the most famous was Acosta's *Historia Natural y Moral de las Indias* that proposes a classification of three types of societies. This work as well as the manual of mission entitled *De Procuranda Indorum Salute* by the same Acosta was a systematic intent to establish a history of customs of the peoples of the world.[13] It proposes a hierarchical outline of three categories of societies based on their civility and capacity to govern themselves, from those possessing states, cities and constituted alphabets to those wandering in the jungle and lacking any sort of *consortium*. Missionaries working in the most remotes parts of the world manifested an awareness of the global reach of their task, and usually compared the capacity of the different peoples to acquire Christian faith.[14] Asia, particularly China, was an idolatric civilization at the core of missionaries' ambitions; while the Americas were considered a radical confine inhabited by both civil societies as the Incas or the Aztecs and gentiles with no faith, no law, and no king.[15]

---

[13] Josef de ACOSTA, *Historia Natural y Moral*. One edition of this book include pictures by Theodor De Bry.

[14] In a passage of his *Spiritual Conquest* of Paraguay, Jesuit RUIZ DE MONTOYA, compares the Japanese with the indigenous peoples of the jungle he is trying to convert: "Y si en el Japon hay cuchillo que hace mártires, no faltan acá saetas que lo forman; hallo ménos acá las casas y palacios, la policía, las sedas los vestidos japoneses, la variedad de comidas y regalos, no digo que los usen los apostólicos varones; pero al fin su visita atrae y entretiene. Acá hay la vestidura y traje que al nacer concede la naturaleza á los humanos, siendo /fuerza que un solícito cuidado de los Padres haga cubrir lo que puede ofender á ojos castos, con cuidado necesario y afán continuo de buscarles lana, cordellate y algodón, y para que con comodidad siembren este, los mismos Padres con sus mismas personas les han enseñado á hender la tierra con arado, cosa nueva para ellos, pero bien lograda." Antonio RUIZ DE MONTOYA, *La Conquista Espiritual*, 194.

[15] In the following paragraph Acosta differentiates societies living in the borderlands with more civilized kingdoms as the Inca and the Aztecs: "[...] muchas naciones y gentes de indios no surgen reyes ni señores absolutos sino viven en behetría, y solamente para ciertas cosas –mayormente la guerra- crían capitanes y príncipes a los cuales durante aquel ministerio obedecen, y después se vuelven a sus primeros oficios. [...] Desta suerte pasa en toda la tierra de Chile, donde tantos años se han sustentado contra españoles los araucanos y los de Tucapel, y otros. Así fue todo lo del Nuevo Reino de Granda, y lo de Guatemala y las islas, y toda la Florida y el Brasil, y Luzón, y otras tierras grandísimas; excepto que en muchas dellas es aún mayor el barbarismo, porque apenas conocen cabeza sino todos de común mandan y gobiernan, donde todo es antojo y violencia y sinrazón y desorden, y el que más puede ése prevalece y manda. [...] En la India Occidental solamente se han descubierto dos reinos o imperios fundados, que es el de los mexicanos en la Nueva España y el de los ingas en el Perú." Josef de ACOSTA, *Historia Natural y Moral*, 212.

The interest for China was particularly strong among Italian Jesuits. In the period 1676–1770 more than 900 *indipetae* of Italian Jesuits are conserved among which only 167 specify a destination. More than the third part of them requested either China or the Philippines. The interest in those regions may have been the extremely positive image they had not only as missionary destinations but as the place for the emergence of societies comparable to Europe.[16] This positive image was the result of the impact of travel literature of the previous centuries. But from the 17th century on, the Jesuits started to produce and promote their own accounts of the missions in Asia. In his return to Europe, Jesuit Nicolas Trigault actively promoted Matteo Ricci's unpublished work on the Jesuits in China and their successful method of accommodation, the collection of *Letres édifiantes et curieuses* had also spread the idea of a moral superiority of the Chinese civilization, and Athanasius Kircher's *China Illustrata*, based on accounts from missionaries, became a reference for idealizing the Chinese world.

Over time, mapping became an important complement to descriptions in texts as it highlighted both the location of places and "nations" and the progress of evangelization. At a certain point, it became an obsession to accurately describe the customs, religion and political organization of the natives. A significant example is a map by Jesuit Jose Quiroga entitled "Mapa de las Missiones de la Compañía de Jesus en los ríos Paraná y Uruguay: conforme a las mas modernas observaciones de Latitud, y de Longitud, hechas em los pueblos de dichas Missiones; y a las relaciones antiguas y modernas de los Padres Misioneros de ambos ríos" (1749). Emphasizing the results of evangelization Quiroga locates in the map "newly founded mission towns" including notes in the margins with information about the various "barbarian nations" incorporated to the missions.[17]

Beyond the Mission: Anthropocentric (Re)turn

According to the missionaries, Christian life was characterized by a rational and natural ordering of space and time. The world was organized in terms of antinomies that radically opposed "Christian civility" to "gentile chaos". Jesuit sources

---

16 "Les missionnaires jéstuites eurent un poid déterminant dans la construction et la diffusion d'une image mythique de la Chine dans la culture européenne, en exaltant l'idée de la 'superiorité morale' de ce peuple. L'idée de la Chine provoqua une profonde crise, spirituelle, religieuse et diéologique: les longues polémiques sur la cronologie universelle, l'universalité du déluge, l'antiquité du monde, une morale chrétienne qui ne devait pas être nécessairement le fruit de la Révélation ou de la théologie occidentale en constituent la preuve." Anna Rita Capoccia, "Le Destin", 93.

17 Cf. Artur H. F. Barcelos, *O Mergulho No Seculum*, 314–315.

presupposed the existence of a radical opposition between the inner and the outer space of the mission town, overlapping a series of dichotomies considered as expressions of the natural ordering of the world. The rain-forest, in the official discourse was related not only to the infidels dwelling in it but also to the indigenous ancestors and memories that threatened mission's stability.

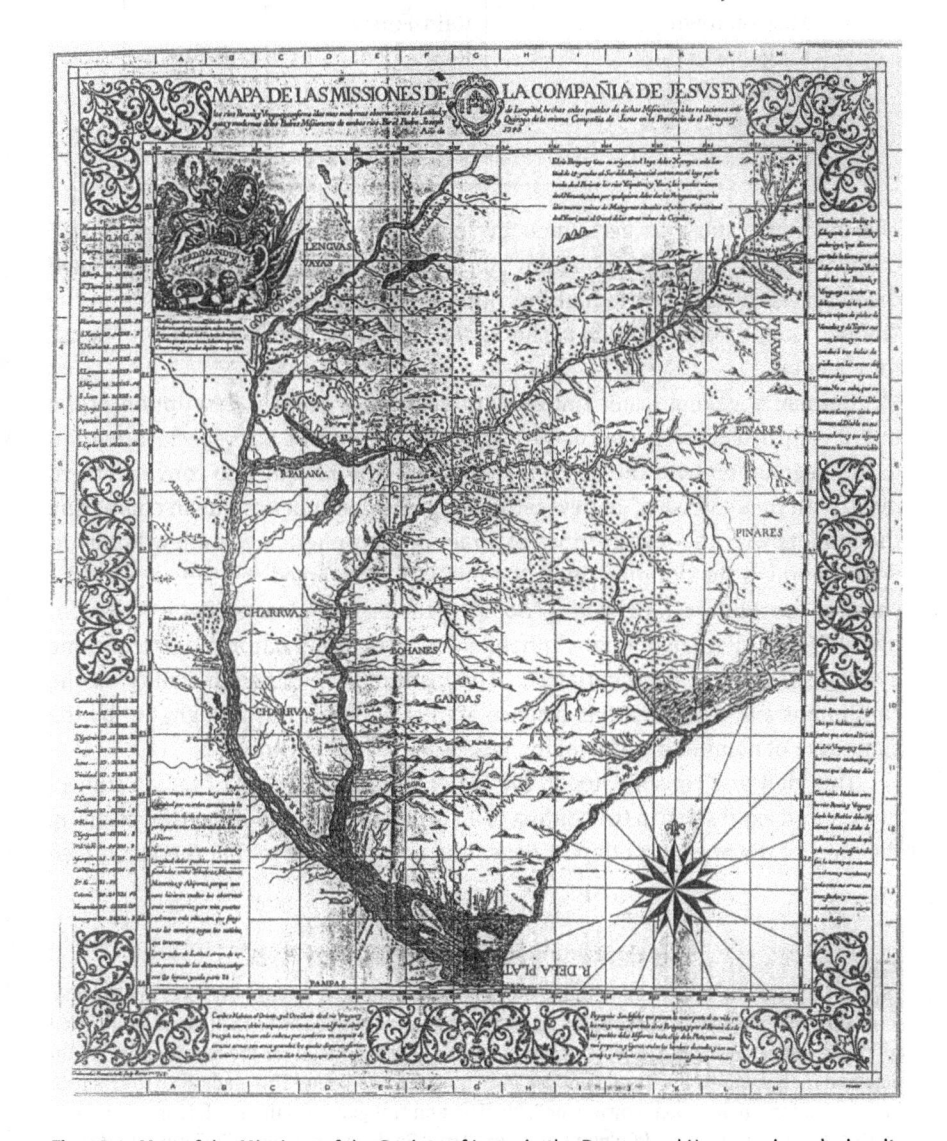

Fig. 12.4: Map of the Missions of the Society of Jesus in the Parana and Uruguay rivers by jesuit Joseph Quiriga with descriptions of the Barbarian Nations, year of 1749

Inner space	Outer Space
Present time (Christians)	Past time (ancestors)
Eternal/Spiritual	Temporal
Heaven	Hell
Order	Chaos
Mission town	Rain-Forest
Kingdom of God	Realm of demons and the devil
Christian Indians	Gentiles, Infidels
Civil life	Savage/Barbarian life
Lambs	Tigers, serpents

The mission history, as accounted by important Jesuit chroniclers of the 17th century was the story of a transition from one pole to the other of the mentioned dichotomies. It was the gradual inscription of the marks of Christianity on the "infidel" soil, a domestication of the Savage mind, the transformation of "lions" into "lambs".[18]

German speaking Jesuit Anton Sepp presents a detailed description of the building up of a mission town at the end of 17th Century. He pays special attention to the negotiation with the indigenous leaders (the *caciques*) to convince them move with their "vassals" to new settlements. He does not hesitate in comparing the Indians with the Jewish tribes of Israel in their pilgrimage to new lands. In Sepp's opinion the building up of the mission represented the control over the chaos of the rainforest. He states: "So many thousands of years after its creation, had this semi-desserted jungle, inhabited only by pagan barbarians, to become a village of catholic paracuarians".[19] The institution of Christian civility on the continuous and undifferentiated space of the rain-forest was brought out by the simple act of nominating and taking possession of the territory.

This view was consolidated in the 18th century. The ideal of Christian subjectivity found expression in the context of an urban life, which was conceived along the lines of the ancient notion of *Polis*. It is not coincidence that the Jesuit José

---

[18] It is important to bear in mind that the Jesuits several times recognize that they are not able to modify the indigenous customs. In many cases they continued with their traditional ritual practices even after having accepted Christian faith. It was difficult for the missionaries to understand indigenous duplicity and ambivalence toward Christianity. This leads as to the issue of how the indians understood "conversion", "belief" and "religion". On this see Eduardo VIVEIROS DE CASTRO, *A inconstancia da alma*; Carlos FAUSTO, "Se deus fosse Jaguar"; Guillermo WILDE, *Religión y poder*.

[19] Antonio SEPP, *Continuación de las Labores Apostólicas*, 194.

Manuel Peramás at the end of 18th century refers to the mission of the Guaraní of Paraguay in terms explicitly drawn from Plato's *Republic*. This vision is probably also informed by other utopias imagined in antiquity.[20]

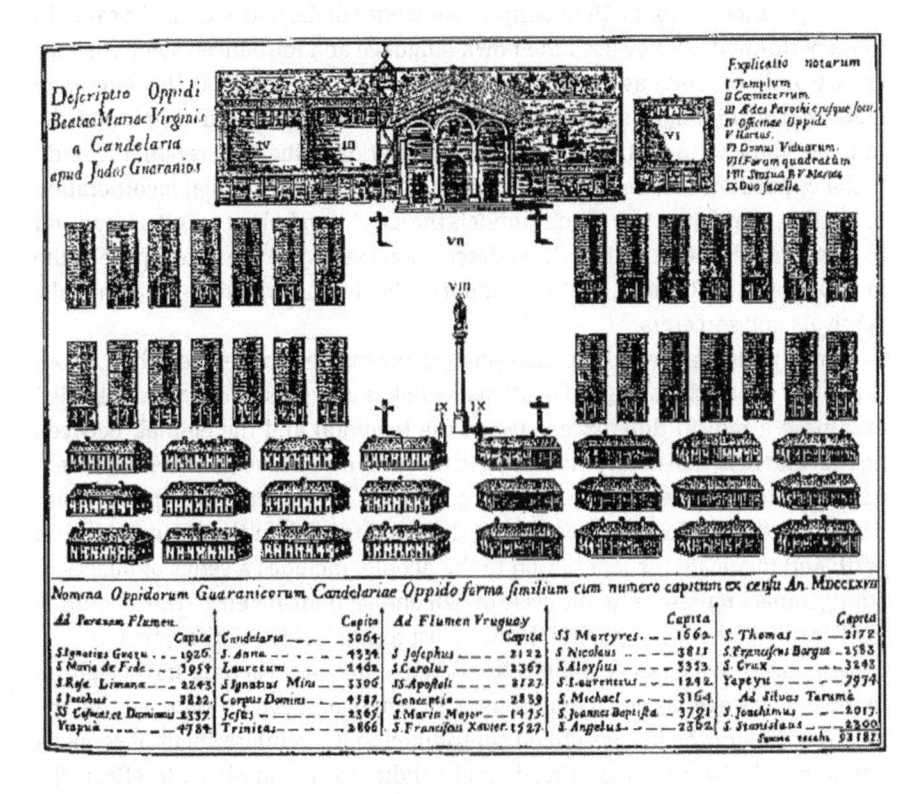

Fig. 12.5: Plane of the Jesuit mission of Candelaria included in Josep Peramás, *Plato´s Republic and the Guarani* (1793).

Frequently, the urban structure became a stage for public performances that pedagogically showed the triumph of the good over the evil through appealing allegories. Sometimes, those performances incorporated local elements in the official narrative, generally elements of nature, such as animals and plants of the land, or eloquent images of the non-converted Indians as symbols of the evil that had

---

20 Much has been written on the links between classical utopias. Among the more important studies see Arno Alvarez KERN, *Missões, Uma Utopia Política*.

to be defeated.[21] A description of one celebration relates that Indian children from the missions used to celebrate with dances and games in which they symbolized the combat between moors and Christians in their typical clothes. They also performed passages from the Holly scripture or scenes of the martyrdom of a saint. In these performances they used their own language and introduced some customs of their nations, such as hunting or "stealing" cattle.[22] Sensorial elements were mobilized to highlight significant moral contrasts that served to instruct the Indians on the virtues of civic life. In the description of the celebration, the traditional opposition between Moors and Christians leads to a gradual incorporation of familiar elements, such as the "infidels indians", symbols of religious, cultural and geographical externality. Other descriptions associate the outer space of the mission town, its beyond, to the kingdom of the devil, undomesticated animals, carnivals and sorcerers.[23]

Once well-established the missions, Jesuits exalted and embellished a conception of civil order and good death using image and music. They also intended to impose a radical difference between the temporal and the eternal, between heaven and hell, insistently inculcated to the Indians. The most conventional representations of heaven and hell also acquire local colorations. The already mentioned treatise by Eusebio Nieremberg, designed to explain the futility of life on earth and inculcate the fear of God in the people, includes a series of images of strong impact representing the cycle of hell and its punishment.[24] The "mouth of hell" is one of the iconographic themes most recognizable in other previous and contemporary works, since it was utilized frequently for preaching and catechism in the modern age, as much in Europe as in America. It can be assumed that the incorporation of the images of hell contributed to the reinforcement of sermons and a visual discourse that already had validity in the missions. In effect, the

---

[21] "Remedan sobre todo con mas perfección las escaramuzas de los infieles y *Charrúas* á caballos: pintándose como ellos los cuerpos desnudos de varios colores y figuras, adornándose cabeza y cintura de penachos de plumas largas de avestruz y capacetes de cuero, y corriendo en pelo, silvando y acometiendo los unos á los otros con las chuzas, con tal celeridad, tendidos sobre el caballo, y haciendo con el cuerpo varios quites, que admiran. Finalmente, el resto del tiempo lo emplean en galopear y correr al rededor de la plaza, haciendo diversos torneos, entradas y salidas, con simetria y órden, á son de trompetas y pitos, en lo que son incansables y tienen sus mas particular y frecuente diversion". Diego de ALVEAR, "Relación geográfica", 485–550, quote p. 535.

[22] In the Saint Ignatius opera, mentioned at the beginning of this article, one interesting element is the presence of the tiger (the jaguar) as a symbol of evil, which may have been part of the daily experience of the indians in the jungle. "Ignatius: Contra este tigre rampante/con mi Dios corro a pugnar/ y con mi escuadrón volante/ quiero guerra presentar (escenas 3 y 6)".

[23] Cf. Mónica MARTINI, "Imagen Del Diablo".

[24] Cf. Guillermo WILDE, "The political Dimension".

subject of the devil and the agonies of hell were commonly exploited by missionaries in their preaching. However, fear to hell was also accompanied by a positive promotion of the reflection on the necessity of having a good devote life and preparing for a good death.

At this point the Beyond of the mission reveals itself as a return to daily life. The initial anthropological desire that triggers the mission ends up anchored to the generation of a practical know-how: the rigid organization of the mission towns, which regulates and administrates the afterlife. The presentation of the topic of death as an experience that may be beautiful introduces an interesting sublimating passage: it manifests a (re)turn to the sensual and earthly (Ignatius' internal fight in the Opera) that acquires a sense linked to an afterlife that remains, once established the missions, too far to be questioned.

"The mission as Beyond" expresses an anthropological desire of overcoming oneself, while "the beyond of the mission" expresses an anthropocentric turn of that desire, represented by the foundation of an anthropological knowledge on the concrete missions, a rationalization, a realization of an imagined order. Desire can be clearly recognized in the very mention of death as a horizon of life. Death takes the place of life, or assumes the role of giving sense to life, endowing it with meaning. This expresses an anthropocentric and sensual (re)turn. At the end, it is in daily life where the sense of the Beyond takes roots. The Beyond becomes diluted in the rigid organization of the missions as imagined by the missionaries; it gets captured by the here and now, making possible the return of desire to the flesh.

Bibliography

Acosta, Josef de, *Historia Natural y Moral De Las Indias. Edición Crítica De Fermín Del Pino-Díaz*. Madrid, CSIC, (1590) 2008.
Alvear, Diego de, "Relación geográfica e histórica de la provincia de Misiones". In Angelis, Pedro de, *Colección de obras y documentos relativos a la historia moderna de las provincias del Río de la Plata*, segunda edición, vol. 3. Buenos Aires, Lajouane, 1910, 485–550.
Barcelos, Artur H. F., *O Mergulho No Seculum: Exploração, Conquista E Organização Espacial Jesuítica Na América Espanhola Colonial*. PH. D. Dissertation, Pontificia Universidad Catolica de Rio Grande do Sul, 2006.
Bargellini, Clara, "At the Center on the Frontier: The Jesuit Tarahumara Missions of New Spain". In *Time and Place: The Geohistory of Art*, edited by Thomas Dacosta Kaufmann. London, Ashgate Press, 2005, 113–34.
Bayne, Brandon, "Converting the Pacific: Jesuit Networks between New Spain and Asia". In *Oxford Handbook of Iberian Borderlands*, edited by Cynthia Radding and Danna Levin. Oxford/NewYork, Oxford University Press, (in press).

Capoccia, Anna Rita, "Le Destin Des *Indipetae* Au-Delà Du Xvie Siècle". In *Missions Religieuses Modernes. "Notre Lieu Est Le Monde"*, edited by Pierre Antoine Fabre and Bernard Vincent. Roma, École Française de Rome, 2007, 89–103.

Castelnau de L'Estoile, Charlotte, "Élection Et Vocation. Le Choix De La Mission Dans La Province Jésuite Du Portugal À La Fin Du Xvie Siècle", *Collection de l'Ecole française de Rome* 376, 2007, 21–43.

Castelnau-L'Estoile, Charlotte de, Marie L. Copete, Aliocha Maldavsky, and Ines G. Županov, eds., *Missions D'Évangelisation Et Circulation Des Savoirs (Xvie-Xviiie Siècle)*. Madrid/Paris, Casa de Velasquez-EHESS, 2011.

Colombo, Emanuele. "Jesuitas Y Musulmanes En La Europa Del Siglo Xvii". In *Saberes De La Conversión. Jesuitas, Indígenas E Imperios Coloniales En Las Fronteras De La Cristiandad*, edited by Guillermo Wilde. Buenos Aires, Editorial SB, 2011.

Corsi, Elisabetta, *Órdenes Religiosas Entre América Y Asia: Ideas Para Una Historia Misionera De Los Espacios Coloniales*. 1. ed. México, D.F.: Colegio de México, 2008.

Fabre, Pierre Antoine. "Un Désir Antérieur. Les Premiers Jésuites Des Philippines Et Leurs Indipetae (1580–1605)". In *Missions Religieuses Modernes. "Notre Lieu Est Le Monde"*, edited by Pierre Antoine Fabre and Bernard Vincent. Rome, École Fran-caise de Rome, 2007, 71–88.

Fausto, Carlos, "Se Deus Fosse Jaguar: Canibalismo E Cristianismo Entre Os Guarani (XVI-XX Séculos)", *Mana* 11, no. 2, 2005, 385–418.

Kern, Arno Alvarez, *Missões, Uma Utopia Política* (Série Documenta 14). Porto Alegre, Mercado Aberto, 1982.

Maldavsky, Aliocha, *Vocaciones Inciertas. Misión Y Misioneros En La Provincia Jesuita Del Perú En Los Siglos Xvi Y Xvii*. Sevilla, Consejo Superior de Investigaciones Científicas, 2012.

Martini, Mónica Patricia, "Imagen Del Diablo En Las Reducciones Guaraníes", *Investigaciones y Ensayos* 40, 1990, 335–60.

Mungello, David E., ed., *The Chinese Rites Controversy. Its History and Meaning* (Monumenta Serica, 33), publ. by Institut Monumenta Serica, Sankt Augustin, and the Ricci Institute for Chinese-Western Cultural History. San Francisco. Nettetal, Steyler, 1994.

Rubiés, Joan Pau, "The Concept of Cultural Dialogue and the Jesuit Method of Accommodation: Between Idolatry and Civilization", *Archivum Historicum Societatis Iesu* 76, no. 147, 2005, 237–80.

Ruiz de Montoya, Antonio, *La Conquista Espiritual Del Paraguay*, edited by Estudio Preliminar de Ernesto Maeder. Rosario, Equipo Difusor de Estudios de Historia Iberoamericana, (1639) 1989.

San Ignacio, L'Opéra Perdu Des Missions Jésuites De L'Amazonie. Ensemble Elyma, dir. Gabriel Garrido. K617 Recordings. Notes by Bernardo Illari. Series: Chemins du Baroque, 1996 (CD Booklet).

"St. Ignatius Loyola – A Mission Opera: An Emblem of the Mission." Introduction. The Jesuit Operas: Operas by Kapsberger and Zipoli. Ensemble Abendmusik. Dir. James David Christie. Dorian Recordings, 2002.

Sepp, Antonio, *Continuación De Las Labores Apostólicas*, Edición Crítica De Las Obras Del Padre Antonio Sepp S.J., Misionero En La Argentina Desde 1691 Hasta 1733 / a Cargo De Werner Hoffmann. Buenos Aires, Editorial Universitaria de Buenos Aires, 1973.

Viveiros de Castro, Eduardo, *A Inconstancia Da Alma Selvagem*. São Paulo, Cosac & Naify, 2002.

Wilde, Guillermo, *Religión Y Poder En Las Misiones De Guaraníes*. Buenos Aires, Editorial SB, 2009.

Wilde, Guillermo, "The Political Dimension of Space-Time Categories in the Jesuit Missions of Paraguay (17th and 18th Centuries)". In *Space and Conversion in Global Perspective.*, edited by Giuseppe Marcocci, Wietse De Boer, Aliocha Maldavsky and Ilaria Pavan. Leiden, Brill, 2014, 175–213.

Zampelli, Michael, "Opera News: Jesuits, Catholic Imagination, and the Staging of Cultural Conversations". In *Catholic Theatre and Drama. Critical Essays*, edited by Kevn J. Wetmore. Jefferson, NY, McFarland, 162–180.

Županov, Ines G., "El Repliegue De Lo Religioso: Misioneros Jesuitas En La India Del Siglo Xvii, Entre La Teología Cristiana Y La Ética Pagana". In *Saberes De La Conversión. Jesuitas, Indígenas E Imperios Coloniales En Las Fronteras De La Cristiandad*, edited by Guillermo Wilde. Buenos Aires, Editorial SB, 2011, 435–58.

Pictures

"The Ignatian Tree" engraving in Athanasius Kircher´s *Ars magna lucis et umbrae* (Rome, 1646).

Engraving from Eusebio Nieremberg´s *De la Diferencia entre lo Temporal y lo Eterno*, translated to Guarani language and printed in the Jesuit missions of Paraguay.

Anonymous, Allegory of the Society of Jesus and the pastoral labor in the four continents, Church of San Pedro, Lima, Peru, 18th century.

Map of the Missions of the Society of Jesus in the Parana and Uruguay rivers by jesuit Joseph Quiriga with descriptions of the Barbarian Nations, year of 1749.

Plane of the Jesuit mission of Candelaria included in Josep Peramás, Plato´s Republic and the Guarani (1793).

Gideon Bohak
Expelling Demons and Attracting Demons in Jewish Magical Texts

The Babylonian Talmud, composed in present-day Iraq between the third and sixth centuries CE, is the foundational text of medieval and modern Judaism.[1] Among the numerous topics it discusses, it also has much to say about demons. One of its more famous statements on this score characterizes them as follows –

> Six things were said about demons – in three (things) they are like the angels of service, and in three (things) they are like human beings. In three things they are like the angels of service – they have wings like the angels of service, and they fly from one end of the world to the other like the angels of service, and they know the future like the angels of service [...] And in three things they are like human beings – they eat and drink like human beings, and procreate like human beings, and die like human beings.[2]

This statement offers an interesting generalization about the demons, their nature, and their place in the world – they have wings and can fly great distances, they have access to various secrets, they procreate and they die. Implicitly, it also tells us where the demons belong in the ancient Jewish conceptualization of the Beyond – first comes the one and only God, then the angels, who are his underlings and messengers, and then the demons, below whom are we, humans, who watch this entire celestial hierarchy from below. The demons, in other words, are up there in the heavenly realms, but on their lowest rungs; this might also explain why encounters with them were deemed to be frequent, as we shall soon see.[3]

While this Talmudic statement tells us much about the demons, it also leaves much that is unsaid. To anyone accustomed to Christian discourse, the absence of any reference to the demons' evil nature might seem like a strange omission, since we might have expected a clear contrast to be drawn here between angels, who are inherently good, and demons, who are inherently evil. But rabbinic literature thinks differently, and although many statements and stories in the Babylonian Talmud make demons seem inherently evil, others imply that they only

---

[1] The research for the present paper was funded by the Israel Science Foundation (Grant No. 986/14). I am grateful to the organizers of the conference on "The Beyond as a Challenge of Life" for their wonderful hospitality, and to the conference participants for their helpful comments on an earlier draft of this paper.
[2] Babylonian Talmud, Ḥagigah 16a.
[3] For the rabbinic views of demons, see Ludwig BLAU, *Das altjüdische Zauberwesen*; Sara A. RONIS, *Do Not Go Out Alone*; Gideon BOHAK, "Conceptualizing Demons".

DOI 10.1515/9783110530773-013

attack people who harm them or invade their territory, and others even make it clear that some demons are inherently good.

This might be the rabbinic view, as expressed in the Babylonian Talmud. But outside the Talmud, yet still in Babylonia, we have abundant evidence of how some Jews viewed demons as malevolent and dangerous, and of the great lengths to which they went in order to lock such demons up or keep them out of their own homes. The evidence for this comes in the form of incantation bowls, that is, standard earthenware bowls on the inside of which were written elaborate spells and adjurations. These bowls were produced in late-antique Babylonia, from about the fifth to about the eighth century CE, and the texts written upon them were intended to ward off demons, and a whole host of other dangers, and keep them away from the bowls' owners, who are often named, and from their children, their cattle, and their other belongings. As a very typical example, we may look at the first four sentences of the text of one such bowl, written in Jewish Babylonian Aramaic –

> This writing to bind, and muzzle, and lock up, and take out, and remove all demons, and *dews*, and howlers, and lilis, and tormentors, and evil spirits, and wicked charms, male idols and female idols, male and female, and all plagues, necklace charms, and ban, and tormentor, and barren spirit, and barren Lilith, male or female. All of you, hear this adjuration and receive this oath. Go out and remove yourselves from Maḥlafta daughter of Imai and from her fetus in her belly, and from her house in which she lives, and from her dwelling. Again, may you not come against her, and may you not appear to her, not in her house and not in her dwelling from this day and this time and forever.[4]

In reconstructing the social realia behind this text, we can easily imagine a situation in which Maḥlafta, daughter of Imai, became pregnant, and – fearing the demons that lurk in her house – went to a bowl producer, who wrote for her an elaborate adjuration (which we did not quote here), aimed against a whole list of demons and evil beings, who are listed at the beginning of the text. To us, it is not always clear what are the exact differences between demons, *dews* (*dew* being the Persian word for a demon), howlers, tormentors, evil spirits, and so on, but it is extremely clear that the bowl producers tried to cover all possibilities, and expel all evil creatures from their clients' homes. In this, the bowls' texts are not unlike those modern insecticides whose producers promise that they kill more than a hundred different bugs, the idea being that the user cannot really know which bug would be attacking his home or his garden, and prefers not to buy many different insecticides. If a single powerful mixture can do the job by itself, the user would surely buy it.

---

4 Dan LEVENE, *A Corpus*, 40–41 (No. M101).

One could adduce hundreds of bowls whose texts list all the different types of demons that the bowls seek to expel and drive away, or to muzzle and bind. But side by side with the texts, some of these bowls carry images of demons, thus enabling us a glimpse of their physical appearance in the Jews' *imaginaire*. Only about 20 % of the bowls carry images (for example, the bowl whose text we just quoted has no image), but the number of images available to us is in the hundreds.[5] In a vast majority of these images, we see bound creatures, often depicted as hybrids, or as composite creatures – a human face, chicken legs, wings, and so on. This feature of the demons is, of course, a recurrent feature in many artistic traditions: think, for example, of Hieronymus Bosch's hybrid demons, or of the depiction of demons in ancient Mesopotamian or Egyptian art. However, in the present paper I am less interested in the common human tendency to depict malevolent creatures as made up of pieces taken from different animals.[6] I am more interested in how the images on the Babylonian incantation bowls reflect the Jewish attitude towards demons in Late Antiquity.

As one very typical example, let us look at Fig. 13.1.[7] The image here is that of a human figure, who is identified in a caption (which is not reflected in the line-drawing), as "an evil Lilith." She seems to be naked, and her breasts are marked by two circlets on her chest; but her "feet" clearly are those of some bird of prey, and the dots on her legs imply that she has chicken legs.[8] Her armpits are not shaven, she wears an unusual hat or an elaborate hairdo, and she is bound with an iron chain that binds her two legs and ties them to her neck. The fact that her hands are crossed is significant, as in most other bowl-images the figures' hands would be crossed and shackled. Thus, just as the bowls' texts seek to expel, or bind, a whole host of demons, the bowls' iconography too seeks to bind them in strong chains, and prevent them from harming their potential victims.

Looking at other bowls, we may easily note how some of the images they carry are those of less human, and more ambiguous creatures, whose very boundaries

---

[5] For a detailed study, see Naama Vilozny, *Lilith's Hair*. See also Erica C.D. Hunter, "Who Are the Demons?"; Naama Vilozny, "Lilith's Hair and Ashmedai's Horns"; Naama Vilozny, "Between Demons and Kings".

[6] For this tendency see, for example, Reuven Tsur, "The Demonic and the Grotesque"; David Wengrow, *The Origins of Monsters*, esp. pp. 99–104.

[7] All the line-drawings presented below were produced by Naama Vilozny, who kindly let me use them.

[8] This aspect of the physical appearance of some demons is amply attested in the Babylonian Talmud, e. g., Berakhot 6a and Gittin 68b.

are extremely fluid (see, for example, Fig. 13.2 and 3), whereas others are quite scary (see, for example, Fig. 13.4 and 5). And what is perhaps most striking about all these images is that they vary so greatly. Clearly, there was not a single way to depict demons, and each artist could imagine them at will, and draw them to the best of his artistic abilities. Thus, they provide us an excellent point of entry into the iconographic *imaginaire* of the Jews of late-antique Mesopotamia.[9]

Fig. 13.1: After Naama VILOZNY, *Lilith's Hair*, 328 (No. 51)

The incantation bowls have much to tell us about how the Jews of late-antique Babylonia conceptualized demons, and how desperately they tried to keep those demons away. In late-antique Palestine, the practice of producing incantation bowls is unattested, but the fear of demons is well documented in the Second Temple period – as may easily be seen from the many exorcisms performed by

---

9 Some of the bowls were written in non-Jewish Aramaic dialects, such as Mandaic, and they too display some images, but these will not be analyzed in the present study.

Fig. 13.2: After Naama VILOZNY, *Lilith's Hair*, 347 (No. 69)

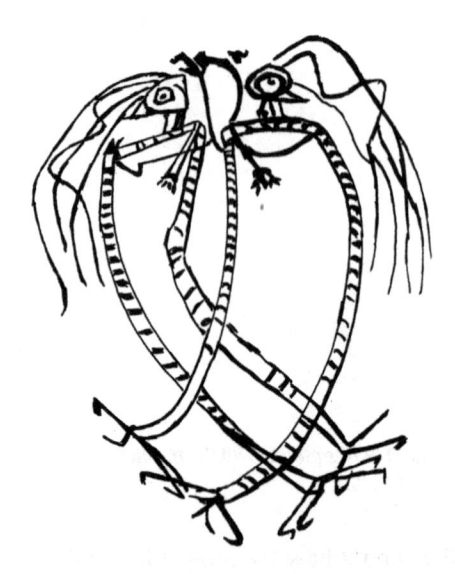

Fig. 13.3: After Naama VILOZNY, *Lilith's Hair*, 307 (No. 30)

Jesus and his disciples, or from the exorcistic manuals found among the Dead Sea scrolls – and it remained pervasive in later periods as well.[10] And while the Jews of Palestine produced no incantation bowls, they did produce written amulets,

---

10 For a fuller survey, see Gideon BOHAK, *Ancient Jewish Magic*, 88–114.

Expelling Demons and Attracting Demons in Jewish Magical Texts — 175

Fig. 13.4: After Naama VILOZNY, *Lilith's Hair*, 339 (No. 62)

Fig. 13.5: After Naama VILOZNY, *Lilith's Hair*, 342 (No. 64)

attested from the third or fourth century CE down to the seventh or eighth century. These amulets, inscribed either on papyrus, which in most cases did not survive, or on thin sheets of metal, which in some cases did survive, tell us much about the fears of the Jews of Palestine, including the many demons against which such amulets were produced.[11] Unfortunately, these amulets are almost never accompanied by images, but the texts upon them suffice to show how pervasive the fear of demons was in late-antique Palestine as well.

Reading the Babylonian Jewish incantation bowls, and the Palestinian Jewish amulets, we get the clear impression that Jews in both communities shared a deep-seated fear of demons. This impression is strengthened when we read the stories found in rabbinic literature, including the Babylonian Talmud, of the harm caused by demons to many different people on numerous occasions. But occasionally, these sources also make it clear that certain people – and especially some famous rabbis, whose sanctity would protect them – were less afraid of demons.[12] And in a few cases, they claim that some people ask the demons various questions, and even imply that some people knew how to coerce demons to do their will.[13] The most famous example is the rabbinic story of how King Solomon had once subdued Ashmedai the King of the demons and used him in his efforts to build the Jerusalem Temple.[14] And yet, such claims are quite rare, and the vast majority of the ancient Jewish sources point to a pervasive fear of demons, and consistent attempts not to provoke them, or to drive them away, rather than subjugate them and use them as one's own servants.

If in the period up to the rise of Islam we have no real evidence of Jews who were actively dealing with demons, in a later period, such evidence becomes abundant, and quite detailed. Displaying the clear impact of the Arabic understanding of *jinn*s and of their potential uses (think, for example, of Aladdin's Lamp), some Jewish texts of the early Middle Ages provide their readers with detailed blueprints for conjuring demons from different places, gathering them to a single location, and forcing them to do one's bidding. Let us look at one typical example -

> If you wish to rule over the demons and all the spirits and evil demons, and the twelve families that descended from Heaven in the days of Satan their father, you should first study this book, and their names, and the names of their families, and each type thereof, and when you want to subjugate them by force and bring them by coercion, whether by day or by night, go to a place where no women live, in a separate, well-appointed house, and sweep

---

11 For broad surveys, and much further bibliography, see Gideon Bohak, *Ancient Jewish Magic*, 114–123 and 149–153; Hanan Eshel and Rivka Leiman, "Jewish Amulets".
12 See, for example, bt Pessaḥim 112b, where both Rabbi Ḥanina ben Dosa and Abaye are said to be immune to demonic attacks; and cf. the story in bt Pessaḥim 111b, of Rav Papa's (temporary) immunity.
13 For claims about consulting demons, see, for example, bt Sanhedrin 101a.
14 For this story, see bt Gittin 68a-b. Similar traditions are found in the *Testament of Solomon*, and in some of the Gnostic texts from Nag Hammadi.

the house floor well, and make a circle in front of the front door. Then make in the circle four openings, to the four cardinal directions, and place on each opening a clay vessel full of coals, and fumigate an incense called Custus (?). And leave the house open for the whole day and the whole night.[15]

The elaborate instructions go on and on; you are supposed to enter the circle while holding a knife made of Indian steel, to write twelve sacred names and place them in your lap, to burn more incense, and to recite an elaborate adjuration, intended to make the demons come "from all the mountains, and all the hills, and all the fields, and all the seas, and all the rivers, and all the streams, and all the lakes, and all the market-places, and all the streets, and all the bath-houses, and all the courtyards," and immediately fulfill your requests and wishes.[16]

Reading such detailed texts – which are found in the Jewish world in Judaeo-Arabic and in Hebrew, and in several different versions – we might detect a U-turn in the Jewish attitude towards demons: From the fear of demons in the ancient Jewish sources, and the almost desperate attempts to exorcize them and drive them away, or to bind them and render them impotent, to the rituals that seek to attract demons and to subjugate them in medieval Jewish sources. This move is in no way unique to the Jewish world, and the rituals for adjuring and coercing demons were extremely popular not only in the Muslim world, whence they came to the Jews' attention, but in the Christian world as well. Thus, to mention just one famous example, the celebrated Florentine jeweler and sculptor, Benvenuto Cellini provides in his *Autobiography* an extremely detailed account of two consecutive nights in which he had such a ritual conducted on his behalf, and in his presence, in the Roman Coliseum, in 1533 or 1534 CE.[17] And yet, for the purpose of the present paper, I wish to focus exclusively on the Jewish evidence, and to highlight the gap between the fear of demons common among ancient Jews, and the eagerness with which some of these Jews' descendants tried to gather demons together and coerce them into their own service. How are we to explain this great transformation of the Jewish attitudes towards demons from one period to the next?

In thinking of the two different attitudes towards demons that we examined above, we may adopt several different strategies. From an historical perspective, we could easily argue that whereas fear of demons is pervasive in many cultures,

---

15 For the Hebrew text, see Gershom SCHOLEM, "Some Sources", 7. The English translation is my own.
16 Gershom SCHOLEM, "Some Sources", 8.
17 See Benvenuto CELLINI, *Autobiography*, 120–121.

the techniques to subdue them are much less common, and arise only in certain times and places. In the Jewish case, it was not some "natural" historical development that led from one set of attitudes to another, but the exposure to a new, and dominant, culture, namely Islam, which brought with it a new set of technologies for the subjugation of demons, technologies that were simply unavailable to the Jews of earlier periods. From a sociological perspective, we must note that the texts we are reading probably reflect two very different social phenomena: On the one hand, we have the ancient incantation bowls and amulets, which were written for hundreds of different clients, and reflect these clients' fear of demons and of many other sources of evil. On the other hand, we have a dozen, or two dozen, medieval manuscripts, copied and used by a small group of learned Jewish practitioners of the occult, for their own benefits and for the benefit of their clients. Thus, the fact that some medieval Jews were conjuring and subduing demons does not mean that other Jews were not trying to thwart and expel such demons at the very same time. In fact, we have much evidence to prove that this indeed was the case. As one example out of many, we may note that the Cairo Genizah (the "used-paper storage room" of a medieval synagogue in Cairo, which yielded some 300,000 textual fragments) preserves several very interesting specimens of demon-gathering texts, but also preserves numerous amulets, many of which are anti-demonic in nature.[18] Thus, we should not say that in the Middle Ages Jews stopped fearing demons, but that many Jews kept on fearing them, while a small group of specialists learned how to lord it over them.

The historical and the sociological perspectives thus go some way towards explaining the seeming anomaly on which we focus here, but one can, and should, also look at this anomaly from a third perspective, that of Religious Studies. For when we look at the Jewish attitudes towards the demonic residents of the Beyond, we must note how in all periods of Jewish history we can sense a certain ambivalence, a dual attitude towards demons, an attitude that mixes fear and attraction, loathing and fascination, a wish to expel the demons, and a desire to see them. In terms borrowed from Rudolf Otto's famous book on *The (Idea of the) Holy*, I would argue that these denizens of the Beyond were both a *mysterium tremendum*, to be feared, and avoided, and a *mysterium fascinans*, attracting whoever saw them or thought of their potential powers.[19] Thus, even in periods when Jews sought to repel demons they also found them quite tempting,

---

18 For Genizah texts for gathering demons see, for example, Peter SCHÄFER and Shaul SHAKED, *Magische Texte*, vol. 1, No. 1; vol. 2, No. 51; vol. 3, Nos. 62 and 66. For Genizah amulets, see esp. Lawrence H. SCHIFFMAN and Michael D. SWARTZ, *Hebrew and Aramaic Incantation Texts*; for amulets against demons, see ibid., Nos. 2, 5, 8, etc.
19 See Rudolf OTTO, *The Idea of the Holy*, chapters 4 and 6.

and even when Jews tried to conjure and subdue demons, they also found them very frightening.

Before turning to some late-antique and early-medieval examples of this ambivalence, we may briefly point to one well-known biblical precedent, which nicely demonstrates this combination of fear and attraction. This is the story of King Saul's visit to the necromancer of Endor, who enables him to talk to the dead prophet, Samuel (1 Sam 28). Here, we are not dealing with demons, but with a ghost, but we can easily sense the same kind of ambivalence that is apparent in the later Jewish attitudes towards demons. On the one hand, we are told at the very beginning of the story (1 Sam. 28.1) that Saul had "removed" all the necromancers, an action which no doubt reflects the age-old biblical prohibition against consulting such practitioners (see Dt 18.10-11). On the other hand, the story informs us that Samuel was dead, the Philistines were getting ready for a major battle, Saul was afraid of their military might, and all his attempts to learn from God what he must do and what is about to happen were answered with a deafening silence (1 Sam 28.3-6). Torn between the prohibition against necromancers, which he himself had enforced, and the desire to talk to Samuel, as he had done when Samuel was alive, Saul decided to consult a necromancer. He went to her, incognito, she raised Samuel's ghost, and Samuel was furious with Saul for having bothered him (1 Sam 28.15). Samuel then accurately foretold of the disaster about to befall Saul, his sons, and his people on the following day, and Saul was extremely frightened (1 Sam 28.20-21). And so, readers of this story are sure to deduce that consulting necromancers is forbidden, but that they can accurately foretell the future, and that ghosts are very frightful, but also very useful. Consulting them may not be for the faint of heart, but in some situations it is simply irresistible

Returning from this biblical example to the later Jewish sources, we may note some pertinent examples of the very same ambivalence. Beginning with the Aramaic incantation bowls, we may note that one recurrent theme, which appears in quite a few bowls, is that the demons are adjured not only to stay out of the homes of the named clients, but also not to appear to them in various forms, neither by night nor during the day. In some cases, it seems as if the reference is to nightmarish apparitions, as the demons are addressed, for example, "... you bark like dogs, you grunt like pigs, you hiss lie snakes... you make yourselves visible to Yawitai daughter of Ḥatai in bad dreams, in a hateful shape," and this is followed by a long list of all the shapes in which they appear, including those of donkeys, lions, wolves, tigers, and so on.[20] But in other cases, it is very clear that

---

20 Joseph NAVEH and Shaul SHAKED, *Amulets and Magic Bowls*, 201 (Bowl 13, ll. 10–13).

the demons who appear in the clients' dreams and visions do not only frighten them, they also seduce them. Note, for example, a bowl that refers to "the evil Lilith, who leads astray the hearts of human beings and appears in a dream by night or a vision by day."[21] Here, we seem to be dealing less with the scary or disgusting appearance of a demon, and more with a demonic apparition that might lead people astray – a notion that is well attested already in the Dead Sea Scrolls and in the New Testament.[22] And in other bowls, the "leading astray" carries explicitly sexual overtones, as in the following adjuration -

> Healing from Heaven for Mihraṭ son of Shaburdukh. I adjure you, male *lili* and female *lili*, who has accompanied Mihraṭ son of Shaburdukh and who dwells in his house, that you not show yourself to him in the form of a man [or] the form of a woman, nor as a related woman or as an unrelated woman, and do not appear to him in any form, and do not lie down with him, not in a dream of the night nor in a dream of the day [...].[23]

Fig. 13.6: After Naama VILOZNY, *Lilith's Hair*, 293 (No. 18).

Here, the reference to the demon "lying down" with the hapless victim is unmistakable, and it ties in extremely well with numerous references in rabbinic literature to the seductive powers of the demons. "If a man sleeps alone in a house,"

---

21 See J.B. SEGAL, *Catalogue*, 99 (No. 068A).
22 For demons who lead people astray, see, for example, the Qumran exorcistic hymns 4Q510-511, or such scenes as Mk 1.12–13 and parallels. Needless to add, later Christian literature provides numerous examples of Saints fighting seductive demons.
23 This bowl was first edited by Christa MÜLLER-KESSLER, *Die Zauberschalentexte*, 40 (No. 10); it was re-edited in James Nathan FORD and Matthew MORGENSTERN, *Aramaic Incantation Bowls*, and my translation follows theirs, with minor modifications.

says the Babylonian Talmud, "Lilith will seize him."[24] Adam, the primordial man, was said by the rabbis to have had sex with quite a few demons.[25] And in the early Middle Ages, we find a famous story – known as "The Story of the Jerusalemite" – of a man who married a female demon, the daughter of Ashmedai, the king of the demons.[26] That the notion of demonic seduction of human beings – and especially of female demons seducing innocent men – was shared by the producers of the incantation bowls is made clear not only by the texts we have just quoted, but also by the images on some of the bowls. Of these, by far the most explicit example appears on a bowl in the Lycklama Museum in Cannes, shown in Fig. 13.6. Looking at such an image, a modern viewer is immediately reminded of Playboy magazine, or of Gustave Courbet's notorious picture, "L'Origine du monde." An ancient viewer probably would have added that depicting a female figure fully naked, and with her hair disheveled, was an act of extreme humiliation for the figure thus depicted. But both would agree that the figure is more demonic than human (note her fingers!), and yet is quite sensual. Thus, it is a fitting example of the seductiveness of some demons in the eyes of some Jewish viewers.

Returning to the image we examined above (Fig. 13.1), we may note that here too the bowl producers seem to have tried to create a seductive image, of a female figure whose hands are raised above her head in a dance-like motion, and with her breasts probably exposed. In another bowl (Fig. 13.7), the image displays a woman who is wearing a dress, but is twisting her body in a dancing motion, and probably banging some musical instrument such as cymbals. Her open mouth suggests that she is singing and her hair is, once again, disheveled. We can easily imagine this as the image of a woman with very loose morals, seductive but also dangerous.[27] And in another bowl (Fig. 13.8), we find once again a naked female demon, this time identified by a caption, "this is the image of Mevakhalta (i. e., "the (female) tormentor"), who appears in dreams and in (different) forms." In this image, the demon clearly is a hybrid creature, but it seems to have a pair of breasts, and it certainly has a large female sexual organ. And, as Guillermo Wilde suggested to me, the artist who produced this image may have been trying to depict the demon as possessing a *vagina dentata*, certainly one of the most

---

24 See bt Shabbat 151b.
25 See Genesis Rabba 20.20 (Theodor-Albeck 195–196). A fuller version of this tradition is found in the *Stories of Ben Sira*.
26 For this story and its many different versions, see Yehudah Leib ZLOTNICK, *Maaseh Yerushalmi*.
27 In this specific case, it is not clear whether the figure is bound, but a similar image (see Naama VILOZNY, *Lilith's Hair*, 288, No. 13) has the figure's feet bound by one chain, her neck and hands by another.

explicit symbols in human history of the mixture of attraction and fear in the male view of the female body.[28]

Fig. 13.7: After Naama VILOZNY, *Lilith's Hair*, 287 (No. 12)

Fig. 13.8: After Naama VILOZNY, *Lilith's Hair*, 326 (No. 49)

In light of this discourse of seduction, in its verbal and pictorial manifestations, I believe that we may safely conclude that ancient Jews feared demons, but were also attracted to them. In fact, we might even suggest that one more reason why the demons had to be expelled, or bound, is that they could be so seductive. And, to wrap up this discussion with one more talmudic example, we may quote the lovely rabbinic explanation of how one may see the demons, who normally are invisible -

---

28 For this motif, see, for example, Jill RAITT, "The 'Vagina Dentata'".

> If one wishes to seem them, he should take the afterbirth of a black cat, born of a black cat, the first-born one, born of a first-born one, and he should burn it in a fire and grind it and fill his eyes with it, and he will see them. ... Rav Bibi, son of Abaye, did this; he saw (them), but was hurt. The Rabbis prayed for him, and he was healed.

That the son of Abaye, who is one of the foremost rabbinic figures in the Babylonian Talmud, was so curious about demons that he badly wanted to see them is in itself an interesting demonstration of their seductive nature. The story claims that he got what he asked for, and indeed saw the demons, but the experiment ended up badly, and the rabbis had to pray for their colleague's son until he regained his health. Clearly, the moral of the story is that one *can* see the demons, but it is much safer not to, even if the temptation to see them is very great. Elsewhere, the Babylonian Talmud has much to say on how to avoid harming the demons and being harmed by them, and even how to write amulets to ward them off.[29]

Thus far, we focused on the incantation bowls of Late Antiquity, and saw that in spite of their anti-demonic rhetoric, they also reflect a certain attraction towards demons, an attraction that makes the need to drive them away even more urgent. Similarly, but much more explicitly, the medieval Jewish texts that seek to gather demons together and use their great powers are just as ambivalent. Returning to the text from which we quoted above, and examining some of its instructions, we find the following warnings –

> But before you enter the circle, examine yourself and your soul, (and) if it is strong and able to sit in the circle, you should sit with a good and strong and powerful heart, and you should be like a man whose sword is drawn in his hand. And do not be afraid, and do not become weak before them (= the demons); when they come, raise your voice, and add on to your words, and know and understand that if they come to you in evil apparitions, you should know that they wish to frighten you; do not become frightened, and sit like a hero and adjure (them).[30]

What is very clear here is that the rituals for adjuring demons should never be taken lightly. If you follow the book's instructions, you will be able to subdue them, and thus reap many rewards. But the demons are extremely dangerous, and if you show them that you are afraid, they will attack you – and you will be greatly harmed. Moreover, they will "come to you in evil apparitions," just as they did to the owners of the incantation bowls many centuries earlier, and you must be strong in order to achieve your goal.[31] In other words, dealing with demons is

---

29 For specific examples, see Gideon BOHAK, *Ancient Jewish Magic*, 366, 373–376.
30 Gershom SCHOLEM, "Some Sources", 7–8.
31 Benvenuto CELLINI, in his *Autobiography* (see above, n. 17), provides striking descriptions of the great fear aroused in his companions when the demons swarmed all around them, so much so that one of the participants shat in his pants for fear.

a very dangerous affair, and yet it is also very lucrative, and so, if you are brave enough, and have the right book, you might just go ahead and do it.

We have seen a handful of examples, to which many more could be added, showing that in different periods of Jewish history, demons posed a great threat, but also were a source of great attraction. Moreover, these two forces could not easily be separated, since it is their ability to attract and seduce people that added to the danger they posed, and it is the danger they posed which only added to their attraction. Living on the lower rungs of *the Beyond*, these creatures provide a clear example of the Jewish ambivalence towards much of that supernal realm, at once both fearful and fascinating, attractive yet very dangerous.

Bibliography

Blau, Ludwig, *Das altjüdische Zauberwesen*. Berlin, Louis Lamm, ²1914.
Bohak, Gideon, *Ancient Jewish Magic: A History*. Cambridge, Cambridge University Press, 2008.
Bohak, Gideon, "Conceptualizing Demons in Late Antique Judaism". In *Demons and Illness from Antiquity to the Early-Modern Period*, edited by Siam Bhayro and Catherine Rider (Magical and Religious Literature of Late Antiquity, 5). Leiden, Brill, 2017, 111–133.
Cellini, Benvenuto, *Autobiography*, translated by George Bull. Harmondsworth, Penguin, 1956.
Eshel, Hanan, and Rivka Leiman, "Jewish Amulets Written on Metal Scrolls", *Journal of Ancient Judaism* 1, 2010, 189–199.
Ford, James Nathan, and Matthew Morgenstern (with Ohad Abudraham), *Aramaic Incantation Bowls in Museum Collections, vol. 1: The Frau Hilprecht Collection, Jena*. Leiden, Brill, forthcoming.
Hunter, Erica C. D., "Who Are the Demons?: The Iconography of Incantations Bowls". In *Magic in the Ancient Near East*, edited by S. Ribichini (Studi Epigrafici e Linguistici sul Vicino Oriente antico, 15). Verona, Essedue, 1998, 95–116.
Levene, Dan, *A Corpus of Magic Bowls: Incantation Texts in Jewish Aramaic from Late Antiquity*. (The Kegan Paul Library of Jewish Studies). London, Kegan Paul, 2003.
Müller-Kessler, Christa, *Die Zauberschalentexte in der Hilprecht-Sammlung Jena, und weitere Nippur-Texte anderer Sammlungen*. Wiesbaden, Harrassowitz, 2005.
Naveh, Joseph, and Shaul Shaked, *Amulets and Magic Bowls: Aramaic Incantations of Late Antiquity*. Jerusalem, Magnes Press, 1985.
Otto, Rudolf, *The Idea of the Holy*, translated by John H. Harvey. Oxford, Oxford University Press, ²1923.
Raitt, Jill, "The 'Vagina Dentata' and the 'Immaculatus Uterus Divini Fontis'", *Journal of the American Academy of Religion* 48, 1980, 415–431.
Ronis, Sara A., *"Do Not Go Out Alone at Night": Law and Demonic Discourse in the Babylonian Talmud*. PhD Diss., Yale University, 2015.
Schäfer, Peter, and Shaul Shaked, *Magische Texte aus der Kairoer Geniza*. 3 vols., (Texte und Studien zum Antiken Judentum 42, 64, 72). Tübingen, Mohr Siebeck, 1994–1999.

Schiffman, Lawrence H., and Michael D. Swartz, *Hebrew and Aramaic Incantation Texts from the Cairo Genizah: Selected Texts from Taylor-Schechter Box K1* (Semitic Texts and Studies, 1). Sheffield, Sheffield Academic Press, 1992.

Scholem, Gershom, "Some Sources of Jewish-Arabic Demonology", *Journal of Jewish Studies* 16, 1965, 1–13.

Segal, Judah B., *Catalogue of the Aramaic and Mandaic Incantation Bowls in the British Museum*. London, British Museum Press, 2000.

Tsur, Reuven, "The Demonic and the Grotesque", *The Psychotherapy Patient* 12, 2003, 111–126.

Vilozny, Naama, *Lilith's Hair and Ashmedai's Horns – Figure and Image in Magic and Popular Art: Between Babylonia and Palestine in Late Antiquity*. Jerusalem, Ben-Zvi, 2017 (Heb.).

Vilozny, Naama, "Lilith's Hair and Ashmedai's Horns: Incantation Bowl Imagery in the Light of Talmudic Descriptions". In *The Archaeology and Material Culture of the Babylonian Talmud*, edited by Markham J. Geller (IJS Studies in Judaica, 16). Leiden, Brill, 2015, 133–152.

Vilozny, Naama, "Between Demons and Kings: The Art of Babylonian Incantation Bowls". In *Orality and Textuality in the Iranian World: Patterns of Interaction across the Centuries*, edited by Julia Rubanovitch (Jerusalem Studies in Religion and Culture, 19). Leiden, Brill, 2015, 400–421.

Wengrow, David, *The Origins of Monsters: Images and Cognition in the First Age of Mechanical Reproduction*. Princeton, Princeton University Press, 2014.

Zlotnick, Yehudah Leib, *Maaseh Yerushalmi*. Jerusalem, The Israeli Institute for Folklore and Ethnology, 1947 (Heb.).

Terry Kleeman
Many Paths, Many Souls: Traditional Chinese Views of the Other World

Chinese have always been fascinated with the idea of death, and provisions for the dead constitute our earliest records of Chinese civilization. As we shall see, the world beyond this mortal realm was intially conceived of as rather similar to our own, with existence continuing much as it had while alive, in the same familial and social groups. This view of the dead was challenged by the emergence of organized religious groups with significantly different ideas about eschatology, the meaning of being human, and the nature of the other world. Indic notions brought in with Buddhism melded with indigenous ideas that had developed within the context of the nascent religion of the Celestial Master Daoists beginning in the second century C.E. Since then, traditional ideas have swirled about these new conceptions, leading to a variety of more detailed understandings of the other world, which were further adumbrated through contact with other world religions and ultimately with the onslaught of modernity and modern scientific thought. This paper will trace the development of China's conception of the world beyond from its inception to modern times, focusing in particular on how individuals were expected to interact with this world and its denizens, which appeared as either ancestors or demons.

The earliest popular tale to survive about the world of the dead concerns a certain Duke Zhuang of Zheng (r. 744–701) during the Spring and Autumn period, who in the midst of an argument vowed to not see his mother again until they met "in the Yellow Springs" (*huangquan*, an early terms for the subterranean world of the dead).[1] He resolved the issue without foreswearing his oath by digging an underground tunnel where they could meet. Still, this tale shows that already the Chinese believed that familial relations survived death, that one would be reunited with dead kin in the other world, and presumably that social status also was preserved in that realm.

Our earliest textual evidence confirms this view of death. The oracle bone inscriptions of the Shang dynasty (ca. 1500–1045 BCE) record divinations made before the Shang king on a variety of matters of significance to the state. The preponderance of inscriptions record concerns about the fate and temperament of the royal ancestors, who are seen as actively interfering in the lives of their descendants. The desires of these ancestors were first augured through changes

---

1 Wu Hung, *Art of the Yellow Springs*, 7, citing *Zuozhuan*, first year of Duke Yin (721 BCE).

in the body of the king or of the state; the king would then order divinations to determine which ancestors was unhappy and how he or she might best be assuaged. Offerings to placate these divine forebears centered on food, meats and grains prepared in a variety of ways and set out for the consumption of the ancestors. Long sets of divinations show the care used to determine precisely which combinations of foodstuffs would fully mollify the dissatisfied individual in the other world.

Although royal ancestors were the primary subject of the Shang oracle bone inscriptions, they were not the only inhabitants of the Shang other world. There is a shadowy figure called Di 帝, which we sometimes translate as "thearch" to reflect his divine and royal identities. Not much is know about this figure.[2] He was far enough removed from mere mortals that even the Shang king could not offer sacrifice directly to him; instead, Shang ancestors would "host" (*bin* 賓) him on the king's behalf. Di determined matters of import like the founding site of a city. Other deities in the Shang records include nature deities like the (Yellow) River or the Mountain (perhaps referring to Mount Song near modern Loyang) and culture heros from the past, represented by semi-zoomorphic pictograms. Shang sources tell us nothing about the life of common people, but at least some few chosen confidants of the Shang royals were buried alive with them in order to continue to serve them in the other world. These commoners or lower nobility, then, also expected to live on in the other world much as they had in this. The fate of non-Shang peoples is less certain. When captured, the Qiang were regularly enslaved and often offered as human sacrifice to the gods or ancestors. Allied peoples, on the other hand, seem to have had their own *di* on high.

Around the middle of the eleventh century BCE, the mighty Shang were overthrown by an upstart group of western barbarians call the Zhou 周. They were of the Rong ethnicity, no doubt Sino-Tibetain speakers, but we have no idea how close their native language was to the early Sinitic of the Shang. While adopting Shang language and customs, they introduced some new beliefs, chief among them a new figure, Heaven (*tian* 天), that was driven by a sense of morality, or at least propriety. Whereas Di had always and inalienably been on the side of the Shang rulers (perhaps because he was in fact a proto-ancestor of the ruling clan), this Heaven was fickle, choosing now one, then another family to rule over the "realm under Heaven" (*tianxia* 天下), a new term for the entirety of the Chinese world.

The Zhou claimed that Heaven was on their side because the last Shang king had committed ritual errors like neglecting the sacrifices and abusing alcohol. They called the favor of this new Heaven its "mandate," the famous Mandate

---

[2] On *di*, see David N. KEIGHTLEY, "China's First Historical Dynasty".

of Heaven (*tianming* 天命) that was used down the centuries in China to justify changes of rule. Later, in the Eastern Zhou period (771-256 BCE), the philosophers Mozi (470-391 BCE) and Mencius (ca. 385-312 BCE) expanded this vision of Heaven as a just god. Mozi spoke of Heaven having a will (*tianzhi* 天志), that demanded justice for all humans. Mencius, a century later, wrote of Heaven hearing with the ears of the common people. There are growing ideas of Heaven not as a willful tyrant, but rather as a bureaucratic system. A tale dating to around 300 BCE tells of a man taken before his time by a divine official called the Director of Fates (*siming* 司命). Once the mistake is discovered, he is returned to life, but does not thrive and dies some time thereafter. Already by the end of the fourth century BCE, Heaven is full of records and recordkeepers.[3]

By this time, the existence of ghosts was widely accepted. Mozi built his system of cosmic justice on them, arguing that they were the enforcers of Heaven's Will and the agents of divine justice. Even Confucius admitted their existence in his admonition to "respect them but keep them at a distance." Most people warded ghosts when they could and placated them when they had to. The "Imprecations" (*Jie* 詰) manuscript found at Mawangdui is a good example of how common people dealt with threats from the other world.[4]

The Warring States period, the Qin, and the early Han was a period of extended military conflict that decimated the populace and raised serious questions about the ritual treatment of the dead. It was believed that the souls of individuals who died in battle away from home became a particularly fierce species of vengeful demon (*ligui* 厲鬼) who roamed the countryside. The state set up official altars to these unknown soldiers, but this did not seem to quiet the fears of the populace. During the Han dynasty, independent buildings were erected as temples to these beings, and the government debated how to deal with them.

The Han saw several changes in mortuary practice that are significant for their understanding of the world beyond. First, the structure of tombs changed from a vertical shaft containing a multi-layer coffin to a horizontal suite of rooms intended to replicate a mortal dwelling. The tombs were decorated with engraved images depicting gods and auspicious signs, entertainers, a dwelling, welcoming officials, in short, everything to sustain an existence as close as possible to that the deceased had experienced while alive. In the Latter Han, a new genre of tomb document appeared, the land contract (*maidiquan* 買地券). Modeled on real world contracts, these documents purchased the subterranean territory occupied by the tomb from gods of the terrestrial bureaucracy and assured the deceased rights in

---

[3] For the growth of this system of supernatural recordkeeping, see Mark CSIKSZENTMIHALYI, "Allotment and Death in Early China".
[4] See Donald HARPER, "Spellbinding".

perpetuity to this otherworldly space.[5] The parcel conveyed by the contract may have been limited in temporal terms, but which in the other world stretched to the limits of space in all directions. One way of representing this was to give the limits as the cyclical characters for that direction, as in this contract from 338 CE:[6]

> Xue, the wife of Zhu Man of Dantu, Jiangling purchases land from Heaven and a home from the Earth. To the east, [the plot] extends to the limit of *jiayi*, to the south it extends to the limits of *bingding*; to the west, it extends to the limits of *gengxin*; to the north, it extends to the limita of *rengui*; above it extends to the limits of the heavens; below, it extends to the limits of springs.
> 晉陵丹徒朱曼故妻薛，從天買地，從地買宅。東極甲乙，南極丙丁，西極庚辛，北極壬癸，中極戊己，上極天，下極泉。

The space, purchased with a mythical two million cash, might have seemed small to mortal eyes, but to the deceased, it was almost limitless. Still, challenges to territorial claims were not unknown in the other world, and for this reason each contract was careful to include a number of well known gods as guarantors of the contract. Another danger was corpses from the past buried in the vicinity. They might conceivably contest the title to the subterranean homestead, so some contracts have provisions that and other dead within the purchased gravesite would become servants to the new occupants.[7]

Thus, by the Han, the dead were clearly understood to pose two sorts of threat: if not ritualized, they starved for lack of sacrifice and resolved to take it by force, wreaking violence on the populace; if ritualized, they entered the world of the dead, where they would be conscripted into fell armies that enforced Heaven's justice by taking in death evil-doers and all those whose time had come. Arrayed against them were the ancestors and the age-old local gods, usually tied to sacred spots like wells or ancient trees. All, demons or deities, were approached and entreated through the offering of food, specifically dead animals or "bloody victuals" (*xieshi* 血食). Ecstatic religious professionals called *wu* 巫, usually identified as shamans, were the primary source of knowledge about these supernatural beings and the primary means of communication with them. Priests, commonly referred to as incanters (*zhu* 祝) oversaw the rituals of sacrifice, guiding the shamans or, in the case of ancestral sacrifice, a young lineal descendant of the deceased who would become possessed by the departed. This basic structure of religious professionals still survives today in traditional Chinese communities.

---

5 On land contracts, see my "Land Contracts and Related Documents"; Anna SEIDEL, "Traces of Han Religion".
6 *Wenwu* 1965.6: 48–9.
7 *Wenwu* 1965.8: Fig. 1.

The Advent of Daoism

Despite a short interregnum, the Han royal house ruled for nearly four centuries. When the dynastic order began to seriously fray in the latter half of the second century CE, it was a shock for the populace, many of whom turned to new religious groups offering innovative answers to the dilemma of a world off its hinges. Most of these nascent groups left a fleeting mark in the historical record, and today these is little we can say of them. One group, the Celestial Masters or Orthodox Unity group founding in West China in the mid-second century, survived long enough to create an organized religion, with an ordained priesthood, a collection of sacred texts, and a network of sacred sites where the faithful would gather for religious observances.

This new religion was founded upon a Covenant with the Powers that was pure and uncorrupted. They believed this required the abandonment of the practice of sacrifice, which they understood to be similar to bribery in a secular context. Because all existing gods had been corrupted by offerings of foodstuffs and other riches, had aided mortals not on the basis of virtue but because of personal debts of gratitude, they were not correct or upright, and did not deserve worship. Instead, the Celestial Master Zhang Daoling revealed a new class of deity occupying previously unknown heavens and enforcing transcendent codes of conduct that applied to mortals, demons, and the lower deities, as well.

The Six Heavens of Han official religion were subordinated in this scheme to a higher order of three Daoist heavens called the Three Pures (*sanqing* 三清) because they were uncorrupted by blood sacrifice.[8] The supernatural denizens of these realms were transformations of the pure pneumas of the Dao, not mortal in any sense, and hence had no need for normal provender. But they also were not the idle aesthetes and inspired artists of the popular imagination, but rather hard-working, nose-to-the-grindstone bureaucrats, who also appeared in court in spotless garments to pass wise judgment on all questioned presented to them. They could be moved only by properly prepared legal documents called petitions, written on behalf of a known member of the church by an appointed officer of the church and expressing pious contrition for whatever misdeed had led to the current predicament.

The early Celestial Master movement was strongly millenarian in character. Seeing the Han empire crumbling around them, they were convinced that the wickedness of the non-Daoist profane, and the hordes of demons that they nourished through their deviant worship of these beings, was bringing about an age of war, pestilence, disaster, and calamity. Only a small group of the most devout

---

[8] See my "Licentious Cults and Bloody Victuals".

Daoists could hope to survive these troubles, to live on as the Seed People (*zhongmin* 種民) who would would repopulate the now purified world as the ideal of Great Peace finally reigned supreme.[9] At that time, secular government would be replaced by a divine administration led by the Supreme Lord Lao and the other world would be fully realized in this one. As prophecies and omens circulated through the Chinese realm, Daoist-inspired rebellions arose sporadically for centuries thereafter. The Daoists, however, eventually reconciled themselves to the non-appearance of Great Peace, turning to more personal paths to apotheosis.

The Supreme Purity movement of the late fourth and fifth centuries marks an important shift.[10] Although the path of pious endeavor and adherence to the precepts remained fundamental to Daoism, the Supreme Purity revelations revealed a number of new paths to even higher levels of self-divinization. Esoteric techniques of astral travel and meditative exercises to absorb cosmic essences provided small groups of elite aspirants with expedited paths to exalted realms. Practices that had been primarily ritual-oriented and communal became individualistic and oriented to experience-based goals. Herbal concoctions and even mineral-based alchemical preparations were part of this new lore. The moral foundation of Daoism was not wholly elided, but it was superseded in this sort of quest for personal apotheosis. Supreme Purity was never a mass movement, however, and it influence on Daoist practice was limited.

Buddhism and Numinous Jewel Daoism

To understand the next development in Daoism, we need to retrace our steps to the Han dynasty, to witness the arrival of the world religion of Buddhism in the first century CE. Buddhism had been founded in the fourth century CE by followers of the Indian teacher Siddhartha Gautama Sakyamuni.[11] It was a revolutionary and strongly evangelical faith that swiftly gained followers across the Indian subcontinent and was transmitted through the Silk Road into Central Asia. Bringing with it an Indic conception of the other world, it was bound to greatly disrupt the Chinese religious realm. But this process took several centuries.

Buddhism first entered China through the Silk Road, and established outposts first in expatriate trader communities in the major cities of North China.

---

9 See Anna SEIDEL, "Taoist Messianism".
10 On the Supreme Purity movement, see Michel STRICKMANN, "The Mao Shan Revelations"; *Le Taoïsme du Mao Chan*.
11 For a current understanding of the founding of Buddhism, see Geoffrey SAMUELS, *The Origins of Yoga and Tantra*; Rupert GETHIN, *The Foundations of Buddhism*.

The capital, Chang'an, was certainly the primary center in China and by the second century, we find teams of foreign Buddhist priests and local Buddhist converts collaborating on the first translations of Buddhist sutras and other sacred literature. A second sea-based route brought Buddhist evangelists to South China, especially after the establishment of the independent Wu kingdom (222–280) in the Southeast China region. Still, it was only in the later half of the third century in South China that we see Chinese elites discussing Buddhism and incorporating Buddhist ideas into their daily life.

Buddhist conceptions of the Other World were quite distinct from traditional Chinese ideas, and to a certain degree the acceptance of Buddhism depended upon a process of accommodation and assimilation between these two views of the divine. Indic conceptions differed in scale, with fantastic trillion-year long eons and thousand-fold multiverses butting up against much more pragmatic Chinese conceptions of an Other World strongly resembling our own. In India, for example, *karma* was a natural process by which actions produced results in later lives. In China, this system depended upon a complex network of reporters of misdeed both within the body and in every physical place as well as a central recording bureau, a series of judges to adjudicate questionable cases, and an extensive, fearsome body of enforcers who detained, managed, and tortured mortals.

The Buddhist concept of transmigration, wherein dead individuals came back as other people, animals, or even hell beings in response to their actions while alive, was not easy for the Chinese people to assimilate. It is only in the fourth century that we start to see the concept discussed outside of Buddhist circles. Still, its significance for Chinese conceptions of the world of the dead was profound. It was always true that the dead might face otherworldly tribunals in which they were judged based on their conduct while alive, but it was an occasional matter, with proceedings held only when an aggrieved party lodged a complaint. Otherwise, life in the other world was conceived of as like that of the living, involving periods of work and leisure. Han tomb bricks depict acrobats and musicians to amuse the dead. Buddhism gave post-mortem existence a teleology: it was all about passing through a series of ten hells where the deceased would be judged for crimes committed while alive and suitable punishment doled out. No longer could one hope that loved ones would rest peacefully in a subterranean home; instead they faced a harrowing ordeal that stretched out, potentially, for eons as they suffered the punishments assigned in each hell in succession.

This gave rise to a great ritual change. Traditional ritual had entreated a specific ancestor or deity for aid in a specific problem. Daoist ritual addressed a pantheon of deities, but a petition still focused on a specific problem or set of related problems facing and individual or family. Buddhist doctrine made clear that the deceased was only one of a mass of individuals at only one time progressing through the courts of hell, all in need of succour. Moreover, although a Buddhist ritual might in theory seek only the salvation of one soul on this path, in fact the same ritual directed to all such beings was much more effective because it produced so much more merit. This merit could then be used to cancel out the deceased's bad deeds and avoid punishment, thus speeding them through the court and on to another existence. It became the custom to offer Buddhist rites for the dead at seven-day intervals for seven weeks, then at one hundred days, three hundred days, and three years after the funeral, thus assuring the passage through ten courts of hell.

These beliefs also exerted a strong influence on Daoist ritual practice. A new scriptural movement appeared near the end of the fourth century that incorporated much of the new Buddhist-inspired worldview into Daoism. This Numinous Jewel (Lingbao 靈寶) movement combined traditional esoteric lore with Buddhism ideas to create a new synthesis. Central to this was a rite of universal salvation (*pudu* 普度) that sought to save all the myriad souls suffering in all of the hells and all of the homeless ghosts wandering through this earth.

Rituals that sought to save all sentient beings were not limited to a single sponsor. Often groups would pool resources to put on a larger ritual, and government sponsorship might mean a festival on a grand scale. These new rites developed into elaborate, multi-day observances, and rituals of three, five or even seven days have been common in Daoism since the Southern Song (1127–1298).[12] Elite or government sponsorship sometimes resulted in extended ritual performances, with multiple Daoist troupes being invited to perform simultaneous or consecutive rituals that could continue for weeks. Today these majestic rituals survive in many regions of China as well as in Taiwan, Hong Kong, Singapore, and other overseas Chinese communities.

Daoist ritual introduced certain innovations that reflected Chinese culture's special focus on the family.[13] Whereas the Buddhist rite transfers the dead directly to the blessed lands of the Buddhas, the Daoists first call their dead relatives home and provide them with special rituals structures where they can bathe away the defilements of death and change into new clothes fitting for their new lives in happy realms. This personal touch brought the dead back into contact with their survivors and there are many tales of pious individuals encountering, in the course of the ritual, dead mothers or fathers, who seemed just as they had

---

[12] See Edward L. DAVIS, *Society and the Supernatural in Song China*.
[13] On Daoist ritual, see John LAGERWEY, *Taoist Ritual in Chinese Society and History*; LÜ PENGZHI 呂鵬志, *Tangqian Daojiao yishi shigang* 唐前道教儀式史綱..

been while alive, and even conversed with them for a time before returning to the other world.

The Buddhist worldview allowed that the deceased might end up in multiple places.[14] Assuming one got through or out of the hells somehow, one might go on to another existence among humans, animals, or the dead. But rebirth among the dead for the Buddhists was not the pale imitation of this life envisioned in the Confucian ancestral cult, but rather a life of constant suffering in penance for some great sins committed in the previous existence. Similarly, rebirth as a god might explain continued worship of local deities (as in Japan's Shinto-Buddhist combinatory religion), but in the Buddhist view, even these gods must one day experience death and judgment again for their actions. True release meant either transfer to a Buddha-land, like the Pure Land of Amitabha or the Western Paradise of Maitreya, or immediate release from existence through the attainment of Nirvana, a goal viewed as unrealizable by a mortal by almost all Buddhists except the followers of Chan. Buddhist funeral ritual came to focus strongly on the Buddha-lands as the desired destination for the deceased. From there, it was thought, the deceased would eventually make their way to Nirvana and a cessation of individual existence.

The Daoist vision was more prosaic. Saved from the torture of the hells and absolved ritually of sin, the deceased was thought to live out a more normal afterlife in the Heavenly Halls (*tiantang* 天堂). If virtuous, he or she might rise in the ranks to attain progressively higher appointments, but existence seems, on the whole, to have been more secure. Barring personal misconduct or unusual misfortune, one's dead after Daoist ritualization were fixed in a good place and required little care. Here we see a certain continuum with Confucian conceptions. If one's ancestors were virtuous enough to receive some sort of divine posting in the other world, they were beyond mortal sustenance and did not require sacrifice. By the Song, rituals called Refinement and Salvation (*liandu* 煉度) were developed to transmute the gross matter of the corpse into a sacred body that had no place in the mortal realm.[15]

The Late Imperial Amalgam

The Chinese religious world is often misunderstood, both by Chinese and outsiders, because the true religion of the vast majority of the Chinese people has never been named. If colonizers had bothered to name this amorphous mass

---

14 On Buddhist conceptions of rebirth, see Stephen F. TEISER, *The Scripture on the Ten Kings*.
15 On *liandu* rites, see the article "Liandu rites" by Maruyama HIROSHI.

of practices and beliefs, which draws freely upon the elite, organized religions of Buddhism, Daoism, and the state cult, while maintaining its own calendar, sacred sites, and ritual practice, we would be speaking of it in parallel with Hinduism or ancient Greek religion. Instead, colonizers followed the government's lead of only recognizing the elite representations of religion and dismissing the rest as superstition or charlatanry.

In fact, for most of Chinese history, the average Chinese of whatever status or regional identity has practiced a ritual life centering on the offering of blood sacrifice to deities and ancestors in hopes of otherworldly support and protection. Each family will draw upon representatives of the organized religions as needed, often at the time of major passages such as birth, severe illness, or death. They may even take on the ritual interdictions of one of the faiths, like refraining from sex, alcohol, and meat, for a specific period of time relative to the ritual. They will usually not, however, convert or transfer their primary allegiance to the faith, because in the next instance, they may need a different faith or cult.

Chinese funerals are, as a consequence, polyvalent, with multiple, conflicting eschatologies represented.[16] On the one hand, a great deal of effort is usually expended to ensure the deceased will have a comfortable resting place in a grave properly sited according to geomantic principles, and subsequent ritual will supply food and drink as well as other needs. Other symbolism expresses a firm faith that the departed will be swiftly reborn into the Pure Land of Amitabha or the Tuṣita Heaven of Maitreya or the Potalaka Heaven of Guanyin (Avelokiteśvara). Other rituals will be performed that assume that the soul is, rather, trapped in one or another of the courts of hell, suffering supernatural justice. A popular exorcist (*fashi* 法師) may perform a short ritual where he leads supernatural warriors to break down the gate of hell, crafted from paper, and frees the imprisoned soul by military might, at the same time that a Daoist priest is submitting a formal memorial to the officers of hell demanding in proper bureaucratic terms the same soul's release forthwith.

Can one make rational sense out of such a welter of conflicting symbols? One attempt was made by Myron Cohen, an anthropologist of China.[17] He noted that the Chinese commonly believed that an individual had a complement of souls, including three *hun* or yang souls and seven *po* or yin souls. Cohen theorized that this division of fates followed the division of souls, so that one *hun* soul was indeed in the Heavens or hells, one remained in the grave, and one inhabited the ancestral tablet, a piece of wood engraved with the name of the deceased, kept in the home and venerated as part of periodic rites. This neat analysis does not,

---

16 Myron COHEN has set forth this confusion in "Souls and Salvation".
17 Cf. ibid.

unfortunately, account for the multilocation of the soul in the Heavens, which might be in the hells, in a pure land, or already consigned to a new corporeal existence. Moreover, if only one *hun*-soul is processed through the hells and sent on to a new incarnation, how does the new individual get a full complement of three *hun*-souls again? Stevan Harrell argues based on his fieldwork that the various souls in these diverse places "can be treated in the same way at the same time" and hence are fundamentally representing the same soul. My own sense is also that most people do not understand the various rituals performed in the home, at the gravesite, or in a temple to be directed to different "souls." Perhaps it is better to understand that the traditional Chinese worldview encompassed mutually incompatible beliefs, as is true in many cultures around the world.

Bibliography

Cohen, Myron, "Souls and Salvation: Conflicting Themes in Chinese Popular Religion". In *Death Ritual in Late Imperial and Modern China*, edited by James L. Watson and Evelyn Sakakida Rawski, Berkeley, University of California Press, 1988, 180–202.

Csikszentmihalyi, Mark, "Allotment and Death in Early China". In *Mortality in Traditional Chinese Thought*, edited by Amy Olberding and Philip J. Ivanhoe, Albany, State University of New York Press, 2011, 177–190.

Davis, Edward L., *Society and the Supernatural in Song China*. Honolulu, University of Hawaii Press, 2001.

Gethin, Rupert, *The Foundations of Buddhism*. Oxford, Oxford University Press, 1998.

Harper, Donald, "Spellbinding". In *Chinese Religions in Practice*, edited by Donald S. Lopez, Jr., Princeton, Princeton University Press, 1996, 241–50.

Hiroshi, Maruyama, "Liandu rites". In *Encyclopedia of Taoism*, vol. 1, edited by Fabrizio Pregadio, London, Routledge, 2004, 642–48.

Keightley, David N., "China's First Historical Dynasty: The Shang". In *Cambridge History of Ancient China*, Cambridge, Cambridge University Press, 252–3.

Kleeman, Terry F., "Land Contracts and Related Documents". In *Makio Ryōkai Hakase Shōju Kinen Ronshū: Chūgoku no Shūkyō, Shisō to Kagaku*, Tokyo, Kokusho Kankōkai, 1984, 1–34.

Kleeman, Terry F., "Licentious Cults and Bloody Victuals: Sacrifice, Reciprocity and Violence in Traditional China", *Asia Major, Third series*, 7.1, 1994, 185–211.

Lagerwey, John, *Taoist Ritual in Chinese Society and History*. New York, Macmillan, 1987.

Lü Pengzhi 呂鵬志, *Tangqian Daojiao yishi shigang* 唐前道教儀式史綱. Beijing, Zhonghua, 2008.

Samuels, Geoffrey, *The Origins of Yoga and Tantra: Indic Religions to the Thirteenth Century*. Cambridge, Cambridge University Press, 2008.

Seidel, Anna, "Taoist Messianism", *Numen* 31.2, 1984, 161–174.

Seidel, Anna, "Traces of Han Religion in Funeral Texts Found in Tombs". In *Dōkyō to shūkyō bunka* 道教と宗教文化, edited by Akizuki Kan'ei 秋月觀英, Tokyo, Hirakawa, 1987, 21–57.

Strickmann, Michel, "The Mao Shan Revelations: Taoist and the Aristocracy", *T'oung-pao* 63, 1977, 1–64.
Strickmann, Michel, *Le Taoïsme du Mao Chan: Chronique d'une révélation* (Mémoires de l'Institut des Hautes Études Chinoises, 17). Paris, Collège de France, 1982.
Teiser, Stephen F., *The Scripture on the Ten Kings and the Making of Purgatory in Medieval Chinese Buddhism*. Honolulu, Univeristy of Hawaii Press, 2003.
Wenwu [Cultural artifacts]. Monthly academic journal on recent archaeological finds. Beijing, Cultural Artifacts Publishing House, 1950-.
Wu Hung, *Art of the Yellow Springs. Understanding Chinese Tombs*. Honolulu, Univeristy of Hawaii Press, 2010.

Klaus-Dieter Mathes
Liberation through Realizing the Emptiness of Dependent Origination
A Modern Interpretation of the Buddhist "Beyond" in the Light of Quantum Physics

The Buddhist "beyond" is best expressed and defined by enlightenment (*bodhi*), or more literally "awakening."[1] This involves a non-conceptual realization of true reality beyond the duality of a perceived object and perceiving subject.[2] In Yogācāra Buddhism, the surrounding we usually perceive as reality is but a product of false imagination.[3] That the things of the world do not appear as they truly are is also an essential point of Madhyamaka philosophy, so essential that our failure to perceive true reality simply as it is constitutes the root of all suffering in cyclic existence. This ignorance underlies the complex process of dependent origination or interconnectedness, which includes any form of interconnectedness, such as logical relationships. In its fully developed form, dependent origination suffuses the entire universe, which is thought of as consisting of innumerable continua of momentary material and mental factors of existence (*dharma*).[4] The most eminent Buddhist philosopher of Madhyamaka Nāgārjuna (fl. 200 CE) equates dependent origination with emptiness[5] and rules

---

1 This is most clear in the *mantra* of the *Prajñāpāramitāhṛdayasūtra* (i. e., the Heart Sūtra): "Oṃ, gone, gone, gone beyond, gone completely beyond, enlightenment, *svāhā*" (translated in Donald S. Lopez Jr., *Elaborations on Emptiness*, 169).
2 See for example the detailed exposition of the Buddha's fundamental transformation on the basis of non-conceptual wisdom in the *Dharmadharmatāvibhāga* (Klaus-Dieter Mathes, *Unterscheidung der Gegebenheiten*, 133–146); and Candrakīrti's *Prasannapadā* on MMK XXV.16 (see further down).
3 MAVṬ 13_{23-25}: "The past, future and present mind and mental factors, which are cause and result, which belong to (i. e., constitute) the beginningless threefold world, which end in *nirvāṇa* and conform with *saṃsāra* are precisely false imagination." (*atītānāgatavartamanā hetuphalabhūtās traidhātukā anādikālikā nirvāṇaparyavasānāḥ [saṃsārānurūpāś cittacaittā aviśeṣenābhūtaparikalpaḥ]*)
4 Cf. Erich Frauwallner, *Philosophy of Buddhism*, 50–51.
5 MMK XXIV 18ab (426_1): "That which is dependent origination – that we call emptiness." (*yaḥ pratītyasamutpādaḥ śūnyatāṃ tāṃ pracakṣmahe* /)

Note: Improvements to my English by Philip H. Pierce (South Asia Institute, Kathmandu branch) are gratefully acknowledged.

DOI 10.1515/9783110530773-015

out any true origination in terms of an "own-nature" (*svabhāva*).[6] This raises the question whether Nāgārjuna reduces dependent origination to a mere nominal construct[7] (metaphysical nihilism)[8] or whether he merely negates the *svabhāva* of the *dharma*s (substance nihilism).[9] In the latter case, existence could be still thought of in terms of dynamic systems of interrelatedness, which precludes any clean separation between any individual component of the system – or any subsystem that is singled out for observation – and all the rest. This calls into question our common-sense view of a universe built up from isolated entities. In this regard, Niels Bohr came to the conclusion that "isolated material particles are abstractions, their properties being definable and observable only through their interaction with other systems."[10] David Bohm and Basil J. Hiley accept the existence of the quantum world only under the provision that a locally determined existence is excluded.[11] Following this position, Jan Walleczek and Gerhard Grössing propose a *"quantum interconnectedness*, e. g., in the form of *non-local influences* across the universe."[12] According to this theory, which goes under the name "emergent quantum mechanics", the quantum is a particle in terms of an emergent resonance phenomenon, which is inseparably connected with its surrounding vacuum (i. e. zero- point field). To be sure, such particles do not exist in an isolated way, i. e., independent of their surrounding vacuum.[13] This interpretation is in opposition to orthodox quantum theory, in which any ontological reality on the level of the quantum is negated.[14]

It is argued in this paper that if we take Nāgārjuna to only deny the *svabhāva* of *dharma*s, i. e., locally determined factors of existence, his philosophy can be brought in line with the position of emergent quantum mechanics. The common

---

6 YṢ 19 (39$_{1-2}$ following YṢV): That which has arisen dependently has not arisen in terms of an own-nature. How can that which has not arisen in terms of an own-nature, truly be called 'arisen'? (*yat pratītyasamutpannaṃ notpannaṃ tat svabhāvataḥ / yat svabhāvena notpannam utpannaṃ nāma tat katham //*)
7 As in MMK XXIV 18c (426$_2$): "The latter (i. e., emptiness) is dependent designation." (*sā prajñaptir upādāya*)
8 A position maintained by Anne MACDONALD (personal communication), Jan WESTERHOFF (*The Madhyamaka Concept of Svabhāva*) and most interestingly the Jo nang school of Tibetan Buddhism.
9 See David SEYFORT RUEGG, *Literature of the Madhyamaka School*, 1–3; this mainly is the position of the dGe lugs pas.
10 Niels BOHR, *Atomic Theory*, 57.
11 David BOHM and Basil J. HILEY, *The Undivided Universe*, cited from Jan WALLECZEK and Gerhard GRÖSSING, "Is the World Local or Nonlocal?", 2.
12 Jan WALLECZEK and Gerhard GRÖSSING, "Is the World Local or Nonlocal?", 2.
13 Cf. Gerhard GRÖSSING et al., "Double Slit Experiment", 422.
14 A position maintained by Anton ZEILINGER (*Einsteins Schleier*, 229).

ground would be then a "physical reality" of dependent origination that can be compared to quantum interconnectedness. What is left, the 'beyond,' then is a dynamic reality that is possible because of its emptiness of *svabhāva* (Buddhism) or its absence of locally determined particles (physics). This beyond is realized by refraining from any form of reification, i. e., wrong denial and superimposition. Candrakīrti (ca. 600 – ca. 650 CE) and much later also Maitrīpa (986-1063) refer to this as wisdom. The *dharma*s that still constitute in their interconnectedness true reality, then, are *buddhadharma*s (i. e., Buddha qualities).[15]

The Role of the Observer: Mind and Matter

A modern interpretation of dependent origination and emptiness in the light of quantum interconnectedness requires acknowledging that mind has some influence on matter, for example in its often-discussed role of the observer. In Mahāyāna Buddhism consciousness is not only influenced by the environment but also influences it. In the Yogācāra work *Madhyāntavibhāga* the dependent nature[16] (which includes the whole universe) thus is explained as being entirely constituted by false imagination (*abhūtaparikalpa*),[17] and in his *Mūlamadhyamakakārikā* XXIV.18, Nāgārjuna includes dependent designation in his equation of dependent origination and emptiness:

> That which is dependent origination—
> That we call emptiness.
> The latter is dependent designation.
> This is the right middle path.[18]

This verse is taught in the chapter on the Four Noble Truths, and in this context, Nāgārjuna defends his doctrine of emptiness against the charge of espousing nihilism. He turns the tables on his opponent by claiming that if *dharma*s existed in terms of an "own-nature" (*svabhāva*), their arising and passing out of existence

---

15 See *Samādhirājasūtra* XXXII.8ab (SRS 195$_{24}$), where phenomena (*dharma*s) are in reality buddha qualities (*buddhadharma*s): "All dharmas are buddha-dharmas [for those] who are trained in *dharmatā*." (*sarvadharmā buddhadharmā dharmatāyāṃ ya śikṣitāḥ*). Note that *ya* is used for *ye* or the like for metrical reasons.
16 Equated with dependent origination in *Sandhinirmocanasūtra* VI.5 (SNS 60$_{25-27}$).
17 Mario D'Amato, *Distinguishing the Middle*, 120.
18 MMK 426$_{1-2}$ (XXIV.18): *yaḥ pratītyasamutpādaḥ śūnyatāṃ tāṃ pracakṣmahe | sā prajñaptir upādāya pratipat saiva madhyamā ||*

would be impossible.[19] In other words, the dynamic process of dependent origination presupposes the absence of a *svabhāva* in any of the involved components. It is for this reason that Nāgārjuna equates dependent origination with emptiness. To be sure, dependent origination is not negated here but declared possible because of its emptiness. That the *dharma*s of dependent origination are not only nominal for Nāgārjuna follows from his *Lokātītastava* where a "physical reality" of fire is clearly distinguished from pure nominalism:

> If a name and its object were not different
> One's mouth would be burned by [the word] fire.
> If they were different, there would be no comprehension of anything.[20]

In other words, one does not bring something into existence by only saying it, but a mutual dependence between the perceived and the perceiver is a necessary condition for comprehension. This line of thought only holds water if the perceiver also has an influence on the perceived. In my opinion, this is what Nāgārjuna's return from emptiness to dependent origination in its aspect of dependent designation in MMK XXIV.18c means. It underlines the role the labeling and conceptualizing mind has as part of the process of a dependently arising world.

The discussion of possible mental components in this process leads to the mind/body problem, or rather the question how mind and matter co-exist and influence each other. Given the eminent role first person experience plays in systems that are mainly based on the concentrated observation and critical investigation of mind and its mental states, not a single Buddhist model of reality has attempted to reduce mind to matter. An idealist current of Buddhist thought known as "Mind Only" even tried to reduce matter to mind on the presupposition that "mind alone" (*cittamātra*) exists. Western scientific models, on the other hand, are inclined to privilege matter to such an extent that extreme proponents of scientific materialism reject the existence of mind including all its mental factors because descriptions of such (epi)phenomena have no place in a naturalistic account of the world.

Can we or should we dispense altogether with discourses about mind? The mere fact that we ponder such a question presupposes first person access to

---

19 MMK XXIV.16–17 (424$_{13-20}$): "If you see the true existence of things as coming from a [supposed] *svabhāva*, then in that case you see things as being without either causes or conditions. You exclude result, cause, agent, doing, action, arising, passing out of existence, and fruit." (*svabhāvād yadi bhāvānāṃ sadbhāvam anupaśyasi / ahetupratyayān bhāvāṃs tvam evaṃ sati paśyasi // kāryaṃ ca kāraṇaṃ caiva kartāraṃ karaṇaṃ kriyām / utpādaṃ ca nirodhaṃ ca phalaṃ ca pratibādhase //*)

20 LS 7abc (LS 130$_{10-11}$): *saṃjñārthayor ananyatve mukhaṃ dahyeta vahninā / anyatve 'dhigamābhāvas.*

complex mental processes. In the case of Buddhism, how could we otherwise give any credence to the advanced stages of meditation, whose observation and investigation are held to be repeatable by anyone ready to apply the technique? A combination of reducing negative influences like hatred or desire, for example, and cultivating calm abiding and insight provides the means for a deeper investigation and eventual understanding of the nature of mind. Buddhist practitioners train in such mental disciplines to realize for themselves what has been discovered by many down through the ages. In short, the attempt to reduce mind with its discernible features and structures to physical and physiological processes would be as absurd for a Buddhist as the reduction of matter to mind would be for a physicist. What is needed then is a model of reality that accounts for both mind and matter, and that seeks to understand the complex interactions between the two better.

While scientific materialists readily accept that consciousness is solely generated by the neuronal activity of the brain, even though no such causal mechanism has been found so far, an influence of mind on matter or the body is not considered possible mainly because this would violate the principle of the conservation of mass and energy. The energy-time uncertainty principle in quantum physics, however, allows for a short violation of energy conservation. Wallace concludes from this that it is possible for a nonphysical mind to engage with matter and raises the question whether individual quantum events are truly random since nonphysical causes, or even nonlocal interactions within entangled systems,[21] for example, cannot be excluded.[22] Given these obvious epistemic elements, it is not completely out of the question anymore, to think of models of reality in which the observing mind has an influence on the world we live in.

Against this background, I propose to accept both, mind and matter. Reducing one to the other makes it extremely difficult to account for a number of processes that can be observed directly. In line with Nāgārjuna, I suggest, though, that one need not subscribe to a substance dualism. Mind and matter, rather, are relational or complementary. Such irreducibility need not be unscientific. In fact, a well-known form of irreducibility can be found within the field of quantum physics, where a single entity such as a photon shows both wave and particle character. We need both to account for light-matter-interaction. When a gamma ray hits a gold atom, the energy and impulse of the involved 'particles' before

---

[21] Particles which have interacted physically remain under certain conditions entangled (in such a way that they are mysteriously twisted together) even after they have become separated over large distances. The shared state of polarization or spin, for example, remains indefinite until measurement.

[22] Cf. B. Alan WALLACE, *Taboo of Subjectivity*, 142–43.

and after the impact conform to the calculations with the ordinary equations of energy and momentum conservation. This suggests that the gamma ray displays its particle character of transmitting momentum, as well as its wave character of transmitting energy by increasing its wavelength.

Different Concepts of Existence

While orthodox quantum physics refrains from ontological commitments on the level of quantum events, taking the latter to be genuinely random and inexplicable without observation, modern followers of David Bohm see quantum events as realistic dynamic processes of interrelatedness, the participating particles not being independent, but emergent phenomena of resonance that interact with their surrounding zero point field.[23] This leads to the question of what we understand by the existence of something (x). Does it require x to be independent and locally determined, or in Buddhist language, to possess a *svabhāva*? Anton Zeilinger's interpretation of the double slit experiment, which is based on the position that information and reality are the same,[24] requires that we deny the existence of the photon on its trajectory between its source and the detector.[25] Arthur Zajonc responded that the continued existence of the photon made good sense to him but that

> [i]f you allow that the photon, or the electron, by nature has that continued existence, then its own intrinsic nature is very strange, and believing this has a big impact on the way you see the world. If you say that it has no continued existence – that only the source, the detector, and certain events exist, and there is nothing that one can say about the particle's intervening existence – that is an easy way to avoid the impact of quantum mechanics. The effects are interesting, but they have no ontological significance. They don't make a statement about reality. For me, I think these experiments make statements about the way the world is.[26]

The reason why the intrinsic nature of the photon is strange for Zajonc, is that we usually expect from an existing (x) that is does so as something locally determined. It is interesting that Nāgārjuna shares the same conventional view on existence. Still, he must have accepted Zajonc's 'strange way' of interrelatedness,

---

23 Email communication with Herbert Schwabl, dated Sept. 8, 2016.
24 Cf. Anton ZEILINGER, *Einsteins Schleier*, 229.
25 This is what Anton ZEILINGER maintained at a Mind and Life Conference in October 1997 in Dharamsala (Arthur ZAJONC, ed., *New Physics and Cosmology*, 139–40).
26 Arthur ZAJONC, ed., *New Physics and Cosmology*, 140.

but preferred not to call this existence anymore. *Mūlamadhyamakakārikā* I.10 can be interpreted in this way:

> Since the existence of entities devoid of a *svabhāva* is not found,
> The formula "when x exists, y comes to be" is not appropriate.[27]

The causal clause in the first part of the verse clearly shows that for Nāgārjuna the concept of existence presupposes an independent existence (*svabhāva*). With such an understanding the traditional formula for dependent origination does not work. To say x exists means x exists independently (*svabhāvena*), but an independent x cannot have any causal relation to anything. Otherwise, it would not have a *svabhāva*. If the building blocks of the universe consisted of completely isolated, independent entities, there could be no interaction at all. Or else anything could arise from anything else – for instance, like darkness from light – as Candrakīrti explains in *Madhyamakāvatāra* VI.14.[28] In other words, when one understands existence as an independent existence and attempts to reify the members of the traditional formula "when x exists, y comes to be", the formula does not work anymore. It could be argued that Nāgārjuna still accepts causality on a pragmatic level. After all, he endorses the principle of dependent origination in his introduction to the *Mūlamadhyamakakārikā*.[29] But what is dependent origination without arising? Nāgārjuna immediately gives an answer in the first verse of his *Mūlamadhyamakakārikā*:

> Nowhere are things found anywhere that have arisen
> From themselves, other, a combination of both, and without a cause.[30]

Given the negation of an "own-nature" (*svabhāva*) and "other-nature" (*parabhāva*) in chapter fifteen of the *Mūlamadhyamakakārikā*[31] this can only mean that in the absence of a locally determined existence, or own-nature, the borderline between "self" and "other" cannot be drawn anymore. It is not possible to say, for example,

---

[27] MMK I.10 (MMK 18₁₋₂): *bhāvānāṃ niḥsvabhāvānāṃ na sattā vidyate yataḥ | satīdam asmin bhavatīti etan naivopapadyate ||*
[28] Cf. David SEYFORT RUEGG, *Two Prolegomena*, 71.
[29] MMK Introduction (MMK 12₁₋₄): *anirodham anutpādam [...] yaḥ pratītyasamutpādaṃ [...] deśayāmāsa saṃbuddhas taṃ vande vadatāṃ varam.* My own translation: "I pay homage to him the fully awakened, the best of all teachers who has proclaimed dependent origination as being without cessation and arising [...]."
[30] MMK I.1 (MMK 12₁₃₋₁₄): *na svato nāpi parato na dvābhyāṃ nāpy ahetutaḥ | utpannā jātu vidyante bhāvāḥ kvacana kecana ||*
[31] MMK XV.3ab (MMK 236₁₃₋₁₄): "Where, in the absence of an own-nature, will there be an other-nature?" (*kutaḥ svabhāvasyābhāve parabhāvo bhaviṣyati*)

precisely where a cause stops being a cause and from which point on we have an effect since locally determined causes and conditions cannot be identified and singled out. This suggests to understand dependent origination as referring to a dynamic system of interrelatedness without concrete building blocks resembling billiard balls. This applies not only to the spatial extension of the building blocks but also their temporal extension. Just as the members of an entangled system appear, upon measurement, to share the same quantum mechanical state – such parameters as position, momentum, spin or polarization – even over long distances in space, so the event of an intentional deed (*karman*) and its effect can be related over a long period of time. In *Madhyamakāvatāra* VI.39 we find a justification of such a long-term relation, namely that nothing passes out of existence:

> Since there is no passing out of existence in terms of an own-nature, you should know that the fruit [of deeds] will arise at some time, even if the termination of the deed [sometimes] lies back a long time. Because of its (i. e., the deed´s) power, [this works] even without a ground [consciousness].[32]

The idea here is that causes that take the form of intentional deeds are not bound by time constraints so that it is impossible to say when precisely they end. Thus, they may link up with an event of maturation in the far future even without a chain of locally and temporally determined factors of existence stored in a ground consciousness (as maintained in the Yogācāra school). The fact that enlightenment, the Buddhist beyond, requires a complete extinction of any ripening process of *karman*, does not necessarily pose a problem for our proposed comparison of this aspect of Buddhist philosophy with quantum interrelatedness, for entangled systems can also collapse. A structured order on a macroscopic level can thus emerge from locally indeterminate quantum states in top-down and bottom-up causal flows.[33]

The Buddhist goal of analyzing and determining true reality as the emptiness of dependent origination is to undermine the process of constant reification or projection of an own-nature into true reality. According to the *karman* theory, this happens due to one's habitual tendencies, namely mental imprints (*vāsana*) left by intentional deeds under the influence of ignorance, attachment, hatred and so forth.[34] In other words, one's mind creates the environment. The common experience of external objects is explained by assuming the idea that a particular

---

32 MA VI.39 (MA 7$_{25-28}$): *yasmāt svarūpeṇa na tan niruddhaṃ ciraṃ niruddhād api karmaṇo ´taḥ | kvacid vinaivālayam asya śakteḥ phalaṃ samutpadyata ity avaihi ||*
33 Cf. Jan WALLECZEK and Gerhard GRÖSSING, "Is the World Local or Nonlocal?", 6.
34 See Erich FRAUWALLNER, *Philosophy of Buddhism*, 82–91 for an explanation of this process according to the *Abhidharmakośa*; and Klaus-Dieter MATHES, *Unterscheidung der Gegebenheiten*, 146–47 for an explanation in the *Dharmadharmatāvibhāgavṛtti*.

group of sentient beings shares common imprints which influence each other so as to give rise to common appearances. Human beings thus share the common imprints for the manifestation of drinking water. For a fish, however, water must be what the troposphere is for land animals. In other words, there is no such thing as an ultimately existing body of water with inherent qualities. What one experiences depends on one's sense faculties, mental imprints, etc. In his *Collected Works* the Tibetan rNying ma master Rong zom chos kyi bzang po (1042-1136) uses the example of "wild herbivores possessing the purity of fire" (Tib. *ri dwags me'i gtsang sbra can*) which wash themselves with fire without burning themselves.[35] The point here is that it is not enough to simply think "I am not burning in fire" but one needs to be such an animal with all the necessary mental imprints.

Within a certain range limited by one's rebirth as a human being and respective set of sense faculties, one's mental imprints lead to this or that determined reality that is characterized by the duality of a perceived object and perceiving subject. Personally created reifications freeze into one's reality, which in turn fortifies or creates fresh mental imprints. Since we share similar patterns of mental imprints with a large group of sentient beings, the resulting reifications are commonly accepted by one's group as true reality. To express this in the words of emergent quantum mechanics, said patterns structure the quantum vacuum (i. e., zero point field) in such a way, that the respective events, which are typical of particular groups of sentient beings, emerge on the macroscopic level.

The Buddhist Beyond

Given these mostly unpleasant distortions of true reality, the question arises how to avoid them and reach the Buddhist beyond. But since any conceptual activity and labeling harbors the danger of reification, one cannot, strictly speaking, think or talk about it. This paradox has been nicely expressed in the *Tattvaratnāvalī* (TRĀ), where Maitrīpa says in his presentation of his favored Apratiṣṭhāna-Madhyamaka:[36]

> The wise know the true reality of things
> As the non-abiding in anything.
> Now, this is not just conceptual [analysis], for a [conceptualizing] mind
> Does not know the nature of mind.[37] (TRĀ 29)

---

35 RONG ZOM CHOS BZANG, *gsung 'bum*, vol. 1, 426.
36 Cf. Klaus-Dieter MATHES, *A Fine Blend*, 71–72.
37 TRĀ 360$_{23-27}$: *sarvasminn apratiṣṭhānaṃ vastutattvaṃ vidur budhāḥ | athaiṣā kalpanā naiva yac cid vetti na cittatām ||*

All superimposition, whatever there is—
All this does not exist in any respect;
The meaning of Madhyamaka is thus the absence of superimposition;
Where is, then, the denial or establishing [of anything]?[38] (TRĀ 30)

This effortless wisdom
Is called inconceivable;
Something 'inconceivable' that one has [been able to] conceive
Cannot truly be inconceivable.[39] (TRĀ 31)

The verses 29 and 30 nicely summarize what has been elaborated so far in this paper. The realization of the true reality of things is only possible by "not abiding" (*apratiṣṭhāna*) in anything. The Sanskrit word *apratiṣṭhāna* also means "lacking foundation" which conveys the idea that there is no foundation to anything whatsoever by which the latter can be reified in any conceivable way. This is made clear in the *Sekanirdeśapañjikā* of Rāmapāla (one of the four main disciples of Maitrīpa),[40] who glosses *apratiṣṭhāna* as "not to become mentally engaged" and "not to superimpose."[41] In other words, one needs to refrain from projecting wrong notions (such as a *svabhāva*, independent existence or characteristic signs) onto anything arisen in dependence, whether *skandha*s, *dhātu*s or *āyatana*s.[42] A mind, however, which is in a state of not superimposing cannot be achieved through analytical thought processes, which are always accompanied by distorting reifications, but only by some inconceivable intellect, i.e., our effortless wisdom of verse 31. In fact, Maitrīpa anticipates the possible objection that thinking about the inconceivable is in itself an obstacle. An answer is not given in the *Tattvaratnāvalī*, but the same verse is also found in Maitrīpa's *Sekanirdeśa*, and Rāmapāla explains in his commentary on this verse that

> [t]his non-abiding is inconceivable wisdom. It does not come from investigation, but is effortless, occurring within its own sphere.[43]

The Buddhist beyond thus is not only negatively defined as the emptiness of superimposed *svabhāva*s, but there is also an inconceivable wisdom behind

---

38 TRĀ 361$_{3-6}$: *yāvān sarvasamāropaḥ sa sarvaḥ sarvathā na hi | madhyamārtho nirāropas tatrāpohavidhī kutaḥ ||*
39 TRĀ 361$_{12-16}$: *anābhogaṃ hi yaj jñānaṃ tac cācintyaṃ pracakṣyate | saṃcintya yad acintyaṃ vai tad acintyaṃ bhaven na hi ||*
40 See George N. ROERICH, *Blue Annals*, vol. 2, 842.
41 SNP 192$_6$: *apratiṣṭhānam amanasikāro ´nāropaḥ*
42 SNP 192$_{5-6}$: *sarvasminn iti pratītyasamutpannaskandhadhātvāyatanādau* [...].
43 SNP 193$_{1-2}$: *tac cāpratiṣṭhānam acintyaṃ jñānaṃ na tad vicārāgataṃ kiṃ tarhy anābhogaṃ svarasābhyāgatam |*

everything. Still, how can Maitrīpa call it ineffable wisdom? This points to a fundamental problem that the Buddha is said to have addressed immediately upon his enlightenment. In *Lalitavistara* XXV.1 we thus find:

> I found a Dharma, profound, peaceful, pure,
> Luminous, nectar-like, and not conditioned.
> Even if I taught it, nobody would understand it.
> I better remain silent and go to the forest.[44]

Even though the Buddha initially doubted whether he could communicate his realization, he spent his remaining life of about forty-five years teaching what he first considered ineffable. In other words, somebody who has an immediate realization of the "beyond" can teach it to an audience of disciples who are aware of the limitations of language in this matter. Maitrīpa's inconceivable wisdom must be understood in this sense. In this context, it is interesting that in his *Amanasikārādhāra*, Maitrīpa takes *amanasikāra* not only as mental disengagement (i. e., Rāmapāla's synonym of non-abiding), but also the cultivation of realization, or self-empowerment (*svādhiṣṭhāna*), to use Maitrīpa's final interpretation of *manasikāra*. The initial *a*- not only represents the simple negation of a privative *a*, then, but also stands for a profound Madhyamaka type of negation, such as non-arising or emptiness, which Maitrīpa understands also in a positive sense as luminosity.[45] The two levels of analysis – *amanasikāra* as (1) the negation of conceptual engagement that results in duality and (2) luminous self-empowerment – skillfully combine a *via negationis* and a *via eminentiae*. The same combination is also found in Maitrīpa's *Tattvadaśaka*.[46]

To sum up, the deconstruction of conceptual duality that involves a perceived object and a perceiving subject does not result in a blank nothingness, but a "transcendent knowing" (*jñāna*) of the ultimate. The latter statement can only be made, though, under the provision that this *jñāna* and the ultimate are not taken as a perceived object and a perceiving subject. Candrakīrti, who is otherwise well known for his radical deconstruction of everything, also claims that the Buddhas abide in objectless wisdom.[47] In his commentary on *Mūlamadhyamakakārikā* XXV.16, Candrakīrti explains:

> [...] It is because consciousness has characteristic signs as support. But in *nirvāṇa*, there is no characteristic sign whatsoever. Therefore it (i. e., *nirvāṇa*) is indeed not to be

---

44 See LV XXV.1 (LV 286$_{10-13}$),: *gambhīra śānto virajaḥ prabhāsvaraḥ prāpto mi dharmo hy amṛto ´saṃskṛtaḥ / deśeya cāhaṃ na parasya jāne yan nūna tūṣṇī pavane vaseyam //*.
45 Cf. Klaus-Dieter Mathes, *A Fine Blend*, 245–47.
46 Cf. Klaus-Dieter Mathes, *A Fine Blend*, 211–13.
47 Cf. Anne MacDonald, *Knowing Nothing*, 156.

apprehended by consciousness. Nor is it known by wisdom. Why is that? Because wisdom must have emptiness as support. It has the nature (lit. 'form') of non-arising only. How then does one grasp through this [wisdom], whose own-nature does not exist, that *nirvāṇa* is neither an existent nor non-existent? It is because of the wisdom´s nature that transcends all mental fabrication.[48]

In other words, Candrakīrti expounds a form of wisdom beyond all mental fabrication and having emptiness as its object.[49]

Conclusion

In conclusion, I suggest that the Buddhist beyond in terms of the emptiness of dependent origination does not necessarily entail a nihilistic position. In my opinion, emptiness should not be compared to the nothingness of a vacuum in classical physics, but rather to a quantum vacuum with infinite potentiality. This not only means that emptiness has the potential to manifest the manifold appearances of the world, but also that its realization discloses the primordial Buddha qualities, as explained in the *Tathāgatagarbhasūtra*s. Depending on whether one's mind is in a mode of reifying or not, it is *saṃsāra* and *nirvāṇa* that emerge from emptiness.

Bibliography

Primary Sources (Indian)

TRĀMaitrīpa, *Tattvaratnāvalī*. Edited by Klaus-Dieter Mathes. See Mathes, *A Fine Blend*, 341–69.
PPCandrakīrti, *Prasannapadā*. Edited by Louis de la Vallée Poussin (Bibliotheca Buddhica 4).
    Contained in *Mūlamadhyamakakārikā*. Delhi, Motilal Banarsidass, 1992.
MACandrakīrti, *Madhyamakāvatāra*. Edited by Xue Zhu Li, *China Tibetology*, No. 1, March 2012, 1–16.
MAVṬSthiramati, *Madhyāntavibhāgaṭīkā*. Edited by S. Yamaguchi. Nagoya, Librairie Hajinkaku, 1934.
MMKNāgārjuna, *Mūlamadhyamakakārikā*. Edited by Ye Shaoyong. Beijing, Zhongxi Book Company, 2010.

---

[48] PP 533$_{14-17}$ (on MMK XXV.16): *yasmān nimittālambanaṃ vijñānaṃ na ca nirvāṇe kiṃ cin nimittam asti / tasmān na tat tāvad vijñānenālambyate / jñānenāpi na jñāyate / kiṃ kāraṇaṃ yasmāj jñānena hi śūnyatālambanena bhavitavyaṃ / tac cānutpādarūpam eveti / kathaṃ tenāvidyamānasvarūpeṇa naivābhāvo naiva bhāvo nirvāṇam iti gṛhyate sarvaprapañcātītarūpatvāj jñānasyeti /*
[49] Cf. Anne MACDONALD, *Knowing Nothing*, 165.

LV *Lalitavistarasūtra* Edited by P.L. Vaidya, Buddhist Sanskrit Series 1. Darbhanga, Mithila Institute, 1958.
LS Nāgārjuna, *Lokātītastava*. Edited by Christian Lindtner. See Lindtner, *Nagarjuniana*, 128–38.
YṢ Nāgārjuna, *Yuktiṣaṣṭikākārikā*. Edited by Li Xuezhu and Ye Shaoyong. Beijing, Zhongxi Book Company, 2014.
SNS *Sandhinirmocanasūtra* (Tibetan translation from the Kanjur) Edited by Étienne Lamotte. Louvain (Belgium), Bureaux du Recueil, 1935.
SRS *Samādhirājasūtra* Edited by P. L. Vaidya. Darbhanga, The Mithila Institute of Post-Graduate Studies and Research in Learning, 1961.
SNP Rāmapāla, *Sekanirdeśapañjikā*. Edited by Harunaga Isaacson and Francesco Sferra in: *The Sekanirdeśa of Maitreyanātha (Advayavajra) with the Sekanirdeśapañjikā of Rāmapāla. Critical Edition of the Sanskrit and Tibetan Texts with English Translation and Reproductions of the MSS* (Manuscripta Buddhica 2). Naples, Università degli Studi Napoli "L'Orientale", 165–204.

Primary Sources (Tibetan)

Rong zom chos bzang, *Rong zom chos bzang gi gsung 'bum*. 2 vols. Chengdu, Si khron mi rigs dpe skrun khang, 1999.

Literature

Bohr, Niels, *Atomic Theory and the Description of Nature*. London, Cambridge University Press, 1934.
Bohm, David, and Basil J. Hiley, *The Undivided Universe: An Ontological Interpretation of Quantum Theory*. London, Routledge, 1993.
D'Amato, Mario, *Maitreya's Distinguishing the Middle from the Extremes* (Madhyāntavibhāga). New York, The American Institute of Buddhist Studies, 2012.
Frauwallner, Erich, *The Philosophy of Buddhism* [first German in 1956], transl. by Lodrö Sangpo. Delhi, Motilal Banarsidass, 2010.
Grössing, Gerhard et al., "An Explanation of Interference Effects in the Double Slit Experiment: Classical Trajectories plus Ballistic Diffusion Caused by Zero-Point Fluctuations", *Annals of Physics* 327.2, 2012, 421–37.
Lindtner, Christian, *Nagarjuniana: Studies in the Writings and Philosophy of Nāgārjuna*. Delhi, Motilal Banarsidass, 1990.
Lopez, Donald S. Jr., *Elaborations on Emptiness. Uses of the Heart Sūtra*. Princeton, Princeton University Press, 1996.
MacDonald, Anne, "Knowing Nothing: Candrakīrti and Yogic Perception". In *Yogic Perception, Meditation and Altered States of Consciousness* (Sitzungsberichte der philosophisch-historischen Klasse, 794), edited by Eli Franco and Dagmar Eigner. Vienna, Austrian Academy of Sciences Press, 2009, 133–68.
Mathes, Klaus-Dieter, *Unterscheidung der Gegebenheiten von ihrem wahren Wesen* (Dharmadharmatāvibhāga) (Indica et Tibetica, 26). Swisttal-Odendorf, Indica et Tibetica Verlag, 1996.

Mathes, Klaus-Dieter, *A Fine Blend of Mahāmudrā and Madhyamaka: Maitrīpa's Collection of Texts on Non-conceptual Realization* (Amanasikāra) (Sitzungsberichte der philosophisch-historischen Klasse, 869; Beiträge zur Kultur- und Geistesgeschichte Asiens, 90). Vienna, Austrian Academy of Sciences Press, 2015.
Roerich, George N., *The Blue Annals*, 2 vols. (Royal Asiatic Society of Bengal, Monograph Series, 7). Kolkata, Motilal Banarsidass, 1949–53.
Seyfort Ruegg, David, *The Literature of the Madhyamaka School of Philosophy in India* (A History of Indian Literature, 7, fasc. 1). Wiesbaden, Franz Steiner Verlag, 1981.
Seyfort Ruegg, David, *Two Prolegomena to Madhyamaka Philosophy: Studies in Indian and Tibetan Madhyamaka Thought, part 2* (Wiener Studien zur Tibetologie und Buddhismuskunde, 54). Vienna, Arbeitskreis für tibetische und buddhistische Studien, 2002.
Wallace, B. Alan, *The Taboo of Subjectivity: Towards a New Science of Consciousness*. Oxford, Oxford University Press, 2000.
Walleczek, Jan, and Gerhard Grössing, "Is the World Local or Nonlocal? Towards an Emergent Quantum Mechanics in the 21st Century", *Journal of Physics. Conference Series* 701, 2016. Accessed September 5, 2016. http://arxiv.org/pdf/1603.02862v1.pdf.
Westerhoff, Jan, "The Madhyamaka Concept of *Svabhāva*: Ontological and Cognitive Aspects", *Asian Philosophy* 17 (1), 2007, 17–45.
Zajonc, Arthur, ed., *The New Physics and Cosmology: Dialogues with the Dalai Lama*. Oxford, Oxford University Press, 2004.
Zeilinger, Anton, *Einsteins Schleier: Die neue Welt der Quantenphysik*. München, Verlag C.H. Beck, 2003.

Faye Kleeman
Here, There, and "Beyond" – Japanese Views on the Afterlife

The Pre-Buddhist Worldview and the Afterlife

The traditional Japanese view of the "beyond" can be found in its earliest myth, recorded in Japan's first history, the *Chronicles of Ancient Matters* (*Kojiki*, 712 CE). The mytho-historical account begins with a section on the creation of Japan. When the pair of founding gods of the island nation, Izanagi (male) and Izanami (female), are separated by Izanami's death in childbirth, her brother/husband Izanagi travels all the way to the Land of the Dead (*yomi no kuni* 黄泉の国) to retrieve her. Izanami informs him that as much as she would like to return to the world of the living with him, she has already partaken of the food there and thus has become an inhabitant of the dark realm. Izamagi, not willing to give up his wife, grabs her hands and tries to force his way out of the Land of the Dead. When he inadvertently sees her decaying body, he is frightened and escapes, chased by thousands of furies. As Izanagi emerges from the Land of the Dead, finally escaping the terrifying furies, he bathes himself in the river, thereby performing the first water purification rite in Shinto history.[1] From his left eye, the Goddess of the Sun, from his right eye, the God of the Moon and from his nose, the trickster god Susanoo no mikoto were born. Many scholars point to the similarity of the Izanagi/Izanami myth to the Greek myth of Orpheus, who also went to hell to retrieve his wife Eurydice. In this ancient myth, the Land of the Dead is identified as being deep below Izumo 出雲 (modern day Shimane Prefecture), under the Land of the Hard Roots (*Nenokatasu kuni* 根の堅洲国).[2]

In other written records from eighth-century Japan, like the Izanagi and Izanami myth in *Kojiki*, the image of the world of the dead is vague and its location ambiguous (somewhere in Izumo, under the Land of the Roots, etc.). Mythical figures like Izanagi could come and go between this world and that other world. In Japanese mythology, there is another site for the great beyond: far away across the sea there is a place known as the Land of Eternity (*tokoyo no*

---
[1] NISHIO YŪ 西尾右, "*Kojiki* no zaiekan 『古事記』の罪穢観".
[2] *Kojiki*, Part I chapter 2 (上巻– 2). In Kurano Kenji 倉野憲司 and Takeda Yūkichi 武田祐吉, eds., *Kojiki Norito* 古事記・祝詞, 73.

kuni 常世の国), where Emperor Suinin 垂仁 is said to have sent his loyal subject Taji Mamori 田道間守 to search for the eternal golden fruit (Tokijuku no kaku no konomi 非時香菓 ときじくのかくのこのみ) that would bring the Emperor eternal life.[3] The Land of Eternity is also sometimes thought of as a dwelling place of the dead, but it seems to convey the sense of an idealistic, Utopian realm quite at variance with the Land of the Dead, which is dark and polluted (thus requiring Izanagi's water purification ritual) and deeply hidden in a mountain forest. Together with the Field of the High Heaven (*Takaamahara* 高天原) where the gods reside, the Land of the Dead (in the mountains) and the Land of the Eternity (across the ocean) form the tripartite "other world" (*ikai* 異界, *takai* 他界), a realm distinct from the living world where humans reside. In this traditional conception of the world of the dead, all the dead go to the same place, without distinction of whether they are good or bad people.[4] The more complex, value-laden system of the afterlife introduced by Buddhism had yet to penetrate popular discourse at this time.

Contemporary literary sources such as Japan's first imperial anthology of poetry, the *Collection of Ten Thousand Leaves* (*Manyōshū*, late 7th century to late 8th century) also provide us with glimpses of Japan's early imagination of an afterworld. Among the twenty volumes, with over four thousand five hundred poems collected in the anthology, there are 263 poems (approximately 5.8%) in the category of elegy (*banka*挽歌, literally "[hearse] pulling songs") that can provide us with a glimpse of how the ancient Japanese perceived the world beyond. The elegiac genre of poems *banka* literally refers to poems/songs/chants that were sung while pulling the mortuary cart (柩車) to the gravesite. Scholars surmise that these songs had there origin in ancient Chinese funeral poems (*zangsongge* 葬送歌) that can be traced back as early as the second century BCE. In *Banka*, as in most early Japanese poems, the invocation of place names and names of deities were informed by the *kotodama* belief that words have inherent magical power and that, consequently, ritual recitation of these elegiac poems could summon back the soul of the departed and pacify the vengeful dead. The poetic imagination of the *Manyōshū* poets, offers some idea how men and women in late 7th and 8th century Japan envisioned the fate of the dead. Here are some examples:

昨日こそ君はありしか　思わぬに浜松が上の雲にたなびく

Only yesterday, you were here. Now unexpectedly, you are the cloud trailing above the pine beach.

(*Manyōshū*, vol. 3)

---

[3] According to the myth, when Taji found and brought back the fruit of eternal life, the Emperor had already passed away. Taji presented the fruits at the Emperor's tomb and later committed suicide.
[4] Cf. MIURA HIROBUMI 三浦宏文, "The Problem of the Life after Death".

佐保山にたなびく霞見る毎に　妹を思いて泣かぬ日はなし
Whenever I see the mist trailing over Mount Saho, I think of you (my wife) and there is not a day I do not cry.

(*Manyōshū*, vol. 3)

隠国の泊瀬の山の霞たち棚引く雲は妹にかもあらむ
The cloud trailing over the mist over the Hatsuse mountain in the hidden country, could it be my lover?

(*Manyōshū*, vol. 7)

These poetic renderings of death focus on the physical transformation of the deceased rather than the geographical location of the dead. As seen in the above examples, the dead are most commonly imagined as clouds or mist, unstable and constantly changing phenomena. The smoke image reflects the early funerary practice of cremation. It also echoes the ephemerality evoked by Buddhist belief that life is constantly changing and by nature transient. However, the impact of Buddhist conceptions of the afterlife would come into full prominence later in the Heian period.

Death in the Heian Period

Continental influence, particularly through Buddhism, resulted in a radically different understanding of the afterlife in the Heian intellectual world. Japanese classical culture reached its apex in the Heian Period (794–1185), when the poetic tradition was universally acclaimed the highest art form and poets enjoyed the patronage and support of high court culture. The *banka* elegy evolved during this period into the class of laments (*aishō no uta* 哀傷歌). The most famous female poet of the day, Izumi Shikibu 和泉式部 (978~??) left us with many such poems, mourning for and reminiscing about those who had passed away. A few examples, first to Tametaka:

亡人のくる夜ときけど君もなし　我が住む宿や魂無きの里
naki hito no kuru yo to kikedo kimi mo nashi wa ga sumu yado ya tamanaki no sato
They say the dead return tonight, but you are not here. Is my dwelling truly a house without spirit?

(*Goshūi wakashū* 10:575)

This poem was written when seeing her daughter Koshikibu no Naishi's name on the Imperial robes the poet received after her daughter's death:

諸共に苔のしたには朽ちずして埋もれぬ名をみるぞ悲しき
morotomo ni koke no shita ni ha kuchizu shite udzumorenu na wo miru zo kanashiki

Seeing her imperishable name, now buried with all the others beneath the moss, I was sad.
(*Kin'yō wakashū* 10:620)

Izumi Shikibu's grief for the deceased seems relevant and relatable to the modern reader. She does not invoke hell or the unknown world of the beyond in her poems; rather, her poems notice either the empty space evacuated by the deceased (as in *Goshūi* 10:575) or the sadness of the commemorative objects left behind by the deceased (as in the last poem).

There was a detailed exploration and depiction of the beyond in this period, related to the rise of the Pure Land sect of Buddhism, which believed that through the Pure Land, Amida granted all human beings, regardless of status or wealth, equal access to the Pure land after death. Founded by the monk Hōnen (1133–1212), it argued that two thousand years after the death of the historical Buddha, the world had as of 1052 entered into the Last Age of the Dharma (*mappō* 末法), a benighted age when no man or woman could hope to attain enlightenment on the basis of their own efforts. Instead, by putting one's entire faith in the salvific power of the Buddha Amida, one could be sure that upon death, he would come at the head of retinue to welcome you into the Pure Land, where there would be no temptation and all would be conducive to enlightenment and spiritual progress. Paintings of the "welcoming approach" of Amida (*raigōzu* 来迎図) were popular, with the Buddha Amida shrouded in purple clouds, accompanied by twenty-five bodhisattvas (some playing beautiful music). The idea of rejecting this profane world, encapsulated in the phrase "leaving in disgust this land of filth, I happily seek the Pure Land" (*enri edo gongū jōdo* 厭離穢土, 欣求浄土) began to spread among the populace.[5]

In previous centuries, depictions of the world of the dead in works such as *Kojiki* had indeed portrayed this realm as polluted by death and surrounded by taboos, such as the one broken by Izanagi in gazing at the decaying body of his wife, but when Izanagi escapes into the world of the living and purifies himself with water, the threat ends. The world of the living is not polluted by its occasional contacts with the world of the dead. Pure Land Buddhism extended the pollution into this mortal realm, which is constantly touched by death; only the Pure Land offers escape. One should eagerly seek the Pure Land. Thus we find that instead of a demarcation between the polluted world of the dead and the pure world of the living, we find the polluted worlds of the mortals, living or dead,

---

[5] KAKEHASHI JITSUEN 梯実円, "Nihonjin no seishikan no ichisokumen: Jōdo kyōdo no baai" 日本人の生死観の一側面 – 浄土教徒の場合 – (An Aspect of Life-and-Death Views of the Japanese: The Case of Adherents of the Pure Land Buddhism).

versus the pure realms of the Buddhas. The afterlife has come to be valued over the world of the living.

Death and the Samurai Class

The medieval period of Japanese history (1185-1600) was marked by the rise of the Samurai class, an educated class of warriors who in this age of socio-political change chose warfare as a profession. Since these elite men lived dangerous lives in direct contravention of the basic Buddhist precept "do not kill" (sesshōkai 殺生戒), the warrior class did not often talk about the afterlife (raisei 来世). An eliding of questions of the afterlife and a focus on the transient nature of this life reflect the warrior consciousness of the time. It is this new outlook that views the distinction of life and death as a thin line that this newly arisen social class embraced. The resolution and resignation of the warrior class can be seen from many "farewell to the world" poems (jisei no ku 辞世の) that express the sentiment:

四十九年一睡の夢一期の栄華は一盃の酒にしかず柳は緑にして花は紅
Uesugi Kenshin 上杉謙信

Forty-nine years just like a dream seen in a nap; a period of glory, no more than a cup of wine. The willow is still green and the blossoms red.

Or as the famous quote from one of the most famous stage dance performance *kōwakamae* (幸若舞) *Atsumori* (敦盛):[6]

「人間五十年　　　　　　　　　化天の内をくらぶれば、夢幻のごとくなり
一度生を受け滅せぬ者の有るべきか」

Fifty years of mortal life is like a fleeting dream to one in the Heaven of Transformation (the lowest heaven of the six heavens). Could there be one who, once born, does not perish?
Atsumori, Act III '*Yūya*'

These literary and performatory traces reveal that, unlike the commoners, who suffering in this material world, purposefully seek to leave it and pursue the utopian Pure Land in the next life, the warrior class focused on the transient, unreliable nature of life ("like that of a dream"). This reflects the rising influence of Zen, which stressed immediate enlightenment rather than gradual progress toward Nirvana. In fact, for the samurai, grasping after life was considered

---

[6] Aoki Shigeru 青木繁, *Kōwakami* 幸若舞, vol. 3, 51–52.

shameful. In this world, the important thing was not to live a long, prosperous life but rather to leave behind a reputation (*na* 名), a value system also influenced by the popularity of Confucianism in early modern Japan.

Recluses and the Aesthetics of Death

Hermits and recluses constitute another important group in medieval and early modern Japanese literature. It is this body of literary and philosophical writings of the recluse discourse that gave birth to two quintessential Japanese aesthetic concepts: *wabi* and *sabi*. Recluses are those who seek peace and tranquility by avoiding socialization with the secular outside world. Living in the deep mountains with minimal material comforts, recluses were motivated by a sense of the impermanence of human life and devoted their life to reading, writing, traveling, and observing natural in general. The sense of beauty is manifest in the love of nature (through simple living and travel) and a simplistic, rustic, minimalist take on aestheticism, focusing on the values of *wabi* (austerity) and *sabi* (rusticity). A poem by the famous traveling poet-monk Saigyō best captures this new sensibility:

> 「津の国のなにはの春は夢なれや蘆の枯葉に風わたるなり」　西行
> Like the spring of Naniwa in the country of Tsu, it's all but a dream, symbolized by the wind that blows through the withered leaves of the reeds.
>
> Saigyō

Here Saigyō's metaphor that this worldly life is like a dream accords well with Heian aristocratic sensibility. The visible difference, however, lies in Saigyō's further association of the "dream" metaphor with a more medieval ideal of rustic beauty: the dry, withered reed leaves. The second half of the *waka* subverts the spring (green, lively, growing) image in the first half of the poem, countering it with an image of brown, desiccated autumn leaves.

For the recluse, the dread of death merged with the new aestheticism and transformed into an aesthetic experience, as Saigyō again wishes that his death would be an event of beauty:

> 願はくは　花のもとにて　春死なむ　その如月の　望月のころ
> I wish to die under flowers in the spring, on a full moon night in the fifth month.

Flowers and the moon are all standard symbols for impermanence in Japan. Here the recluse literature accentuates the splendor of impermanence, thus making impermanent life itself (represented by the ultimate death) a part of that splendor.

This medieval sensibility, which treasures austere beauty and the final resolution of death, is prominent in medieval Nō theater. One of the most common tropes in Nō theater is for a dead spirit (usually a warrior who is either embodied in a natural object such as a tree or takes the forms of a woodcutter or local old man) to reveal itself to a traveling monk/poet. The spirit would tell of his/her life and their unfortunate death. As their stories are being told, often the storyteller would transform, taking up their original form as he relived the experience. Usually, a resolution is achieved and the spirit is finally able to return to the realm of the death in peace. The theater stage was traditionally set in a Buddhist temple or Shinto shrine and the performance served as part of the requiem to ritualistically calm the dead spirits.

Visualizations of the Great Beyond

When, in 985, the monk Genshin 源信 (942–1017) collected materials related to belief in the Pure Land into a collection called *Collected Essential for Rebirth in the Pure Land* (Ōjō yōshū 往生要集), he included a detailed description of the hells and the torments to be suffered after death.[7] As Buddhism became popular with the masses in the medieval period, visual representations of Hell also become prominent. The Hell (*jigoku*) was viewed as the lowest realm in the six realms (*rokudō*).[8] In Japanese Buddhist belief, when a person dies, he or she crosses the River of Three Forks (*santo no kawa* 三途の河) and is tried by the King of Hell (*enma*) and the Ten Kings (*jūō*) every seven days for a total of seven times. At the end of the seventh trial, a verdict would be issued. According to the seriousness of the crime and indiscretions, each was assigned to a level of hell. There were Eight Grand (Hot) Hells with a gate on each of four sides. Outside of each gate there were four smaller hells (The Sixteen Hells).[9] After fulfilling their karmic debts through torturous suffering, they are allowed to reborn into the world again. (See Appendix image 2)

---

[7] Cf. Allan A. Andrews, *The Teachings Essential for Rebirth*.
[8] The Six realms consist of the Heaven Realm (*tendō*), Human Realm (*ningendō*), Shura Realm (*shuradō*), Animal Realm (*chikushōdō*), Hungry Ghost Realm (*gakidō*), and Hell Realm (*jigokudō*). The last three realms are collectively referred to as the Three Evil Realms (*san akudō*). See Appendix, image 1.
[9] These include: the Hot and Burning Hell, Cold and Frozen Hell, Screaming Hell, Grilling Hell, etc. There are also sixteen smaller hells and other various hells that form an extremely complex system.

Belief in Hell spread together with the popularity of the Pure Land belief. In order to promote belief in Hells and the *mappō*, temples would put on Hell Pictorial Sermons (*jigoku etoki*) using vividly illustrated Hell Picture Scrolls to teach about bad deeds and their consequences. (See Appendix image 3) This type of illustrated hell tale is probably the most vivid and detailed depiction of the beyond.

Early Modern Popular Views of the Afterlife

During the Tokugawa period (1603–1868) the social structure was rigidly separated into four classes: samurai, peasants, artisans, and merchants, each with distinct societal obligations and duties. In this era, two divergent trends on life and death developed. On the one hand, we see the development of strict and highly elaborate rules for ritualistic self-immolation (*seppuku*) for the samurai class; on the other, the merchant class and commoners adopt a lifestyle based upon the evanescence of life and a determination to make the best use of it. The Tokugawa regime was heavily influenced by Confucianism, which prized loyalty toward one's lord more than anything. Loyalty demanded that one serve only one's lord and be willing to sacrifice one's life for that goal. In his famous treatise on samurai *Hagakure* (1716), the author Yamamoto Tsunetomo proclaimed: "The way of the samurai is found in death."[10] This fostered ideals such as "learning death" (死習う) "to live like a dead (body)" (常住死身に成る). In this sense, the attitude toward death in the way of the samurai was to blur the line between life and death, in other words, to normalize the end and control their death.

As much as the samurai class valorized death for honor, they rarely talked about the world of the afterlife. Perhaps again due to the influence of Neo-Confucian doctrines that emphasized this-worldly empiricism, the samurai discourse did not develop a well-formed vision of the beyond.

The Tokugawa feudal system, which required regional nobility to spend much of their time in the capital, fostered the growth of a merchant class of city dwellers or *chōnin*. Though they were formally of low social status, their wealth for the first time formed a middle class that demanded to be entertained. One of the signature terms used in this period is *ukiyo* 浮き世 or "floating world", an ironic allusion to the homophonic "sorrowful world" (*ukiyo* 憂き世), a Buddhist term for the earthly plane of death and rebirth from which they sought release.

---

10 YAMAMOTO TSUNEYOSHI, *Hagakure*, 17.

The term describes the pleasure-seeking aspect of the urban lifestyle, turning its original Buddhist connotation of the impermanence of the world into a positive living philosophy of "life is short and uncertain, enjoy it as you can." This secularization of the Buddhist idea of *ukiyo* permeated popular culture, especially in the *bunraku* puppet theater and *kabuki* stage performances.

Particularly in theatrical or novelistic contexts, the term "floating world" came to be associated with romantic relationships between men and women. When the love affair does not come to fruition, whether because of money, a disparity in social rank, to the protagonists' social obligations (*giri* 義理), the star-crossed lovers often take their own lives in a dramatic double suicide (*shinjū* 心中, "love suicide"), hoping that they will be united in love in the afterlife. The double suicide trope is further highlighted by the highly ornate lyrical passages called "journey to death" (*michiyuki* 道行き) in which the lovers proclaim their love to each other, their fear for the impending death and their hopefulness to be united after death. The "journey to death" in one of the most famous plays *Double Suicide at Sonezaki* by the great dramatist Chikamatsu Monzaemon (1653–1725) express these sentiments in an elegant and eloquent way:

> Farewell to the world, and to the night farewell.
> We who walk the road to death, to what should we be likened?
> To the frost by the road that leads to the graveyard,
> Vanishing with each step ahead:
> This dream of a dream is sorrowful.
> Ah, did you count the bell? Of the seven strokes
> That mark the dawn, six have sounded.
> The remaining one will be the last echo
> We shall hear in this life. It will echo
> The bliss of annihilation.
> Farewell, and not to the bell alone,
> We look a last time on the grass, the trees, the sky,
> The clouds go by unmindful of us,
> The bright Dipper is reflected in the water,
> The Wife and Husband Stars inside the Milky Way.[11]

The star-crossed lovers, inching toward their final death, look longingly at the world they are leaving behind, but there is hope for their eventual reunion as the narrator/chanter (*gidaiyu*) informs the audience that death may, in this case, releases the lovers from suffering and provide them with untroubled rest.

---

11 Donald KEENE, *Anthology of Japanese Literature*, 404.

However we think, however lament,
Both our fate and the world go against us.
Never before today was there a day
Of relaxation, and untroubled night,
Instead, the tortures of an ill-starred love.[12]

There is also joy expressed that they will soon be reunited with their dead parents in the other world. At the end, the two lovers vow to die a beautiful death, "Wouldn't it be a good idea" they ask "if we fastened our bodies to this twin-trunked tree and *died immaculately*? Let us *become an unparalleled example of a beautiful way of dying.*"[13]

Like the honor suicide performed by the samurai class, the working class Edo commoners also prized the ritualistic and aesthetic aspects of death and wanted to do their part in living up to that standard. The act of death took on a metaphysical aspect. It was no longer the end of a life due to aging, illness, accident, and misfortune that cannot be controlled by individuals. Rather, in the Tokugawa period, death became a volitional act, a mechanism that could be employed by an individual of high or low birth to control their fate, to pay back their debt to their lord or to society, and to claim relief for oneself from the travails and suffering of life. But, as much as these practices mythologizing and aestheticizing the act of death, there was little talk in these circles of the life after death. But whether voluntary or not, death always leaves behind regrets as we see in the male protagonist Tokubei's final lamentation: "I am ashamed of myself that I am dying this way without repaying my indebtedness to him (ref. to his uncle who raised him)."[14]

Modern Worldview of the Beyond

In 1868, more than two and a half centuries of rule by the Tokugawa Shogunate came to an end as a constitutional monarchy was established. The era ushered in Western ideals and science. With the modernization project and the decline of Buddhism as a central belief in everyday life, attitudes toward death evolved rapidly.

One of the masterpieces of modern Japanese literature is Akutagawa Ryūnosuke's novella *Hell Screen* (*Jigokuhen*), in which a talented but difficult painter

---

[12] Ibid., 405
[13] Ibid., 405. Emphasis added.
[14] Ibid., 408.

Yoshihide is determined to paint a masterpiece depicting Hell. He is able to enlist his servants in enacting various cruel and frightening hell scenes, but when comes to portraying the last scene, in which a beautiful court lady is burned in a chariot, he is at a loss. He demands that his Lord, Horikawa, arrange for a real person to be burnt to death in front of him so that he can capture the true essence of the horrific scene. Lord Horikawa had lusted after Toshihide's beautiful, gentle daughter, but was rejected; now he selects the daughter for the human sacrifice. The artist is thrilled that his wish will come true and paints enthusiastically. At the moment when he discovers it is his beloved daughter in the chariot, he hesitates a moment, then proceeds to finish his painting while his daughter is burned to death. Akutagawa's piece is thus less about Hell than about Hell on earth. The brutal lord Horokawa's malicious revenge over his unrequited love, and the artist's devotion to his craft over the love of his child, both reveal that the human ego can create a living hell. Akutagawa's writing is often based on medieval Buddhist didactic tales, a genre called *setsuwa*, which is quite concerned with the afterworld. Nevertheless, this piece is exceptional; in the modern Japanese literary canon one rarely finds any concrete depiction of the great beyond.

In the following section, I will use several films, the new artistic medium of the contemporary Japan, to examine the modern conception of death and the afterlife. The first film is the director Kore'eda Hirokazu's *After Life* (Japanese title: *Wonderful Life*, 1999), the most innovative take on the transition to the beyond in contemporary Japanese cinema. The film depicts a sort of waystation where people remain for the first seven days after death. The staff aid the deceased in compiling a short film composed of their most treasured memories from their past life. After the film is completed, the person watches the film and relives those moments of bliss, then they move on to their final destination, which is not described.

By focusing on the first seven days after death, *After Life* does not really address the question of where we ultimately go after death; instead it asks: What is life? What is memory? How does memory constitute human identity and existence? The director Koreeda wrote the script based on six months of interviews of five hundred random people on the street, on college campus, in retirement homes, and in offices. The interviewees were asked: "If you had to choose one memory to represent your life, what would it be?" Out of the five hundred interviewed, ten were chosen to appear in the film, becoming its primary subjects. The bulk of the film consists of interviews of these subjects and the mixture of actors and non-actors give the film a documentary-like look. The director Koreeda reflected upon this unconventional film making process:

> In the first half of the film, which mostly is scenes of characters who speak about their memories, I mixed actors who spoke according to the script, actors who spoke from their own

experience, and non-actors who tell of their real experiences. Even when it was a non-actor speaking from his own experience, when he was in front of the camera and in character, his words became mixed with variations. What I wanted to do is to capture the expressions of human emotion tinted by the real and the fake memories in a documentary way.[15]

Oftentimes, the actors and non-actors were given a situation and a rough plot by the director but left to improvise the scene, which further enhanced the realistic, documentary style.

The subjects take great care in choosing their cherished memories. One man chooses a memory of when, as a young soldier for the Japanese Imperial Army in the Philippines during the World War II, he was captured by the US military and offered some white rice. The delicious taste of the rice made a deep impression on the hungry soldier's mind. A housewife chooses the moment when she gave birth to her child; an old women remembers dancing with her brother in a red dress. Someone recalls the sun shining in while he was a baby less than one year old. An office worker remembers the clouds he saw when he was taking flying lessons, with his goal set on becoming a pilot. A high school girl originally chooses a common memory of going to Disneyland with friends, but after some thought, changes to a memory of when she was three years old, resting her head on her mother's knee while smelling her scent.

But there are also people who cannot think of any one significant memory to put into the film. A young man refuses to come up with anything at all. An old man named Watanabe looks back at his long life and finds everything mundane and ordinary and nothing worth remembering. As long as they cannot find a memory for the film, they cannot move on, and remain trapped in a perpetual limbo. The surprise ending of the film reveals that the facility's staff is composed of individuals in limbo, people who were unable to pick their own favorite memory.

This idea of unresolvedness and lack of closure is also the main theme of a more recent film, *To Live with my Mother* (*Haha to kuraseba*, 2016) by the veteran director Yamada Yōji.[16] The film is set in Nagasaki where the second atomic bomb fell on August 9th, 1945. The protagonist Nobuko is a middle-aged widow who lost one son, Kō'ichi, to the Pacific War, another, Kōji (who had been a student at the Nagasaki Medical University) to the atomic bomb, and now lives alone, with occasional companionship provided by Machiko who was Kōji's girlfriend. On the third anniversary of the atomic bombing, Nobuko visits Kōji's tomb. She laments: "That child disappeared in an instant. All I can do is be resigned to the fact."

---

15 Cited from: www.kore-eda.com/w-life/index.htm.
16 The director Yamada Yōji based his film on the idea of the writer Inoue Hisashi, who passed away in 2010 but left a novel titled *Living with Father* (*Chichi to kuraseba*) that was set in the author's hometown, Hiroshima, which also suffered an atomic bomb blast.

That evening, the deceased Kōji suddenly appeares in front of Nobuko. Nobuko asks him "Are you OK?" Kōji laughs out loud: "How could I be OK? I am dead!"

Since that day, Kōji appeared frequently to his mother. The mother and son talked and comforted each other just like back in the old days, sharing their memories, deep thoughts, music and tea. When Nobuko asks Kōji why he did not appear earlier, he says, "Mother, you are someone who does not give up easily (*akirame ga warui* 諦めがわるい) and that impeded my coming to you."

The night her oldest son had died, Nobuko had dreamed about him coming to say farewell. Kōji compared his own death, which was sudden and without warning, to that of his older brother, who had wandered in the tropical jungle on a South Pacific island for days before dying. Kōji regretted that his death was so sudden that he did not have time to bid farewell to his mother. The mother, fully aware of Kōji's love for his girlfriend Machiko, nevertheless encourages Machiko to move on and advises Kōji to "Give up." (*akirameru* 諦める). Yet, for a while, Kōji cannot get over the fact that Machiko has moved on and is about to marry someone else. He cannot face the fact that the living keep on living he cannot really accept the fact that he is dead himself. He still desires to eat when he watches his mother having dinner.

As winter approached, the mother's health declined. As a ghost, Kōji realized that his mother was about to die. He comforts her and escorts her to the world of the dead. The film ends with the neighbors crying over the hard life of this woman, in particular that she passed away all alone with no family around her.

The key to understand this film is the concept of *akirameru* (to be resigned to; give up)." The mother gives up hope of seeing her children again and the dead become resigned to the fact that they are dead. Though the temporal progression of the filmic time, the ghost Kōji comes to realize and embrace his own death.

As the two contemporary films demonstrate, much thought has been given to the meaning of life and death. What does it mean to be alive? What makes living worthwhile? What are some of the essential matters that one needs to take care of before facing death? In these films, the focus is on death as a vantage point from which to see life. They rarely touch upon life after death nor speculate about the beyond.

Conclusion

In 2008, the highest-grossing Japanese domestic film and one that received the Japanese Academy Award for the best film was a small film called "The Departures" (*Okuribito* "One who sends off") by the director Takita Yōjirō. Loosely based on Coffinman,[17] a memoir by Aoki Shinmon, the film depicts an unemployed young orchestra musician who returns to his hometown and takes a job as a mortician (*nōkanshi*). His friend and even his wife object, citing Japanese social taboos against people who deal with death, but the protagonist is able to overcome this prejudice and find beauty and dignity in his work. This film highlights a recent phenomenon call "lonely death" (*kodokushi*), because increasing numbers of the elderly die alone. Through his enlightenment and perseverance, the protagonist is able to bring the final ritual of a human being back into our everyday consciousness and by normalizing this even, emancipate the people around him from the taboo on death as a source of pollution, which has been deeply rooted in the Japanese psyche since the time of *Kojiki*.

Another ongoing social change is a new mode of death ritual for unmarried women (whose numbers increase daily) or married women who refuse to be buried in their husband's family tomb. In order to serve these women, a new type of communal cemetery has been created for anyone who would like to be buried alone as an individual. These two phenomena demonstrate that the social-familial structure in Japan has been transformed since the bursting of the economic bubble in the mid-1990s. The economic downturn has made young people reluctant to get married and start their own families. These new ways of thinking about where to go after death were unthinkable a generation ago. This reflects the crumbling of the traditional familial structure and newly assertive women's demands to control their own fate.

The concept of death and the afterlife is inevitably molded by historical and cultural contexts. In this article, we looked at how this concept transmuted and transformed, from ancient Japan, where death was a vague, cloudlike existence to very concrete and vivid visualizations of Hell in medieval times. Whereas in the early modern period, death ritual and conceptions of death differed depending on class, modern contemplations of life and death focus on individual autonomy in forging one's path to "the beyond." Present throughout this development has been an urge to communicate with the other world and a respect for the transition between the two worlds.

Bibliography

Andrews, Allan A., *The Teachings Essential for Rebirth: A Study of Genshin's Ōjōyōshū*. Tokyo, Sophia University, 1973.
Anonymous, Kowakamai Atsumori幸若舞 敦盛. In *Zoku Nihon zuihitsu taisei* (Great Japanese Notebook Collection) 続日本随筆大成, vol. 8. Tokyo, Yoshikawa Kōbunkan, 2008.

---

17 Aoki Shinmon, *Nōkanfu Niki*.

Aoki Shigeru青木繁. Kōwakamai 幸若舞. Vol. 3. Tokyo: Heibonsha, 1983.
Aoki Shinmon青木新門, Nōkanfu Nikki 納棺夫日記. Tokyo, Bungei shunjusha, 1996.
*Haha to kuraseba*母と暮らせば (*To Live with my Mother*), dir. by Yamada Yōji, Shōchiku, 2016 (film).
Kakehashi Jitsuen 梯実円, "Nihonjin no seishikan no ichisokumen: Jōdo kyōdo no baai 日本人の生死観の一側面 – 浄土教徒の場合 – "(An Aspect of Life-and-Death Views of the Japanese: The Case of Adherents of the Pure Land Buddhism), *Shinrigaku hyōron* 心理学評論 (*Japanese Psychological Review*) 37.4, 1994, 400–418.
Keene, Donald, *Anthology of Japanese Literature*. New York, Grove Press, 1955.
Kurano Kenji倉野憲司 and Takeda Yūkichi武田祐吉, eds., *Kojiki Norito* 古事記・祝詞 (Nihon bungaku taikei日本文学大系 series, 1). Tokyo, Iwanami Shoten, 1958.
Miura Hirobumi 三浦宏文, "The Problem of the Life after Death: A Study of The View of Life and Death in Asian Thought", *The Bulletin of Jissen Women's Junior College* 33, 2012, 13–23.
Nishio Yū 西尾右, "*Kojiki* no zaiekan 『古事記』の罪穢観", *Journal of the UOEHAssociation of Health Science* 11, 1.1989, 43–48.
Okuribito おくりびと ("The Departures"), dir. by Takita Yōjirō, Shōchiku, 2008 (film).
*Wandafururaifu*ワンダフルライフ (*After Life*), dir. by Koreeda Hirokazu, Terebiman Union, 1999 (film).
Yamamoto Tsuneyoshi, *Hagakure*. New York, Kōdansha International, 1979.

Web Pages

www.kore-eda.com/w-life/index.htm

Here, There, and "Beyond" – Japanese Views on the Afterlife — 227

Appendix

Fig. 16.A1: Six Realm Reincarnation Chart

Fig. 16.A2: Trials before the King of Hell (Enma)

Fig. 16.A3: Hell Scroll (illustrations with text)

Uriya Shavit
Can the Metaphysical Be Rationally Proven?
Islamic Modernism Revisited

At the end of the 19th century and the beginning of the 20th century, three Muslim theologians, Jamal al-Din al-Afghani (1838/9–1897), Husayn al-Jisr (1845–1909), and Muhammad 'Abduh (1849–1905), reflected on the crisis of the Muslim world and laid the foundations of the modernist-apologetic school in Sunni-Arab thought. Determined to defend their belief in Allah, the afterlife and the inerrancy of the Islamic revelation and its ability to serve as an all-encompassing guide also in modern times, they pointed to the absence of scientific and political progression in their societies as the root of that crisis, and offered a unique approach to its resolution. Drawing a historical distinction between Christianity and Islam, and introducing mechanisms for accommodating revelation to new scientific and political concepts, their literature suggested that an Islamic society can be revelation-based without being theocratic and without forfeiting any of the blessings of reason and freedom. This approach was further developed and propagated by a number of paramount thinkers throughout the 20th century, including 'Abduh's and al-Jisr's disciple Muhammad Rashid Rida (1865–1935) and the founder of the Muslim Brothers, Hasan al-Banna (1906–1949). No single intellectual contribution has had a prevailing impact on Arab societies as much as has that of the early modernist-apologists. And no set of ideas has been misconstrued to the extent that those associated with this group have been.

The modernist-apologetic project was not the first to recognize that something had gone wrong for the Muslim world. It was also not entirely original in identifying freedom and reason as important assets of Western societies, and in explaining them in Islamic terms; the Tunisian politician Khayr al-Din al-Tunisi (1822-1890) made these claims already in the late 1860s.[1] However, early modernist-apologetic literature, starting most prominently with 'Abduh, took a bold step further by drawing a direct link between the diminishing role of religion in the West and its ascendance; it suggested that the strong position of Western societies was due to a scientific revolution that had rationalized explorations of the natural world and freed them from the arbitrary interventions of religious authorities, and to a political revolution that had made decision-making more

---

[1] Khayr al-Din al-Tunisi presented these ideas in his book *Aqwam al-Masalik fi Ma'rifat Ahwal al-Mamalik*.

inclusive, restricted the powers of rulers, and separated between Church and state. This view was encouraged, in part, by several French and Arab liberal analyses, including those authored by the French scholar of the Orient, Ernst Renan (1823-1892),[2] the French historian and politician, Gabriel Hanotaux (1853-1944),[3] and Farah Antun (1874-1922),[4] a Lebanese Christian-Arab journalist, who settled in Cairo in 1897. The analyses of these Christian scholars convincingly made the case for the separation between religion, science and politics as the cornerstone of national ascendance in the Christian world.

The originators of the modernist-apologetic approach believed that there is God, that He had sent to humanity a final Prophet, Muhammad (570–632) and that the final Prophet provided humanity with a final revelation and with Prophetic examples, all of which are absolute truths that must serve as the premise for conduct in all aspects of life, including the scientific and the political. But if the experience of the West instructed that science, technology and politics were greatly advanced only after the Church lost its power to delegitimize ideas, what were the implications for Muslim societies? Perhaps that those societies, too, must become doubt-based?

This option was inconceivable for the modernist-apologists. The solution to what seemed an unsolvable paradox was the Islamizing of modernity as a means of making a case for the possibility of modernizing Muslim societies without relinquishing revelation as the foundation of the mind and of social life. This approach offered much, and asked for little. The promise of an Islamic revelation-based society that will be as strong as, and in fact stronger than, any doubt-based Western society is a promise to meld the best of all worlds without giving anything up: tradition and modernity, a life of virtue and an afterlife of reward, faith and reason, authenticity and reform.

The Early Modernist-Apologists

A few biographical notes follow. After a period of study in India in the 1850s, where he became acquainted with modern sciences, and a short spell as an

---
[2] For an Arabic translation of Renan's ideas on "Islam and Science" and commentary on these ideas by Muhammad al-Haddad, "al-Nass al-Haqiqi wal-Kamil lil-Munazara bayna Raynan wa al-Afghani".
[3] "Maqal Misye Hanotaux, Wazir Kharijiyyat Faransa"; "Hadith Hanotaux ma'a Sahib Jaridat al-Ahram".
[4] Farah ANTUN, *Ibn Rushd wa-Falsafatuhu*.

advisor to rulers of Afghanistan, the Persian-born al-Afghani stopped in Egypt on his way to Istanbul in 1869. There he met, for the first time, with the young Muhammad 'Abduh. During his two years in Istanbul he demonstrated his lifelong talent for charming and associating with powerful individuals, and then irritating and falling from grace with the same or other powerful individuals. He then left for Egypt once again, where he remained for eight years. In Cairo, he became the unofficial mentor on religion and politics for a group of young individuals, mainly students at al-Azhar, including 'Abduh and the future leader of the nationalist liberal party, al-Wafd, Sa'd Zaghlul.[5] In 1879, he was forced into exile for political subversion and returned to India, where he authored a defense on the concept of a revelation-based society, *The Refutation of the Materialists*. 'Abduh translated it into Arabic in 1886.[6] In 1883, by then in Paris, he debated Renan's argument that a society cannot be Muslim and scientifically advanced at the same time. His response to this accusation constituted an ambiguous defense of the possibility for an Islamic society that is guided by reason and freedom. In 1884, still in Paris, he joined 'Abduh in the publication of *al-'Urwa al-Wuthqa*, a bi-monthly journal that, in half a year of existence, critically reported on imperialist policies and debated possible approaches for Islamic revival. In 1885, al-Afghani moved to London, where he participated in discussions on the future of Egypt. His declining years were spent as an advisor to the Iranian Shah and then to the Ottoman Sultan, where the pattern of becoming a close advisor and then falling from grace was repeated.[7]

A student at al-Azhar from 1869 to 1877, 'Abduh reflected on his mentor al-Afghani's time in Egypt as a transformative event that enlightened the minds and purified the faith of many religious scholars, including 'Abduh himself.[8] In the early 1880s, after gaining some repute as an essayist for *al-Ahram*, 'Abduh was appointed editor and then editor-in-chief of Egypt's official gazette, *al-Waqa'i' al-Misriyya*. In 1882, following his role in the 'Urabi uprising, he was sentenced to three years in exile.

'Abduh began, and ended, his exile in Tripoli. There, he met Husayn al-Jisr, who in the summer of 1882 became the headmaster at Beirut's al-Madrasa al-Sultaniyya. An educator and journalist, al-Jisr's life effort was to introduce a

---

5 Nikkie R. KEDDIE, *An Islamic Response to Imperialism*, 87.
6 Jamal al-Din al-Afghani, *Al-Radd 'ala al-Dahriyyin*.
7 For a concise biography of AL-AFGHANI: Albert HOURANI, *Arabic Thought in the Liberal Age*, 108–129; Nikki R. KEDDIE, *An Islamic Response to Imperialism*, 11–35.
8 Muhammad 'ABDUH, "Kitab Ta'rikh al-Ahdath al-'Urabiyya", 481–482. On al-Afghani's great impact on the young 'ABDUH in the 1870s see also: 'Abbas Mahmud al-'Aqqasd, *Al-'Ustadh al-Imam Muhammad 'Abduh*, 122–133.

curriculum that combined modern sciences and religious studies as a means of fighting the appeal of missionary schools and materialist ideas.[9] Their encounter was a milestone in the development of a distinct modernist-apologetic approach to reason and freedom. In 1888, al-Jisr, who was inspired by 'Abduh's teachings, published *al-Risala al-Hamidiyya*, an anti-materialist apologia that included the first methodological introduction on establishing the commensurability of Islam's revelation and modern science; 'Abduh read the book and praised it.[10] In 1897, 'Abduh published *Risalat al-Tawhid*, an apologetic rationalization of God's and Islam's truth that, according to 'Abduh, relied on the lectures he had given at al-Madrasa al-Sultaniyya, and bears some resemblance to al-Jisr's work.[11] During the 1890s, 'Abduh led reforms at al-Azhar and, in 1899, was appointed grand mufti of Egypt.[12]

Can the Metaphysical be Rationally Proven?

Early modernist-apologetic texts accumulated to a two-pronged defense of the possibility of a revelation-based society that enjoys all the benefits of a doubt-based, rationalist and modern one. They established that the metaphysical assumptions upon which Islam is based can be rationally proved and that the Islamic revelation is commensurate with, and even encouraging of, all the desirable aspects of modernity, including complete freedom to pursue investigations of the natural world and reach conclusions that challenge the literal and conventional meaning of revealed passages. It is understandable why the latter effort has been given much more attention in academic studies and judged as the essential historical contribution of the modernist-apologists. Telling Muslims that there is no God but Allah, Muhammad is His final Prophet, and the Quran is the final, divine, perfected revelation, was hardly a novelty in the annals of Islam. Still, the main objective of the formative treatises of this approach, the stepping stone upon which their defense of the concept of revelation-based society was built, was rationalizing the

---

9 'Ismat NASAR, "Taqdim", 27–34; Johannes EBERT, *Religion und Reform in der Arabischen Provinz*, 79–86.
10 'Ismat Nasar, "Taqdim", 38.
11 Muhammad 'ABDUH, author's preface in *The Theology of Unity*, 27–28; for the Arabic version: Id., "Risalat al-Tawhid", 353–354; on 'ABDUH's time at the school also: 'Abd al-Halim al-Jundi, *Al-Imam Muhammad 'Abduh*, 7–85.
12 On ABDUH's biography: Albert HOURANI, *Arabic Thought in the Liberal Age*, 130–160; 'Abd al-Aziz Ahmad AYYAD, *The Politics of Reformist Islam*, 1–27; 'Abd al-Halim al-Jundi, *Al-Imam Muhammad 'Abduh*, 7–85.

metaphysical premises of Islam. Al-Afghani's *Refutation* was written in response to a letter he received in December 1880 from Muhammad Wasal, a math teacher in Hyderabad who was concerned with the spread of materialism among Muslims in India,[13] and the book was intended to shock its readers with the implications of a world without God. Al-Jisr's *al-Risala al-Hamidiyya*, published according to its author in response to growing interest in Islam in England,[14] was in large part a rationalist discussion on the reality of a Creator and His Prophet and His Revelation. So, too, was 'Abduh's *Risalat al-Tawhid*.

The prominence of rationalizing Allah, His Prophet and His revelation is curious, considering that there was never a moment in the late 19th century in which open disbelief ceased to be a taboo or was propagated by a dominant faction in the Arab speaking world. Materialist notions were articulated in Egypt and Syria during the late 19th century mainly by Christian Arab intellectuals, and remained a negligible phenomenon.

Still, providing rationalist proofs for the reality of Allah, His Prophet and His revelation was essential for a worldview that stressed the idea that true Islam in no way negates the scientific methods that have dominated European thought since the Renaissance and have led to Western triumphs, or else the approach would contradict itself. Furthermore, while atheism and materialism existed only on the fringes of Arab-Muslim societies, the moment of learning of these views would have been an unsettling one for the modernist-apologists. In their childhoods, the reality of God was as obvious as the reality of New Zealand: they have never seen Him with their eyes, but were completely confident of His existence. The moment of being acquainted with an alternative that denied that reality was a shocking one. At stake was the certainty that there is meaning to life; that this world is followed by an eternal afterlife; and that devotion and goodness are rewarded.

The first modernist-apologetic treatment of atheism, al-Afghani's *Refutation*, was different from what followed. This book, in which al-Afghani first emerged as a defender of the Islamic faith,[15] focused on utilitarian arguments about the essentiality of religion for the prosperity of nations, offering no more than a general commentary on the rationality of Islam. Herein its weakness as proof for the existence of God, because even the most compelling case for the benefits of a social order based on metaphysical faith constitutes no proof for the reality of a creator, let alone for the truth of the Muslim revelation, a matter the treatise was not directly concerned with.

---

13 See 'Abduh's introduction in Jamal al-Din AL-Afghani, *Al-Radd 'ala al-Dahriyyin*, 33–35.
14 Husayn al-Jisr, *Al-Risala al-Hamidiyya*, 4–5.
15 Nikkie R. Keddie, *An Islamic Response to Imperialism*, 22.

Al-Afghani introduced faith in God or in a metaphysical order in general as a Hobbesian leviathan that safeguards social cohesion (however, Hobbes was not explicitly mentioned). He suggested that all religions, even in their lowest forms, are better than a philosophy that deprives humans of the virtues provided by faith.[16] According to his treatise, by reducing man to an animal that is no different than other animals, materialism releases beastly desires and aggressions.[17]

In al-Jisr's and Abduh's foundational apologetic treatises, materialism was attacked further, and rationalist proofs for the existence of a Creator, rather than merely arguments about the desirability of believing in one, were introduced. As in al-Afghani's apologia, al-Jisr presented utilitarian arguments according to which life without recognition of an afterlife inevitably leads to the rule of lust, beastly desires and egoism, and, ultimately, to the end of civilization as we know it.[18] To these justifications al-Jisr added, in a scattered and unsystematic fashion, rationalistic counter-materialist reasoning, including that there must be an original source that created matter, as it could not have been created by itself;[19] that the inability to observe something with the senses (God, the soul) does not imply that it does not exist (or else the materialists would have to concede that ether also does not exist);[20] and that the complex structure of our world, the marvelous constancy, order and harmony, implies the existence of a purposeful Creator.[21]

As al-Jisr, 'Abduh was impressed with the constancy, order and harmony of the world, considering them to be proofs for the existence of a purposeful creator. He insisted that when one observes the natural world, whether plants or animals, and the perfect functional operation of their abilities, one cannot but accept the facts of a Creator and an intended creation for which He is responsible.[22]

The main logical proof presented in early modernist-apologetic literature for the truth of the Prophet and of the revelation is the strength of the message and the weakness of the messenger. The humble background of Muhammad, an illiterate, was offered as evidence that he could not have composed the Quran, a marvel of literature that no human being has ever been able to match. 'Abduh wrote that the Prophet Muhammad was an illiterate orphan, born and raised among idol-worshippers. Normally, people with such background are molded in the shape of their surroundings, all the more so if there is no book or teacher to

---

[16] Jamal al-Din al-Afghani, *Al-Radd 'ala al-Dahriyyin*, 94–105.
[17] ibid., 64.
[18] Husayn al-Jisr, *Al-Risala al-Hamidiyya*, 351–353.
[19] ibid, 158.
[20] ibid., 329.
[21] ibid., 172–174, 206–209, 263–264.
[22] Muhammad 'Abduh, *The Theology of Unity*, 49 (in Arabic "Risalat al-Tawhid", 374).

guide them toward the right path. However, from his earliest years, Muhammad felt deeply repulsed by paganism. Upon receiving the revelation, he had no property, army, supporters, literary talent or rhetorical skills to aid him. The only possible explanation for his rise was that an awareness of the world's need to recover true belief was infused in him by Allah and led him to act and, ultimately, to be victorious. Divine revelation illuminated the path before him and led him in its heavenly authenticity.[23]

Reconciling Revelation with Scientific Freedom

The early modernist-apologists argued that in maintaining the rationally-ascertained belief in Allah, His Prophet and His final book as the premise for all aspects of life, Muslim societies would not hinder progression. They suggested that Islam is the religion of reason and freedom, and encourages rational, scientific research, and technological innovation. They introduced Islam as a precursor and foreseer of modernity, including its methods of administration and governance, suggesting that the reason for the failures of Muslim societies is not their faith, but their neglect of it.

Islam as presented by the modernist-apologists constitutes an alternative to the daunting model of secularization – and its inevitable implications – that had challenged Muslim thinkers since the late 19th century. At one end of the spectrum delineated by the secularization model are revelation-based societies, doomed to backwardness due to the oppressive tendencies of religious establishments and their privileging of metaphysical predispositions over empirical, rationalist depictions of the natural world. At the other end are doubt-based societies, prosperous and advanced due to their separation of religion from the scientific and political spheres.

The modernist-apologists defined a radically different spectrum as an alternative to the abovementioned. At one end are Muslim societies that are not loyal to the true teachings of Islam and are thus backward. At the middle of the spectrum lie secularized Christian societies that have been inspired by Islam to establish scientific and political freedoms but have rejected the foundations of Islamic faith. While more Muslim than Muslim societies in this sense their future downfall is, nevertheless, inevitable. At the other end of the spectrum is the ideal Muslim society, which Muslim societies have the ability to become. Should

---

[23] ibid., 112–119 (in Arabic, "Risalat al-Tawhid", 429–36). And also Muhammad ʿABDUH, *Al-Islam Din al-ʿIlm wal-Madaniyya*, 108.

Muslim societies return to Islam, true to itself as the modernist-apologists understand it, they will advance, and rise once again to lead humanity because of, rather than in spite of, the revelation.

As far as apologetics are concerned, this is a sophisticated spectrum. It tells Muslims that the choice between revelation-based and doubt-based social orders is artificial and biased, and suggests that Islam has a way of providing the advantages of the latter without compromising the former.

The modernist-apologists substantiated their theorizing through historical and theological narratives. Historical narratives laid out in modernist-apologetic literature emphasized Islam as a force for progression rather than a hindrance. 'Abduh's narrative, which was adopted by the Muslim Brothers and others in the Muslim world throughout the 20th century, is the one that had the most enduring impact. He argued that while Christianity is an irrational religion,[24] Islam is rational,[25] and places great importance on the pursuit of knowledge.[26] Whereas in Christianity the Pope held oppressive powers, including the authority to depose Kings, ban princes, levy taxes and enact divine legislation, Islam did not establish the rule of religion. Islam eliminated it. Only Allah and His Prophet have control over Muslims' faith, and it is only Allah that they worship. While individual Muslims may seek the advice of experts in understanding Allah's commands, they must not accept any opinion unless supported by evidence. Thus, while Europeans could indeed only achieve progress after they separated their political and religious authorities, their experience is not relevant for Muslims.[27]

'Abduh argued that the time in history when Muslim scientists could research freely, and the Muslim world was more scientifically advanced than the Christian world, was the time in which Muslims were actually loyal to their religion. Those more advanced Muslims, who were encountered by Christians in Andalusia, enlightened Christian societies, who were at that time oppressed by the Church, with the spark of scientific knowledge that had led to the rise of Christian civilization. The Church did all that it could to extinguish the spark, and maintain the ignorance that protected its rule. However, it did not prevail in the bloody battle that ensued.[28] Meanwhile, the Muslim world witnessed the rule of despots and subsequent decline, whose origins was traced to the first infiltration of Turks to positions of leadership in the Muslim world. Nothing concerned those despots more than science, because knowledge enlightens people of their situation; so

---

24 Muhammad 'Abduh, "Tabi'at al-Din al-Masihi", 260–262.
25 ibid., 282; Muhammad 'Abduh, *Al-Islam Din al-'Ilm wal-Madaniyya*, 109–110.
26 ibid., 90.
27 ibid., 97, 112–115.
28 ibid., 63–64.

science was oppressed.[29] Thus, the so-called persecution of science in Islam is really no more than Muslim ignorance of Islam. A Muslim return to Islam – that is, to Islam true to itself – will constitute a return to science.[30]

Along with history as evidence for the commensurability of Islam with the advances of modernity, the modernist-apologists have also provided theological evidence. The concept of scientific marvel (*al-i'jaz al-'ilmi lil-Qur'an*) suggests that numerous scientific facts and technological innovations that were unknown, and entirely inconceivable in the lifetime of the Prophet, are alluded to in the Quran, testifying to its divinity. The point intended is to assert that the revelation is not alien to modernity and, most definitely, is not a rival of modernity; in a sense, it is a precursor of modernity.

Al-Afghani, for example, noted that humanity time and again discovers and develops things that were not held to be true before, but which appear in the Quran. One example for this marvel is Q. 27:38, which tells of Solomon asking for the throne of the Queen of Sheba to be brought to him before her arrival. According to al-Afghani, the Quran did not detail what means enabled the throne to be speedily transferred to King Solomon's realm because, at the time of its revelation, the instantaneous transfer of communiqués was incomprehensible. In the age of telegraph, they are – and the possibility mentioned in the Quran can be appreciated by those who read it.[31]

The most vital aspect of the modernist-apologetic effort to establish the commensurability of a revelation-based Muslim society with modern, free, rational, empirical scientific methods is their method of applying *ta'wil* – allegorizing, or shifting from the literate meaning of a verse to a concealed meaning.[32] Modernist-apologetic literature suggested that given that the Quran is the revealed word of Allah, and thus an inerrant truth, it is not logically possible that a scientifically proven theory, model or fact that describes the natural world will contradict any of its verses. In cases where a seeming contradiction exists, a pertinent verse or verses should be allegorized so as to accommodate scientific truths. Alternatively, human powerlessness should be acknowledged. The implication is that nothing scientists have discovered, and nothing that they will discover, can potentially undermine the integrity of the Quran. Thus, religious scholars have no reason to fear modern science, and scientists can rest assured that their ability to pursue their studies will not be injured by religious scholars.

This seems a classic case of "heads I win, tails you lose." The logic is almost painfully cyclical: science cannot contradict the Quran because it is the inerrant

---

29 ibid., 157–161.
30 ibid., 193.
31 Jamal al-Din al-Afghani, "Al-Siyasa wal-'Ulum fi al-Qur'an", 268.
32 For this definition: 'Abas AMIR, *Al-Ma'na al-Qur'ani bayna al-Tafsir wal-Ta'wil*, 98.

revealed word of God, and the Quran is the revealed, inerrant word of God because science cannot contradict it. But if one accepts the modernist-apologetic statement that one can rationally and beyond any doubt prove that the Quran is a revelation, one must accept *ta'wil* as sensible and essential. Otherwise, scientific facts will have to be rejected when they conflict with revealed passages, and doing so undermines the revelation itself, which is rational and speaks of the importance of pursuing knowledge.

Applying *ta'wil* opened the door for the integration of any desired aspect of modernity into revelation-based Muslim societies. No matter how radically a discovery challenges clear and unambiguous words, and no matter how radically new findings shake centuries-old conceptions, their potential reconciliation with the Quran, as well as with confirmed Prophetic traditions, is assured. One reason for the relative ease with which this method was introduced and received since the late 19th century is that it was not revolutionary or ground-breaking; on the contrary, already in medieval Ash'ari Islamic thought it was invoked as a means to defend the revealed essence of the Quran and the integrity of confirmed Prophetic traditions, and to resist the infiltration of foreign, ostensibly non-Islamic worldviews.

The first systematic introduction of allegorizing as a method of reconciling science and revelation produced by the modernist-apologists was al-Jisr's in *al-Risala al-Hamidiyya*. He argued that (a) one must not doubt a revealed word of the Quran, or a confirmed Prophetic tradition, as doing so amounts to infidelity. (b) In cases in which a piece of conclusive rational evidence contradicts the literal meaning of a passage from the Quran or a confirmed tradition, allegorization should be applied as a means of reconciling the two. If *ta'wil* is not applied in such cases, the implication is that reason, the basis upon which the truth of the revelation is accepted, will be destroyed. (c) It is imperative not to confuse conclusive evidence with hypotheses; only the former legitimizes distancing an interpretation from the literal meaning of revealed words.[33]

'Abduh introduced similar ideas about allegorizing and its implications. Islam, he wrote, is based on rational investigation as a means to attain the correct faith. There is broad agreement among Muslims, save a small group, that when the literal meaning of the revelation contradicts reason, reason must be given precedence. In such cases, the germane revealed verses should be treated in one of two ways: either the human inability to grasp their true meaning should be acknowledged, or they should be allegorized, in line with the rules of the Arabic language, in a way that reconciles their meaning with what reason established.[34]

---

[33] Husayn al-Jisr, *Al-Risala al-Hamidiyya*, 278–79, 292–93.
[34] Muhammad 'ABDUH, *Al-Islam Din al-'Ilm wal-Madaniyya*, 109–10.

For 'Abduh, the existence of this method is the ultimate demonstration of Islam's compatibility with modern scientific methods. He argued that it opens every path and removes any hindrance for inquisitive philosophical minds. Scholars and students of the sciences cannot wish for greater freedom of investigation than that provided by the option of *ta'wil*. If they will not be satisfied with what it allows, nothing shall satisfy them.[35] Perhaps more than any other statement in the immense body of modernist-apologetic literature, the latter reveals the concerns that motivate the propagators of this approach and their convictions. It conveys 'Abduh's recognition that the ability to freely and rationally investigate the natural world is the most essential aspect of the West's ascendance; and his confidence and great relief thereof that he had discovered a way that makes it possible to maintain a revelation-based social and philosophical order while providing Muslim societies with similar conditions as those allowed in the West by secularization.

While of great appeal, there is an inherent dissonance in the modernist-apologetic defense on revelation-based freedom of thought and inquiry. The method of allegorizing, as suggested by al-Jisr and 'Abduh, is dependent on determining the status of scientific ideas as proven, disproven and yet-to-be-proven. Thus, if one follows the modernist-apologetic line of thinking, absolute scientific freedom is not guaranteed at all; rather, the freedom that exists is that allowed by the criteria set in order to determine *what* qualifies a theory, model or fact as absolutely scientifically proven, and *who* has the authority to determine it qualifies as such. Indeed, the modernist-apologetic concept of allegorizing allows room, potentially even much room, for the religious legitimization of any scientific finding, model or theory, even if such findings seem to contradict revealed passages. But whether or not the room allowed provides scientists with freedom from theocratic interference entirely depends on the nature of the authority that determines the status of scientific notions. If that role is reserved for theologians, or for politicians, judges and even scientists who ground their decisions in theological argumentations, then scientific studies become hostage to theological considerations.

Early modernist-apologetic thought only implicitly treated the issue of authority. But analyses of scientific innovations highlighted the fragility of its promise for a reconciliation of revelation and freedom. One example is 'Abduh's treatment of evidence regarding the Flood. The story of Noah's ark is narrated in two chapters of the Quran – Hud (11) and Noah (71). Q. 11:43 and 71:26 suggest that the Flood was universal, eliminating all of humanity rather than a certain people in a particular region. So does Q. 37:77, which states that Noah's descendents were

---

35 ibid., 110.

the only ones left on the face of the earth. In 1900, a Palestinian from Nablus, 'Abdallah Qadumi, sent 'Abduh a query about the compatibility of scientific evidence demonstrating the Flood was not universal with the Quran.

In his response to Kadumi, 'Abduh wrote that many scientists accepted the view shared by Muslims, Jews and Christians, that the Flood was universal and, as evidence, those scientists pointed to fossils of shells and fish on mountaintops. However, some contemporary scientists argued that the Flood was not universal, introducing evidence whose discussion, 'Abduh argued, required more space than he could allow. According to 'Abduh, scientific findings permit allegorizing revealed passages and reliable Prophetic traditions that contradict them only if they are decisively and logically proven. As no such decisive proof regarding the non-universality of the Flood was presented, it is not permitted to accept or to teach others that the Flood was a local event.[36]

The response by 'Abduh implies that (a) scientific findings should be evaluated against the revelation; (b) proven scientific facts legitimize the allegorizing of conflicting revealed passages; (c) and the non-universality of the Flood has not been sufficiently proven, and thus it is illegitimate to adapt the Quran to this thesis. What is missing in this decision, as in 'Abduh's more theoretical writing on the relation between science and revelation in general, is a clear conception as to how the yet-to-be-proven scientifically is to be distinguished from the proven and disproven: what precisely is the methodology that determines what has been satisfactorily proven and thus justifies allegorizing? What weight of evidence is required to transform the yet-to-be-proven to the status of proven or disproven?

'Abduh did not explain what qualified him, a highly educated theologian and religious jurist but no scientist, to pass judgment on a polemic pertaining to fossils, the layers of the earth and the composition of comets. Given his unequivocal opinion that the time was not ripe for allegorizing the verses germane to the universality of the Flood, and that true believers should not do so, one also wonders what did he, the Grand Mufti of Egypt, think should be done about Muslim scholars and educators who would beg to differ on the point and teach the non-universality of the Flood.

Conclusion

The present essay introduced the modernist-apologetic school as an anxious response to the temptation of a world without an existential force. This response

---

[36] Muhammad 'Abduh, "Tufan No'ah...Hal 'Amma al-Ard Kulha?", 511–513.

rests on two foundations: (a) rational proofs for the truth of Allah, His Prophet and His final book; (b) historical and theological argumentations in support of the potential of Muslim societies to progress scientifically, technologically and politically whilst maintaining revelation as an all-encompassing, binding guide for all aspects of life.

Modernist-apologetic thought has been associated with liberal impulses. Its understanding as such owes, in large part, to Albert Hournai's classic textbook, *Arabic Thought in the Liberal Age*, which introduced al-Afghani and 'Abduh as crucial links in a liberal chain.[37] Indeed, as the present discussion demonstrated, the modernist-apologetic project did have liberalizing implications, especially in the vast opportunities it has provided for accommodating revealed verses to scientific discoveries. However, the discussion also demonstrated that the essence of the project is not liberal. Liberal theory sanctions a continued pluralistic contest between truths and ideas, which the modernist-apologists denied. Their project was about asserting the supremacy of one truth as ultimate and undeniable.

The modernist-apologists impacted generations of Muslims to come by convincing them that a revelation-based society may be as advanced as Western secular societies. This conviction has hardly been an option for Christians in the 19th century. Catholics were struggling with a Church whose legacy was infamously hostile or hesitant toward important scientific works, and, while growing more open, still insisted on its authority to censor scientific and philosophical studies. Protestants were largely left to choose between fundamentalist literalism that denied the need to reconcile science and revelation at all, and Liberal Theology, which in most of its articulations injured to some extent or another the inerrancy of Christian scriptures, thus creating the option of faith that is not grounded in revelation. Herein lies, perhaps, part of the explanation why secularism has had far less appeal in the Arab world than in the West.

Bibliography

'Abduh, Mahmud, "Risalat al-Tawhid". In *al-A'mal al-Kamila lil-Imam Muhmmad 'Abduh*, vol. 3, edited by Muhammad 'Imara. Beirut, al-Mu'assasa al-'Arabiyya lil-Dirasat wal-Nashr, 1972, 351–476.

'Abduh, Muhammad, "Kitab Ta'rikh al-Ahdath al-'Urabiyya". In *al-A'mal al-Kamila lil-Imam Muhammad 'Abduh*, vol. 1, edited by Muhammad 'Imara. Beirut, al-Mu'assasa al-'Arabiyya lil-Dirasat wal-Nashr, 1972, 475–560.

---

37 Albert Hourani, *Arabic Thought in the Liberal Age*.

'Abduh, Muhammad, "Tabi'at al-Din al-Masihi" (his response to Farah Antun). In *al-A'mal al-Kamila lil-Imam Muhammad 'Abduh*, vol. 3, edited by Muhammad 'Imara. Beirut, al-Mu'assasa al-'Arabiyya lil-Dirasat wal-Nashr, 1972, 259–281.

'Abduh, Muhammad, "Tufan No'ah…Hal Amma al-Ard Kulha?". In *al-A'mal al-Kamila lil-Imam Muhmmad 'Abduh*, vol. 3, edited by Muhammad 'Imara. Beirut, al-Mu'assasa al-'Arabiyya lil-Dirasat wal-Nashr, 1972, 511–513.

'Abduh, Muhammad, *Al-Islam Din al-'Ilm wal-Madaniyya*. Beirut, Manshurat Dar Maktabat al-Haya, 1989.

'Abduh, Muhammad, *The Theology of Unity*, translated by Ishaq Musa'ad and Kenneth Cragg. London, George Allen & Unwin, 1966.

Al-'Aqqad, 'Abbas Mahmud, *Al-Ustadh al-Imam Muhammad 'Abduh*. Cairo, Maktabat Misr, 1960.

Al-Afghani, Jamal al-Din, "Al-Siyasa wal-'Ulum fi al-Qur'an". In *al-A'mal al-Kamila li-Jamal al-Din al-Afghani*, edited by Muhammad 'Imara, n.d., 266–270.

Al-Afghani, Jamal al-Din, *Al-Radd 'ala al-Dahriyyin*. Cairo, Dar al-Karnak, n.d.

Al-Haddad, Muhammad, "Al-Nass al-Haqiqi wal-Kamil lil-Munazara bayna Raynan wal-Afghani", June 30, 2015. Accessed April 19, 2017: https://www.il7ad.org/vb/showthread.php?t=4453.

Al-Jisr, Husayn, *Al-Risala al-Hamidiyya fi Haqiqat al-Diyana al-Islamiyya wa-Haqqiyyat al-Shari'a al-Muhammadiyya*. Cairo/Beirut, Dar al-Kitab al-Misri, Dar al-Kitab al-Lubnani, 2012 (originally published 1888).

Al-Jundi, 'Abd al-Halim, *Al-Imam Muhammad 'Abduh*. Cairo, Dar al-Ma'arif, 1979.

Al-Tunisi, Khayr al-Din, *Aqwam al-Masalik fi Ma'rifat Ahwal al-Mamalik*. Al-Dar al-Tunisiyya lil-Nashr, n.d. (originally published 1867).

Amir, 'Abas, *Al-Ma'na al-Qur'ani bayna al-Tafsir wal-Ta'wil*. Beirut, Mu'ssasat al-Intishar al-'Arabi, 2008.

Antun, Farah, *Ibn Rushd wa-Falsafatuhu*. Alexandria, Idarat al-Jami'a, January 1903.

Ayyad, 'Abd al-Aziz Ahmad, *The Politics of Reformist Islam: Muhammad 'Abduh and Hasan al-Banna*. Ann Arbor, Mich., University Microfilms International, 1991.

Ebert, Johannes, *Religion und Reform in der Arabischen Provinz*. Frankfurt am Main, Peter Lang, 1991.

"Hadith Hanotaux ma'a Sahib Jaridat al-Ahram." In 'Abduh, Muhammad, *Al-Islam Din al-'Ilm wal-Madaniyya*. Beirut, Manshurat Dar Maktabat al-Haya, 1989, 49–59.

Hourani, Albert, *Arabic Thought in the Liberal Age, 1798–1939*. London/New York, Oxford University Press, 1962.

Keddie, Nikki R., *An Islamic Response to Imperialism: Political and Religious Writings of Sayyid Jamal al-Din "al-Afghani"*. Berkeley/Los Angeles, University of California Press, 1968.

"Maqal Misye Hanotaux, Wazir Kharijiyyat Faransa". In 'Abduh, Muhammad, *Al-Islam Din al-'Ilm wal-Madaniyya*. Beirut, Manshurat Dar Maktabat al-Haya, 1989, 23–39.

Nasar, 'Ismat, "Taqdim". In al-Jisr, Husayn, *Al-Risala al-Hamidiyya fi Haqiqat al-Diyana al-Islamiyya wa-Haqqiyyat al-Shari'a al-Muhammadiyya*. Cairo/Beirut, Dar al-Kitab al-Misri/Dar al-Kitab al-Lubnani, 2012 (originally published 1888), 21–83.

Pablo Wright
Ontological Thresholds in Contemporary Shamanisms

Introduction

Anthropological studies on religion confront dominant assumptions of Western modernity, which are based on an illuminist and evolutionist dogma of reason as supreme. Reason here is constructed as a cultural artifact of Western tradition, one step above the uncontrollable and savage emotion attributed to primitive people and to all the societies considered "others" in the West. Evolutionism as a philosophy of history also reveals the ostensibly dry and inevitably academic discussions on secularization, disenchantment and the primacy of reason. If we rethink the evolutionist stages predominant during the nineteenth century, magic-religion-science, we see that science represented the self-evident – and we could say "cosmological" – triumph of truth, reason and the scientific spirit.[1] In any case, something different occurs if we approach religious phenomena from different starting premises that necessarily involve the sacred in the case of anthropology as a relational and historically modeled phenomenon where human finitude is symbolized through innumerable symbolic devices, always in specific socio-historic contexts, wherein the dimensions of experience and identity also are key to understanding religions today.

In this article, I propose an analytical perspective of religion that considers these aspects, providing more context and meanings to the religious phenomena connected with shamanism. In the contemporary world, there are multiple manifestations of shamanism that go beyond Mircea Eliade's classic vision.[2] For Eliade, shamanism is one of the oldest religions in the world, mainly centered on the shaman, a word taken from the Tungus šaman (Siberia). The shaman is an expert in ecstatic techniques who embarks upon spiritual journeys to different cosmological sites in order to restore the souls (and thus the health) of his patients. From Eliade's perspective of comparative religion, he proposed universal characteristics that people in all classes of society share. Although shamanism expresses historical conditions specific to each society or region where it exists,

---

1 Cf. Edward Evan EVANS-PRITCHARD, *Teorías de la Religión Primitiva*, 41–77.
2 Cf. Mircea ELIADE, *Shamanism*.

there are certain characteristics that repeat across cultures.[3] These are related to what Michel Foucault referred to as the technologies of the self[4] that involve altered states of consciousness, which people defined as the spiritual states produced after an initiation process involving symbolic experiences of death and resurrection through which the new initiate can travel through the cosmos using these spiritual technologies. The initiate thus enters a new cosmological but also social dimension since his status changes, allowing him to gradually being working to heal the sick; in some cases, this may also modify his political status and functions. In the actions of the shaman, as Winkelman notes,[5] there are universal aspects of symbolic healing in which the personal circumstances of the patient are situated within a context of mythology and the cosmology of the reference group or society. Through the use of ritual drama, the shaman works to modify problematic emotions, relationships and existential knots in order to cure the patient. In short, cultural symbols always come into play in all shamanisms through specific technologies of the self that produce an ontological modification allowing the shaman to carry out the cosmological actions required for his/her therapeutic goals. This takes place within a community where these symbols are viewed as sacred entities, powers and territories that hold the key to individual but also to collective wellbeing.

In the case of shamanism, as DuBois argues[6] various expressions of shamanism exist in specific social and cultural practice. Moreover, they are ways of approaching reality that entail connections between beings and objects, between people and the universe, and conceptions about people, health, illness, life and death, and the afterlives of different types. While these visions are rooted in ancient knowledges, they are also creations and recreations that dialectically interact with conditions of specific social existences; therefore, today's versions of shamanism synthesize a symbolic dialogue between social and cultural imaginaries and specific historical contexts.

In this work we explore these fluid ontological nuances of certain forms of contemporary shamanisms in Latin America and Europe. The idea is to analyze expressions that range from the traditional – ethnic shamanism in the case of the Qom or Toba in Argentina's Chaco region – to more eclectic forms of neoshamanism where there is a fusion of indigenous and mestizo cultures, like the Brazilian Santo Daime movement. Finally, we will pause to compare certain neoshamanic manifestations of the so-called neopaganism in Lithuania, which

---

[3] Cf. Michael WINKELMAN, "Shamanism in Cross-Cultural Perspective", 47–49.
[4] Cf. Huck GUTMAN, "Rousseau's Confessions", 99–109.
[5] Michael WINKELMAN, "Shamanism in Cross-Cultural Perspective", 57.
[6] Cf. Thomas DuBois, "Trends in Contemporary Research", 100–105.

has particular connotations of nationalist ethnopolitics combined with a unique spiritual worldview.

I

Among the *Takshek Qom* or Toba in the east of Argentina's Chaco region, the dominant religiosity is known as Evangelio (literally, "the Gospel"), a set of what were originally Pentecostal churches. Towards the middle of the 1940s, a religious institutional model lead by the *Qom* has formed in an unorganized, non-centralized way. In this model, Christian elements merge with elements of shamanism.[7] Today, it is the hegemonic institutional model in the *Qom* religious field and since its origins, shamanic practices have been gradually stigmatized, associated first with the world of the devil, but also with the "ignorant," "pagan," and "poor" past of the old aboriginals.[8] However, in spite of the public condemnation of shamans by Evangelio parishioners, shamanism persists as a therapeutic and social practice. Evangelio and its churches represent the new system of political and sacred power among *Qom* communities. This system is based, first, on male and female pastors entrusted with the powers once attributed to the shaman, pastors who present the Bible and the Christian worldview. What is unique about Evangelio, however, is that it has incorporated elements of the traditional *Qom* mythical imaginary.

The cosmology and the rituals of the Evangelio Church are particularly interesting because they possess shamanic elements within Christian morphology. The Bible, for example, is an object with extreme sacred power, given that it contains the words of God, words that are powerful in their written version. The same goes for prayer (spoken words with power) and the laying of hands on the altar in gestures similar to those of the shaman (hands as therapeutic instruments); when the hands are placed on the altar, shaman breathing techniques, insufflation and exsufflation can also be observed. In essence, the fact that a pastor is associated with the Christian god guarantees his power to heal, in keeping with the logics of shamanism.

In terms of other current religious specialists in the Chaco region, there are those who follow an ancient tradition that roughly correspond to Eliade's description of shamanism. These figures are known as *pi'oGonaq* (fem. *pi'oGonaGa*),

---

[7] Cf. Edgardo J. CORDEU and Alejandra SIFFREDI, *De la Algarroba al Algodón*, 124–146; Elmer S. MILLER, *Pentecostalism among the Argentine Toba*, 108–137; Id., *Los tobas argentinos*, 151–163.
[8] Cf. Pablo WRIGHT, *"Ser en el sueño"*, 178–205.

which could translate as "sucker," according to Miller,[9] in reference to the sucking technique they once used to remove illness from a patient's body. The *pi'oGonaq* coexists with the pastors and although they are often subjected to public scrutiny, they are also respected, feared and sought out for consultations. Initiation begins when a powerful *jaqa'a* being (see below) shares his/her power. This experience often takes place after an individual suffering from an illness and is healed by the *jaqa'a*; during the healing process, the initiate suffers a mutation that results in him or her receiving the power usually called *haloik* (lit. "knack, ability").[10]

Ontologically speaking, what type of world makes the Qom shamans possible? Within their life philosophy or *qom lataGak* (lit. "Qom way of living"), there is a distinction that is linguistically expressed by the term *jaqa'a* (lit. "other", "stranger") that marks an existential slope that separates humans from the powerful beings that live in different parts of the world. These beings, generically defined as owners (*looGot*) or as fathers (*lta'a*) or mothers (*late'e*) are characterized by their power; they control specific domains in the world both "natural" and "social" (land, water, countryside, forest, night, palm groves, music, games of chance, sports, seduction). Thus any power humans possess stems from the *jaqa'a* and life itself can be seen as a continual process of gaining *haloik*. People can receive this power under different circumstances, though the most common occurs while dreaming. Dreams, which are conceived of as real and significant experiences, serve as a cosmological channel in which humans and powerful beings communicate with one another and establish relationships that will later be important to individual identity and one's social profile. There is a spiritual component of a person asleep known as *lk'i* (lit. "his/her image") that enters the dream. In this regard, for the *Qom*, humans are considered an existential field comprised of different spiritual entities that dynamically interact over the course of one's life; there is an intimate relationship between the person, society and world.[11]

In contrast with the Westernized Christian notion of person, a *Qom* is comprised of a set of existential areas that can include one's name (*lenaGat*), soul-image (*lk'i*), soul-shadow (*lpaqal*), and thought (*lkwennataGa*). Some individuals may also receive a certain type of power from other entities (*ltawa*, lit. "his/her helper") and also *lowanek* (lit. "one under his/her command"). As a dynamic symbolic structure, the existential field of being also includes any object the person has used, their footprint and even their body fluids.

---

9 Elmer S. MILLER, "Shamans, Power Symbols", 481.
10 Pablo WRIGHT, "Ser en el sueño", 135.
11 Cf. Pablo WRIGHT, "Being-in-the-dream", 536–546.

Conceptually, the word used for the physical body (*l'ok*) is also used to refer to the peel or skin of vegetables, the hide of animals or any outer coating while the "interior" of the flesh (*lapat*) includes the organs, bones, muscles and blood, where the heart (*lkillakte*) is the center (*laeñi*) of a person's life and *haloik*. This is where a person's power is centralized and where the entities that empower him or her are located.

How do the *pi'oGonaq* differ from other people? Besides possessing more *haloik*, they also have powerful beings located throughout their body, not just in their heart. These beings, which are generated by the power they have received, are usually known as *lowanek*, which are the illnesses they can cure. In addition, they have lucid dreams. For this reason, it is said that the *pi'oGonaq* know how to "walk at night," that is, travel to any part of the cosmos while dreaming. During such journeys, they can determine what illnesses their patients are suffering while also competing with others for power in ferocious battles using light balls known as *le'eraGa*, which hold the *haloik* of each *pi'oGonaq*.

The world according to the *Qom* thus has different regions controlled by powerful beings with which the *pi'oGonaq* communicate according to the *jaqa'a* that has given them power. According to the *Qom*, the day is for humans (*shiaGawa qom*, lit. "*Qom* people") and the night is for non-humans (*shiaGawa jaqa'a*, lit. "other people"). This polarity of light-darkness or day-night permeates the *Qom* ontological classifications, which also include the east and the morning as the human realm and the west and twilight-night for the *jaqa'a*. In general terms, the presentation or manifestation of a *jaqa'a* is always conceived of as real. It is unlike the Western approach to visions, as there are no "false" states of consciousness here; a vision can hold any revelation in the world according to the *Qom*. For the *Qom*, the world can reveal its power at any moment in life, and the *pi'oGonaq* have particularly close ties with the powerful beings. In fact, their range of practices and notions fosters a sense of familiarity with the multiple dimensions of the numinous, which takes shape in experiences of initiation, healing and damage – another possibility that is also present in the shamanic world – competition for power and at times, collaborations with other therapeutic specialists.

II

As a socioreligious expression where elements of Amazonian shamanism mix with diverse influences of traditional medicine, spiritism and esoterism, we will now analyze the Brazilian Santo Daime. Once a phenomenon rooted in indigenous society, it has gone on to become a case of eclectic neoshamanism. Santo Daime[12] is a religion founded by Raimundo Irineu Serra, a son of slaves from Maranhao, Brazil. After working as a rubber tapper in the Amazonian region common to Peru and Brazil, and also working as border patrol, he discovered the medicinal use of ayahuasca among the Campa and the Ashánika between 1910 and 1920. He learned to use the substance and began having visions and receiving songs of revelation. In around 1920, he started organizing spiritual ceremonies where participants drank ayahuasca. His followers were initially all African descendants though later the movement attracted indigenous followers and Brazilians (of European descent). Due to the founder's ties to a group called the "Esoteric Circle of the Thought Community," masonic and Rosicrucian influences were added. In around 1940, he formally founded the movement he called the "Center of Universal Christian Illumination" (CICLU), which later adopted the word used to refer to the ayahuasca beverage, "Daime." The basic rituals Mestre Irineu introduced include concentrations, hymnals (structured singing and dancing similar to a military or disciplined exercise) and the *feitio* (concoction of the beverage). These are the technologies which the Daimist initiate, who is referred to as *aparelho* and has experience taking Daime, aims to generate. The aparelho is someone with regular contact with the spiritual world.

When Mestre Irineu passed away in 1971, some of his followers split with the group to found CEFLURIS, led by Padrinho Sebastián Mota de Melo. Padrinho Sebastián proposed that their spiritual work involved building a New Jerusalem in the rainforest, the only place where the practice could be done correctly. They constructed a spot in what is now Céu do Mapiá (state of Acre), a place where the members would support one another economically and worship. Self-sufficiency was a key element of this utopian community, since if any human catastrophe occurred, New Jerusalem would be protected both materially and spiritually. It is considered a place where salvation is possible, out near the rainforest, far from modern life. At the same time, New Jerusalem is a state of being, a state of spiritual harmony that is achieved by participating in the rituals and in the communion produced by the sacred brew.

Thus, the mythical locus par excellence is the rainforest, which is inhabited by extremely powerful and knowledgeable entities. These include the plants used to make ayahuasca (the liana, the feminine component, which is called *rainha*; the

---

[12] In this section, I have mainly drawn on two recent doctoral dissertations, one by Isabela Lara OLIVEIRA, *Santo Daime*, the other by Victor Hugo LAVAZZA, *Ideología y Utopía*. Concerning the field of ayahuascan religions in Brazil, the three most conspicuous are *União do Vegetal*, *A Barquinha* and Santo Daime.

masculine component, another vine that is gathered in bunches called *jagube*); and also the Queen of the Forest or Our Lady of the Conception, the most important of the female entities of the rainforest. These are master plants conceived of as numinous beings that the aparelhos are in contact with; they sometimes receive songs (referred to as hymns), which are sacred words and melodies, from the "astral" beings (the name used to refer to the numinous dimension). These allow healing to take place during the temple rituals. The hymns are paths for spiritual elevation and doctrinal pedagogy, the sources of sacred and political prestige that can sometimes lead to disputes among the main leaders of the movement. The Daime opens up these channels of communication with the astral, continuously reconfiguring the ontological structure of the individual. This can be observed in the modification of the individual's sensorial map, increasing his or her range of perception, while at the same time transforming one's individual and social life as a terrain where the sacred is revealed. The aparelho is integrated in the Daimist community and this belonging embodies the movement's utopian ideal, where there is symbolic feedback between the being and the geographical space. The principal beliefs include reincarnation, the protection of the rainforest and its natural species, and its pantheon includes Jesus, the Virgin Mary, angels, saints, animals, plants, and even extraterrestrial beings. This Amazonian retreat embodies a spiritualized ecosophy that is practiced by the religion's initiates, where the rainforest is the chair of multiple hierophanies that produces its master plants for people's development. The material here is an expression of the spiritual at all levels, not vice-versa; that is, the invisible is what gives shape to the visible.

In this Daimist community, the aparelhos embark upon the path of the initiate, where any number of diverse spiritual symbols, norms and practices come together; their fusion and creative reworking aim to transmit a technology of the self that turns people into "aparelhos of the doctrine," as they say in Ceu de Mapiá. This is expressed in different Daimist rituals, where the community enters a high level of intersubjectivity facilitated by the sacred brew. The members of the church thus work to perfect their ontological integrity and if they reach a certain level, they are transformed into agents of healing and wellbeing for people suffering from all sorts of illness and for the community as a collective spiritual entity.

For this reason, this branch of the Santo Daime can be viewed as a neo-shamanic initiate school where different spiritual traditions converge. The Amazonian ayahuasca shamanism is dominant, though it is organizationally reworked based on the Catholic and military influences of Mestre Irineu, its founder. Finally, given the expansion of CEFLURIS across Brazil and the different branches of Santo Daime in many countries, there has been a growing globalization of this church. This subjects New Jerusalem to dogmatic redefinitions. Some groups maintain a territorial utopia and its symbolic seal; others, more open to expansion and dogmatic liberation, propose to open up its sealed doctrine and facilitate sacred decentralization. Global modernity comes with pressure and – for the moment – there is no adequate way to alleviate this pressure.

III

The final case to analyze here will be Lithuanian Neopaganism. As Michael Strimska mentions,[13] in recent years several neopagan movements have appeared in different parts of Europe in response to the sociopolitical transformations of European postmodernity and the fall of the USSR. The principal movements include Norwegian revitalization groups known as Asatru, which have appeared in different parts of Scandinavia, along with similar movements in England, Australia and the USA. In Latvia, there is an important neopagan movement known as Dievturi. All of these movements can be seen as examples of neoshamanisms in which elements from the old shamanisms are selectively reappropriated as part of new sociohistorical contexts, yielding novel cosmologies and mythologies that demand an imagined historic continuity with those ancestral traditions.

It could be said[14] that the initiator of Lithuanian paganism in the modern era is Wilhelm Storotsa; known as Vydunas, this Lithuanian writer and philosopher was the first to celebrate the traditional Saint John's day at the end of the nineteenth century. Vydunas, whose name means "he who sees clearly," tried to synthesize theosophy with the local Pre-Christian pantheist tradition. Mazeikis claims[15] that in 1967, Ramuva was founded – the subtle change of name tried to avoid Soviet ideological control.[16] The name of this association for the preservation of indigenous culture made reference to a pagan sanctuary in Prussia. Following Lithuanian independence in 1991, political, ethnic and cultural processes of different kinds began, allowing neopaganism and multiple forms of neo-tribalisms to expand rapidly. Romuva aims to popularize national folklore and ritual activities like the performance of ancient Lithuanian celebrations. Jonas Trinkunas, a charismatic former researcher with the Lithuanian Academy of the Arts, was the high priest or *krivių krivaitis* of Romuva until his death in 2014.

Sociologically speaking, this movement arose from social actors who came from the urban intelligentsia – mainly writers and artists – where one of the most

---

[13] Michael F. STRMISKA, "Modern Paganism in World Culture".
[14] Piotr WIENCH, *Neo-Paganism in Central-Eastern Europe*.
[15] Gintautas MAZEIKIS, "Challenge of imagined societies".
[16] Rasa PRANSKEVIČIŪTĖ, "Contemporary Paganism in Lithuanian context", 78 and 90.

important bonding factors is the imaginary of an archetypical Lithuanian nation. In other words, there is a nostalgic search for a pagan, utopian life to counter the evils of modernity, Christianity, consumerism, and Soviet atheism. Thus, as Victor Shnirelman argues,[17] neopaganism in Lithuania, the rest of the Baltic countries and in a great part of the former Soviet republics of North Caucasus and Transcaucasia represents neotraditionalist movements of ethnic nationalism. The spiritual dimension best contributes to legitimizing and consolidating a worldview that fosters the new ideologies of the nation, creating the dream nation. This new mytho-practical horizon, to borrow the term of Sahlins,[18] is applied to reconstruct faith in the native gods. Life in communities begins; churches and entire villages are built; and religion intervenes in both community education and in the education provided by the state.[19]

According to Pranskeviciute,[20] within the communities there is a hierarchy of ritual specialists known as vaidilas (or the elderly) who are experts at ancient beliefs and both family and collective rites. The communities celebrate seasonal and national festivities, building altars and temples; they organize summer camps in old sacred Lithuanian sites (*alka*); and also host scientific conferences. Within the Romuvian reconstructionist culture, there is also a redefinition of material culture that includes archeological discoveries that the Romuvians associate with ethnic spiritual culture; these discoveries serve as confirmations of beliefs about daily life in the past (rituals that used to be carried out, the gods worshipped, etc.). These discoveries include different weapons, jewelry and clothing found in cemetery by the archeologists and are used in contemporary reconstructions.

It is said that Romuva is a lifestyle and a worldview that is based on a unified conception of reality as sacred and alive, thus nature itself is a hierophany.[21] The identifying symbol of the movement is a mythic oak tree that represents the structure of the world, serving as a true axis mundi at three levels: the ancestors are on the lower level (the past), human beings are in the middle (the present) and the divine (the future) is on the upper level.[22] Ancestors are worshipped since their descendants prolong their existence on earth. It is believed that the souls of the dead continue their life after death, staying with their living family members and descendants until their reincarnation.

---

17 Victor SHNIRELMAN, "'Christians! Go Home'", 198.
18 Marshall SAHLINS, *Islands of History*, xi, 145–151.
19 Gintautas MAZEIKIS, "Challenge of imagined societies", 61–65.
20 Rasa PRANSKEVIČIŪTĖ, "Contemporary Paganism in Lithuanian context", 79.
21 Cf. Rasa PRANSKEVIČIŪTĖ, "Modeling the Sacred in Nature", 46–55.
22 Introduction to Lithuanian Paganism, http://www.romuva.lt/en.html, official webpage of the Romuva movement.

The main Romuvian rituals are coherent with this view of nature as sacred. They are organized according to a pagan calendar associated with the solstices: the summer solstice is called Rasa or Kupolé, in honor of the goddess of fertility, and the winter solstice honors the ancestors. The worshipped gods considered unique to the old Baltic tradition are conceived of as the enshrinement of nature, where everything has a soul. Fire is a key religious symbol and for that reason, every home must have a sacred fire burning at all times. The Romuvians believe that one can gain awareness of the presence of the gods through experience and ritual performance. In this regard, anyone can meet the gods at any time in the human setting, and gods are constantly monitoring to ensure that human beings observe laws of morality.[23] Birth, marriage and death – that is, the stages of the life cycle that the vaidilas are entrusted with – are ritualized as well. The sacred texts are musical pieces called dainas, hymns that have mythical and mystical elements associated with rural life. They play a key role in religion, as the keepers of life experiences and thoughts that embody its doctrinal principles.

To summarize, within the Romuvians the idea of ethnic religion necessarily correlates with the enshrinement of the national territory where Lithuania itself is considered a sacred land.[24] Through neopagan religiosity, then, a true Lithuanian national essence is revitalized through the reinterpretation of a remote European past that contributes an important symbolic and cultural capital for its own contemporary legitimacy. The very pagan otherness that materializes the mythic substance of a nationality that must be rebuilt is redeemed here. Without a doubt, this is a traditionalist neoshamanism that is expressed through an ethnic nationalism that aims at the spiritual at its most basic level all the way up to the public and political sphere, forging important ties with the Lithuanian state and imposing its prerogatives since the country's independence in 1991.

Final Words

In this work, we analyzed three ethnographic cases in which different contemporary shamanisms elaborated theoretical and practical frameworks for conceiving reality and acting on/in it, and the types of borders they establish in these proposed worlds. The first case was one of indigenous ethnic shamanism rooted in Qom tradition in Argentina's Chaco. A case of intergenerational transmission, this movement suffers from a crisis as the result of cultural censorship by

---
23 Cf. Rasa Pranskevičiūtė, "Contemporary Paganism in Lithuanian context", 84–85.
24 Cf. ibidem, 83.

indigenous Pentecostalism, the hegemonic religion in the region. Here the shamans (*pi'oGonaq*) and their activities are viewed as part of a "sinful" past that must be overcome and forgotten. In the second case, the Santo Daime, its roots are not ethnic but mestizo and Brazilian (of European origin); because of its characteristics, it can be considered a case of neoshamanism that combines diverse cultural traditions. Another important aspect of Santo Daime is the technologies of the self, which point to the ontological metanoia that we consider an essential element in this religious system. The last case, Lithuanian neopaganism, illustrates how neoshamanism can become a national ethnic religion within a historical-political context of subalternity and oppression. Here ancient regional traditions are reinvented and combined with aspects of Hindu traditions and its theosophical version.

In all cases, we observed a topology of ontological thresholds very different from what institutional religions and science define as reality, human and nature – and the limits between them. In each case, we found fluid thresholds between the multiple dimensions of human history, social life, essential and inevitable relationship with nearby "natural" surroundings and with the cosmos. In addition, all of the movements conceived of nature not as an external dimension separate from humans but as part of closely connected systems; in summary, nature is enchanted. Within the dimensions of reality, classic distinctions like material-spiritual, visible-invisible, word-world, awake-asleep, and life-death take on different meanings or simply lose their potential to serve as classifications; other cosmological principles are at work in each of the movements analyzed. In terms of specifically religion, all of the movements aim to form or transform individuals – and by extension, entire communities – through specific technologies of the self to achieve a direct connection with the numinous. The nuances of these experiences can be found in their respective master narratives: the mythical-shamanic outlook of the Qom; Amazonian wisdom, popular Catholicism and esoterism among the Daimists; Pre-Christian paganism and Baltic folklore traditions among the Romuvians.

The different shamanisms analyzed in this work have allowed us to show social and cultural worldviews based on different ontological and cosmological conceptions. Passages, communication, sociability and exchanges between the real and the numinous – passages that have been sealed off or suspended in the scientific vision or in hegemonic religions – become possible in these shamanic and neoshamanic phenomena. Like many other religious movements across the world, these dialectically address the challenges of modernity but resist – either proactively or more covertly, depending on the case – the apparently inevitable move towards the rationalization of the world. In the view of anthropology, this move can be seen as one of many myths that, once identified as such, lose their power, yielding a philosophy of history increasingly decentered from Western evolutionism.

Bibliography

Cordeu, Edgardo J., and Alejandra Siffredi, *De la Algarroba al Algodón. Movimientos Milenaristas del Chaco argentino*. Buenos Aires, Juárez Editor, 1971.

DuBois, Thomas, "Trends in Contemporary Research on Shamanism", *Numen* 58, 2011, 100–128.

Eliade, Mircea, *Shamanism: Archaic techniques of ecstasy*. New York, Pantheon Books, 1964.

Evans-Pritchard, Edward Evan, *Las Teorías de la Religión Primitiva*. Madrid, Siglo XXI, 1976.

Gutman, Huck, "Rousseau's *Confessions*: A Technology of the Self". In *Technologies of the Self. A Seminar with Michel Foucault*, edited by Luther H. Martin, Huck Gutman, and Patrick Hutton. Amherst, The University of Massachussetts Press, 1988, 99–120.

Lavazza, Victor Hugo, *Ideología y Utopía en procesos socio-religiosos contemporáneos. Modernidad y Milenarismo en el culto brasileño del Santo Daime*. Ph.D. Dissertation, Facultad de Filosofía y Letras, Universidad de Buenos Aires, 2014.

Mazeikis, Gintautas, "Challenge of imagined societies for political anthropology in Lithuania", *Acta Historica Universitatis Klaipedensis* 29, 2006, 57–70.

Miller, Elmer S., "Shamans, Power Symbols, and Change in Argentine Toba culture", *American Ethnologist* 2 (3), 1975, 477–496.

Miller, Elmer S., *Los tobas argentinos. Armonía y Disonancia en una sociedad*. México, Siglo XXI, 1979.

Miller, Elmer S., *Pentecostalism among the Argentine Toba*. Ph.D. Dissertation, University of Pittsburgh, 1967.

Oliveira, Isabela Lara, *Santo Daime: um sacramento vivo uma religiâo em formação*. Ph.D. Dissertation, Universidade de Brasilia, Instituto de Ciências Humanas. Programa de Pos Graduação em Historia, 2007.

Pranskevičiūtė, Rasa, "Contemporary Paganism in Lithuanian context: principal beliefs and practices of Romuva". In *Modern Pagan and Native Faith Movements in Central and Eastern Europe*, edited by Kaarina Aitamurto and Scott Simpson. Durham, Acumen Publishing Limited, 2013, 77–93.

Pranskevičiūtė, Rasa, "Modeling the Sacred in Nature among Nature-Based Spirituality Movements: the Case of Vissarionites, Anastasians and Romuvians". In *Walking the Old Ways: Studies in Contemporary Paganism*, edited by A. Anczyk and H. Grzymała-Moszczyńska. Katowice, Sacrum, 2012, 37–60.

Sahlins, Marshall, *Islands of History*. Chicago, University of Chicago Press, 1985.

Shnirelman, Victor, "'Christians! Go Home': A Revival of Neo-Paganism between the Baltic Sea and Transcaucasia (An Overview)", *Journal of Contemporary Religion* 17 (2), 2002, 197–211.

Strmiska, Michael F., "Modern Paganism in World Culture. Comparative Perspectives", In *Modern Paganism in World Culture. Comparative Perspectives*, edited by Id. Santa Barbara CA, ABC-CLIO, 2005, 1–56.

Wiench, Piotr, *Neo-Paganism in Central-Eastern Europe*, published February 9, 2007. Accsessed April 2012. http://www.uclan.ac.uk/ahss/education_social_sciences/social_science/society_lifestyles/files/pagan9.pdf.

Winkelman, Michael, "Shamanism in Cross-Cultural Perspective", *International Journal of Transpersonal Studies* 31 (2), 2013, 47–62.
Wright, Pablo, *"Being-in-the-dream". Postcolonial explorations in Toba ontology.* Ph.D. Dissertation, Temple University, 1997.
Wright, Pablo, *"Ser-en-el-sueño". Crónicas de historia y vida toba.* Buenos Aires, Editorial Biblos-Culturalia, 2008.

Web Pages

www.romuva.lt/en.html

Raquel Romberg
The Beyond as Partner of the Here and Now
The Actuality and Indeterminacy of a Spiritual Semiotics within Spiritism

Abstract: Drawing on extensive archival and ethnographic research among Puerto Rican Spiritists and vernacular healers, this paper focuses on the ever present and quotidian hermeneutical practices performed by many Puerto Ricans of various social classes and backgrounds in deciphering the *"manifestaciones"* (manifestations) assumed to have been produced by a host of spirits and ancestors. Since these invisible agents are assumed to communicate with humans on a regular basis in indirect ways (dreams, unexpected occurrences and sudden events, such as the death of a pet or the loss of an object) this requires a constant deciphering of, and acting on, a "spiritual semiotics" composed of impromptu sings of the "beyond." Most importantly, these are viewed not just as explanations and warnings of misfortunes but also as ethical guides for everyday action following the Spiritual Laws of Spiritism – considered a spiritual philosophy not a religious dogma. My argument centers on "religious" individual and collective subjectivation processes that these kinds of everyday interventions of the" beyond" produce in the lives of individuals, even those who might otherwise define themselves as "modern" and "secular." A theoretical discussion about the extent of a spiritual semiotics that is predicated neither on a binary, arbitrary, or closed system of meaning is launched in conversation with contemporary semiotic theories that address the dynamic, actuality, and agentive power of an indefinite number of objects and subjects, human and non-human, material and spiritual, all tied in meaning making processes informed by specific semiotic ideologies that act on the world in pragmatic yet also, most surprisingly, indeterminate ways.

"There is No Coincidence, there is Causation" On Spiritist Subjectivation Processes in Everyday Life

Espiritismo (Spiritism) and *brujería* (heterodox Spiritism or witch-healing) are very much embedded in the quotidian practices and collective memory of Puerto

Ricans, even among those who do not define themselves as *espiritistas*.[1] As a colleague at the University of Puerto Rico said to me at the beginning of my fieldwork while scratching his arm, "if you scratch the surface a little, all of us in Puerto Rico are Spiritists."[2] He was referring to the routine deciphering of dreams perceived as messages from the spirits, the lighting of candles and incense in commemoration of the dead, the cleansing of the home from spirits, and the occasional appearance of goose bumps that are interpreted as a manifestation of the spirits or *"los fluídos"* (spiritual fluids).[3] All these practices reflect the idea of *manifestaciones*: the beyond manifests in this world and thus it is imperative to constantly decipher its messages.[4] It implies a quintessentially timeless and spaceless ethos that guides the cosmic order. Both the beyond and the here and now are thereby ruled by a set of spiritual laws: The Law of Cause and Effect, The Law of Love, and The Law of Reincarnation. They entail, respectively, that every action has its effect (in this and subsequent lives), that our actions should be motivated by love (following the model set by Jesus), and that reincarnation gives us subsequent opportunities to improve our karma through the exercise of our free will. In a nutshell: If a misfortune in the present is thought to have its cause in the recent or remote misdeeds of an ancestor or of oneself in a previous life, we can amend such past misdeeds in the present through a correcting action inspired by our indisputable free will, and thus have an active role in determining how our future will be played out. This ethos lay at the basis of a pervasive causal folk theory that guides the interpretation of *manifestaciones*, the perception and

---

1 Although the premises of Spiritualism and Spiritism are similar with regard to the belief in the communication with spirits, the later includes (as encoded by Allan Kardec) East Asian reincarnation philosophies. See Raquel ROMBERG, "'Enlightened' Spirits of the Dead."
2 In contrast to orthodox (Kardecean) Spiritism (also called Scientific Spiritism), heterodox Spiritism (also called *brujería*) includes African-based, indigenous, popular Catholic and Christian religious practices. This difference is also found in other parts of Latin America and the Caribbean. Elsewhere I have discussed the cultural significance of these differences, see Raquel ROMBERG, "Whose Spirits Are They?"; "From Charlatans to Saviors"; and *Witchcraft and Welfare*. For the inclusion of African elements, see Raquel ROMBERG, "Glocal Spirituality"; "Today, Changó is Changó"; "Legitimate and Illegitimate Vernacular Religions."
3 See Rosario FERRÉ, "La brujería en la literatura Puertorriqueña" for the metaphoric power of *brujería* in the expressive culture of Puerto Rico.
4 My fieldwork in Puerto Rico (1995–1996) included both archival and ethnographic research of the practices of both orthodox and heterodox Spiritists in various metropolitan and countryside areas. I purposely refer to all as Spiritists; for the politics of labelling Spiritists, see Raquel ROMBERG, "Whose Spirits Are They?"; "From Charlatans to Saviors"; *Witchcraft and Welfare*; and "Today, Changó is Changó."

evaluation of social realities of followers, and the solution of life predicaments.[5] In sum the beyond becomes an active, dynamic partner of the here and now by providing the ethical horizon against which interpretations, actions, and decisions are made on a daily basis.

The motto that heads this section, "*No hay casualidad hay causalidad*" ("There is no coincidence, there is causation"), conveys the idea that spirits and the spiritual world guiding reincarnation have idiosyncratically infinite ways of influencing the world of the living; whatever may seem incongruous, random and inexplicable might in fact have a reason and purpose. It can refer to apparently meaningless occurrences such as losing a ring, finding an object more appealing than others to us, finding the presence of a person we hardly know unbearable or cheering. Often whatever seems to be inconsequential, such as a candle being put out by a sudden draft, a candle that doesn't light up easily with a match, or that emits a black smoke, becomes the object of interpretation and spiritual significance; for example, that there are obstacles to our offerings, that it is not the right offering, or that it is consumed by evil not enlightened spirits, respectively. Manifestations can also be embodied in sudden illnesses, accidents, the death of a pet, or banal everyday occurrences such as sudden dislikes or likes of a person or place. Illustrating one such unexpected banal contexts, Julia, an 80-year-old woman I met at the beginning of my fieldwork in Puerto Rico, gifted me with an umbrella on the first day I had met her, after I was caught unprepared for mid-Summer sudden Caribbean showers. She explained nonchalantly that for some inexplicable reason, "today I bought 2 for 2 $, and then God brought you to me because I had two umbrellas, and one was meant for you."

Sometimes manifestations, embodied in sudden illnesses, small accidents, or love and work mishaps, require that the deciphering be raised up a few notches, in which case experts are consulted because of their not so self-evident meanings, often times assumed to be the result of bewitchments, angry *muertos* (the recently dead), or discontent ancestors. Unethical behaviors in this world, in relation to peers, family members, or friends, might be the cause for such manifestations. This was the case of Manuel, a man whose ulcerated leg relentlessly failed to heal regardless of doctors' interventions, until he consulted a *bruja* (witch healer) who unraveled, in trance, that until he visits his neglected mother the spirits will keep punishing him. In some other cases, spirits' manifestations warn people of impending dangers, or about the cosmic consequences of not behaving ethically

---

[5] It also becomes evident in the discourse of divination and cleansing rituals, and the making of magic works (*trabajos*). See Raquel ROMBERG, *Witchcraft and Welfare*; and *Healing Dramas*.

according to the Spiritist Laws of Love, Reincarnation, and Cause and Effect, mentioned above, and may also command people to forgive a neighbor, drop an unjust law suit, and the like. In less frightening occasions, spirit manifestations may just assure humans that they are protected, that their paths are cleared of obstacles and good fortune will ensue. On one such occasion Haydée, the *bruja* I worked intensely with for more than a year, had a dream about two plantains, an avocado, and a plant of *guanábana* [soursop, *annona muricata*]. Her dead mother had a dove on her lap, "which I caressed, picked up, and kissed as a baby, and [said to her], 'You will shelter me, protect me, and free me of all that is black around me.'" Having had inexplicable headaches the day before, Haydée interpreted this dream as a recipe for a cleansing ritual given to her by her mother's spirit.

As these vignettes show, a limitless yet openly-defined semiotic system, composed of anything from dream narratives, found objects, somatic reactions, and physical occurrences, might mediate the communication between spirits and humans in various forms and channels. Whereas much of my previous work has been focused on extraordinary contexts of spirit presence among healers during spirit possession, divination, exorcising, cleansing and healing rituals, and the making of magic works, in this essay I focus on the more ordinary kinds of contexts of spirit presence. Inspired by the colloquium Beyond as Challenge of Life, which generated this collection, I discuss the agency of such manifestations of the beyond in directing individuals into action and to making choices in everyday life, all of which are navigated by the premises of the Spiritist ethos and its spiritual laws.

Spiritist interpretations of manifestations are thus seen here as agentive forces that operate on moral, affective, and pragmatic grounds, and as such are viewed as compelling yet subtle modes of Spiritist subjectivation processes.[6] Similarly to the effects of visitational dreams described by Vincent Crapanzano, Spiritist *manifestaciones* may provide "a primary orientation point" for the "articulation of experiences that are central to the individual's personal history."[7] In this same vein, Katherine Ewing shows that certain dreams, recognized among Pakistani Muslims as "initiation dreams," have a culture-specific transformative power on the dreamers, following a culturally defined semiotic template.[8] Even though Spiritists are not equipped with a clear cut semiotic template for deciphering *manifestaciones*, the Spiritist Laws mentioned earlier, as well as past and present collective interpretations might be recruited in the deciphering of manifestations. In other words, the interpretation of manifestations, whatever these may be, becomes a non-human yet

---

[6] Elsewhere I expand on religious subjectivation processes within Spiritism; see Raquel ROMBERG, "'Gestures That Do'".
[7] Vincent CRAPANZANO, *Hermes' Dilemma and Hamlet's Desire*, 245, 257.
[8] Cf. Katherine EWING, "The Dream of Spiritual Initiation."

material "actant" or agent (following network theory terminology). As they come into existence, interpretations have the power of creating new realities, including people's state of mind, emotional reactions, and actual behaviors.[9] Put bluntly, the interpretation of spiritual signs is itself a "performative," following Austin's illocutionary acts and related speech-act theories.[10] Further, the model suggested by Richard Bauman and Charles Briggs for conceptualizing shifts of performative strategies from linguistic to extralinguistic contexts is relevant for my purposes.[11] "Recontextualization" and "entextualization," they propose, are two interrelated performative embedding modes of meaning making. In spite of being based on a textual model for social action, these two modes might operate in imbuing specific meanings to Spiritist manifestations by either making them speak in a new context or by making them appear in a different form, respectively. For example, if the flames of a candle turn black (meaning the spirits refuse this offering), its effects may be transported to a productive reflexive state that asks why it is being refused, or it can be the basis for changing the course of some recent action or inaction that might be suspected as the cause of such a spirit manifestation. In this sense, *manifestaciones* are agentive forces originating in the beyond, which give an opportunity for human beings to modify the course of their reincarnated lives, in line with the ethos of Spiritism, in this here and now world. As such, the beyond becomes a partner in shaping the here and now in various positive and negative ways. For instance, when no action follows a premonitory dream, tragic consequences might follow – as will be shown below. Indeed, following the idea of "free will" (one of the central principles of Spiritism), there are always consequences for both taking or not taking seriously the messages of the beyond.[12] Haydée, the *bruja* (witch healer) I worked with, painfully reminisced that the spirits revealed to her in a dream that her eldest son was going to be killed by a bullet. "I told him. But he didn't listen to me: I gave him the remedy but he didn't buy it (*le dí la medicina pero no la compró*), and was killed."

Dreams, Visions, Revelations and Confirmations

Mani, a man in his thirties I met through a mutual friend, told me about his unforgettable, life-changing, healing dreams, as soon as he heard about my research

---

9 See Ruy BLANES, and Diana ESPÍRITO SANTO, *The Social Life of Spirits*; and Diana ESPÍRITO SANTO, and Nico TASSI, *Making Spirits*.
10 Cf. John L. AUSTIN, *How to Do Things with Words*.
11 Richard BAUMAN, and Charles BRIGGS, "Poetics and Performance."
12 See Vincent CRAPANZANO, *Imaginative Horizons*.

in Puerto Rico. These dreams, he said, always involved his *protecciones* (guardian spirits), especially his long-dead grandmother. Once, she performed a "singing rosary" (*rosario cantado*, healing prayer) in his dream for his aunt who had cancer. "Sometime later, when my aunt underwent all sorts of tests, everything came out negative!" After such "healing dreams," he added, he wakes up "with an incredible sense of peace."

Clara, a woman I also met in Old San Juan told me about her Spiritist mother, who used to "see a lot in dreams"; that is, was able to decipher the messages of the visions she was given in dreams. When people are unable to decipher dreams that they feel contain important messages, they seek expert Spiritists such as Clara's mother. This is what Eric, a man in his twenties did when he had an "unsettling dream." But once the interpretation or the decoding is given, everybody knows that it is the responsibility of the dreamer to follow through.

Intrigued by this dream-deciphering folk system at the beginning of my fieldwork, I purchased a cheap booklet on dream symbols with the hope of having a sort of handy, if popular, consulting resource. I immediately noticed that my hopes were unfounded. The level of folk dream-interpretation supersedes any simple cataloguing of symbols; it engages, in contrast, assemblages of images, words, and personal contexts. Also mistakenly I thought that, since I was not a medium or for these purposes a native Puerto Rican, I was exempted from offering my dream interpretations during fieldwork. To my utter surprise, I was sometimes asked to intervene in dream interpretation sessions. Trying not to disappoint my interlocutors I often piggybacked on the interpretations of others with careful additions as, I guess, any pressured novice would have done.

But on one memorable occasion, when I was alone with Chelo, the manager of a Kodak store where I regularly took my fieldwork photos to develop, she looked at the photos I just developed and which disclosed my research with Spiritists. She then nonchalantly asked me to interpret the dream she had the previous night. "Let see what do you have to say about this," she challenged me before telling me the details of her lengthy dream. I now recall the dream in broad strokes (of course, I was not taking notes at the store), full of unpleasant, dangerous, situations that ended with her immersing in water and then somebody (she could not see who) "came from behind and covered me from head to toe with a yellow cape." Remembering at that moment – I had been working for a few months already with Haydée – what was the spiritual meaning of "being covered" (*ser arropado*), of water, and the color yellow in Spiritist parlance and ritual, I ventured: "Whichever misfortune might be hitting [you], La Caridad (a Saint associated with the river and the color yellow) is protecting you."

The next vignette also involves the intervention of spiritual protections (*protecciones*) that appear in a dream in order to help the dreamer deal with a difficult situation. Basi, the owner of a *botánica* (store that sells herbs and religious paraphernalia) was in her mid-sixties when I lived with her for several months during my fieldwork. We used to spend many hours a day talking about her life as a Spiritist and healer, her memorable and current dreams, and her daily consultations of clients at the *botánica*. On one occasion, she reminisced about a revelatory dream she had when she was still married.

> In that dream I was shown exactly where my husband's lover lived. I woke up the next morning and, as if guided by an invisible hand, I went directly to her house. As I was walking, I recognized the streets as I had seen them in my dream; I knew exactly the way to her house – my *protecciones* led me directly to her house.

When the truth of a dream or vision is confirmed, it is a confirmation of the spiritual faculties (*facultades espirituales*) of the dreamer. When I first met Haydée, she stressed the power of her spiritual faculties and the need of sharing them with her loved ones saying,

> I have revelations [*revelaciones*] in my dreams; one day, one week passes by and the thing happens, it is seen. Already as a child I had *revelaciones*. I always felt I liked *espiritismo*; I was born for this. Already as a child I had *fluídos*. [The spirits] used to present me with situations, which I deciphered. Whenever I had dreams I felt the need to tell about them. And then I saw them happening: If [I dreamt that] an accident was going to happen, I didn't see it [happen] the same day or the next, but after some time, I did, the same way as I had seen it [in my dream]. Exactly as had seen it, I used to see it happen. I always had to share it [my dream]. I used to tell my mother, and then my ex-mother-in-law and my children.

The fact that people tell and retell the premonitions given to them in dreams suggest that dream-telling is a culturally-specific narrative-genre intimately bound to the numinous. Not only among devout Catholics but especially among Spiritists, having premonitory dreams be confirmed by actual events shortly thereafter (*confirmaciones*) indicates the dreamer's godly gift of mediumship. Although the knowledge given in dreams is empowering, it also establishes the moral obligation to share it with those involved in the dream.[13] An incident in Haydée's life four years earlier illustrates this double-edged nature of premonitory dreams:

> It was revealed to me that my ex-husband's daughter would be involved in a car accident. I saw her in the cemetery. I told her my dream. One has to be fearful of dreams. After a week, she called me from the hospital; she had an accident!

---

[13] Cf. Vincent CRAPANZANO, *Hermes' Dilemma and Hamlet's Desire*, 242–243, described in a similar fashion how dreams are valued by Moroccan fellahin for their prognostic as well as directive powers – both of which have the potential of influencing the dreamer's future.

Somatic Manifestations

Different forms of spirit presence or manifestation mark the practices of Puerto Rican Spiritists, among them somatic manifestations imply that the human body becomes a communication channel for spirits. In addition to possession and trance, in which case spirits momentarily take over the bodies of mediums, researchers have documented four types of somatic manifestations in which the medium's body receives messages form the spirits but is still in some state of consciousness. These are *videncias* (seeing the spirits), *audiciones* (hearing the spirits), *inspiraciones* (sensing immediately what's on the client's mind), and *plasmaciones* (feeling the pain and distress caused in the client by spirits).[14] The latter can take various forms, from vibrations and tingling in the body, to headaches, stomachaches, accelerated heart rate, extreme fatigue, and the like.[15] Most importantly, healers can "learn about the problems and emotional states of their clients through bodily experiences thought to parallel those of the afflicted."[16] These somatic manifestations are interpreted as spiritual signs that require some form action, varying from placing ice cubes on the forehead, taking a cleansing bath, avoiding contact with certain people and the like. I have heard healers announce, "I have nausea. Which of you here is pregnant?"; "Which one of you has a headache? I didn't have one, but my face feels fatigued now"; "This headache is not mine!" Healers often feel in their bodies when someone *reclama* (invokes) their help, in which case they might have sudden headaches and insomnia for no other apparent reason. But healers, unlike most people, have the spiritual power to be aware of and counteract these effects. For other people, it can be the cause not only of headaches but also of unusual havoc and distraction, or a sense of extreme rejection or empathy when meeting a person. This was the subject discussed at a lecture series at a Centro Espiritista (Spiritist Center) I visited in Puerto Rico during my fieldwork. The main idea, evidenced by reading selected sections of the *Evangelio según el espiritismo*, was that the spiritual laws of Reincarnation and Love give us infinite opportunities to raise to higher spiritual levels by placing certain obstacles in our paths, such as reincarnated spirits with whom we had some issues in past reincarnations "*y con los que chocamos*" ("and with whom we clash") as an opportunity to solve them and thereby raise our Karma. I remember one person adding, "*Al que no le gusta el caldo le dan tres tazas*" (lit., "To those who hate soup, one gives three cups"; viz., obstacles should be seen

---

14 Cf. Thomas J. CSORDAS, "Somatic Modes of Attention", 143.
15 Compare with Robert DESJARLAIS, *Body and Emotion*; and "Presence".
16 Thomas J. CSORDAS, "Somatic Modes of Attention", 142-143; Raquel ROMBERG, *Healing Dramas*.

as opportunities to enlighten our spirit). This is what happened on one occasion with Haydée, who kept postponing for no apparent reason a woman who came to consult with her. After many days in which the woman sat in the waiting room for hours and was sent home, Haydée finally met with her. The subject of the consultation soon became the inexplicable rejection that this woman had caused her – a somatic manifestation that was interpreted and treated spiritually by means of cleansing and healing rituals.

Concluding Discussion: An Amplified Indeterminate Semiotics?

In this paper I have straddled the material and spiritual sides of spiritual manifestations by means of which the beyond intervenes in the everyday. As a form of partnership, I have suggested, the interpretation of manifestations shapes the ethical attitudes and behaviors of lay and practicing Spiritists. In this concluding discussion, I propose to assess the characteristics of a "spiritual semiotics" in order to address the performative and pragmatic significance of manifestations. Drawing on the notion of performatives from speech-act theory and the philosophy of language, mainly on Austin's illocutionary speech acts, spirit manifestations such as visions, dreams, revelations, odd occurrences, unexpected physical phenomena, and somatic responses can "do" something in this world. But what they "do" depend on how these manifestations are interpreted. Considering the lack of a prescribed Spiritist semiotic system – as my vignette about the uselessness of the dream-interpretation booklet showed – and the highly contextual mode in which manifestations acquire their significance, I venture the viability and limits of an indeterminate semiotics in my concluding discussion.

Without birddogging semiotics to its full theoretical consequences, I propose to approach the specificity of a Spiritist spiritual semiotics by recourse to Webb Keane's notion of "semiotic ideologies."[17] They reflect on specific "representational economies" that determine "the dynamic interconnections among different modes of signification at play within a particular historical and social formation." Semiotic ideologies thereby define "how people handle and value material goods" and "how they use and interpret words, and vice versa, reflecting certain underlying assumptions about the world and the beings that inhabit it." Particularly relevant for my purposes here, semiotic ideologies determine "what will

---

[17] Webb KEANE, "Semiotics and the Social Analysis", 411.

or will not count as a possible agent."[18] Human beings, spirits and their manifestations, in the case of Spiritism, are such possible agents. Indeed, the semiotic ideology behind Spiritist manifestations establishes that any textual, oneiric, and sensuous phenomena – be it visual, auditory, olfactory, gustatory, or proprioceptive – might be significant in connecting the beyond with this world. Readers attentive to Actor Network Theory (ANT) – as articulated by Latour – will also recognize the implicit lack of hierarchy of "actants" within the spiritual semiotics proposed here, for human and non-human subjects as well as materialities of various kinds (linguistic, sensorial, organic) are entangled in different yet related semiotic "bundles" and forms of action.[19]

Since spirits and their manifestations appear suddenly and spontaneously and might be embodied in unexpected and unfamiliar objects, the spiritual semiotics proposed here encompasses actualities (past interpretations) and unbounded future possibilities or potentialities (potential interpretations).[20] It requires at each time the evaluation of unknown signs with a repertoire of both known and unknown interpretations. This evidently forfeits the promise of interpretative coherence and certainty assumed by the early semiotics of the 1960s, adducing instead an actual indeterminacy and openness that may correspond to the agentive capacities of a host of shifting agents within the representational economy of Spiritism.

Specifically, within this semiotic ideology, manifestations of the beyond – whether fully interpreted and acted upon or not – entail agentive capacities that by virtue of their spiritual commanding significance and authority may become "partners" of the here and now. When followed, the contingent mode in which this partnership may take place encompasses all aspects of a person's life, as stipulated by the ethos of Spiritism and its Laws, linking the past, the present and future. If one considers manifestations as impromptu instances of spirit presence, and their agency and effect as dependent on open-ended interpretations, it becomes clear that the spiritual semiotics proposed here is both sustained and endangered by its indeterminacy. Highly empirical, though circumstantial, flexible, open ended, and rhyzomatic, the spiritual semiotics proposed here has been offered as an amplified semiotic model that is attentive to both the actuality and futurity of the indeterminate effects of the beyond in the here and now.

---

18 Webb KEANE, "Semiotics and the Social Analysis", 410.
19 Cf. Bruno LATOUR, *An Inquiry into Modes of Existence*; Webb KEANE, "The Evidence of the Senses"; Raquel ROMBERG, "Sensing the Spirits" and "'Enlightened' Exchanges" (under review).
20 See Webb KEANE, "Semiotics and the Social Analysis", 414.

Bibliography

Austin, John L., *How to Do Things with Words*. Cambridge, Harvard University Press, 1975.

Bauman, Richard, and Charles L. Briggs, "Poetics and Performance as Critical Perspectives on Language and Social Life", *Annual Review of Anthropology* 19, 1990, 59–88.

Blanes, Ruy, and Diana Espírito Santo, *The Social Life of Spirits*. Chicago, University of Chicago Press, 2014.

Crapanzano, Vincent, *Hermes' Dilemma and Hamlet's Desire. On the Epistemology of Interpretation*. Cambridge, Harvard University Press, 1992.

Crapanzano, Vincent, *Imaginative Horizons. An Essay in Literary-Philosophical Anthropology*. Chicago, University of Chicago Press, 2014.

Csordas, Thomas J., "Somatic Modes of Attention", *Cultural Anthropolog* 8 (2), 1993, 135–156.

Desjarlais, Robert R., *Body and Emotion. The Aesthetics of Illness and Healing in the Nepal Himalayas*. Philadelphia, University of Pennsylvania Press, 1992.

Desjarlais, Robert R., "Presence". In *The Performance of Healing*, edited by Carol Laderman and Marina Roseman. New York, Routledge, 1996, 143–164.

Espírito Santo, Diana, and Nico Tassi, *Making Spirits. Materiality and Transcendence in Contemporary Religions*. London, I.B.Tauris Publishers, 2013.

Ewing, Katherine P., "The Dream of Spiritual Initiation and the Organization of Self Representations Among Pakistani Sufis", *American Ethnologist* 17 (1), 1990, 56–74.

Ferré, Rosario, "La brujería en la literatura Puertorriqueña", *El Nuevo Día*, November 9, 1989, 3–7.

Keane, Webb, "Semiotics and the Social Analysis of Material Things", *Language and Communication* 23, 2003, 409–425.

Keane, Webb, "The Evidence of the Senses and the Materiality of Religion", *Journal of the Royal Anthropological Institute* 14, 2008, 110–127.

Latour, Bruno, *An Inquiry into Modes of Existence. An Anthropology of the Moderns*, translated by Catherine Porter. Cambridge, MA, Harvard University Press, 2013.

Romberg, Raquel, "Legitimate and Illegitimate Vernacular Religions in Colonial and Postcolonial Times. Historical and Anthropological Explorations of Ritual Indeterminacy". In *Religious Diversity Today. Experiencing Religion in the Contemporary World*, vol. 2: *Ritual and Pilgrimage*, edited by Anastasia Panagakos. Santa Barbara, CA, Praeger, 2016, 189–214.

Romberg, Raquel, "'Enlightened' Spirits of the Dead. Revisiting the Modernity of Nineteenth-Century Spiritualism and Spiritism". Research funded by the Minerva Center for Interdisciplinary Studies of the End of Life, Tel Aviv University, 2015.

Romberg, Raquel, "Sensing the Spirits. The Healing Dramas and Poetics of Brujería Rituals", *Anthropologica* 54 (2), 2012, 211–225.

Romberg, Raquel, *Healing Dramas. Divination and Magic in Modern Puerto Rico*. Austin, TX, University of Texas Press, 2009.

Romberg, Raquel, "Today, Changó is Changó, or How Africanness Becomes a Ritual Commodity in Puerto Rico", *Western Folklore* 66 (1 & 2), 2007, 75–106.

Romberg, Raquel, "Glocal Spirituality. Consumerism, and Heritage in an Afro-Caribbean Folk Religion". In *Caribbean Societies and Globalization*, edited by Franklin W. Knight and Teresita Martínez Vergne. Chapel Hil, University of North Carolina Press, 2005, 131–156.

Romberg, Raquel, "From Charlatans to Saviors. Espiritistas, Curanderos, and Brujos Inscribed in Discourses of Progress and Heritage", *Centro Journal* 15 (2), 2003, 146–173.

Romberg, Raquel, *Witchcraft and Welfare. Spiritual Capital and the Business of Magic in Modern Puerto Rico*. Austin, TX, University of Texas Press, 2003.

Romberg, Raquel, "Whose Spirits Are They? The Political Economy of Syncretism and Authenticity", *Journal of Folklore Research* 35 (1), 1998, 69–82.

Romberg, Raquel, "'Gestures That Do'. Spiritist Manifestations, and the Technologies of Religious Subjectivation and Affect", *Journal of Material Culture*, forthcoming.

Romberg, Raquel, "'Enlightened' Exchanges between the Living and the Dead: A Historical-Anthropological Perspective on Spiritism and the Ongoing Vitality of Spirits." In *Articulate Necrographies: Comparative Perspectives on the Vices and Silences of the Dead*, edited by Anastasios Panagiotopoulos and Diana Espírito Santo, under review.

Stewart, Charles, "Fields in Dreams: Anxiety, Experience, and the Limits of Social Constructionism in Modern Greek Dream Narratives", *American Ethnologist* 24 (4), 1997, 877–894.

About the Authors

Araos San Martín, Jaime
Philosophy
Pontificia Universidad Católica de Chile
Santiago de Chile, Chile

Baquedano Jer, Sandra
Philosophy
Universidad de Chile
Santiago de Chile, Chile

Bohak, Gideon
Anthropology
Tel Aviv University
Tel Aviv, Israel

Breitenstein, Mirko
Medieval history
Sächsische Akademie der Wissenschaften / FOVOG
Dresden, Germany

Burucúa, José Emilio
Cultural History
Universidad Nacional de San Martín-IDAES
Buenos Aires, Argentina

Gianneschi, Horacio
Philosophy
Universidad Nacional de San Martín-EdH
Buenos Aires, Argentina

González Casares, Santiago
Philosophy
Universidad Nacional de San Martín-EdH
Buenos Aires, Argentina

Kleeman, Faye
Japanese Literature and Culture
University of Colorado,
Boulder, USA

Kleeman, Terry
Chinese and religious studies
University of Colorado
Boulder, USA

Lazzari, Axel
Anthropology
CONICET / Universidad Nacional de San Martín-IDAES
Buenos Aires, Argentina

Ludueña, Gustavo
Anthropology
CONICET / Universidad Nacional de San Martín-IDAES
Buenos Aires, Argentina

Mathes, Klaus-Dieter
Tibetan and Buddhism Studies
Universität Wien
Vienna, Austria

Melville, Gert
Medieval History
Technische Universität Dresden
Dresden, Germany

Romberg, Raquel
Anthropology
Tel Aviv University
Tel Aviv, Israel

Ruta, Carlos
Philosophy
Universidad Nacional de San Martín
Buenos Aires, Argentina

Shavit, Uriya
Islamic Studies
Tel Aviv University
Tel Aviv, Israel

Sonntag, Jörg
Medieval history
Sächsische Akademie der Wissenschaften / FOVOG
Dresden, Germany

Vogt-Spira, Gregor
Classical (Latin) philology
Philipps-Universität Marburg
Marburg, Germany

Wilde, Guillermo
Anthropology
CONICET / Universidad Nacional de San
    Martín-IDAES
Buenos Aires, Argentina

Wright, Pablo
Ethnology
CONICET / Universidad de Buenos Aires
Buenos Aires, Argentina